S0-ACN-942

IRAN

PERSIA: ANCIENT AND MODERN

IRAN

PERSIA: ANCIENT AND MODERN

by
Helen Loveday, Bruce Wannell
Christoph Baumer & Bijan Omrani

Principal Photography by
Anthony Cassidy
Christoph Baumer

A NOTE ON TRANSLITERATION

To help travellers with the correct pronunciation of Iranian names and words, all Farsi vocabulary has been transliterated in the main text according to the Tehrani standard. As a part of this, macrons (ˆ) have been used to indicate the presence of long vowels. Thus, for example, in the main text 'Farsi' becomes 'Fârsi', with a long 'a', 'Tehran' becomes 'Tehrân', and 'Iran' becomes 'Irân'. See p. 95 for further details.

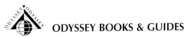

ODYSSEY BOOKS & GUIDES

Distributed in the USA by
W.W. Norton & Company, Inc.,
500 Fifth Avenue, New York, NY 10110, USA
Tel: 800-233-4830; Fax: 800-458-6515
www.wwnorton.com

Distributed in the UK and Europe by
Cordee Books and Maps, 3a De Montfort St.,
Leicester, LE1 7HD, UK
Tel: 0116-254-3579; Fax: 0116-247-1176
www.cordee.co.uk

Iran—Persia: Ancient and Modern © 2005 Airphoto International Ltd.
Odyssey Books & Guides is a division of Airphoto International Ltd.
903 Seaview Commercial Building, 21–24 Connaught Road West, Sheung Wan, Hong Kong
Tel: (852)2856 3896; Fax: (852)2565 8004; E-mail: sales@odysseypublications.com

ISBN: 962-217-751-4 Library of Congress Catalog Card Number has been requested.

All rights reserved. No part of this book may be translated, reproduced or transmitted in any form, or by any means, electronic, mechanical, photocopying or otherwise, without the prior permission of the publisher, except for brief passages for inclusion in critical articles or reviews.

Although the publisher and author(s) of this book have made every effort to ensure the information was correct at the time of going to press, the publisher and author(s) do not assume and hereby disclaim any liability to any party for any loss (including loss of life) or damage caused by errors, omissions or misleading information.

The opinions expressed in the Special Topics (or sections attributed to one specific contributor) are those of the individual contributor unless otherwise cited. They do not necessarily represent the views of the Publisher or the authors, all of whom pass no opinion as to the content, nor do they accept responsibility for the claims or statements made.

Grateful acknowledgement is made to the authors and publishers for permissions granted:

Serpent's Tail, London for An Iranian Odyssey by Gohar Kordi © 1991 Gohar Kordi; HarperCollins for In Xanadu by William Dalrymple © 1990 William Dalrymple; Oxford University Press and Peters, Fraser & Dunlop for The Road to Oxiana by Robert Byron © 1966 The Estate of Robert Byron; Random House, New York, for Reading Lolita in Tehran, by Azar Nafisi, © 2003 Azar Nafisi; Oneworld, Oxford, and Franklin Lewis for Rumi, Past and Present, East and West, © 2000 Franklin Lewis.

Editor: Bijan Omrani
Design: Au Yeung Chui Kwai
Map Design: Mark Stroud

Cover photographs by Anthony Cassidy
Photography courtesy of Christoph Baumer 14–5, 53, 56–7, 196–7, 216–7, 229, 230–1, 235, 237, 238, 244–5, 248, 249, 252–3, 259, 264, 265, 266, 267, 268, 269, 270, 271, 290, 388–9, 391, 393, 394; Anthony Cassidy 1, 2, 4, 7, 12–3, 17, 29, 47, 64, 81, 83, 87, 91, 93, 96, 98, 105, 107, 109, 112, 116, 119, 146, 155, 158, 159, 166, 171, 178–9, 186, 187, 190, 191, 198, 199, 201, 227, 298, 299, 312–3, 315, 317, 319, 321, 325, 332–3, 336, 337, 338, 339, 340, 341, 342, 346, 347, 348–9, 351, 352, 353, 356, 357, 359, 360, 362–3, 364, 365, 366, 367, 375, 378, 379, 381, 382, 383, 384, 387, 400; Gita Shenasi Cartographic & Geographic Organization, Tehrān 396; Paul Harris 132–3, 144, 224, 328, 368; Helen Loveday 151, 154, 203, 225, 275, 278, 361; Jacqueline Mirsadeghi 11, 123, 128–9, 306; The Board of Trustees of The Victoria & Albert Museum 60

Production and printing by Twin Age Limited, Hong Kong
E-mail: twinage@netvigator.com
Manufactured in China

(Right) Dome of the Árámgáh-e Sháh Nematolláh Vali Dome, Máhán

CONTENTS

(Pages 12–13) *View of the Friday Mosque, Yazd*
(Pages 14–15) *The Dare Rosh mountain west of Orumieh*

PREFACE TO THE THIRD EDITION

The old Shakespearian adage that was spoken originally of Caesar—"The evil that men do lives after them, The good is oft interred with their bones"—is equally applicable to nations as it is to individuals. Of the truth of this, there is perhaps no better example we can turn to than Irân. For every television report with chanting crowds and slogans of "Death to Israel, death to America", we forget that Cyrus the Great, the first king of one of the earliest incarnations of the Irânian state—the Achaemenian Empire—guaranteed the religious liberties of his subject populations, and stood as a pioneer in the field of human rights; for the controversies over the evolution of a program of nuclear technology, we forget the contributions made by Irân over the last 3,000 years in the fields of theology, poetry, art, philosophy, music and architecture; and for every stentorian editorial, breathing dire imprecations against the malign influence of the Islamic Republic, we forget that Irân is more than its government: a people young and aware, critical and well-educated; of diverse faiths, and of diverse understandings and reactions to their faiths.

Bearing this in mind whilst preparing the new edition of the Odyssey Guide, we have attempted to enlarge and revise the work with two equal intentions: for those who do not propose to make their way to the country, it should illuminate and inform about the fullness of Irânian culture; for those who have decided to journey there as visitors, it should act as a detailed and reliable handbook to aid them in their travels. To this end, the original 1999 text produced by Dr Helen Loveday has been thoroughly updated by two travellers with great experience of Irân—Dr Christoph Baumer and Bruce Wannell—to include new and further details about sites of interest, hotels, and other practicalities. Both authors also contribute new essays: the former on the earthquake-stricken city of Bam and the history of Christianity in Irân; the latter on cinema, music, and food. The historical introduction to Irân has been also completely re-written and greatly expanded, so as to give those who are new to the subject a comprehensive grasp both of the history of Irân, and as well of its role in the wider region. For those readers who wish to follow the contemporary happenings, a list of useful websites is included as an appendix.

We have also attempted to update the system of transliteration throughout the work, taking as our standard modern Tehrâni pronunciation; this is explained in further detail in the Fârsi language guide, now moved closer to the front of the book (p.95). We hope that readers will refer to this early so that—whether travelling to Irân or not—they will be able to pronounce Irânian words and place-names correctly, and with confidence.

Bijan Omrani, Hong Kong, July 2005.

INTRODUCTION

Since the political and social upheavals that Irân has been undergoing since the revolution in 1979, Western tourism in Irân has shrunk to a mere trickle. Even today, many people simply do not realize that it is possible to travel in Irân. And yet, for several years now, tourism has been developing at a steady rate and the attraction of Irân's cultural and historical riches is proving stronger in the long run than the preconceived ideas that exist about the Islamic Republic.

Those who knew Irân in the 1960s and 1970s will be struck as soon as they arrive by the most obvious changes that have occurred: the growth in the population, unrestrained urbanization, pollution. In addition, a revolution and ten years of war have inevitably left their mark on the people, although these deeper scars are not always immediately visible. Despite this, the quality of the welcome has lost none of its earlier warmth and modern Irân can be as interesting as ancient Persia.

At the beginning of the 21st century, more than two decades after the Islamic Revolution, Irân stands at another turning point in its history. This vast country with enormous economic potential—it contains the third largest oil reserves in the world—is on the verge of becoming one of the most powerful states in the Middle-East. Whatever the long-term evolution of its policies, it can no longer be ignored by the West nor by the rest of the world. Let us then learn to understand it rather than fear it.

IRÂN—A BRIEF HISTORY

"As a beginning you must know precisely what the material of the elements was in origin. God created matter out of nothingness in order that his power might be manifested; out of it was produced the substance of the four elements, without effort and without expenditure of time... When these four elements were once in existence they came together to form the fleeting abode of the world. With sea, mountain, desert and meadow the earth became as bright as a shining lamp. With the mountain towering high, waters coalesced and the heads of the growing plants reared upwards... Overhead, the stars displayed their wonders, casting their brightness on the earth. Fire ascended, water poured down and the sun revolved around the earth..."

Ferdosi, *Shâhnâmeh*

PREHISTORIC IRÂN

Fifteen thousand years before the beginning of the present era, whilst glaciers lay deep upon the face of Europe, the land of Irân, or much of it, was covered by the waters. Rainfall, at that time, was heavy, and near perpetual; lakes stood even in the highest of the mountain valleys; and on the central Plateau of Irân, where now extends a great and hostile desert, an inland sea once rested, collecting the rivers as they flowed down from the heights.

Towards the end of this age, described by geographers as the 'pluvial period', we find the first evidence of man's habitation on the soil of Irân. The rains became less frequent, the inland sea began to recede, and along its coasts or in the foothills of the mountains dwelt early man as a hunter, taking shelter in the caves. Professor Roman Ghirshman, the French archaeologist, leading a campaign of excavation in 1949, unearthed the remains of one of these early settlers at Tang-e Pabda, near Shustar in the Bakhtiâri Mountains. These ancient inhabitants carried implements of bone and already possessed a coarse variety of dark pottery, using weapons fashioned from stone, axes and hammers, to seek after and dismember their prey. It is perhaps also during this period, around 6,000 BC, that the first experiments were made in the cultivation of crops. Cereals, such as wild emmer, the ancestor of wheat, already grew native on the mountain slopes of Irân, and it was a small but important step—taken, many conjecture, by the sedentary women whilst the men were absent on the chase—to collect their seeds, sow them, and harvest their fruits in an organised fashion. It is from these small beginnings that agriculture, as we know it today, began to grow.

As the climate changed, so civilisation evolved. The inland sea dried out fully and disappeared. In its wake was left an earth of rich and heavy silt, fertile for vegetation and attractive to animals. Man too, seeing the newly-uncovered pasture-lands, productive in plant-life and abundant in game, made his way down on to the Iránian Plateau, and across it took up his abode. Fully-fledged settlements appear for the first time. One of these, at Siyalk near Káshán, inhabited from around 5,000 BC into the historical period, reveals the story of man's development. Crude huts made from the branches of trees give way to houses constructed of compacted earth, and later of mud-brick. Their inner walls are painted white; beneath their hearths are buried the bones of the family dead. Outside the houses begins the domestication of animals; cattle, sheep and oxen, are herded and bred. In the field of pottery, a new red ware is now introduced, to which is applied a white slip, decorated with geometrical patterns in imitation of woven baskets. Stone and finely carved animal bone is used for the manufacture of tools; when of the latter, the handles are sometimes exquisitely fashioned also into abstract forms or the heads of animals. Pebbles, bone, and even turquoise are incorporated into necklaces and other pieces of jewellery; personal adornment goes even as far as the application of cosmetics, crushed and prepared in a pestle and mortar.

Although by 4,000 BC we note the appearance of further innovations—copper, both hammered and smelted; the potter's wheel; vases with patterns now also in black—it is more the evolution of trade that has a bearing on the history of the region, rather than the advancement of technology. Merchants, guaranteeing their goods with the newly-invented stamp seal—and later, the cylinder seal—dispatched their wares over international distances; not just luxury items, such as lapis lazuli mined from the mountains of distant Badakhshán, but also more every-day commodities, such as barley, and wheat. The importation of these crops to the Mesopotamian Plain (modern-day Iraq), more fertile and more hospitable for habitation with the onset of time, was to have an important effect. The dwellers in the settlements along the great rivers of antiquity, the Tigris and Euphrates, aided by the introduction of the art of agriculture, were soon to outstrip the inhabitants of the Iránian Plateau. Although it is to the latter that we must look for the invention of farming, it is to the former that we owe the subsequent steps in the progress of civilisation: writing, art, science, and the emergence of the great cities.

THE STATE OF ELAM: 3000–645 BC

The ready abundance of water and the supply of food, the ease of travel over the plains and the navigable rivers, the nearby presence of the sea, the need for learned men and stable governments to administer and co-ordinate the irrigation of the land—through these conditions, in all of which the Irânian Plateau was quite deficient, came into being on the Plain of Mesopotamia the first great urban centres of civilisation. In the southern territory of Sumer began to rise the towns of Erech, Ur, and Larsa. In the northern land of Akkad appeared the settlements of Sippar, Kish, and Babylon. While these progressed as pioneers of mathematics, of literature, and law, the scattered communities on the Plateau of Irân—where oases were few, rivers were scarce, and journeys were difficult—continued as before, unchanging in their ways. Nonetheless, such was not the case for the whole of Irân. Below the mountains in the south-west, the environment was more benign. As with Mesopotamia, though less significant in scale, a number of rivers—the Kârun and the Karkheh—watered a region by the sea, low-lying and fertile. And, as with Mesopotamia, in these surroundings cities also began to grow, and from those cities, the first great empire in the history of Irân: the State of Elam.

The word Elam in the Assyrian language signifies "mountain", and originally denoted only the area to the north, where ran the ranges of the Zagros. The land by the sea where the cities were established was known to the Classical geographers as the Plain of Susiana, taking its name from Susa, the principal city in the district. In early times, the Plain and the mountains were distinct entities. It was only when Susa, in the third millennium BC, began to extend the sphere of its influence to include the mountainous territories to the north, that the name "Elam" came to describe the state in its entirety.

Of the Elamites, we know the names of their principal cities—Susa, Madaktu, and Khaidalu. We know that these cities were governed by Patesis, or Priest-Kings. We also know that their principal god—Inshushinak, or "the Susian", for his real name was never to be uttered—was worshipped in sacred groves, to which the priests and Patesi alone had access. Of these, the holy places of the Elamites, we perhaps have a portrait in the Epic of Gilgamesh, where the hero and his companion Enkidu set out to destroy their enemy Humbaba, who dwells in such a haven:

"Together they went down from the gate and they came to the green-mountain. There they stood still, they were struck dumb; they stood still and gazed at the forest. They saw the height of the cedar, they saw the way into the forest and the track where Humbaba was used to walk. The way was broad and the going was good. They gazed at the mountain of cedars, the dwelling-place of the gods, and the throne of Ishtar. The hugeness of the cedar rose in front of the mountain, its shade was beautiful, full of comfort; mountain and glade were green with brushwood."

Aside from Inshushinak in his sanctuaries, a multitude of other gods and lesser deities were worshipped with ceremonies not dissimilar to the Babylonian. And, moreover, as with the other empires in Mesopotamia, the Elamites would leave for them votive offerings and plaques, inscribed in their own language and a script of their own devising: proto-Elamite, which still today awaits to be deciphered.

For all this, however, the Mesopotamians looked down on the Elamites, considering them to be backward, dangerous, and a threat to their stability. The history of the state, as far as the sources allow us to unravel it, is one of endless conflict with the neighbouring empires. Indeed, one of the earliest-known letters in existence, written in Sumerian around 3000 BC, is a complaint by a priest of the mother-goddess Ninmar that a band of Elamites had ravaged a territory belonging to his city, Lagash, and that he had scattered them only with the grievous loss of his own men. Fearful of the Elamites, but looking greedily at the natural wealth with which their land abounded—timber, copper and gold—it became the policy of the empires which flourished on the Mesopotamian plain to subdue the Elamites, and hold them as a tributary. The first ruler to achieve this feat was Sargon of Akkad, perhaps around 2300 BC; not long after, hegemony over Elam, and also over Mesopotamia, passed into the hands of the Sumerians, and the third dynasty of Ur. The Elamites, however, managed to shake off the yoke of foreign domination towards the end of that millennium. Their resurgent power and the wars they waged against the other cities are thought to have caused more general instability in the area, the movement of refugees, and also—as it was formerly held by many— the flight of Abraham "from Ur of the Chaldees to go into the land of Canaan."

It was at this point, at the beginning of the 2nd millennium BC, that the Elamite state attained its apogee. Free from the rule of outsiders, its boundaries extended as far as the Tigris in the west, and under its authority came all the areas encompassed by the modern Irânian provinces of Khuzestân, Luristân, and Fârs. However, its golden period was to be short-lived. Again, it was overcome, this time by Hammurabi, King of Babylon (author of the famous code of law) around 1700 BC, and despite various periods in the ascendant, particularly around the 12th century BC, it was never again able to obtain its former prominence. When, in 750 BC, the Assyrian Empire came to be the dominant nation in the Mesopotamian Plain, a perennial conflict was joined against Elam; the Assyrians held them responsible for stirring up the inhabitants of subject cities to revolt. The strength of the Elamites was fatally damaged at the battle of Tulliz in 659 BC, and not long after, the state having been rendered irredeemably unstable, Assurbanipal, King of the Assyrians, was able to sack the capital Susa in 645 BC, denude it of its treasures, and raze it to the ground. On the obliteration of this once-great empire, the Prophet Ezekiel wrote:

> *"There is Elam and all her multitude round about her grave, all of them slain, fallen by the sword, which are gone down uncircumcised into the nether parts of the earth, which caused their terror in the land of the living; yet have they borne their shame with them that go down to the pit."*

THE COMING OF THE ARYANS

The balance of power in Irân and the Plains of Mesopotamia was irredeemably to be altered with the arrival from the east of a new and vigorous people: the Aryans. Their place of origin, which they themselves called 'Aryanem-Vaejo', is thought to have been the steppe land between the Oxus and the Jaxartes (the Amu Darya and the Syr Darya), and that a change in climate after 2000 BC compelled them to leave their native territories to seek out a new and more congenial home. The first wave of Aryan immigrants is believed to have arrived in the north of Irân not long after the beginning of the second millennium BC, making their way to the foothills of the northwest by way of the northern coast of the Caspian. Erupting from this district perhaps as little as a hundred years later, a new empire—the Kassite—likely to have been composed of an Aryan aristocracy with a native subject population, was able to dominate the region of southern Mesopotamia until 1100 BC. Indeed, it is the presence of this new people—of whom we know little except that they reverenced a Sun-God, Suryash—that prevented the Elamite realm from any expansion beyond the bounds of the Tigris during this time.

It was in 1500 BC that a second and significant tide of Aryans began to quit Aryanem-Vaejo. This time, making their way directly south across the Oxus, they sojourned for a time in the vicinity of Herât and, as their legends would have it, Balkh 'of the beautiful high-lifted banners', before splitting into two groups. The former continued its way through the land of modern-day Afghânistân, taking the road south of the Hindu Kush to reach Arachosia (Qandahâr) before crossing the Bolan Pass to debouch into India. The latter, on the other hand, proceeded westwards, spreading out across the Plateau of Irân, making it, along with the mountainous terrain of the Zagros and the Alborz, their new and more permanent home.

The incoming settlers were, for the most part, nomadic in their way of life, deficient in many of the arts of civilisation which had, by then, come into being in the Mesopotamian world. Nonetheless, they are thought to have had an advantage over the original population of the Plateau in one important respect: a proficiency in horsemanship. With the aid of this ability and by other means as well, by expulsion, by massacre, and by assimilation, they were able to supplant and surpass the primeval inhabitants of the country, learning from them agriculture and the use of settlements, whilst causing the Aryan language to replace those which had come before it.

With the onset of the 9th century BC, the Aryans begin to make their appearance in the written records of Assyria—then the leading power in Mesopotamia—and thus their disposition throughout the area begins to be understood with a greater clarity. In 844 BC, the Assyrian ruler King Shalmaneser led an expedition to the north of Lake Orumieh, where he found and fought against an Aryan people, the Parsua, or Persians; seven years later, he mounted a similar attack on another Aryan group further to the south—the Madai, or Medes. Other such groupings to be found are the Zikirtu—the Sagartians—in the modern district of Azerbaijân, and the Parthava—the Parthians—in the region of the Caspian gates. We learn that although their land was well-populated and fertile—the great number of prisoners led away by the Assyrians, as well as horses, sheep and cattle, bears testimony to this—the Aryans were a disunited people, divided into tribes, ineffective for defence. This state of affairs was to continue for many years, as were the raiding parties of the Assyrians. The most notable of these, perhaps, was led by Sargon II, who, after laying waste much of the Median territory, in 722 BC "took Samaria, and carried away Israel into Assyria, and placed them... in the Cities of the Medes."

Nonetheless, in time, the Aryans were to take action to defend themselves from the menace of Assyria. The Persians, following the range of the Zagros, migrated south, taking up their residence in an area of the Bakhtiâri mountains near Shushtar, to which they gave the name 'Parsumash' (modern-day Fârs); here, they

Black
Sea

Granicus

LYDIA

CAUCASUS

Aral
Sea

SOGDIANA

Aleppo
Tabriz
ARMENIA
ASSYRIA
Arbela
Caspian
Sea
KARA KUM DESERT
Samarqand

Alexandria
Damascus
MEDIA
Ecbatana
PAMIR
HINDU KUSH

Jerusalem
Rey
Hecatompylos
Bactra
BACTRIA

Babylon
PARTHIA
Haraiwa
(Herât)
Kapisa

EGYPT
Susa
Taxila

SUSIANA
Arachosia
(Qandanâr)

Red
Sea

Persepolis

Persian Gulf
PARSA

Gulf of Oman
Karachi

Arabian
Sea

Indian Ocean

Indus

Tigris
Euphrates
Oxus
Volga
River

ACHAEMENIAN
PERSIA

Achaemenian Empire

Modern Political Boundaries shown in gray

0   200   400   600   800   1,000
Kilometres

© Airphoto International Ltd

hoped to be less vulnerable to attack. The Medes, by contrast, took a more political solution. One of their chiefs, Daiukku, known to the Greeks as 'Deiocies', emerged as a leading figure amongst the people—they trusted beyond all others, says Herodotus, his judgements in law—and from this position was able to unite, with himself as king, a number of the Median tribes. Having taken under his control the Busae, the Parataceni, Struchates, Arizanti, Budii, and the Magi, he chose a site for a new capital—Ecbatana (modern-day Hamadân)—and caused a new city to be built: "...a place of great size and strength fortified by concentric walls, these so planned that each successive circle was higher than the one below it by the height of the battlements... The circles are seven in number and the innermost contained the royal palace and treasury... The battlements of the five outer rings are painted in different colours, the first white, the second black, the third crimson, the fourth blue, the fifth orange; the battlements of the two inner rings are plated with silver and gold respectively." However fanciful Herodotus' description of the capital might be, it is beyond doubt that the foundations had been laid for a challenge on the power of Assyria.

Deiocies' son, Phraortes, came to the Median throne around 655 BC. Continuing the work of his father, he conquered the Persian tribes to the south—a feat allowed by their disunity—before turning his attention to the west, with an attack against the Assyrians. In this attempt, however, he was premature. The might of the Assyrians was still too great to overcome, and he was killed whilst waging his campaign. It was left to his successor, Cyaxares, to throw off, as the Prophet Nahum described it, "The burden of Nineveh." Having reorganised the army of the Medes, converting it from a feudal to a professional, standing force, and seeing off the assaults of a number of Assyria's allies, he marched his troops into Mesopotamia, besieged the Assyrian capital, and finally, in 606 BC, brought about its downfall. The Assyrian Empire, now defunct, was dismembered, the southern lands being allotted to the Babylonians, with the Medes continuing to hold the north, and, by 584 BC— the year of Cyaxares' death—the domain of the Medes extended from Fârs in the east to the River Halys in distant Anatolia. The Irânian plateau now ceased to be a backwater; rather, it harboured, for the first time in recorded history, the seat of power of the leading empire of the East.

THE ACHAEMENIAN EMPIRE: 550 BC–330 BC

Cyaxares was to be succeeded by his son, Astyages, the last of the monarchs of the Median line. Although the empire which he inherited was by no means to be lost, and indeed, was further to expand, control of the kingship was to pass from the Median tribes to those whom once they had held in subjection: the Persians.

Of the Persian tribes which had migrated to the district of Fârs, we know the names of ten: The Pasargadae, the Marphians and the Maspians 'upon which all the other tribes were dependent'; the Panthialaens, the Derusiaens, and the Germanians 'who were all attached to the soil'; and the Daans, the Mardians, the Dropicans, and the Sagartians, who were nomads. The Pasargadae, reports Herodotus, of all of these were the most noble, and it is from them that sprang Achaemenes, the founder of the Royal line.

Although little can be said of Achaemenes—and, indeed, many consider him to be more mythical than real—we can be more certain of the achievements of his son, Teispes, who ruled sometime around 650 BC. Biding his time, he waited for the Assyrian army to finish its destruction of the Elamite realm, before moving in to conquer the territory which they had devastated, and abandoned. The kingdom of Elam, which in the Persian was called 'Anshân' after one of the cities of the region, became a possession of Teispes, who, aside from being the ruler of Fârs, assumed the style of 'Great King, King of Anshân'. However, beyond the lands of the Elamites, there were to be no further additions to the domain of the Persians; rather, the Persians themselves were to become a prey. As mentioned above, Pharortes overwhelmed them, and turned them into a vassal of the empire of the Medes. On the death of Teispes around 600 BC, his kingdom was divided amongst his sons, the elder taking the district of Anshân, and the younger, the district of Fârs, founding, as one inscription puts it, 'a double line of kings.'

It was the third king of the Anshân line, a great-grandson of Teispes, who was to reverse the order of things, wresting power from the Medes and seizing it for the Persians. Of the date of birth of Cyrus the Great, we cannot be certain. However, his coming into the world was, according to Herodotus, accompanied by such portents, dreams, and visions, that he seems, to a modern reader, to be more of the order of prophets than of kings. Like Moses, or so the legend relates, he was abandoned after birth and raised by strangers, his identity a secret; like Christ, a vengeful king—Astyages—hearing prophecies from the wise men of his court that the child would overcome him, ordered his servants to put the babe to death.

Whatever the truth of these stories, we can declare for sure that Cyrus was able to unite the Persians, lead them against the Median King Astyages in three battles, and after the third in 550 BC, march into Ecbatana and claim for himself the throne.

Cyrus, now at the head of the head of the most powerful empire in the East, the ruler of the Medes as well as the Persians, was determined still that his dominion should be enlarged. He marched, in 546 BC, to Asia Minor in the west, and in a daring raid took Sardis, the city of Croesus, the richest monarch of the age of antiquity. Between 545 BC and 539 BC, he turned to Central Asia and the East, subduing the tribes in the regions of Afghânistân, Pakistan, and beyond the bounds of the Oxus. In 538 BC, he returned with his men to Mesopotamia to secure the capitulation of Babylon, and the surrender of its lands. And, all the while, the Greek cities along the coast of Asia Minor were one by one besieged, and taken under his control.

Although Cyrus was one of the greatest conquerors the world had seen to date, he should be remembered for more than his accomplishments on the battlefield, 'so very different was he,' said the Greek writer Xenophon, 'from all other kings.' He showed a generosity to his subject populations that was quite unprecedented, with the result that 'he was able to awaken in them so lively a desire to please him, that they always wished to be guided by his will.' He released the Jews from their captivity in the cities of the Medes, and allowed them to return to Jerusalem to rebuild the Temple. And, when he took the city of Babylon in 538 BC, he did quite the opposite of the Assyrians, who, in 689 BC, had razed it to the ground. Instead, he forbade his troops to loot it, and, sparing the lives of the citizens, acclaimed himself its lawful king according to the ancient customs of the place—an act which led to their hailing him as a liberator and a saviour. All in all, as Donald Wilber wrote, he was the first to display 'that spirit of tolerance which is typical of the Irânian character.'

Cyrus died in 529 BC during a skirmish against a tribe in the east, and the empire devolved to his son, Cambyses. Although Cambyses possessed the martial ability of his father, it seems that he was not treated with the same affection by his subjects, and indeed, according to ancient sources, for much of his life he was plagued by mental illness. In 525 BC, he was able to extend the empire with the annexation of Egypt; however, after further expeditions into other parts of Africa were rewarded with failure, he received the news that an uprising had broken out at home, and, driven to despair, he took his own life.

It seemed at this point that the empire constructed by Cyrus and his Median predecessors was unlikely to survive. Rebellions arose in a number of the provinces, and pretenders to the throne staked out their claims, or prepared to carve out their own personal domains. However, one of the cousins of Cyrus, a descendant of Teispes and king of the ancestral land of Fârs, Darius the Great, was to salvage and rescue the empire from collapse. Claiming the throne in 521 BC, he led a devoted army to crush the revolts, putting down as many as eight in all, in Elam, Media, and Babylon. At length, the dominions were pacified, and in 518 BC, when Darius was universally acknowledged as king, he set out to re-organise the empire so as to enhance its stability and make the prospect of further sedition less likely. He caused it to be divided into twenty satrapies, or districts. To each of these was assigned a satrap, or lord, and, to check the power of the satrap, a general to control his armies, and a secretary of state to control the administration and collect the taxes. Each of these officials was responsible to the government of Darius, and served regular terms, being shuffled around the empire to prevent them from building up a power base. Moreover, also responsible to Darius was a wandering group of peripatetic inspectors, the royal eyes, who journeyed from satrapy to satrapy, listening to complaints, reporting to the centre, and ensuring that all was in order. To facilitate their movement round the empire, a network of roads was built, complete with inns and imperial post stations along the way. The most important of these, the Royal Road from Sardis to Susa, the latter of which was one of the primary venues of the court of Darius, could be traversed by a courier on horseback in around a fortnight. Aside from this, he also ordered irrigation works to be constructed throughout the empire, and splendid buildings to be raised at Susa, as well as at Persepolis.

Darius, however, was not to be universally successful in his military exploits. He led a campaign in 512 BC across the Bosphorus to subdue the Scythian tribes in the south of Russia—the first known expedition of the Persians into Europe—and, aside from the annexation of Thrace, he was unable to engage his enemies in battle. Worse than this, had it not been for the support of the Greek cities of Asia Minor, his force would have been stranded, and indeed obliterated, on the European shores of the Sea of Marmara. It was from this incident—the realisation of the Greeks that the Persians were not invincible—and not, as Herodotus claims, the Siege of Troy, that ultimately came the enmity between the Greeks and the Persians. The Ionian Greek cities under the control of Darius felt emboldened to revolt, the Persian rulers were expelled, and finally, in 498 BC, the city of Sardis, the seat of the Satrap, was burnt. It was five years before the uprising was to be repressed, and Darius, angry at the support which the Greeks on the mainland had lent to the rebels—

including the Athenians, who had despatched to them twenty ships—decided that the Hellenic world in its entirety should be brought to submission. To this end, in 492 BC, a naval expedition was dispatched, but it ran into storms by the rocks of Mount Athos, and was forced to return. Two years later a second attempt was launched, but despite both the numerical superiority of his forces, and various intrigues made with a pro-Persian party in Athens, Darius' army was put to flight on the plain of Marathon (490 BC). In the wake of this defeat, he planned to assemble a grander and more formidable host to visit on the Greeks the revenge he thought they deserved. However, his energies were diverted by a rising in Egypt, and, by reason of his death in 485 BC, he was unable to bring his intentions to fruition.

It was to fall to Darius' son and successor, Khshayarsha—better known by his Greek name Xerxes—to fulfil the designs of his father. It seems, in actual fact, that he himself had little desire of any sort to mount a campaign against the Greeks, and it was only the urging of his counsellors, pointing out that the prestige of Persia would suffer if nothing was done, that led him to assemble his forces. The first few years of his reign were spent in the pacification of

*Two Persian officials,
from a relief carving, Persepolis, 4th Century BC*

Egypt, after which, in 480 BC, a great army, with contingents from every satrapy of the Empire—1,700,000 men according to Herodotus, but more realistically likely to have been 250,000—was assembled in Asia Minor. Bad omens, we hear, were the constant companion of its journey. When a bridge of boats built across the Hellespont to allow the passage of the marching column was blown away in a storm, Xerxes in a fury ordered the river to be given 300 lashes, crying out "Xerxes the King will cross you, with or without your permission." He eventually did manage to cross after the construction of a second bridge, but the invasion was further delayed by the heroic action of 4,000 Greek soldiers at the Pass of Thermopylae; and, although this time he was able briefly to capture the city of Athens, his navy was put to rout at the Battle of Salamis. Not pausing to save face, Xerxes immediately retreated to Asia, nevertheless leaving behind a detachment of troops hoping that they would be able to maintain the gains which had been made. Yet, these were comprehensively defeated at the Battle of Plataea (479 BC), at which point Persian military involvement on the Greek mainland came to an end. Although the Persians would, in the future, by means of diplomacy and finance, continue to interfere in the internal affairs of Greece—the phrase "Persian gold" was often to be heard in Greek politics—never again did they attempt to stage such an invasion as this.

Xerxes' return to his capital might be said to mark the onset of the decadence of his dynasty—a pattern which few of its successors were able to escape. We have a picture, believed by the historians to be authentic in colour, of the latter part of his reign in the Book of Esther (in which he is called Ahasuerus). He was little inclined to depart from Susa, despite the constant attacks of the emboldened Greeks on the distant borders of his empire; rather, he would stay in his palace where he would make feasts "unto all the people that were present... both great and small, seven days in the court of the garden of the king's palace; Where were white, green, and blue hangings, fastened with cords of fine linen and purple to silver rings and pillars of marble: the beds were of gold and silver, upon a pavement of red, and blue and white, and black marble. And they gave them drink in vessels of gold (the vessels being diverse one from another,) and royal wine in abundance, according to the state of the king." The reforms put in place by his father Darius began to unravel: the satraps refused to relinquish their offices on the completion of their terms, but rather continued to hold their provinces as personal fiefdoms and familial possessions; rebellions abounded and lands were lost; and, in the palace itself, the Achaemenian House was riven and enervated by intrigues, plots, and murder.

Xerxes himself was assassinated in 466 BC by the Captain of his Guard, Artabanus, and his successors were never to regain the initial vigour with which his forebears had established the line. Although one of the later kings, Artaxerxes III, was able, to a certain extent, to pacify the rebel territories and re-establish some semblance of central control, the empire was not much longer to survive: the work of Cyrus and the achievements of Darius were ready to be undone by the advent from the west of Alexander the Great.

ALEXANDER THE GREAT AND THE SELEUCIDS

It would not be unjust to say that one of the factors which preserved the Achaemenian Empire for so long was the disunity of their rivals, the Greeks. For all their sense of a strong and shared Hellenic identity, with a common language, literature, and customs of religion, their sense of loyalty to their individual *poleis*, or city-state, was even more prevalent. Every attempt up to the 4th century BC to bind into a federation the little cities which, as Plato said, sat around the Aegean 'like frogs round a pond' was doomed to failure, and, egged on by pride and the ubiquitous presence of 'Persian Gold', they were suspended in an unending round of wars and petty rivalries, quite unable to think of agitating more further afield. However, this was all to change. One of the regions to the north, Macedon, the dwellers of which many of the Greeks regarded as semi-barbarian, with only a veneer of Greek culture, found itself in the ascendant. By the latter half of the 4th century BC, under their gifted leader King Philip, by means of a highly-trained army, innovation in the field of military strategy and tactics, the seizure of a gold-mine and a collection of vital sea-ports, the exploitation of their opponents' lassitude and lack of foresight, diplomatic acuity, cunning, and, when necessary, unmitigated brutality, the Macedonians could lay claim to an unparalleled achievement: the unity of Greece, with them at the head.

In 337 BC, Philip summoned from the city-states their representatives to sit on a Federal Council, whose duty would be the wider government of the region. To them, he announced a new and grander plan: the conquest, by an army of Greeks, of the Empire of Persia. The council, perhaps after some hesitation, assented to his proposal; yet, in spite of their support, he was never to see his plans through to fruition: the next year he fell victim to the dagger of an assassin. His son Alexander, nonetheless, was by no means reluctant to assume control of the venture. At the age of twenty, he might have been regarded as somewhat immature in terms of years to

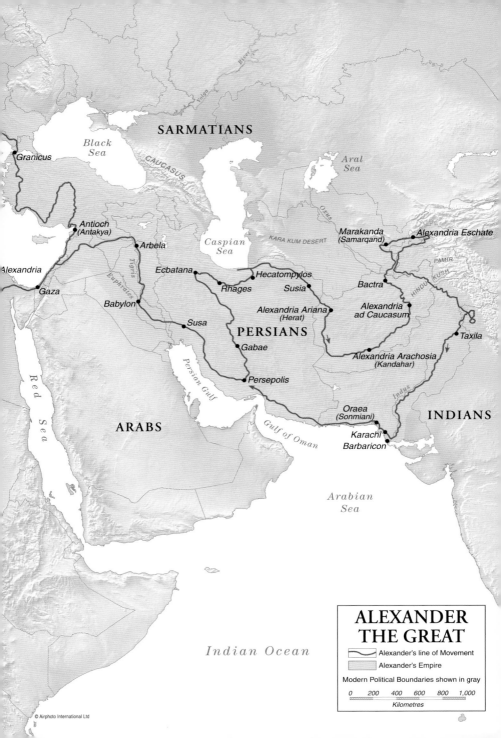

SARMATIANS

Black Sea

Granicus

CAUCASUS

Volga River

Aral Sea

Antioch
(Antakya)

Arbela

Caspian Sea

KARA KUM DESERT

Oxus

Marakanda
(Samarqand)

Alexandria Eschate

Alexandria

Ecbatana

Hecatompylos

Susia

Bactra

PAMIR

Gaza

Tigris

Euphrates

Rhages

Alexandria Ariana
(Herat)

Alexandria
ad Caucasum

HINDU KUSH

Babylon

Susa

PERSIANS

Gabae

Taxila

Persian Gulf

Alexandria Arachosia
(Kandahar)

Indus

Persepolis

Red Sea

ARABS

Gulf of Oman

Oraea
(Sonmiani)

Karachi
Barbaricon

INDIANS

Arabian Sea

Indian Ocean

ALEXANDER THE GREAT

Alexander's line of Movement

Alexander's Empire

Modern Political Boundaries shown in gray

0   200   400   600   800   1,000

Kilometres

© Airphoto International Ltd

embark on an invasion of the largest empire the world had seen to date; yet, in other respects, this was by no means the case. His tutor at school had been Aristotle; he had served in father's campaigns against the Greeks with distinction, demonstrating not just courage and an ability to endure hardship, but also an excellent grasp of strategy; and, perhaps most importantly of all, his fanatical devotion to the *Iliad*, along with the persuasions of his mother, had engendered in him the belief that he was marked out for greatness, that he was destined, like Achilles, to bestride the world as a hero.

To this end, after he had pacified the Greek mainland (for a number of rebellions had broken out on the death of his father), Alexander assembled his men—a mere 30,000 infantry and 5,000 cavalry—and made his way across the Hellespont. Having paused at the site of Troy to contemplate the ruins of the city—and indeed to pay tribute to the tomb of Achilles with the laying of a garland and a dance in the nude—he joined his first battle against the armies of the Persians on the banks of the River Granicus (334 BC). This fight was little more than a skirmish with a small detachment of local troops in which the Persians did badly, as a result of which two of the region's satraps were killed, and the third committed suicide. As Alexander proceeded to free the Greek cities nearby from the control of the Persians, and furnish them with democratic constitutions, news of the invasion and the early defeat was brought to the Persian capital. The new King, Darius III— a distant scion of the royal line, installed after the murder of Artaxerxes III—realising that he had no alternative but to act, collected together his household troops, cavalry, and archers; with these, and a detachment of Greek mercenaries, he began the march northwards to meet the invaders. Battle was eventually joined near the Issus in the region of Syria (November 333 BC). Although in number the Persian forces were far superior—some estimates place them as high as 600,000—in other respects, the advantages were with the Macedonians. Their troops were more highly trained and better drilled; they employed the latest developments in military tactics including the phalanx, or infantry formation of overlapping shields and long pikes; and, both the cavalry and the infantry could boast of a greater mobility than their Persian counterparts. Moreover, specific to Issus itself, Darius had foolishly chosen to offer battle on a narrow plain, confined on one side by a range of mountains, and on the other by the sea. In such circumstances he was quite unable to deploy his full forces, and the numerical superiority which he possessed was turned to no account. Alexander placed his phalanx in the middle of the battlefield with his own companion cavalry to the right flank. Whilst the former occupied the attention of the Persians in the centre of the field, he ordered wave after wave of his cavalry to attack at the edge of the Persian lines. After a period of heavy fighting during which the outcome of affairs still hung in doubt, Alexander, at the head of his horsemen, smashed his way through the Persian cordon, and Darius, becoming fearful of the breakthrough, turned from the battlefield, and fled. His men, now without their leader, began to retreat in disarray, and the Macedonians, seeing their disorder, threw themselves into a charge, killing perhaps as many as 100,000 Persians in the confusion. Not only did Alexander carry the day; he also captured the baggage and harem of the King, taking into his custody the Queen Consort and Queen Mother. Although he treated them honourably, he refused to release them, despite Darius' offer to cede to him the western half of his empire in exchange for peace and their return; he was determined on victory outright.

Alexander, however, was in no hurry to bring the campaign to a conclusion. He continued southwards down the Levant, securing the cities towards his rear, before making his way into Egypt. Here, in 332 BC, as the population who were weary of the sovereignty of the Persians acclaimed him as a liberator, he paused to sail down the Nile, mark out the bounds of a new city—Alexandria—and finally visit the desert oracle of Zeus Ammon, who hailed the Macedonian as a son of the god. In the meantime Darius had returned to his heartlands to summon up the full forces of the Empire, ready to meet Alexander with, as the historian C.E. Robinson put it, 'a true Oriental host.' When Alexander finally made his way out of Egypt towards Mesopotamia and Persia to meet Darius for a second time at the Battle of Arbela (October 331 BC), Darius arrayed before him an army of a million men, embellished with a fleet of scythe-bearing chariots, and fifteen war elephants imported from the satrapies of India.

For all the might laid out before him, Alexander was contemptuous. "Look at the disorganised army of the Persians," he is reputed by Quintus Curtius to have said, "some only armed with a javelin, others with stones in slings, only a few with regular weapons. There are more men standing on the Persian side, but more are going to be fighting on the Macedonian." And so it proved to be. Indeed, the battle was in essence no more than a repeat of their previous encounter. The elephants were ineffective; the perfectly-drilled Macedonian phalanxes, when confronted with the scythe bearing chariots, merely stepped aside to let them harmlessly through, before again closing their ranks and resuming their attack. And Alexander, leading his elite cavalry before the standards, broke through the flank of the Persians, and, making his way towards the vanguard of Darius, terrified his rival once more into flight. Darius' army disintegrated, and his claim to be the 'Great King', in effect, was forfeit to the invader.

Alexander was now free to make his way through the great cities of the Empire at his leisure. He was welcomed at Babylon, which he treated in the same fashion as Cyrus had done two hundred years earlier. Susa as well admitted the conqueror without incident, surrendering to him the wealth that had accumulated in its vaults over the age of empire—50,000 talents, or roughly 650 tonnes of gold. One of the Satraps, Ariobarzanes, determined to fight to the death, put up a stern resistance to Alexander before he could enter Persepolis; yet, the city was eventually taken, and —whether as revenge for Xerxes' devastation of Athens, or just an accident at a drunken orgy is unclear—the opulent Palace was put to the torch.

It only remained for Alexander to pursue and capture the fleeing Darius as he made his way to the satrapies of the east, hoping there to raise another army and return to confront the invaders. Alexander therefore set off northwards via Ecbatana, making his way towards the Caspian Gates—the route to the plains of Central Asia. However, despite his speed, riding up to 50 miles in a day, he was never to see Darius alive. One of the members of the Persian court, Bessus, the Satrap of Bactria (Northern Afghânistân), had killed the king, leaving his body abandoned in an ox-cart near Dâmghân. Alexander, we hear, was mortified to discover his opponent in such a disgraceful state, and, pausing only to order for him a funeral befitting his rank, proceeded eastwards to punish this Bessus for disloyalty to his king.

Bessus was finally captured, tried, and executed in 330 BC. In spite of this, Alexander continued his campaigns in Afghânistân and beyond the bounds of the Oxus, before turning back at the River Hydaspes (modern-day Jhelum) in India— his men refused to go any further into the unknown—and reaching Babylon, where he died in 323 BC.

It is the view of many historians—though by no means of all—that Alexander's intention was, by his conquests, to eradicate the distinction between barbarian and Greek, and, by the promulgation of a great and universal empire, to make available to all the benefits of the civilisation of the Greeks. However, he died too young and too suddenly fully to realise this vision, and his successors were not of a stamp to bring it to pass. The rule of Irân, and, at the beginning, the whole of Asia devolved to one of his generals, Seleucus, but although a large number of Greek immigrants came to settle in the Irânian cities, bringing with them their culture, art, institutions and language, they were unable to leave a truly lasting impression on the nature of the country. As for the Greek dynasty founded by Seleucus, it was to be short lived, ceding ground in the east to breakaway states and nomadic invasions, and in the west (Syria and Mesopotamia) to the waxing power of the Romans. Into the hands of one of the dynasties of these nomadic invaders—the Arsacid, or Parthian dynasty —was to fall the rule of Irân itself.

THE PARTHIANS: 250 BC–AD 224

The Roman historian Justin wrote of the Parthians that, at the time of their rise to power, they were "the most obscure of all of the people of the East." The Epic Poet of Irân, Ferdosi, is even more at a loss: "...the learned narrator holds no record of their annals. I have heard nothing of them but their name, nor seen anything in the Book of the Kings." We are, however, in a position to say a little more than this. It appears that, as the Seleucid Dynasty began to lose its hold over the eastern districts of Irân, the native Parthian folk—an Aryan people, as mentioned before, living in the south-eastern coastal region of the Caspian—were conquered by the Parni, a tribe which hailed from the steppe land between the Oxus and the Jaxartes. Around 250 BC, Arsaces, the chief of the tribe and founder of the Parthian royal dynasty— the Arsacids—taking advantage of the decline in central government control, drove out the Greek satrap Andragoras, and seized the area for himself. In 247 BC, he was succeeded by his brother Tiridates, who was not only to extend the sphere of Parthian control to include the neighbouring region of Hyrcania on the southern coast of the Caspian, but also to fortify the existing cities, and found a new capital for Parthia: Dara. Its location is unknown, but, according to Justin, "no place can be more secure or more pleasant, for it is so encircled with steep rocks, that the strength of its position needs no defenders; and such is the fertility of the adjacent soil, that it is stored with its own produce. Such too is the plenty of springs and wood, that it is amply supplied with streams of water, and abounds with all the pleasures of the chase."

The Parthian soldiery, it seems, made a fearsome and difficult opponent for the troops of the Seleucids. They were masters of horsemanship—"on horses they go to war, and to feasts; on horses they discharge public and private duties; on horses they go abroad, meet together, traffic and converse", says the historian—and this skill they put to good use on the battlefield, being able to ride at full speed and fire arrows both ahead of them, and behind. Conventionally, they would feign retreat in the midst of an engagement, and then "return to the battle afresh; so that when you feel most certain you have conquered them, you still have to meet the greatest danger from them." Building on these abilities, they were able to fend off or overcome the attempts on the part of the Seleucids to regain their primacy in Irân. By the reign of Mithridates I (171–138 BC), the Parthians could claim an empire including the districts of Media, Elymais, Persis, and Babylonia. His successors secured their borders in the east against a new wave of nomadic invaders, the Sakae, and in the west against the last of the Seleucids, with the result that, by the beginning of the 1st century BC, they came to share a common boundary with the other emerging power in the region: the Empire of Rome.

The relations between Irân and the Romans over the next few centuries were never to be very happy. Their dealings were to be poisoned by the location of the frontier between them, and, as Sir Percy Sykes put it, "the constantly recurring Armenian Question." The northern kingdom of Armenia, sitting as a buffer between the two empires in that area, was an endless source of dispute. On the one hand, the Parthians desired to hold it to gain access to the Black Sea, and there, to challenge the dominance of the Romans; on the other hand, the Romans wished to keep it as a vassal state, so as to project their power against the neighbouring Parthians. These problems were to be an endless source of diplomatic wrangles and military campaigns, both difficult to remember and complex to relate. The two empires, at the beginning, maintained a quiet and non-too cordial truce, agreeing to hold the Euphrates as the demarcation line between them. However, in 53 BC, Marcus Licinius Crassus, the Roman proconsul of Syria, acting somewhat on his own initiative and perhaps eager to rival the achievements of his predecessors such as Pompey, marched 40,000 men across the river into Parthian territory, thinking to win an easy victory. However, he was unacquainted with the Parthian manner of fighting, and his troops, although skilled in combat at close-quarters, against the horsemen and archers of the Parthians were of little or no avail. 20,000 men, including Crassus himself, are thought to have died at the Battle of Carrhae, and at least another 10,000 were taken captive to Hyrcania, along with—to the shame and chagrin of the Romans—three legionary standards. The shock in Rome was expressed by the poet Horace: "has the soldier of Crassus lived on, a husband disgraced by a barbarian wife, and, alas… does an Italian live happily under a Persian king, forgetful of the shields and the toga and eternal Vesta, while Jupiter and the city of Rome stands safe?" Despite attempts to retrieve the standards, including an expedition led by Marc Antony himself in 34 BC, they were not to return to Rome for another 15 years, when Augustus consented to acknowledge the Euphrates as the border, and to leave the Parthians in peace.

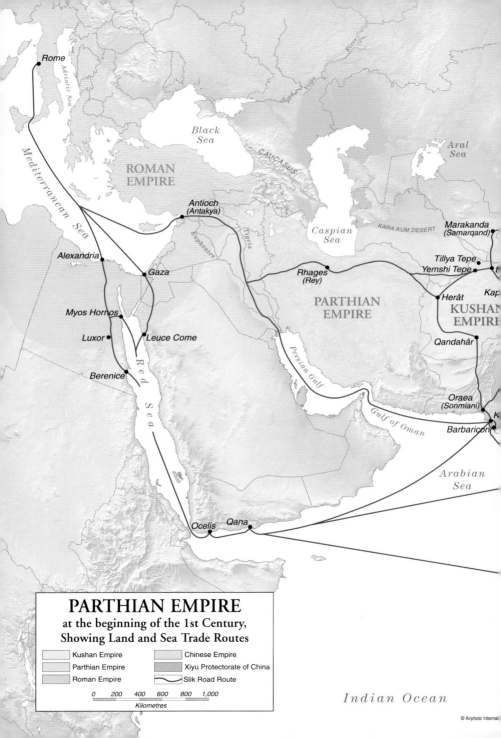

Rome

Adriatic Sea

Mediterranean Sea

Black Sea

ROMAN EMPIRE

CAUCASUS

Caspian Sea

Aral Sea

Volga River

KARA KUM DESERT

Marakanda (Samarqand)

Antioch (Antakya)

Euphrates

Tigris

Tillya Tepe
Yemshi Tepe

Alexandria

Gaza

Rhages (Rey)

PARTHIAN EMPIRE

Herât

KUSHAN EMPIRE

Kap

Myos Hornos

Luxor

Leuce Come

Qandahâr

Berenice

Red Sea

Persian Gulf

Gulf of Oman

Oraea (Sonmiani)

K

Barbaricon

Arabian Sea

Ocelis

Qana

PARTHIAN EMPIRE
at the beginning of the 1st Century,
Showing Land and Sea Trade Routes

	Kushan Empire		Chinese Empire
	Parthian Empire		Xiyu Protectorate of China
	Roman Empire		Slik Road Route

0   200   400   600   800   1,000
Kilometres

Indian Ocean

© Airphoto Internat

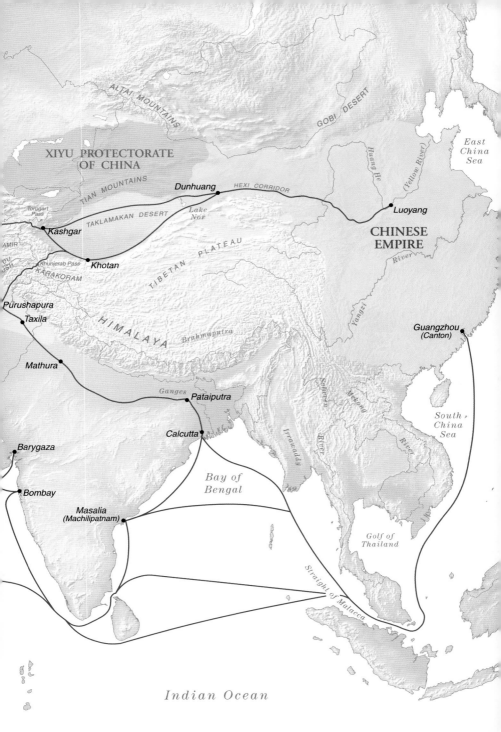

ALTAI MOUNTAINS

GOBI DESERT

Huang He

(Yellow River)

East China Sea

XIYU PROTECTORATE OF CHINA

TIAN MOUNTAINS

Dunhuang

HEXI CORRIDOR

Luoyang

Torugart Pass

TAKLAMAKAN DESERT

Lake Nor

CHINESE EMPIRE

AMIR

Kashgar

DU JSH

Khunjerab Pass

Khotan

River

KARAKORAM

TIBETAN PLATEAU

Purushapura

Taxila

H I M A L A Y A

Brahmaputra

Guangzhou (Canton)

Mathura

Ganges

Pataiputra

Yangzi

Calcutta

Salween

Mekong

South China Sea

Barygaza

Bay of Bengal

Irrawaddy River

Bombay

Masalia (Machilipatnam)

Golf of Thailand

Straight of Malacca

Indian Ocean

In spite of the period of relative calm ushered in by this truce, the Parthian state began to grow weak, rent apart, it seems, by revolts and a vying for power between the king and his nobles. In AD 114, the Romans under the Emperor Trajan, hoping to exploit this open dissent, invaded afresh, capturing the new capital Ctesiphon on the Tigris, and crowning a puppet king to rule on their behalf. However, the Parthian nobles, galvanised into action by this defeat, united, and drove the Romans back beyond the boundaries of Mesopotamia. Not long after, in AD 161, King Vologases IV staged a counter-invasion of the Roman territories, and similarly was beaten back by the Romans under Marcus Aurelius. This pattern of warfare, attack and counter-attack, was to continue without ceasing, until the Parthian House itself, worn out by the combat and unable to maintain its authority at home, was unseated from power in a sudden civil war. The last great dynasty of pre-Islamic Irân, the Sasanian, rose up to take its place.

THE SASANIANS: AD 224–AD 650

On the origins of the Sasanian dynasty, legend is more forthcoming than verifiable fact, and even the most careful historians to write on the subject are apt to be nothing less than contradictory. It seems to be generally agreed, however, that, in the latter half of the 2nd century AD, a man named Sasan attained eminence as the high priest of the temple of Anâhitâ at Istakhr; this, it should be noted, was in the land of Fârs, the heartland of the Achaemenians, not far from Persepolis itself. His son, called Bâbak or Pâpak, was married to the daughter of the local ruler; yet, in spite of this familial connection, he overthrew his father-in-law from his position, and claimed the title for himself. Artabanus V, the king of the Parthian Empire, protested against this usurpation, but engaged in his struggle with the Romans, was unable to do anything more. Bâbak, it seems, and Ardeshir, his son after him, convinced a number of the nobles of the region to accept him as their lord, and to go on to fight against the Parthian king for control of the empire. By persuasion or conquest, the number of his followers increased, with the result that by AD 224, he was able to challenge Artabanus in battle, and, killing him in single combat, bring an end to the rule of the Parthians.

The myths recorded by the Irânian epic poet Ferdosi suggest that the Sasanians were descended from the Royal Achaemenian line; moreover, the stories with which he surrounds the ascent of Ardeshir to power are reminiscent in spirit to those with which Herodotus embellishes the early years of Cyrus the Great. And indeed, the achievements of the two monarchs were not dissimilar. Like Cyrus, he led an army to the east, reaching into India and making the Kushan Empire, which then held the lands of Afghânistân, his tributary. Turning to the west, he attacked in 229 the Emperor of Rome, Severus Alexander, and, defeating him, acquired Armenia as a possession. At home, he reorganised the army, seizing for himself and centralising the authority of the regional commanders. He confirmed Zoroastrianism, which had also been adhered to by the Parthians, as the religion of state, and is credited by Ferdosi with a reputation of justice: "Consider the altar and the throne as inseparable; they must always sustain one another. A sovereign without religion is a tyrant." (For more on the position of the various religions in the Sasanian empire see p. 256) Perhaps of interest to the contemporary advocates of a free market would be his reputed statement: "There can be no power without an army, no army without money, no money without agriculture, and no agriculture without justice." However, Ferdosi also imputes to him the saying: "Hold money in contempt. Sell no man for gain, for this fleeting world lasts for nobody. Seek ever for honesty and wisdom; let greed and folly be remote from you."

The son of Ardeshir, Shâpur, who came to the throne in AD 240 continued a perennial war against the Romans, making sallies deep into Asia Minor, taking Antioch for a time, and even, near the city of Edessa, capturing Valerian, the Emperor of Rome himself. This event, which caused as great a shock in the West as the defeat at Carrhae 300 years previously, was an undoubted fillip for the Sasanians. The defeated Emperor was depicted in carvings at Naqsh-e Rostam near Persepolis, and, according to the Roman writer Lactantius, to add to his humilia-tion: "Whenever Shâpur chose to get into his carriage or to mount on horseback, he commanded the Roman to stoop and present his back; then, setting his foot on the shoulders of Valerian, he said, with a smile of reproach, 'Forget the scenes of triumph your painters paint in Rome: this is how it really is.'" On his death, claims Lactantius, Valerian was flayed, the skin stripped from its flesh, dyed vermillion, and "hung in a barbarian temple, to serve as an admonition... lest the Romans should trust too much in their strength."

After many efforts, and indeed, the death of Shâpur, the Romans for a time were to regain much of ground that they had lost in the Middle East. The first attempt in AD 283, although initially successful, was brought to nothing after the commander of the army of invasion, Carus, was struck by lightning. His successors under the Emperor Diocletian, however, were able to wrest a number of provinces from the Persians, but, powerless to escape from the pattern of history by now well established,

Rome

Adriatic Sea

*Black
Sea*

CAUCASUS

Volga River

*Aral
Sea*

Oxus

Granicus

**BYZANTINE
EMPIRE**

Trabzon

Tabriz

*Caspian
Sea*

KARA KUM DESERT

*Mediterranean
Sea*

Aleppo

Arbela

Ecbatana

Hecatompylos

Damascus

Rey

Herâ

Alexandria

Ctesiphon

Jerusalem

Babylon

Susa

**SASANIAN
EMPIRE**

Nile

Tigris

Euphrates

Persian Gulf

Persepolis

*Red
Sea*

Gulf of Oman

Gulf of Aden

Indian Ocean

© Airphoto International Ltd.

ALTAI MOUNTAINS

GOBI DESERT

Huang He (Yellow River)

TIAN MOUNTAINS

• Dunhuang

• Luoyang

Lake Nor

TAKLAMAKAN DESERT

TIBETAN PLATEAU

• Samarqand

PAMIR

HINDU KUSH

KARAKORAM

RIVER

• Bactra

Kapisa

HIMALAYA

Qandahár

Indus

Pataiputra

Calcutta

• Karachi

Arabian
Sea

Golf of
Thailand

Indian Ocean

SASANIAN
EMPIRE

Sasanian Empire

Modern Political Boundaries shown in gray

0   200   400   600   800   1,000
Kilometres

lost them again to King Shâpur II (309–379). Endless campaigns, and even a force of 100,000 men under the Emperor Julian in 363 were unable to make a permanent inroads into the territory of the Persians, and it was at this time that their Empire saw, as Sykes declares "the zenith of her power and glory." Yet, they too in the following century suffered reverses, particularly in the eastern areas and Afghânistân, where a new group of nomadic invaders—the Hephthalites, or White Huns—began to cross from Transoxiana and attack the Sasanian possessions. They were at first held off, but during the reign of King Firuz (459–484), through a number of causes were able to gain the ascendancy. The Sasanian Empire was weakened by famine—"the water in the channels became as scarce as musk," says Ferdosi, "and, because of the multitude of dying men and cattle, there was not room to set foot on the surface of the earth". Moreover, the Persian monarch, through a number of diplomatic errors—for example, sending a slave-girl in place of his daughter to wed a Hephthalite ruler—managed to alienate his followers as well as infuriate his opponents. Undergoing a number of defeats, the Persian Empire was reduced to the status of a vassal kingdom until one of Firuz's successors, Noshirwan, with the aid of an alliance with the Turks of Transoxiana, was able to destroy in the 6th century ad the rule of the Hephthalites.

Noshirwan (531–579), known to the historians of Irân as Noshirwan the Just, was to inaugurate the final period of prosperity that the Sasanian Empire was to see before its ultimate destruction. The incursions into Roman territory continued, and although the sack of such cities as Antioch and Edessa brought money for the treasury and glory for the king himself, the policy of incessant conflict began gradually to exhaust in every respect the resources of the Persians. Nonetheless, this gradual decline was masked by a number of reforms in the system of government. The Empire was divided into four substantial satrapies, whose affairs were monitored, as in the time of Darius, by an extensive system of spies. Powers, lost by the central administration over the previous century, were reacquired. The rural areas, which had suffered grievously over the previous century not only in the famine and wars, but also through a number of internal revolts (see p. 168 on the Mazdakites) were restored to their former conditions, with the rebuilding of villages, the repair of roads, and the excavation of canals and channels of irrigation that had fallen into disuse. The system of taxes and was re-ordered to be more equitable, and, to facilitate its collection, a regular survey of the land was made, and its agricultural production was noted. Moreover, to ward off the Hephthalites and the nomadic wanderers of the east, fortifications were constructed, and even, by the south-eastern shore of the Caspian, an Irânian version of the Great Wall of China (see p. 226).

Aside from his achievements in government, Norshirwan was also renowned for his erudition. He hosted in his court a number of Greek Neo-Platonist philosophers exiled from Byzantium, commissioned and studied a translation into Persian of the works of Aristotle and Plato, and established at Gondeshâpur in Khuzestân a University for the study of medicine and the liberal arts. More than this, he ordered the composition of a *Khudhay–Namak*, or "Book of the Kings," to record the known history and legends of Persia; it was from this that the great epic poet of Irân, Ferdosi, would in time draw for his work. Noshirwan's famous Vizir, Bozorgmehr, is also credited with the invention of backgammon, devised, it is said, in response to the Indian invention of chess; he hoped by it to baffle a delegation of ambassadors from that country, and was most certainly successful in his endeavour.

The Sasanian Empire was to expire in a final blaze of glory. It is almost strange to relate, in the face of the previous history, that with the accession of Khusro II in 591, relations with the Romans were good, and that there was a real prospect of a true and enduring peace. This new cordiality was more than an empty expression of the diplomats: the Roman Emperor, Maurice, had supported Khusro against a military coup, and helped him to attain the throne with the aid of the Roman army. Khusro, as a result, saw the Emperor as a personal benefactor, and was by no means inclined to attack him. Thus, when Maurice was assassinated, Khusro, by an invasion of the Roman Empire, was determined to avenge him. Aided by one of the Roman generals who had helped him back to power, he began a march into Syria, and, in a campaign of conquest reminiscent of an earlier heroic age, he led his armies to Jerusalem, capturing the relic of the 'True Cross'; to Alexandria, drawing the bounds of the Sasanian Empire level with those of the Achaemenian; and into Asia Minor, where Chalcedon, near Constantinople, was taken: the capital of the Roman Empire of the east was driven near to collapse.

However, from the chaos was to come a saviour in the person of Heraclius. The new emperor, first having raised the siege of Constantinople, in 622 embarked an army in his ships—the one asset which was still lacking to the Persians—and landed them (perhaps thinking of Alexander) in the vicinity of the Issus. In a brilliant campaign, he won several victories over the forces of the Persians, and, in 627, again like Alexander, defeated them conclusively in a battle near Arbela, from which Khusro, his courage failing like Darius, escaped in flight. A settlement was negotiated in the next year by the Persian nobles, who deposed their King, and executed his heirs. No recovery, however, was to come with the peace. The exploits of Khusro, his death, and the crisis of succession which this brought about, along with

FERDOSI AND THE *SHÂHNÂMEH*

The *Shâhnâmeh*, or *Book of Kings*, is the national Irânian epic. About fifty thousand distichs long, it relates the history of the country from the creation of the world to the Arab conquest in the seventh century. The figures in the *Shâhnâmeh* and their adventures—sometimes glorious, sometimes pathetic—are known to all in the Persian-speaking world, and even further afield, in India and Turkey. The most famous episodes have become the favorite subject-matter of miniature painters: the battles of the hero Rostam against the Turks of Turân; the death of Sohrâb, killed by Rostam, his father, unaware of his son's true identity; the revenge of the young prince Siâvush; the love of King Khusro and Shirin; the fight between King Bahrâm Gur and a fearsome dragon. The main themes of the *Shâhnâmeh* are those of the Sasanian period: the legitimacy of the ruling king; the loyalty of vassals; the inexorability of fate; and the fight between Good and Evil symbolized by the battles between Irân and Turân.

The author of the *Shâhnâmeh*, Ferdosi, was born near Tus, in Khorâsân, between AD 932 and 942. For twenty-five years he worked on this vast epic. In 1010 he presented the finished work to the ruling Ghaznavid sultan, Mahmud, but, after a disagreement with the king, he was forced to flee the court. He returned to his native village to die in 1020. According to tradition, Sultan Mahmud, realizing too late the poet's genius, sent him as a reward a caravan-load of treasure, but it arrived after Ferdosi's death.

While writing the *Shâhnâmeh*, Ferdosi drew from a very rich and varied literary—and probably oral—corpus. From these sources he produced a work that represents the pre-Islamic memory of the Irânian people. In the tenth century, heroic oral narratives were still very much alive in Irân, despite the Arab conquest. In addition to the ancient histories written in Pahlavi (Middle Persian) and the royal chronicles of the Sasanian Dynasty, there existed a Book of Kings from the end of the Sasanian period as well as several *Shâhnâmeh* written in prose in the ninth and tenth centuries, including one begun by Abu Mansur in 957. A few years later, at the request of a Samanid emir, the poet Daqiqi began a verse *Shâhnâmeh*. After his sudden death in 975, Ferdosi took over the project, incorporating Daqiqi's verses into his own work.

Ferdosi's verse has retained many archaic Persian words, close to the Pahlavi, which fit perfectly its heroic tone. Although the author uses hyperbole and metaphors, his style is nonetheless simple and the cadence of the verse grand.

Statue of Ferdosi in Ferdosi Square, Tehrân

the unending centuries of war against the Romans, had utterly enfeebled the empire of the Sasanians. Weakened by strife and without any leader of authority, their kingdom was to make an easy prey for the next opponent to rise against it—the warriors of the Arabs, and the Empire of Islam.

THE ISLAMIC CALIPHATE AND THE INDEPENDENT DYNASTIES

Engrossed in their interminable wars, the Sasanian Empire and the Roman Empire of the east (by this point, it would be more correct to say the Byzantine Empire) became recklessly heedless of the developments to the south. The tribes of Arabia, who beforehand were accustomed to expending their energies in quarrels amongst themselves, had been united by the agency of the Prophet of Islam. Galvanised by his proclamation of a new faith, and ceasing—at least for a time—to feud against each other, they turned their attention outwards, and settled their intention on a campaign of territorial conquest. It is perhaps unsurprising that they should have come to such a decision at this point in history. The Arabian Peninsula, it seems, was suffering from disorders and the movement of population brought about by economic and even climatic upheavals: an exodus to the north became, in the circumstances, expedient. Moreover, with the absolute enervation of the Byzantine and Sasanian forces, an attack against them by the Arabs was more likely to succeed in the 630s than in any previous point in time. Not hesitating, therefore, to take advantage of the weakness of their enemies, the Arabs boldly attacked on two fronts, not fearing to take on both of the great empires at once. Whilst in the west, they pushed towards Damascus and Jerusalem, in the east the general Khalid ibn Walid, leading a troop of Bedouin fighters, began in 633 his march against the Sasanians. Approaching the border post of the Sasanian Empire at al-Hafar near modern-day Kuwait, he sent, according to the historian al-Tabari, a letter to the local Sasanian governor Hormuz, demanding surrender: "Whoever worships the way we worship, faces the direction we face in prayer, and eats meat slaughtered in our fashion, that person is a Muslim who obtains the benefits we enjoy and takes up the responsibilities we bear." Should Hormuz fail to send hostages to the Arabs and place himself under his protection, then, Khalid warned "by Him other than Whom there is no god, I will most certainly send against you a people who love death just as you love life."

Hormuz was unwilling to accede to the demands of the invader; indeed, as their armies joined battle, he challenged the Arab leader to engage in single combat. This, however, lead to the death of the Persian commander, and the rout of his forces. The loss of this battle—known to Muslim history as the 'Battle of the Chains' on account of the number of Persians led away shackled as prisoners—marked the beginning of the final collapse of the Sasanian Empire. A number of engagements between the armies of the two nations followed, culminating in the four day Battle of Qadisiyya in 636, and the fall of the administrative capital Ctesiphon two years later. Unable to call upon the resources or revenues of the lost province of Mesopotamia, the inhabitants of the Plateau of Irân found themselves even less capable of self-defence than before. Again, they were defeated at the battle of Nehâvand in 641, the final Shâh Yazdgerd III went into flight, and little more could be done. The Arab armies occupied the land province by province, some of the cities surrendering freely, and others, such as Rey and Susa, putting up resistance. For all this, the country—aside from the region of Tabaristân on the coast of the Caspian, difficult of access on account of its forests and unwelcoming terrain—was quickly captured, and Yazdgerd III was murdered near Merv. The Sasanian Empire had come to an end.

The history of Irân in the immediate years after its fall to the Arabs is perhaps best summed up in the words of Sir John Malcolm: "Its history, during that period, is to be found in that of its conquerors, and even there it occupies but a small and unimportant space. The only events of consequence are petty revolts of insubordinate governors, who, when the power of the Caliphs declined, tried to render the provinces to which they were appointed hereditary principalities, and humbled themselves to that paramount power when it was strong and efficient." Thus, from 661, Irân was ruled by the Umayyad Caliphs (successors to the Prophet) from their seat in Damascus, overseen by Arab governors appointed to administer the individual regions, and taxed on behalf of authority at the local level by *dehqâns*—local Persian gentry, native to the land.

On account of the lack of hard evidence, it is difficult to say anything substantive about the rate of conversion from the original faiths to Islam. While it appears that there was little in the way of forced conversion, and that Zoroastrianism was tolerated as the faith of a conquered minority, many indeed decided to accept the beliefs of their conquerors over time. The position of Zoroastrianism was perhaps weakened on account of the complexity of its rituals, its connections to the lost Sasanian government, and the tax disadvantages to which non-Muslims were compelled to submit. On the other hand, Irân is striking in comparison to the other regions overwhelmed by the Islamic invaders, in that it was able to preserve much of its culture from assimilation and disappearance. Many of the languages spoken in the areas taken over by the Muslims, for example Aramaic or Syriac, dwindled into virtual extinction, whereas Persian, possibly thanks to its essential dissimilarity to Arabic—the former is of the Indo-European family, the latter of the Semitic—was able to survive. Babylon, Egypt, and Persia all had high cultures and periods of imperial dominance, but perhaps, as Bernard Lewis suggests, because the Persian was so fresh in the memory of the people, it was ultimately able to endure.

If not militarily, then at least in the spheres of culture and government, the Persian element was soon to reassert itself. As the 8th century went on, discontent with the Umayyad Caliphate in the north-eastern region of Khorâsân began to surface. Scholars are by no means agreed on the reasons for its appearance; nonetheless, many contend that its ultimate cause was the disgruntlement of non-Arab converts to Islam, who were being treated by the invaders as second-class Muslims. At any rate, they were stirred to revolt by a charismatic leader, Abu Muslim, who led them to sweep away the Umayyad ruler in 750, and establish a new line of caliphs—the Abbâsids—who were descended from an uncle of the prophet, named Abbâs. When one of the greatest of their number, al-Mansur, decided to found a new capital for the Islamic Empire at Baghdâd in 766, Persian culture finally found an outlet for self-expression. Itself near the old Sasanian capital of Ctesiphon, it made free use of Persian architecture, and precedents of design. The city was round, like Sasanian Firuz Âbâd; the royal palace had a great arch or *eivân* as did the earlier residence of the Shâhânshâhs; and also, following the Persian example, it was built in secluded isolation, cloistered at the centre of the settlement. Court procedure also changed in nature. The Caliph now became an elevated and inaccessible figure, only to be approached—more truly in the style of an eastern potentate—with difficult and elaborate ceremony. Moreover, in the field of government, he now came to be aided by the holder of another office which owed much to the Sasanians: the Vizir, or chief minister. The possession of this office for 50 years by a Persian family—the Barmecides or descendants of Barmak—who did much to patronise the work of Persian scholars, did much to revive the study of literature, medicine, and astronomy. It was through their work that Baghdad was able to attain one of the most glorious periods in the history of Islam.

With the advent of the 9th century, the Abbâsid Caliphs, deciding that it was too dangerous to rely any longer on the troops of Khorâsân who had earlier brought them to power, began to import from Central Asia Turkish slaves to act as mercenaries. Their increasing dependence on these mamluks, or slave soldiers, in fact made it more difficult to control the affairs of the Islamic empire. As a result, various parts began to break away. Although they might have been controlled by rulers who declared their allegiance to the Caliph in Baghdâd, they were de facto independent, and could wield far greater power than the authority to which they nominally would bow. In Irân and beyond, a confusing cascade of dynasties arose, destroying others in their wake before being swept away themselves. The first of these to appear, in 822, was the Tâherid, in Khorâsân, descended from a *deqhân* family who had been long in the service of the Abbâsids. The control of much of Persia was wrenched from them after 870 by the Saffârids, a dynasty hailing from the southern regions of Afghânistân; yet, these too lost their primacy in the region to the Sâmânids, a dynasty ruling from the Transoxianan city of Bokhârâ. In the middle of the 10th century, much of the country came to be divided between the Ziyârids, and the Buyids, whose spheres of influence shifted throughout the region with the passing of time. Perhaps the most interesting attribute of these flickering powers, is that—particularly in the case of the Saffârids, the Buyids, and the Ziyârids—conscious attempts were made to hark back to the Sasanian past. Although they were Muslim, or, as one scholar says of the Buyids 'some kind of Muslim', genealogies were forged to link their rulers back to the Sasanian house, the Pahlavi language and script of the Sasanian period were used in royal inscriptions, and Sasanian crowns and titles were used for their kings. These houses would be the last indigenous Persian dynasties for several hundred years to rule over the country, and indeed the last until the 20th century to look back to a pre-Islamic past for legitimacy. Control over the land was now to pass to a new wave of invaders: the Turks from Transoxiana.

THE SALJUQ TURKS

The Saljuqs, who would, after conquering Irân, "once again unite Islam under a single and powerful sway," are first heard of in the latter half of the 10th century as one of the nomadic tribes of Ghuzz Turks, dwelling in the vicinity of the lower Jaxartes (Syr Darya) in Central Asia. It was here that they were converted to Islam by groups of itinerant Sufi missionaries, and around this time that they are thought to have begun their migration southwards towards Persia. Periodically, they would act as mercenaries for the Transoxianan principalities through which they were passing, and although they were well-reputed as fighters they were often seen as unruly, and difficult to control. In 1025 a group of them moved to the northern region of modern-day Afghânistân, and took service with the Ghaznavid Kingdom which then controlled the area. However, within a few years, as was the trend, they rebelled. By 1037, they had managed to wrest for themselves the city of Nishâpur, and three years later—after a great influx of Saljuqs to the province of Khorâsân— they routed the Ghaznavids at the battle of Dandanqan, and took the district for themselves.

Two brothers at this time were leaders of the Saljuqs. The elder, Chaghri Beg, remained to rule in Khorâsân, whereas the younger, Toghril Beg, with a powerful army proceeded westwards across Irân. In 1044, he took Rey and Hamadân. Not long after, he continued on his course into Iraq, and within five years was in a position to strike even into the Byzantine territories of eastern Anatolia. A people who, a mere 25 years before, had been little more than wanderers, were now the leading and most dynamic force in the House of Islam. Seeking recognition for their conquests, in 1055 he presented himself before the decadent Abbâsid Caliph, al-Qa'im, who, although now unable to wield any temporal authority, was able to endow him with the religious legitimacy which he desired. An elaborate ceremony, without precedent in Islamic practice, was devised to regularise his position. Having been enthroned in the presence of the Caliph, he was invested with seven robes and seven slaves as a symbol of the seven regions of the Caliphate. A double crown, to signify the kingship of Arabia and Persia, was placed upon his head, and finally he was girded with two swords in acknowledgement of his new position as "Ruler of the East and of the West". A declaration also credited him with the titles of "Sultan", "Vice-regent of the Successor of the Prophet", and "Lord of all Muslims". By 1060, the year of Chaghri's death, Toghril had established the rule of the Saljuqs throughout the whole of Irân, and, for the last three years of his life, controlled the new empire alone.

The rest of the century under the next two Sultans—Alp Arslan (1063–1072) and Malek Shâh (1072–1092)—was to see a brilliant period in the history of Irân. In military terms, the Saljuqs were able to conquer as far as Mecca and Medina in the south, and, somewhat inadvertently meeting the Byzantines in battle at Mantzikert (1071), even captured the Emperor Diogenes Romanus; their occupation of some of the most fertile and populous parts of the Byzantine lands dealt a blow to that empire from which it would never be able to recover. In the field of government, the administration throughout the two reigns was efficiently overseen by the talented Persian Vizir Abu Ali Hasan bin Ishak, better known by his honorific

The mountain ridge of Alamut, on which was built the famous Ismaili fortress

title of Nezâm ol-Molk or 'Regulator of the State'. The qualities of this hugely capable minister are perhaps best seen in the Treatise on Government (*Siyâsat-nâmeh*) which he wrote towards the end of his life. Here, drawing on examples both from the pre-Islamic Sasanian period as well as more recent times, he advises on everything from the disposition of wine-bearers in the court and the training of pages, to broad principles of government and the necessity of justice. To kings and those in power, he makes the admonition: "To the best of his ability, let [the king] ever acquaint himself, secretly and openly, with the condition [of his people]; let him protect them from extortionate hands, and preserve them from cruel tyrants, so that the blessings resulting from those actions may come about in the time of his rule and benedictions will be pronounced upon his age until the resurrection... A kingdom may last while there is irreligion, but it will not endure when there is oppression." Nezâm ol-Molk is also notable for his foundation of schools, particularly in Baghdâd, his patronage of some of the building work at the Friday Mosque of Esfahân (indeed, the whole Saljuq period saw a blossoming of architecture throughout Irân), and his support of thinkers such as the mystic al-Ghazâli, and the scientist and poet Omar Khayyâm.

The stability of the Saljuq kingdom was not long to survive the death of Malek Shâh. Several threats, both external and internal, arose to unsettle it. Of the former, these included disputes over succession, and the seizure by Ismâ'ili Shi'as of mountain strongholds, from which they launched unconventional armed campaigns (which perhaps might be described as 'terrorist') to overthrow the Sunni Saljuq state. Indeed, one of the first victims of the Ismâ'ili assassins was the Vizir Nezâm

ol-Molk himself. (For more information on the Ismâ'ilis, see p. 232) Of the external threats, the greatest were posed by the peoples of Transoxiana. Fearful of the danger posed by an invasion of other branches of the Ghuzz tribesmen, Sultan Sanjar (1118–1157) moved his capital to the north-eastern city of Merv, so as to be ready to ward off any assault that should be made against the Saljuqs. However, in spite of being able to reduce for a time the Transoxianan territories to tribute, he suffered an overwhelming defeat in 1141 at the hands of the Qara-khitay—a confederacy of Central Asian tribes—and twelve years later was captured by the Ghuzz themselves. During the years of his imprisonment, the Ghuzz were able to ravage much of Irân, including Merv and Nishâpur, and after his death, the empire consequently began to break up. Parts of it were to remain, even until the 14th century, in the hands of petty princes of the Sajluq dynasty, and others were to fall into the hands of the Khwarazm-Shâhs—a kingdom which arose in Transoxiana from the chaos of the age. Yet, nothing established in that time was to be of long duration: from the steppes of the north was to come the advent of Genghis Khân, and the hordes of the Mongol horsemen.

THE MONGOL INVASION AND THE IL-KHÂNID DYNASTY

The Mongols were originally a group of nomadic peoples who dwelt in the steppe land north of China, between Lake Baikal and the Gobi Desert. The Chinese held them in contempt, regarding them as nothing more than a lot of warring barbarians, and spent much of their energy in attempting, by bribery and diplomatic intrigue, to prevent them from encroaching on the Empire of China. However, as the 12th century wore on, their policy was increasingly less successful, and they suffered greatly as the Mongols staged an incessant series of attacks against them and their allies in the north of the region. One of the chiefs to be killed in these conflicts was named Yissugay Khân; his son, Temuchin, who succeeded to his father's place at the age of 13, was able, by defeating his rivals and making a number of alliances, to assume the paramount position amongst the Mongols. In token of this fact, and to recognise their new-found unity with him as their leader, in 1206 a Great Council of chiefs was convened, and Temuchin was acclaimed by them to be 'The Very Great Khân', or Genghis Khân.

In the following years, the Mongols captured large areas of Northern China, and by 1218 found themselves sharing a border with the Central Asian empire of the

Khwarazm-Shâhs. After Genghis sent a message to its ruler, addressing him as a vassal and subordinate, relations between the two empires broke down. When, in the same year, a Mongol merchant caravan was impounded and a number of ambassadors summarily executed, Genghis found the pretext to attack his new rival. Declaring himself outraged at the impiety of the murder of his ambassadors, he assembled an enormous army—perhaps as large as 150,000 men—and led a campaign of conquest and devastation throughout the territories of the Khwarazm-Shâhs. Having destroyed the cities of Bokhara, Samarqand and Urganj, he ordered a force under his son Tolui to proceed south-west into the Irânian province of Khorâsân. Here, in 1220, the cities of Merv and Nishâpur were besieged, razed to the ground, and their populations—even the very cats and dogs—massacred in their entirety. The cities, in the words of a 13th century Muslim traveller, "were effaced from off the earth as lines of writing are effaced from paper, and those abodes became a dwelling for the owl and the raven." The Mongols, not as yet sharing the Islamic faith with the conquered peoples, felt no compunction in wholesale slaughter. Moreover, by the utter destruction of cities, they hoped to secure their lines of communication, and to ruin the lands under cultivation which they administered; by this latter expedient, they intended that the land would degenerate into pasture, suitable for the flocks and herds which accompanied the Mongol army.

Even after the return of Genghis to his native lands in 1225 and his death shortly afterwards, two detachments of the Mongol force remained in Irân. One of these, after attacking Qom, Hamadân, Zanjân, Qazvin, and Tabriz, continued northwards as far as modern-day Daghestân on the coast of the Caspian Sea. The other remained within Irân itself, either besieging other cities such as Rey and Kâshân, or else completing the work of massacre and desolation left unfinished by their colleagues. The land itself—aside from those districts which remained in the hands of the local Saljuq princes or the sect of the Ismâ'ilis—was now controlled by a series of Mongol governors. Yet, it was not until the middle of the century that any serious attempt was made by the Mongols to hold and govern Irân as a part of their new empire. In 1251, at a great council of the Mongols, Genghis Khân's grandson, Hulagu, was ordered to mount a fresh expedition, with special instructions utterly to extirpate the Ismâ'ilis, and then to extinguish the Caliphate itself. The former task, by destroying the Ismâ'ili castles in the Alborz Mountains, was achieved in 1256. The latter, after a march to Baghdâd, was completed in 1258, and the final Abbâsid Caliph, Muntasim al-Billah, more worried about keeping his gold in the

(Following pages) *The peninsula of Kazim Dashi (formerly an island) on which the Mongol ruler Hulagu (1256–1265) is supposed to have hidden his treasures*

treasury than paying for a proper army to defend him, was put in a sack and trampled to death by the Mongol horsemen—the shedding of royal blood was a practice that they would not at all condone. At length, when the Mongol advance towards the Mediterranean was checked by one of the last remaining Islamic polities—the Mamluk Sultanate of Egypt—Hulagu made his way back towards Marâgheh, in modern-day Azerbaijân. This became the first capital of the il-Khânid Empire of Persia. Although the il-Khânid Empire was in theory subordinate to the Great Mongol Khâns in China (such a state of affairs was signified by the designation of 'il-Khânid'), in fact, it was to evolve into an independent polity in its own right, destined to remain in control of Irân until the middle of the following century.

The early part of the il-Khânid rule was perhaps not the happiest period of Irânian history. The rural areas had been depopulated, the agricultural land damaged almost beyond repair, and the population treated by the Mongol rulers as little more than a milch-cow, whose exclusive function was to provide for them a stream of revenue whenever they should demand it. More than this, the country was still plagued by incessant wars—or the threat of war—with the Mamluks in Egypt, or indeed other branches of the Mongols: the Golden Horde in the Caucasus, already converted to Islam, or the other Mongol dynasties now established in Transoxiana. On the other hand, the tradition of Mongol tolerance in matters of faith allowed different religions to flourish. One ruler, Arghun (1284–91) became a Buddhist, and his unpopular but efficient Vizir, Sa'd ol-Dawla, was a Persian Jew. The Nestorian Christian community in the northwest was especially favoured, and ambassadors were even exchanged with the west to explore the possibility of an alliance against the Mamluks. Besides this, the age could lay claim to some of the greatest writers of Persian literature. In the field of poetry, the Sufi Mystics Jalâl od-Din Rumi and Sa'adi of Shirâz; in history, Juwayni, who chronicled the rise of Genghis Khân; and in science and philosophy, Nâser od-Din Tusi, who not only wrote commentaries on Euclid, Plato, and Aristotle, but also constructed in Marâgheh an astronomical observatory to compile tables on the movement of the stars.

The position changed somewhat with Ghâzân Khân (1295–1304), who decided, on his accession to the throne, to declare himself a Muslim. The earlier policy of religious tolerance was reversed: Buddhists were expelled from the empire; Buddhist sites, as well as a number of Jewish and Christian buildings were destroyed, and the jizya, or poll-tax on non-Muslim 'People of the Book' was reintroduced after a lapse of fifty years. However, with the aid of his Vizir Rashid od-din, who was also an eminent historian and patron of the arts, he enacted a series of reforms designed to remedy the misgovernment of the previous Mongol rulers. Arbitrary extractions of money from the people were forbidden. Exact dates were set for the collection of taxes, and the levels of payment decided by an open assessment of the wealth possessed by the population. The activities of the *qadis*, or Islamic judges, were regulated. The postal service and the system of coinage was reformed, weights and measures standardised, and incentives were offered to bring areas of barren land back into agricultural cultivation. Ghâzân's new capital, Tabriz, was adorned with a number of new buildings constructed both by himself and his Vizir. The arts and scholarship continued to flourish, and commercial envoys from as far afield as Genoa and Venice established themselves, conducting their trade with Europe. However, this golden age, as some have described it, was to come to a sudden end. The ruler Abu Said (1316–1335), who came to the throne at the age of twelve, died suddenly without an heir, and disputes over the succession caused the empire suddenly to fracture, with none of the contenders being able to seize for themselves the paramount power in the state. Broken apart by strife and rent with unending conflict, the land of Irân was to persist in a condition of disunity for more than a century and a half.

THE TURKOMAN DYNASTIES, TAMERLANE, AND THE RISE OF THE SAFAVIDS

The history of Irân after the fall of the Mongols is particularly confusing, even by the standards of the region, and not even the appearance of another great conqueror —Tamerlane—was able to lend clarity to the situation.

With the effective end of the il-Khânid Dynasty in 1335, a number of petty houses, predominantly Persian and constantly at war, arose to usurp the power now free. Most notable amongst them were the Jalayirids in the west, who ruled from Baghdad and often could command the province of Azerbaijân, and in the centre—including Yazd, Esfahân, and Shirâz—the family of the Muzaffarids obtained the government. Other peculiarities emerged also from the chaos. The city of Sabzevâr, for example, controlled by a Shi'a order of Sufis, which every day would lead a riderless horse to the gates in expectation of the return of the Madhi, is regarded by a number of historians—particularly Marxists—as the world's first egalitarian republic. A similar entity is also known to have existed in the area of Mâzanderân. However, if there was any semblance of an evolving stability, it was soon to be dispelled by Tamerlane. Born in 1336 in Shahr-i-Sabz near Samarqand, a noble member of the

Turkish-speaking Barlas tribe, he was able to exploit the gathering disorder beyond the Oxus to garner himself a following. Sometimes acting as an official of the declining Mongol administration, and sometimes as the leader of a band of mercenaries, he used his ruthlessness, courage, and ability in formulating strategy to such good effect, that by 1380 he could be called the master of all Transoxiana. With a powerful army of horsemen at his back, he was now in a position to embark on an unparalleled career of conquest.

Although the military achievements of Tamerlane are far in excess of those attained by Genghis Khân or Alexander the Great, his political legacy is, by contrast, of no equivalent stature. Whilst he was able twice to march through Irân (in 1384 and 1392), and to attack without defeat such places as Moscow, Delhi, Baghdad, Syria, and Georgia—often causing as much damage as the Mongols before him—he took little care for the foundation of a stable administration in his wake. Much of the time, his campaigns were little more than expeditions for plunder, seeking wealth wherewith to adorn his capital of Samarqand. Many historians suggest that the policy of keeping his armies perpetually in the field and preventing any rivals from building authority in the provinces was calculated to see off the danger of a challenger. Whilst in this he was successful, it meant that his heirs—once they had finished fighting each other for the title—had little to show for the efforts of their father. For all the distant marches to India and Russia, the only real remains of the empire he had

Thirteenth-century brass ewer inlaid with silver and gold

founded—the Timurid Empire—were his native Transoxiana and Afghânistân. As for Irân, whilst he left it nominally under the control of his successors, his primary impact on the place was to weaken or obliterate a number of the dynasties which had risen from the wreckage of the il-Khânids. The Jalayirids were enfeebled, the Muzaffarids destroyed, and appearing in their place were a number of Turkoman tribal configurations—the Qara-Qoyunlu 'Black Sheep', and the Aq-Qoyunlu 'White Sheep'—which paid their allegiance to the ruler of the Timurids. This allegiance, however, counted for little, and the times were to continue turbulent. After the death of Tamerlane in 1405, the capital of his empire was eventually moved to Herât, now within the modern-day border of Afghânistân. From here, the Timurid emperor would hold directly the region of Khorâsân (it is to this time and to this dynasty that we owe the development of the Shrine of Emâm Rezâ at Mashhad), but beyond, the Qara-Qoyunlu and the Aq-Qoyunlu would struggle amongst themselves to rule the land of Irân. The latter, by 1467, had managed to overcome the former, yet their victory portended little. Not only did the Aq-Qoyunlu manage to spend their strength in an unsurprising civil war, but also a new threat in the west— the nascent realm of the Ottoman Turks—began to press on them hard. It was in this milieu of decadence and disarray that the House of the Safavids began to rise to prominence, and on this state of turmoil that they were to re-impose a unity long-forgotten.

The dynasty of the Safavids began its career not, like many others, as leaders of tribes or regional governors answering to an imperial overlord. Rather, the family embarked on the *cursus honorum* as masters of a mystical Sufi order. Although much about their origins and their ascent to the royal dignity is unclear, it is nonetheless known that its earliest apparent ancestor, Shaykh Safi od-Din (1252–1334) was a figure of some note in the latter days of the il-Khânid kingdom. Having attached himself to a Sunni Sufi organisation at Talish, south-west of the Caspian, he rose to be its leader in 1301, giving it his name, and moving its head-quarters to Ardabil, not far from the capital Tabriz. The rule over this order passed to the descendants of Shaykh Safi, and over the next 150 years, it continued prosperous but not unconventional, accruing members and accumulating wealth. However, in the middle of the 15th century, as the general situation of the country deteriorated, the institution took on a character more military, and political. A dispute within the organisation over leadership led to one of the claimants, Junayd, to travel through eastern Anatolia and northern Syria gathering followers for support. The Turkoman tribesmen who rallied to his cause were drawn to him not only because they did not wish to be subject to the taxes and bureaucracy of the

Ottomans; they also, it seems, venerated the figure of Junayd himself, believing him—like the Emâms of Shi'a Islam—to be a partaker in the nature of the divine.

The Aq-Qoyunlu ruler in Tabriz, conscious of the developing strength of the Safavid Order and the fanatical devotion it bore to its leader, decided that it would be prudent to enter into an alliance with Junayd. To this end, both Junayd and his son Haydar were given princesses of the Aq-Qoyunlu house in marriage, and Haydar himself was raised at the royal court. However, as was not uncommon at the time, the pact did not endure. Haydar, who succeeded to the headship of the Safavids in 1460, was killed by an ally of the Aq-Qoyunlu in 1488 whilst attempting to conduct a raid on the Christians of the Caucasus, and his sons were thrown into prison. Nevertheless, one of them, Ismâ'il, managed to escape at the age of seven, and take refuge with a minor Shi'a potentate in the province of Gilân. Four years later, in 1499, he sallied forth at the head of an army of 7,000, and by 1501, still only fourteen, unseated the Aq-Qoyunlu from Tabriz, and proclaimed himself the Shâh: the Safavids were now not only the masters of a religious order, but also of the land of Irân.

At the beginning of his reign, victory followed fast upon victory. By 1503, Aq-Qoyunlu resistance to the Safavids had been crushed; by 1510, after a number of successful campaigns, Shâh Ismâ'il's authority had been established over an empire which reached from Eastern Anatolia, to Baghdâd, to Herât in the former territory of the Timurids. Yet, he was unable to maintain this early momentum. An invasion of his lands by the Ottoman Turks in 1514 culminated in the Battle of Châldirân—a disaster for the Safavids, whose forces, composed primarily of cavalry, were unable to withstand the modern weaponry of the Ottomans, artillery and hand-guns. Until well into the 17th century, particularly at the time of the accession of new shâhs, war on the western front against the Ottomans was to be a theme of the Safavid rule. Both empires laid claim the territories of Eastern Anatolia, Azerbaijân and Iraq—especially the former, from which much of the original Safavid support was elicited. A final settlement was to come only in 1639 with the treaty of Zuhab, which established the position of the boundary between the two empires until the advent of the First World War. A permanent peace was assured for the Safavids at the price of all of the disputed lands except Azerbaijân, and thus the borders of Irân began to assume the form with which we are familiar in the present day.

The enmity which arose early between the Ottomans and the Safavids was a product of more than just a contest over territories, and their resources of manpower. It also owed its genesis to religion. The Ottomans bore strict adherence to the Sunni version of Islam; consequently, they viewed many of the developments which were unfolding in the Safavid sphere with distrust. Although originally, the order of the Safavids was also Sunni, with the passing of time they began in addition to venerate the twelve Emâms of Shi'a Islam. Whilst this was not, in the medieval days of doctrinal fluidity, strictly contrary to orthodoxy, the treatment of the Master of the order began stray beyond the pale of acceptability. As has been related, Junayd in the previous century was treated by his Turkoman followers with nothing less than veneration; by the time of Shâh Ismâ'il, the Safavid leader was now regarded as a 'hereditary and living emanation of the Godhead', with all the powers and prerogatives which this entailed. A genealogy reaching back to Emâm Ali, the cousin and son-in-law of the Prophet, was constructed for Shâh Ismâ'il, and it was with this as a support, that he claimed legitimacy as a ruler. None of this the Ottomans could abide, and the situation worsened when Ismâ'il took the decision to convert his whole domain—most of which was still Sunni—on pain of death to Twelver Shi'ism. His motives for doing this are not at all clear. Conventional Twelver Shi'ism would not have approved of his claim to divine status—although many of the clergy he imported from places such as Syria and Lebanon to uphold the conversion were happy to turn a blind eye to the contradiction—and it could well be the case that it was merely the memory of his upbringing in the Shi'a court of Gilân caused him to embark on this course. Although it had the beneficial effect of forging a strong and common identity for his empire which over the previous generations had been quite absent, it was bought at the cost of an exodus of his subjects who refused to change their beliefs, and a war which was to plague the Safavids for the best part of a century and a half.

For all of these disturbances, and indeed the other conflicts which the Safavids were compelled to dispute on their eastern borders as well as the western, this period in the history of Irân is generally regarded by many as being the most felicitous. The reign of Shâh Abbâs the Great (1587–1629) saw an unparalleled efflorescence in every field of the state, in the patronage of the arts, in administration, and in the realm of international trade. One of his first and most important contributions to the empire was the establishment of a fully-fledged standing army. He relied for the composition this force not on the native subjects of Irân, but rather Christian slaves taken as booty in the Caucasus and forcibly converted, or the offspring of Christian women who had been led away in the same fashion. That they were without connection to any of the tribes, and paid directly from the revenues of the crown ensured their undivided loyalty to the Shâh; that the Shâh and his successors no

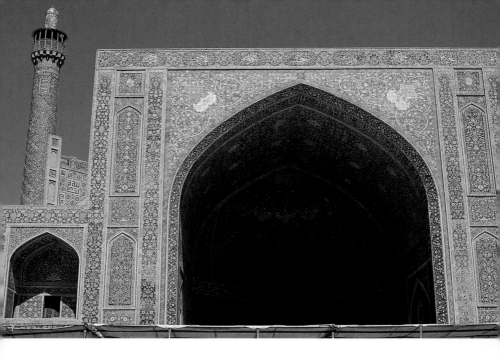

longer had to rely for their position on the support of the tribes whose allegiance may have been divided between their leaders and the crown did much for the stability of the dynasty.

Shâh Abbâs chose for his capital the city of Esfahân. Whilst other cities of the empire such as Shirâz, Ardabil and Tabriz were embellished thanks to his munificence, and whilst places of pilgrimage, particularly Mashhad, received also his special support, it was Esfahân that was, in the expression of Sykes, 'the golden prime of medieval Persian architecture'. Commerce flourished also. The markets of Esfahân were, in the words of a traveller, 'as spacious, as pleasant, and aromatic… as any in the universe.' 3,000 Christian Armenians were moved to the suburb of New Jolfâ, providing a population of skilled artisans and merchants. The Shâh's protection of this talented minority, and of the other foreigners and visitors that came to his court, ensured a resurgence of trade the like of which had not been seen in Irân since the time of the Prophet. Gentlemen adventurers, such as the brothers Sir Robert and Sir Anthony Sherley, presented themselves to the Shâh, bringing with them knowledge of the latest military technology, and offering to act as emissaries back to the rulers of Europe. The letters which Shâh Abbâs entrusted to Sir Anthony, offering them an alliance, speak volumes for the spirit of the time: "…all you princes who believe in Jesus Christ, know you that [Sir Anthony] has made friendship between you and me. This I had long desired, but there was none that came to make the way, and to remove the veil that was between us and you, but only this gentleman... The entertainment which [he] had with me is that daily... we have eaten together of one dish, and drunk of one cup, like two brethren." Privileges were granted to foreign tradesmen, and the English Navy, which, after a struggle with the Portuguese, won control of the Persian Gulf with the capture of the Island of Hormuz, protected brokers who exchanged cloth in the station of Jask, and spices in the port of Bandar Abbâs.

On his death in 1629, Shâh Abbâs bequeathed an empire that in its foundations was stable, well-defended, just, and perhaps more prosperous than it had been since the days of glory in the ancient world. Had it not been for a single flaw in his character—for which, one might argue, he could not at all be held responsible—it is not beyond the bounds of possibility that his achievements might have endured for many more years than they were, in reality, otherwise to do.

THE FALL OF THE SAFAVIDS—AFSHÂR, ZAND AND QÂJÂR DYNASTIES

Although Shâh Abbâs was to preside over one of the happier periods in the history of Irân, his coming to the throne had only occurred after an episode of civil conflict and a great deal of familial blood-letting during which the young Abbâs himself had been in serious danger. The unfortunate circumstances surrounding his accession, it seems, endowed him with a suspicious and distrustful turn of mind. In 1615, suspecting unjustly that his eldest son, Safi Mirzâ, was plotting revolt, he ordered him to be put to death; two of his other sons besides were blinded to exclude them from the line of succession. Other princes of the Safavid house, who ordinarily would have been given posts in the administration of the provinces, instead were confined to the harem, and grew up with no knowledge whatsoever of government, the army, or the wider world. Often emerging quite addicted to drink and drugs, weak-willed and open to manipulation by the women and the eunuchs, they were quite unfitted when the time came to lead the life of the sovereign. Although one of Abbâs's descendants, Abbâs II (1642–1667), was able to escape early from this malign education, and vigorously maintain the prosperity of Irân by upholding the policies of his illustrious namesake, the other Safavid monarchs of the 17th and 18th centuries were not at all of an equal stamp. The successive rulers which were engendered mediocre, thanks to the paranoia of Shâh Abbâs, allowed the standards of justice to decline, and with it, the volume of commerce; corruption became endemic, and the army also was permitted to fall into a state of dilapidation. Only the efficiency of the bureaucracy which Shâh Abbâs had instituted prevented the disintegration of the kingdom, and had a credible invader presented himself more promptly, more promptly, many believe, would the dynasty have collapsed.

The challenge which in the end did indeed overthrow the dynasty is one that can hardly be said even to have been credible. In 1694, Shâh Soltân Hosein inherited the Safavid crown. Being exceptionally under the influence of the clergy, he gave them free rein in the dictation of policy—a decision that was to cause much resentment. Immediately after his coronation, he banned the drinking of wine and the sport of pigeon-flying. Not long after, the state brought to an end its toleration of religious minorities. Not only did Christians and Jews, Sufis and philosophers find themselves the subject of persecution, but also, more importantly, Sunnis who had not yet converted to Shi'ism in the outlying districts of the Empire now were put under pressure to comply. A number of areas rose up in revolt, most notable among them Qandahâr, in the southern part of modern-day Afghânistân. The best efforts of its repressive governor to quell the tribe which inhabited the city—the Ghilzai—came to nothing; in fact, they seized him and put him to death in April 1709. A similar occurrence took place not long after in Herât. Ten years later, the Ghilzai put together a force numbering perhaps not more than 10,000 under Mir Mahmud, their chief. Marching into the Empire's heartlands, they attacked Kermân and Yazd, defeated an opposing Safavid force more than three times their size, and then went on lay siege to the capital Esfahân. Capitulating after six months at the cost of significant damage, the loss of 80,000 lives and—perhaps most grievous to the historian—the state records of the dynasty, Shâh Soltân Hosein forwent the throne, and, in 1722, invested Mir Mahmud with his power.

The new king, however, was not long to enjoy it. Becoming unbalanced, he murdered a number of the remaining princes of the Safavids and committed a series of atrocities, before going on to be assassinated by his own followers in 1724. Neither was there any great longevity in the rule of his nephew and successor, Ashraf. Not only did the Ottomans and the Russians decide to embark on opportunistic invasions; in Qazvin, one of the last Safavid claimants—Tahmâsp II— had been taken into the protection of Nâder Quli Khân, a chief of the Turkoman Afshâr tribe, and proclaimed the legitimate sovereign.

Nâder Khân was successful not only in beating back the Ottomans and the Russians, but also was able to defeat Ashraf, and the Ghilzai warriors. From 1729, he ruled in the name of Tahmâsp II, whose role was little more than that of a puppet king designed to give him legitimacy. However, in 1736, sensing that his position was secure, he decided to do away with this pretence, and rule as the Shâh in his own right; this was the foundation of the Afshâr dynasty. Nâder, encouraged by his victories and confident in the loyalty of his followers, was not content with what he had won to that moment. Instead, rallying his armies, he began on what was to be the last great conquest of Central Asia. Within ten years, he had reduced to submission the cities of Qandahâr, Kâbul and Qunduz; attacked and plundered India, reaching the capital of Delhi and taking as booty the famous Peacock Throne of the Moghul Emperors; and finally crossed the Oxus, where Bokhârâ and Khiva, surrendering, tendered their allegiance. Yet, in spite of the military glory he won for Irân, his popularity swiftly disappeared. He attempted to incorporate Irân into the wider Islamic world by a curious attempt at a merger between the Sunni and Shi'a traditions—a move which was poorly received, and promptly abandoned. His concentration on campaigning, with high demands for taxation and little thought given to the reconstruction of a land enfeebled by civil war, caused the beginnings of resentment. And, when, like his predecessors, he began to behave in a fashion both cruel and deranged, his officers at length mutinied and put him to death.

The customary pattern of bewildering disintegration ensued. A number of Nâder's officers from Qandahâr fled back to their homeland, establishing an empire in that region which was to evolve into the modern state of Afghânistân. Transoxiana, too, recovered its independence. And as for Irân itself, a number of factions began to squabble for primacy. For much of the second half of the 18th century, the country was effectively divided into three parts: Khorâsân, which was held by Shâh Rokh, a blind descendant of Nâder; Mâzanderân, and parts of the north, which were controlled by the Turkoman Qâjâr tribe; and the rest of the country, which answered to another transient dynasty, the Zand. Irân enjoyed the rule of its longest-lived ruler, Karim Khân (1750–1779), in both senses of the word. His assumption not of the title of Shâh, but rather *Vakil ol-ra'aya*, or 'Deputy of the People', perhaps gives an indication as to the nature of his temperament. He avoided unnecessary conflict, encouraged the restoration of agriculture, and licensed the East India Company to set up a factory at Bushehr. Besides this, he greatly embellished his chosen capital, Shirâz, and is even said to have paid for musicians to play in the streets whenever the sound of revelry was wanting. However, his dynasty was not long to survive his death, and by 1796, the Qâjârs, under Âghâ Mohammed Khân, had extinguished their rivals, and set themselves up alone as the rulers of all Irân.

The Russian invasion and annexation of Irânian-controlled Georgia was to set the theme for the 19th century: a time of inferiority and decline. Irân found itself party to a myriad of disadvantageous treaties and shifting alliances, entirely dependent on the will of the European superpowers who strove above all to expand and preserve their imperial interests. The main protagonists of the period were the Russians and the British: the former both hoped to gain access to a warm-water port, and would periodically cast a covetous eye over the riches of India in the distance; the British, not dissimilarly, were eager to protect India, which they now in the main possessed, and moreover to safeguard their lines of communication by maintaining their control of the Persian Gulf. France also, whilst Napoleon was in the ascendant, was a happy participant in the farrago of diplomatic and military gamesmanship. In 1807, hoping also to march a force by way of Turkey to British India, the French promised to support Irân against Russia, with the pledge of advisors and instructors to train the Irânian army. Within seven years, however, the French having been unable to fulfil many of their obligations, the British ousted them from the pact and took their place; envoys from London agreed to help protect Irân and pay subsidies on condition that they forbid the troops of foreign powers from entering their territory. Regardless of this, ill-advised attempts by Irân to regain its lost regions led to further Russian aggression. Russian troops in 1826 penetrated as far as Tabriz, and two years later compelled Irân to sign the humiliating Treaty of Turkamanchai, ceding Armenia and the lands north of the River Aras, as well as an indemnity payment of 30 million silver roubles. With help and encouragement from Moscow, Irân twice attacked the city of Herât in western Afghânistân—a recognised staging post on the way to India—and each time only the threat of a British expedition landing at the head of the Persian Gulf was sufficient to compel an Irânian retreat.

The consequences of this increasing intercourse with the western nations would be varied. The British and French officers who arrived to train the Irânian army brought with them not only knowledge about modern developments in science, but also progressive and liberal notions about the role and conduct of the nation state and government. Such ideas were also to return with the Irânian students who went to study for the first time in the universities of Europe, and later be more widely disseminated with the foundation of a polytechnic college in Tehrân—staffed by Austrians and Prussians—in 1851. Some development of infrastructure in addition was encouraged, notably the telegraph line laid down by the British across western Irân after 1863. However, the overwhelming Irânian memory of this period is one of exploitation—an impression which was to have a profound effect on the future development of Irânian politics. The Treaty of Turkamanchai in 1828 made provision for Russia to import goods from Irân at a preferential rate of customs duty, and also stipulated that none of its subjects in Irân would be accountable to Irânian jurisdiction. Later agreements between Irân and foreign powers would follow these unfavourable precedents. By 1900, the citizens of 15 different countries resident in Irân possessed these 'capitulation rights', remaining immune from arrest and prosecution by the Irânian government. In the commercial field, Irân was similarly at a persistent disadvantage. In 1872, the Shâh, Nâsereddin, eager for Irân to engage in a programme of industrial and economic development, granted an extraordinary monopoly to a British citizen, Baron Reuter. The concessions allowed him to establish a national bank, railway lines, and to exploit the mineral resources of the country for 70 years; so as to finance his venture, the customs of the country were also to be pledged to him for a period of 24 years. Although adverse reaction in Russia and the rest of Europe caused the Shâh immediately to cancel this agreement, Reuter was nevertheless able to bring later schemes to fruition. In particular, he was responsible in 1889 for the creation of the Imperial Bank of Persia, which was vested with the right to issue banknotes and again to exploit Irân's mineral resources, except precious stones and metals. A similar Russian institution, the *Banque d'Escompte de Perse*, allowed Moscow to strengthen its financial hold over the north of Irân.

The Shâh fell into the habit of selling these concessionary rights whenever he needed to replenish his perpetually depleted treasury. However, anger began to grow amongst the people in reaction to this wasteful and exploitative policy. Open rebellion broke out in 1891 when rights to buy the entire tobacco crop of Irân was granted to the British Imperial Tobacco Company, in return for an annual income of £15,000 and one quarter of the profits. A declaration by a leading cleric that, whilst this concession was in place, the use of tobacco by any Irânian was to be "reckoned as war against the Twelfth Emâm", led not only to popular protest, but also the cessation of smoking in Irân until the Shâh relented. The necessity for the Shâh to borrow half a million pounds to pay compensation for the cancellation of the concession was the essential beginning of the Irânian National Debt.

The situation worsened with the assassination in 1896 of Nâsereddin. His son and successor, Mozaffareddin, was not only sickly, but profligate, happy to exhaust the resources of Irân to pay for trips to resorts abroad. His courtiers like-wise were corrupt and rapacious, and were able to amass fortunes and add to their

THE MAGNIFICENCE OF FUTTEH ALI SHAH

*H*e *entered the saloon from the left, and advanced to the front of it, with an air and step which belonged entirely to a sovereign. I never before had beheld any thing like such perfect majesty; and he seated himself on his throne with the same undescribable, unaffected dignity. Had there been any assumption in his manner, I could not have been so impressed. I should then have seen a man, though a king, theatrically acting his state; here, I beheld a great sovereign feeling himself as such, and he looked the majesty he felt.*

He was one blaze of jewels, which literally dazzled the sight on first looking at him; but the details of his dress were these: a lofty tiara of three elevations was on his head, which shape appears to have been long peculiar to the crown of the Great King. It was entirely composed of thickly-set diamonds, pearls, rubies, and emeralds, so exquisitely disposed, as to form a mixture from its surface. Several black feathers, like the heron-plume, were intermixed with the resplendent aigrettes of this truly imperial diadem, whose bending points were finished with pear-formed pearls, of an immense size. His vesture was of gold tissue, nearly covered with a similar disposition of jewellery; and, crossing the shoulders, were two strings of pearls, probably the largest in the world. I call his dress a vesture, because it sat close to his person, from the neck to the bottom of the waist, showing a shape as noble as his air. At that point, it devolved downwards in loose drapery, like the usual Persian garment, and was of the same costly materials with the vest. But for splendour, nothing could exceed the broad bracelets round his arms, and the belt which encircled his waist; they actually blazed like fire, when the rays of the sun met them; and when we know the names derived from such excessive lustre, we cannot be surprised at seeing such an effect. The jewelled band on the right arm was called The Mountain of Light; and that on the left, The Sea of Light; and which superb diamonds, the rapacious conquests of Nadir Shah had placed in the Persian regalia, after sacking Delhi, stripping Mahomed Shah, the eleventh emperor of the Moguls, of his dominions, and adding to Persia all the provinces of Hindostan, north of the Indus. In the horrible spoliation of the Mogul capital, which took place hardly eighty years ago, upwards of a hundred thousand Indians were massacred; and the treasure transported thence to Persia, is computed to have been worth sixty million tomauns; but no part of it was so highly prized as these transcendant precious stones.

Sir Robert Ker-Porter, (c.1822)

Sir Robert Ker Porter, (1777–1842), a British diplomat, painter and artist, visited the Persian court at the beginning of the 19th century, leaving behind this important description of the Persian crown jewels at the time of the Qājār Dynasty.

great estates whilst public officials went unpaid. The economy began seriously to falter, and the works of agriculture and irrigation started to decay. With the government unable to reimburse its creditors, it turned to Russia, borrowing repeatedly in an attempt to meet its obligations. For all this, the deficit continued to increase, and both the treasury as well as the ordinary people lost money to incompetence and extortion. Escalating disturbances after a dispute between merchants and the authorities led in 1906 to a full-scale revolt. The Tehrân Bazaar shut down, and a crowd of 12,000 took refuge in the gardens of the British legation. Drawing on their new-found western ideas of government, they demanded a written constitution for Irân, an end to injustice and the arbitrary behaviour of the state, and the establishment of an elected parliament, or Majlis. The ailing Shâh in the end had little option but to accept. Close to death he signed a new constitution, and opened the first Majlis in October of the same year: the 'Constitutional Revolution' had been accomplished.

THE PAHLAVI DYNASTY

The establishment of the new constitution was, however, neither to bring peace, nor to save Irân from the interference of outsiders. In 1907, so as to put an end to the Anglo-Russian rivalry in Central Asia, the two countries came to an arrangement, dividing Irân into uneven spheres of influence. The British, who received the south-eastern portion, and the Russians, who were assigned much of the north including the cities of Tabriz, Rasht, Tehrân, Mashhad and Esfahân, whilst agreeing to respect the sovereignty and territorial integrity of Irân, consented not to pursue any interests in each other's domains. Following this, the new ruler of Irân, Muhammad Ali Shâh, decided to enlist Russian help in order to destroy the constitution and its supporters. Following his orders, the Persian Cossack Brigade—a military detachment trained, commanded and aided by the Russians—entered Tehrân in June 1908 and bombarded the Majlis, which the Shâh then proclaimed dissolved. The people reacted to this abuse with fury. Tabriz rose against the Shâh, and remained hostile until a Russian unit stormed it and suppressed the dissention with violence. Uprisings nonetheless continued across the north, and after a force of several thousand was raised a march was made on the capital, causing the expulsion of the Shâh, the accession of his twelve year old son, and the re-instatement of the Majlis. Even so, the strife continued. Russian forces remained in the north, and when, in 1911, an energetic American financial specialist, Morgan Shuster, was appointed by the Irânian cabinet to re-order and resurrect the national economy, their hostility again was aroused. Demanding his dismissal, they again advanced southwards, taking Qazvin and perpetrating massacres at Tabriz and Mashhad, where they bombarded the Shrine of the Emâm Rezâ. His departure after these atrocities caused the Irânian economy further to slide into chaos.

Irân's avowed neutrality in the First World War did little for its stability. Tehrân swarmed with foreign spies, especially Germans, attempting to agitate for their respective causes. In the west, a Turkish force came within an ace of invading, only to be repulsed by the Russians before reaching the border. The British took the decision to subject their zone of influence to a military occupation; by raising a native force, the South Persia Rifles, British and Indian officers assumed control of the south by 1916. The Communist revolutions in the following year caused the Russian troops suddenly to withdraw, but the essential result of this change was to leave, by the end of the war, the British as the predominant power in Irân. After the end of hostilities, the Foreign Secretary in London, Lord Curzon, offered to the Irânian government in 1919 a new treaty. Fearing the new regime in Moscow, and hoping to protect Irân from any malign influence, Curzon proposed to Tehrân that Britain should be vested with full authority over the military and economic affairs of the country. In return, Britain would not only undertake to construct roads, railways and other parts of the national infrastructure still wanting, but also more generally to protect Irân's 'independence and integrity'; an immediate loan of two million pounds would also be supplied. The Shâh and his cabinet were happy to accept the proposal; the people, in general, were not. The Majlis, furious at the idea of Irân overtly reducing itself to the status of a client, rejected the treaty. Beyond the capital, moreover, the central authorities could barely project their power. Anarchy took hold throughout the land, British troops skirmished with Bolsheviks on the margins of the Caspian, and provinces on the outskirts threatened to secede.

From this climate of disorder—as is not untypical—a strongman emerged. Rezâ Khân, the commanding officer of the Qazvin detachment of the Persian Cossack brigade, marched to Tehrân, and entered the city on the 21st February 1921. Announcing that he had come to save both the monarchy and the nation, he demanded the dismissal of the cabinet, and the appointment of one of his allies, Seyyed Ziâ Tabatabaie, a liberal journalist, to the office of Prime Minister. Rezâ Khân himself was given the new post of Army Commander, and soon after acquired as well the position of Minister for War. Using his authority rapidly to re-organise the army, he led a series of campaigns against the rebellious peoples and provinces around Irân, and, successful at this endeavour, was hailed by many in the country as a saviour. He rose to be Prime Minister by 1923, and within two years had prevailed on the Majlis to depose the House of the Qâjârs, and to expel its weak and final Shâh. Not long after, Rezâ Khân, who had taken the surname of 'Pahlavi'—the name given to the language spoken in the time of the Sasanians—took his place on the throne as Rezâ Shâh, the founder of a new dynasty.

The new ruler was determined on a speedy programme of modernisation. He believed that by these means, and the maintenance of a strong and centralised authority, he could regain for Irân a position of robust independence. Shortly after he claimed the government with Seyyed Ziâ, the Soviets agreed to relinquish their Irânian assets and cancel their exploitative concessions. In 1927, the regime of capitulations was abolished in its entirety, and the *Bânk Melli*, "National Bank", was established to rival the British-owned Imperial Bank of Persia. There was also the question of Irân's recently discovered reserve of oil. After its discovery in Khuzestân in 1908 by William Knox-D'Arcy, a British concern—the Anglo-Persian Oil Company—had been given a concession to extract it for a royalty payment of 16%. In 1932, Rezâ Shâh increased this payment to 20%, and secured a commitment that Irânians be trained to take over in the long-term the administration of the business. Indeed, the manner of employment of the Irânian population as a whole changed radically throughout the time of his reign. The number of workers at modern industrial plants rose from 1,000 in 1925 to over 170,000 by 1941, and the number of factories from 23 to 346 over the same period. The introduction of conscription along with a significant increase in the level of the military budget caused the man-power of the army to increase to 127,000, and allowed for the establishment of a small air-force, and a navy for the Persian Gulf. These were aided in their work by the construction of 14,000 miles of new road, and the completion of the Trans-Irânian Railway. Other reforms included the major extension of education at all levels, the formation of Tehrân University, and attempts at extending the provision of healthcare.

Despite these achievements, the reign of Rezâ Shâh was to cause much discontent. To many of the traditional elite—in particular the land-owning nobility and the clergy—he often displayed his contempt. The changes in the order of society and its rapid industrialisation tended to leach from them their power. In the case of the former, a number of tribal revolts led to the imprisonment of leaders, and even a number of executions. In the case of the latter, the Shâh withdrew from them their role in the legal system, establishing secular codes of law, marriage and divorce, and appropriating control over the substantial religious trust funds which paid to maintain them. They would openly express their discontent at what they saw as the secularising trends in society, but often would be rebuffed. The most extreme example is their reaction to the ill-administered outlawing of the veil, and the imposition of western dress—a measure which caused anger amongst the clerical class, and hardship and anxiety more generally. A demonstration in the Shrine at Mashhad against the Shâh's refusal to meet a senior religious scholar who wished to protest against these measures was attacked by troops with machine guns, at the cost of hundreds dead. The army, it should also be mentioned, beyond this specific incident was poorly regarded, and seen as overbearing, able to act arbitrarily with impunity. Much of society picked up, over the age, a militaristic tinge. Drill was practised at primary schools; other institutions of learning were subject to a policy of 'Persianisation'. The use of minority languages, dialects and customs was discouraged, a standardised version of the Persian tongue was taught, and a nationalist ideology—with the monarchy at the heart of it—relentlessly was propagated. Dissent at the university, amongst the wider intelligentsia, the press, and the growing classes of the educated workforce, was something that the authorities were less than willing to countenance.

In the end, however, Rezâ Shâh was to fall not at the hand of his disgruntled subjects, but rather at the insistence of those foreign powers which he had endeavoured by his policies to keep at bay. Throughout the 1930s, he had grown increasingly close to the Nazi regime in Germany. He was not, despite his authoritarianism, interested in transplanting fascism to Irân—indeed, Irânians who advocated such a move invariably fell foul of the police. The links came rather from a shared interest in the ideas of a common Aryan origin (it is most likely this which prompted the Foreign Ministry to request, in 1935, that foreigners refer to the country not as 'Persia' but as 'Irân', which derives from the word 'Aryan') and a number of commercial and industrial ties. With the advent of the Second World War, Irân declared its neutrality; however, the Allies, fearing that Germany would be able to attack British India and Russia by way of Irân, decided to reoccupy it in a fashion not dissimilar to that envisaged in the 1907 agreement. The two nations invaded on 26th August 1941, the army capitulated within three days, and Rezâ Shâh, abdicating, fled for South Africa. He was succeeded by his 21 year old son, Mohammed Rezâ Shâh.

Irân served, during this period, as a vital conduit for supplies to the beleaguered Soviet Union. Tehrân also played host, in 1943, to a conference between Churchill, Roosevelt, and Stalin. Even though the leaders acknowledged the contribution that Irân was making to the war effort, the country suffered considerable hardship from shortages and inflationary pressures. The only compensation, whilst cabinet ministers and whole governments frequently were replaced, was the great increase in political awareness and participation amongst the people in general; for the first time, although only for a short while, freedom of debate and fair elections were possible.

Further difficulties presented themselves after the war. The occupying powers had agreed to withdraw within six months of the end of hostilities, yet the Soviet Union prevaricated, refusing to set a date for the removal of its troops. Moscow hoped to put pressure on Irân both to secure for itself a concession for the exploitation of oil reserves in the north, and besides was also supporting communist-inspired secessionist movements in the regions of Kordestân (Kurdistan) and Azerbaijân. The departure of their forces came in May 1946 only after pressure from the Security Council of the newly-founded United Nations—one of the first matters to be brought before it—and Irânian authorities were only able to bring these areas back under central control at the end of that same year.

The free spirit which characterised Irânian politics after the war was soon to be lost with the onset of the Oil Nationalisation Crisis. The Majlis approved a development plan in 1949 for further modernisation in the agricultural and industrial sectors; much of this was to be financed by the proceeds generated by the sale of oil. Many Irânians, however, were becoming conscious of the extreme disparity between the royalties earned by the Irânian government for the sale of oil, and the revenues taken by the British government (between 1932–50, the former received £100 million, the latter £194 million) and hence began to agitate for at least a renegotiation of the 1933 treaty on the matter. The British had little inclination to make any radical changes beyond offering an even division of the profits, and a series of Irânian politicians were unwilling to seek more than this, viewing it as impractical. However, with popular feeling growing ever more vehement against the British presence, the Prime Minister, Dr Mohammed Mossadeq enacted a law for the nationalisation of the oil industry. Diplomatic relations as a result broke down between the UK and Irân; oil production ceased as British technicians left the country, and the economy was damaged as Irânian assets in UK banks were frozen, and exports embargoed. A ruling by the International Court of Justice in The Hague in favour of Irân failed to bring an end to the crisis, and the United States showed some sympathy to Tehrân. However, this evaporated as Dr Mossadeq began to act in a more autocratic fashion, attempting to take control over the army from the Shâh, and dissolve the Majlis so as to rule by decree; this being done with the help of the Tudeh party—the Irânian Communists—America took fright, and ordered the CIA to organise a coup. The Shâh, who had agreed to participate in this, accordingly sent a letter to Mossadeq on 13th August 1953, commanding his resignation.

Mossadeq, however, refused to accept it, and his supporters flooded on to the streets, many crying 'death to the Shâh'. This attempt to remove Mossadeq having failed, the Shâh fled to Rome. However, a backlash against Mossadeq arose—partly organised by the CIA—and pro-monarchist crowds fought to gain control of the capital and the support of the armed forces. Within a week, they had won success, and the Shâh returned to Tehrân. Mossadeq was jailed for attempting to overthrow the dynasty, and an agreement was finally reached for the equal sharing of oil profits between the Irânians, and an international consortium of petrochemical companies: British dominance in this field in Irân hence was brought to an end.

A large number of dissidents were imprisoned after the conclusion of the oil crisis, particularly left-leaning activists and those from the Tudeh party. Free speech was heavily curtailed, the democratic institutions increasingly became nothing more than a series of façades, and the position of the Shâh in government consequently was strengthened. He received significant subsidies from the United States, who were eager to prevent Irân from falling under the influence of the Soviets; with these monies, he not only augmented the strength of the army from 120,000 to 200,000, but also established a state security service—in essence a secret police—known by its Persian acronym, SAVAK. He was, nonetheless, conscious of the need to give the appearance of legitimacy to his rule—the overthrow of the monarchy in Iraq in 1958 made him acutely aware of this problem—and he determined to do so by appearing more progressive than his opponents. Since the start of his reign, he had attempted to portray himself as the champion of the poor of Irân, and in 1963, with increasing general discontent at the state of the political system, the Shâh instituted a series of radical reforms to be known as the 'White Revolution'; such would, he hoped, be sufficient to counteract the possibility of a socialist or 'Red Revolution'. This included, at first, six commitments: the redistribution of land from great proprietors to the country peasants, the nationalisation of forests, the sale of state-owned factories to finance the land reform, profit-sharing for workers employed in industry, suffrage for women, and the establishment of a Literacy Corps to further the cause of education beyond the cities. Much opposition to this, unsurprisingly, was expressed by the clergy, which attacked women's emancipation and the land reform. Particularly conspicuous was the denunciation by the Âyatollâh Khomeini of the report that, in return for a $200 million loan, the United States was seeking again the return of capitulations for their workers in Irân—a protest which led to rioting in the city of Qom, and the exile of Khomeini to Iraq.

The White Revolution—aided by the increasing revenues generated by the sale of oil—was able, for a time, to deliver a rapid rate of economic growth and a certain, though uneven, prosperity. The Shâh, believing that he was shepherding Irân into a new and golden age, arranged for what he calculated to be the 2,500th anniversary of the Irânian monarchy to be celebrated with a lavish festival at Persepolis. This event, attended by dozens of heads of state and government and costing an enormous sum of money to organise, culminated in an address by Mohammed Rezâ Shâh to the tomb of Cyrus the Great: "sleep in peace," he proclaimed, "because we are awake and we will always be awake to look after our proud inheritance." Nothing better than this tableau can illustrate the problems into which Irân fell towards the end of the 1970s. The Shâh, increasingly obsessed by the idea of his own sacral kingship, became progressively more detached from the world, and less willing to listen to advice. Inflation rocketed, as did the population of cities; this served to emphasise the increasing gap in income between the poor and the rich. Traditional networks, which allowed the poor to seek support, particularly in rural areas, broke down with the land reform, and the classes which customarily held a degree of power—bazaar merchants, landowners, clergy—were disenfranchised by the Pahlavi court. The increased levels of education and literacy only worked to heighten the popular awareness of the repression and corruption. The publication of a government-sanctioned article attacking the Âyatollâh Khomeini in 1977 acted as a spark to open rebellion. Disturbances arose first in Qom, and spread to other cities including Tabriz and Tehrân before the vacillating government attempted any action. However, their decision to put tanks on the streets in May 1978 merely heightened the tension, as did a fire at the Cinema Rex at Abâdân on 19th August—a disaster leading to the death of 400 people, for which SAVAK was blamed, although Islamic activists are now known to have been responsible. Khomeini shortly after this moment proceeded to Paris, where he was able to gain access to the international media, and send taped messages to his followers in Irân. Confidence in the Irânian government began to collapse, as even members of the government began to move their money out of the country; yet still the Shâh remained incapable of acting decisively to stem the crisis. Attempts at violence were used to crush the growing demonstrations, but in a manner so haphazard and without conviction that they only served to exacerbate the problem. At the end of 1978, with oil workers on strike, two million people on the streets and most of the army wavering, Mohammed Rezâ Shâh was left with no viable option but exile: he left Tehrân airport on 16th January 1979, and the era of Irânian monarchy was brought to an end.

The Islamic Revolution and the Irân–Iraq War

The Âyatollâh Khomeini returned to Irân on 1st February 1979 to be welcomed by a million people on the streets of Tehrân. Thanks to his agency, an Islamic Revolutionary Council was set up, and also a transitional government under Prime Minister Bâzargân. After Khomeini's associates had secured the loyalty of the army and seen through the execution of many members of the former regime, they promptly sought by referendum the approval of the people for the establishment of an 'Islamic Republic'. Having obtained a positive outcome to this vote, they turned to the question of a written constitution, and began to debate amongst themselves as to the specifics of the new regime. It should be borne in mind that the coalition which brought the revolution to pass embraced every point of view from the secular leftist to the Islamic radical; hence, the constitution, when first drafted, assigned far less power to the clerical classes than later was to be the case. Drawing much from the precedents of 1906, the early versions of the constitution made provision for freedom of speech and association as well as other liberties familiar to the West; arbitrary behaviour on the part of the authorities, as well as torture, were to be banned. Twelver Shi'ism would be recognised as the faith of the state, but the role of religion was nevertheless strongly qualified: sovereignty was in the hands of God, but this was delegated by Him as a free gift to the people; legitimacy therefore rested with the president and their elected representatives in the Majlis, not the clergy. Parliament would have the right to pass laws concordant with the Shari'a, but the Shari'a did not necessarily have to be the source of laws. A Guardian Council would ensure that the bills enacted by the Majlis were "Shari'a compliant"; on this body, the clergy would find their only official role in the machinery of government, but even here they would be outnumbered by laymen. Yet, against a background of continuing unrest, the document was redrafted to include a concept that Khomeini had evolved during his period of exile in Najaf: *velâyat-e faqih*, or "guardianship of the jurisconsult." This innovation, which was in essence the culmination of a certain strand of Shi'a thought which had been evolving over the previous few centuries, held that in the absence of the Twelfth Emâm—who would inaugurate a new age of justice—authority devolved on the most learned of jurists, who alone could correctly unravel and decree the law. Relying on this principle, which many scholars held to be a violation of the traditions of Shi'ism, Khomeini, as the leading jurisconsult, was vested with a multitude of powers: power to appoint the Guardian Council as he pleased; supreme command over the army and security services; the power to declare war; and the power to confirm or disallow the election of the president. The legal system also passed fully into the hands of the clergy. The democratically-elected political arm of the state consequently dwindled in authority, and the "strong president" evolved into little more than a cipher.

In spite of these trends, the international community, and the United States in particular, would most likely have come to terms with the new government, had it not been for the events which were to unfold from the wanderings of the now stateless Shâh. Advancing in years and terminally ill with cancer, he was allowed entry into America on compassionate grounds, so that he might have access to medical care. The Irânians, furious, claimed that the CIA were planning to repeat the coup of 1953, and reinstall Mohammed Rezâ Shâh on a reinstated throne. When a group of armed students occupied the US embassy, taking the staff as hostages, Khomeini refused to condemn the action or call for its abandonment, seeing that it would serve the purpose of uniting the still unstable country against a foreign enemy; he did not see, however, the future repercussions that the event was to bring. The opposition to the Islamic Republic in America became implacable with a botched rescue attempt sanctioned by President Carter, and the exhibition of the charred bodies of the US Special Forces who died on the mission being displayed in Tehrân. Although the hostages were eventually released after the death of the Shâh and the inauguration of President Reagan, diplomatic relations between the two countries came to an end, and Washington thenceforth saw Irân as nothing else besides a threat.

It was in this atmosphere of international hostility towards Irân that the war against Iraq was to arise. The government of the Iraqi President, Saddam Hussein, became conscious that the armed forces in Irân were in a poor state of repair, and could not turn to their traditional suppliers—the US and Britain—for new equipment. The provinces, moreover, were still in disorder, as was usual at times of new regimes, and were unlikely to be able to resist any attack. Hoping, therefore, to re-shape the border between Irân and Iraq to his advantage, and also to capture the oil-rich region of Khuzestân—formerly known as 'Arabistân' thanks to its predominantly Arab population—the Iraqi government seized on a number of pretexts. Citing the calls of Iraq's ambassador to Baghdâd for the Islamic revolution to be exported to Irân, and the seizure of the Irânian Embassy in London by Irânian Arabs from Khuzestân calling for 'liberation'—an episode, incidentally, organised by Iraqi intelligence—Saddam Hussein launched his invasion of Irân in September 1980. Although, it should be noted, the United States did little to restrain Iraq, they gave, at this stage, no active support. However, Irân, shocked by the turn of events, denounced the attack as an American plot. The war, as wars often do, served well the purposes of the fledgling Islamic state. The external threat caused the people to rally round the concept of the revolution, and the Islamist elements were able to bring about the virtual elimination of their leftist rivals in Irân by a campaign of terror and public executions. The army, stricken with desertions and poorly equipped, quickly coalesced and fought tenaciously against the Iraqi advance.

The early gains of the invaders were entirely reversed, and, by 1982, Irân had managed to reoccupy all of its territory back up to the original border. In spite of this, Khomeini decided not to stop there, but rather, perhaps hoping to export the revolution further, to fight on across into Iraq. Little advantage, however, was to be had from this. A terrible stalemate was entered into: Iraq received subsides and support from a wide range of Arab regimes unsettled at the prospect of being under-mined by revolution, and thus was able to hold Irân at bay, but not to drive it back. The West also openly supported Iraq with arms and intelligence; the help they lent to Iraq in the development of a chemical weapons programme—used, amongst other things, for the gassing of the Kurds in Halabja—shows the western nations to no credit. The conflict, as time went on, spread to other regions. Irân used its agents to destabilise Arab states which supported Iraq, and to assail US interests, particularly by the taking of hostages. This led to the curious Irân-Contra affair, in which America attempted to win back its citizens in captivity by covertly appeasing Irân with the offer of new weapons. Iraq, meanwhile, began to strike at civilian areas, and cities along the border found themselves targets for rocket attack. The Persian Gulf also found itself to be a new theatre of the war. The US Navy took up station in its waters, ostensibly to protect the deteriorating security of the shipping lanes, but rather with the intention of maintaining pressure on Irân from a different front. At first merely harassing the Irânian gunboats, they were eventually to bring the hostilities to a conclusion by a terrible escalation of their action. On 3rd July 1988, the USS Vincennes, in circumstances which have not yet been adequately explained, shot down an Irân Air flight on its way to Dubai with the loss of all 240 civilian passengers. Despite the official American explanation that a mistake was made, Irân and Khomeini believed that this event was nothing but the prelude to a full-scale attack. Wearying of any further extension to the already protracted war, the Âyatollâh ordered a cease-fire, and accepted the rulings of the Security Council calling for the cessation and resolution of the conflict.

Martyrs' Cemetary, Qom, 2004

IRÂN TODAY

The conclusion of the war with Iraq allowed many problems which were suppressed by the conflict to come to the surface; these, the passing of time has done little to alleviate, and in many instances, much to exacerbate. Relations with the West continue difficult. Although the European nations have attempted to improve their ties with Irân in the aftermath of the Salman Rushdie affair (where the Anglo-Indian author resident in England was condemned to death by Khomeini in 1989 for allegedly disparaging remarks about Islam made in his book, the *Satanic Verses*) the government in Washington has remained adamantly distant. Since 1995, it has maintained sanctions against Irân, charging the Islamic Republic with involvement in terrorism throughout the Middle East and engaging on a programme to manufacture nuclear weapons. Domestic difficulties, however, are also pressing, and indeed bear some comparison to the situation before the advent of Khomeini. The population is growing rapidly; many are young, and whilst they have little or no knowledge of life under the Shah, and few memories of the Irân-Iraq war, they nevertheless are highly educated and well informed. 60% of the university population are women. The growth of the internet allows them access to easy communication with each other, and experience and news of the outside world; the social strictures of the Islamic regime do not sit easily on their shoulders. In spite of their learning and undoubted ability, employment for them is extremely difficult to come by, and many find themselves trapped in work which hardly befits their level of education; discontent, as a result, is palpable. The economy is sclerotic and over-reliant on the revenues from oil production; corruption also is endemic, as well as glaring disparities in income. Little relief has yet been found in the democratic process. The press is increasingly subject to restriction and censorship; those most critical of the government are more than likely to suffer violations of their human rights. Candidates for the *Majlis* with any serious pretension to reforming the state have consistently been prevented from standing by the Guardian Council. As for the presidency, Âyatollâh Mohammed Khâtami, who came to office by a landslide in 1997 as a reformist, achieved little in the face of clerical opposition. His successor, Dr Mahmud Ahmadinejâd, elected in June 2005 as a champion of the 'pious poor', has declared himself committed to government by Islamic Revolutionary principles. However, his stated intention of re-distributing oil wealth and rooting out corruption is likely to unsettle members of the establishment clergy, many of whom are closely related to business interests; and the fear that he will re-impose conservative social legislation has disturbed the liberal classes. How he will proceed in the midst of this tense and confusing situation remains at present a matter for speculation.

HER HUGE GOLD EARRINGS...

*H*ow can I create this other world outside the room? I have no choice but to appeal once again to your imagination. Let's imagine one of the girls, say Sanaz, leaving my house and let us follow her from there to her final destination. She says her good-byes and puts on her black robe and scarf over her orange shirt and jeans, coiling her scarf around her neck to cover her huge gold earrings. She directs wayward strands of hair under the scarf, puts her notes into her large bag, straps it on over her shoulder and walks out into the hall. She pauses a moment on top of the stairs to put on thin lacy black gloves to hide her nail polish.

We follow Sanaz down the stairs, out the door and into the street. You might notice that her gait and her gestures have changed. It is in her best interest not to be seen, not to be heard or noticed. She doesn't walk upright, but bends her head towards the ground and doesn't look at passersby. She walks quickly and with a sense of determination. The streets of Tehran and other Iranian cities are patrolled by militia, who ride in white Toyota patrols, four gun-carrying men and women, sometimes followed by a minibus. They are called the blood of God. They patrol the streets to make sure that women like Sanaz wear their veils properly, do not wear makeup, do not walk in public with men who are not their fathers, brothers or husbands. She will pass slogans on the walls, quotations from Khomeini and a group called the Party of God: MEN WHO WEAR TIES ARE U.S. LACKEYS. VEILING IS A WOMAN'S PROTECTION. Beside the slogan is a charcoal drawing of a woman: her face is featureless and framed by a dark chador. MY SISTER, GUARD YOUR VEIL. MY BROTHER, GUARD YOUR EYES.

If she gets on a bus, the seating is segregated. She must enter through the rear door and sit in the back seats, allocated to women. Yet in taxis, which accept as many as five passengers, men and women are squeezed together like sardines, as they saying goes, and the same goes with minibuses, where so many of my students complain of being harassed by bearded and God-fearing men.

You might well ask, What is Sanaz thinking as she walks the streets of Tehran? How much does this experience affect her? Most probably, she tries to distance her mind as much as possible from her surroundings. Perhaps she is thinking of her brother, or of her distant boyfriend and the time when she will meet him in Turkey. Does she compare her own situation with her mother's when she was the same age? Is she angry that women of her mother's generation could walk the streets freely, enjoy the company of the opposite sex, join the police force, become pilots, live under laws that were among the most progressive in the world regarding women? Does she feel humiliated by the new laws, by the fact that after the revolution, the age of marriage was lowered from eighteen to nine, that stoning became once more the punishment for adultery and prostitution?

In the course of nearly two decades, the streets have been turned into a war zone, where young women who disobey the rules are hurled into patrol cars, taken to jail, flogged, fined, forced to wash the toilets and humiliated, and as soon as they leave, they go back and do the same thing. Is she aware, Sanaz, of her own power? Does she realize how dangerous she can be when her every stray gesture is a disturbance to public safety? Does she think how vulnerable the Revolutionary Guards are who for over eighteen years have patrolled the streets of Tehran and have had to endure women like herself, and those of other generations, walking, talking, showing a strand of hair just to remind them that they have not converted?

We have reached Sanaz's house, where we will leave her on her doorstep, perhaps to confront her brother on the other side and to think in her heart of her boyfriend.

These girls, my girls, had both a real history and a fabricated one. Although they came from very different backgrounds, the regime that ruled them had tried to make their personal identities and histories irrelevant. They were never free of the regime's definition of them as Muslim women.

Whoever we were—and it was not really important what religion we belonged to, whether we wished to wear the veil or not, whether we observed certain religious norms or not—we had become the figment of someone else's dreams. A stern ayatollah, a self-proclaimed philosopher-king, had come to rule our land. He had come in the name of a past, a past that, he claimed, had been stolen from him. And he now wanted to re-create us in the image of that illusory past. Was it any consolation, and did we even wish to remember, that what he did to us was what we allowed him to do?

Azar Nafisi taught English literature in Tehrân during and after the revolution; she was expelled from the University of Tehrân for refusing to wear the veil. Her book *Reading Lolita in Tehran* recounts a weekly private class she held at home for some of her most devoted students, and gives a fascinating view of the state of Irân through the prism of some of writers they studied, including Jane Austen, Henry James, and Vladimir Nabokov.

Reading Lolita in Tehran is published by Random House, available in the USA at $13.95, in the UK at £7.99

CHRONOLOGY

IRAN	BC	REST OF THE WORLD
First city built at Susa	c. 3900 BC	
	c. 2700–2300 BC	Old Kingdom in Egypt, pyramids of Giza
	c. 2350 BC	Reign of Sargon, founder of the Akkadian Empire
Akkad annexes Susa	c. 2300 BC	
Susa becomes part of Elam	c. 2200 BC	Fall of Akkad
	2065–1785 BC	Middle Kingdom in Egypt
	c. 1730–1680 BC	Reign of Hammurabi, king of the first Babylonian Empire
	16–12th centuries BC	Kassite Empire of Babylon
Height of the Elamite Empire	13–12th centuries BC	
	1193–1184 BC	Trojan Wars (traditional dates)
Destruction of the Kassite Empire of Babylon by Elam	1160 BC	
	800 BC	Composition of the *Iliad* and *Odyssey*
Median capital established at Ecbatana	673 BC	
Assyrian sack of Susa (Elam) under Assurbanipal	645 BC	
Medes' capture of Niniveh and Fall of the Assyrian Empire	612 BC	
	605–562 BC	Reign of Nebuchadnezzar II in Babylon
Persian Achaemenian Empire	550–331 BC	
Reign of Cyrus the Great	558–529 BC	
Reign of Darius I	522–486 BC	
Rebuilding of Susa	521 BC	
	509 BC	Establishment of Roman Republic
Building of Persepolis	500 BC	
Reign of Xerxes I	486–465 BC	
	490 BC	Greek victory over the Persian army at Marathon

	480 BC	Greek victory at Salamis
	431–404 BC	Peloponnesian War between Athens and Sparta
	336–323 BC	Reign of Alexander the Great
Persian defeat at Arbela Death of Darius III, last Achaemenian ruler	331 BC	
Seleucid Dynasty	312–44 BC	Punic Wars between Rome and Carthage
Parthian Dynasty	250 BC–224 AD	
Reign of Mithridates I	171–138 BC	
Parthian victory over Rome at Carrhae	53 BC	
	27 BC	Founding of the Roman Empire by Augustus

AD

Mani, founder of Manichaeism	216–277	
Sasanian Empire	224–642	
Reign of Shâpur I	241–272	
Roman emperor Valerian taken prisoner at Edessa	260	
	330	Constantinople becomes capital of the Roman Empire
	395	Division of the Roman Empire into east and west
	410	Sack of Rome by Alaric
Massacre of the Mazdakites	c. 528	
	622	Prophet Mohammed flees to Medina (Hegira)
	632	Death of the Prophet
Defeat of the Persian army at Nehâvand by the Arabs	641	
Umayyad Caliphate	661–750	
	680	Death of Emâm Hosein at Kerbalâ
	732	Victory of Charles Martel over the Saracens at Poitiers
Abbâsid Caliphate	750–1258	

Reign of Caliph Hârun al-Rashid	766–809	
	768–814	Reign of Charlemagne
Irânian Dynasties:		
Tahirid	821–873	
Saffârid	867–903	
	871–899	Reign of Alfred the Great
Sâmânid	892–999	
	909–1171	Fatimid Caliphate in Egypt
Ziyarid	928–1077	
Buyid	945–1055	Schism between Roman
Ghaznavid	962–1186	Catholic and Eastern
Reign of Toghril Beg, founder of the Saljuqs	1038–1063	Orthodox Churches
	1066	Battle of Hastings
Battle of Mantzikert, Capture of Byzantine Emperor	1071	
Occupation of the castle of Alamut by Hasan Sabbâh	1090–1124	
	1096–1099	First Crusade, capture of Antioch and Jerusalem by the crusaders
	1171–1193	Reign of Saladin in Egypt and Syria
Arrival in Irân of Genghis Khân's Mongol army	1221	
	1271–1295	Travels of Marco Polo
	1304–1377	Ibn Battuta, Arab traveller
Collapse of the il-Khânid Dynasty	1336	
	1337–1453	Hundred Years' War
	1336–1405	Tamerlane, Turko-Mongol conqueror
Timurid Dynasty in Persia	1405–1506	
Shâh Ismâ'il founds the Safavid Dynasty	1501	
Battle of Châldirân against the Ottomans	1514	

	1520–1566	Reign of the Ottoman sultan Soleimân the Magnificent
Reign of Shâh Abbâs I, recon-struction of Esfahân begins	1587–1629	Reign of Queen Elizabeth I of England
Anti-Safavid uprising by Afghâns in Qandahâr	1709	
Siege of Esfahân, collapse of Safavids	1722	
Reign of Nâder Shâh	1736–1747	
Zand Dynasty, capital moved to Shirâz	1747–1779	British expansion in India under Lord Clive
	1789	Beginning of the French Revolution
Qâjâr Dynasty, capital moved to Tehrân	1794–1925	
	1815	Battle of Waterloo
	1861–1865	American Civil War
Adoption of a constitution	1907	
	1922–1923	Atatürk abolishes Ottoman Sultanate, proclaims the Turkish Republic
Reign of Rezâ Shâh Pahlavi	1925–1941	Second World War—Irân occupied by Allied powers
Reign of Mohammed Rezâ Shâh Pahlavi	1941–1979	
Nationalization of oil; Mosaddeq becomes Prime Minister	1951	
Fall of Mosaddeq government	1953	
'White' Revolution	1964–1978	Âyatollâh Khomeini exiled to Iraq
	Oct 1971	Celebration at Persepolis of the 2500th anniversary of the Persian Empire
	Oct 1978	Âyatollâh Khomeini arrives in France
Return of Âyatollâh Khomeini to Tehrân	1 Feb 1979	

Proclamation of the Islamic Republic	1 Apr 1979	
	Oct 1979	Soviet invasion of Afghânistân: many refugees enter Irân
	1979–2001	Civil war in Afghânistân after Russian pull-out; emergence of Taliban
Irân–Iraq war	Sept 1980–July 1988	
Death sentenced issued by Khomeini against writer Salman Rushdie	Feb 1989	
Death of Âyatollâh Khomeini; Seyyed Ali Khamenei becomes Guide of the Revolution	4 June 1989	
Âyatollâh Hashemi Rafsanjâni becomes President	July 1989	
	1990	Iraq invades Kuwait
The moderate Âyatollâh Mohammed Khâtami elected president	May 1997	
Student riots in Tehrân after closure of reformist newspaper	July 1999	
Liberals win landslide	Feb 2000	

FACTS FOR THE TRAVELLER

Since the end of the Irân–Iraq war, and since 1990 in particular, tourism has slowly picked up again in Irân. The great majority of foreign visitors are still Turkish and Pakistani nationals, but the renewed interest in Irân in some European countries and in Japan has lead to a big increase in the number of tourists from those regions too. Even before the 1979 Revolution, Irân was not a destination for mass tourism, and although tourism is tolerated today it should be remembered that a policy of openess to the outside world is still far from unanimously accepted in the government. Outside the main cities, tourists are relatively rarely seen and likely to attract attention, particularly when they arrive by the bus load, with expensive cameras at the ready.

Tourists in Irân have to face certain problems caused by the inadequacy of the infrastructure, and by the strict rules concerning clothing which apply in this Islamic republic. Lack of hotel rooms, especially in the better categories, difficulties in obtaining aeroplane tickets, the unreliability of flight schedules, long distances by road between the main towns, sudden changes in the opening days and times of museums and historical sites, the obligation to wear hejâb (correct and modest dress, either châdor or headscarf for women, legs and arms kept covered for men), and frequent checkpoints on the roads are just some of the problems that can occur.

Expect the unexpected and be ready for delays. Having said that, the situation in Irân is changing very quickly and some of these problems may well be sorted out or at least have improved in the near future.

LANGUAGE

The official language of Irân is Persian, or Fârsi, an Indo-European language which was spoken in the province of Fârs, hence its name. Old Persian of the Achaemenid period was written in the cuneiform script. After the conquest of Alexander, Greek script became paramount. However, Aramaic as an international trade language of the middle east had already penetrated Irân in the Achaemenid period, and by the Sasanian period, gave the script for middle Persian, or Pahlavi. The Arab invasions of the 8th century imposed the Arabic script, which has remained to this day. Words borrowed from Arabic are written in their original form, though may be pronounced slightly differently. However, Persian is not a Semitic language, and therefore has at least four consonants which require separate signs (zh, ch, g, p), which are regularly used in modern script, though were often ignored in medieval manuscripts.

While Fârsi is the national language, other Irânian languages, such as Kurdish and Baluch, are also spoken in some regions. Arabic is spoken in Khuzestân, on the Iraqi border, Turkish Azeri in Azerbaijân and another Turkish language, Turkoman, in the northeast. The tribal communities generally speak their own dialects, such as Luri or Bakhtiâri, as well as Fârsi. However, English is spoken in most hotels and in many shops in the main towns.

LANGUAGE GUIDE

PRONUNCIATION

Except for a few letters, the pronunciation of the Persian language does not present any great difficulties for English-speakers.

VOWELS

a	as in 'hat' or 'map'
â	a long 'a', akin to that of 'wash' or 'what', somewhat like the 'o' in 'o'; in the spoken language, this letter has a tendency to be pronounced like an 'oo' before the letter 'n'; so Irâni (Irânian) often becomes 'Irooni'
e/eh	short as in 'get' or 'end'. The same sound transcribed as 'eh' for final syllable, and 'e' for freestanding (verb—'is')
i	long, as in 'speed'
o	short as in 'hot' or long as in 'bone'
u	always 'oo' as in 'who', not as in 'use'

All the vowels are pronounced separately; thus 'ai' is pronounced 'sight' and 'ei' is pronounced as in 'say'. An apostrophe indicates a glottal stop, for example Nâ'in.

CONSONANTS

b, p, t, l, m, n, v, z are pronounced as in English.

gh	like a thickly pronounced French 'r'
q	pronounced like a 'g' from the back of the throat (N.B. some Irânians tran scribe 'q' as 'gh')
kh	like the Scottish 'ch' of 'loch' or the German 'ich'
ch	as in 'rich'
sh	as in 'show'

r	trilled
g	hard as in 'get', never as in 'page'
s	always as in 'sand', never as in 'rise',
h	always pronounced
j	as in 'judge'
zh	as in French 'juge' or 'agence'

VOCABULARY
USEFUL PHRASES

Hello	*salâm, salâm aleikum*
Good morning	*sobh bekheir*
Good evening	*shab bekheir*
Goodbye	*khodâ hâfez*
How are you?	*hâle shomâ chetor-e?*
Well, good	*khub*
Thank you	*mersi*
Thank you very much	*kheili mamnun*
Please	*lotfan, befarmâyid*
Excuse me	*bebakhshid*
Have a nice trip	*safar bekheir*
Yes	*baleh*
No	*na, nakheir*
My name is...	*esmam...e*
I am English	*man Engelestâni am*
I am a tourist	*man turist/jahângard am*
student	*dâneshju am*
Do you speak English?	*shomâ engelisi baladid?*
I do not speak Persian	*fârsi balad nistam*
What is that?	*ân chist?*
Do you have...?	*shomâ... dârid?*
Where is.../are...?	*...kojâst?*
Where are the toilets?	*tuâlet kojâst?*

tuâlet kojâst?

TRAVEL

Car	*mâshin*
Coach	*otobus*
Train	*qatâr*
Station	*istgâh*
Airplane	*havâ peimâ*
Airport	*furudgâh*
Taxi	*tâksi*
Ticket	*bilit*
Town	*shahr*
Village	*dehkadeh*

DIRECTIONS

Right	*dast-e râst*
Left	*dast-e chap*
Straight	*mostaqim*
There	*ânjâ*
Here	*injâ*
North	*shomâl*
South	*jonub*
East	*mashreq*
West	*maghreb*
Far	*dur*
Near	*nazdik*

TIME

Day	*ruz*
Today	*emruz*
Yesterday	*diruz*
Tomorrow	*fardâ*
Morning	*sobh*
Midday	*zohr*
Evening/night	*shab*
Week	*hafteh*
Month	*mâh*
Year	*sâl*
Date	*târikh*
Hour	*sâ'at*

THE DAYS OF THE WEEK

Friday	*jomeh*
Saturday	*shambeh*
Sunday	*yek shambeh*
Monday	*do shambeh*
Tuesday	*se shambeh*
Wednesday	*chahâr shambeh*
Thursday	*panj shambeh*

ACCOMMODATION

Hotel	*hotel*
	mehmânkhâneh
Guesthouse	*mosaferkhâneh*
Single room	*otâq-e yek nafari*
Double room	*otâq-e do nafari*
With shower/bath	*bâ hammâm*
Bed	*takht*
Blanket	*patu*
Towel	*holeh*
Soap	*sâbun*
Clean	*tamiz*
Dirty	*kasif*

SHOPPING

Market	*bâzâr*
Open	*bâz*
Closed	*tatil*
Money	*pul*
How much?	*chand e?*
Expensive	*gerân*
Cheap	*arzân*

Big	*bozorg*	Spoon	*qâshoq*
Small	*kuchek*	Plate	*boshqâb*
Pretty	*qashang*	Glass	*livân*
Very	*kheili*	Water	*âb*
Carpet	*farsh, ghâli*	Coffee	*qahveh*
Wood inlay	*khâtam*	Tea	*châi*
Caviar	*khâviâr*	Non-alcoholic	
		drinks	*nushâbeh*

MEALS

		Bread	*nân*
Restaurant	*restorân*	Butter	*kareh*
Tea house	*châi khâneh*	Jam	*morabbâ*
Breakfast	*sobhâneh*	Honey	*asal*
Lunch	*nahâr*	Soup	*sup*
Dinner	*shâm*	Yoghurt	*mâst*
Hot	*garm*	Cheese	*panir*
Cold	*sard*	Meat	*gusht*
Knife	*kârd*	Chicken	*jujeh*
Fork	*changâl*	Lamb	*barreh*
		Vegetables	*sabzi*
		Salad	*sâlâd*
		Fruit	*miveh*
		Fruit juice	*âbmiveh*
		Apple	*sib*
		Pomegranate	*anâr*
		Orange	*portaqâl*
		Water melon	*hendevâneh*
		Pistachios	*pesteh*

HEALTH

Doctor	*doktor, pezeshk*
Ill	*bimâr, mariz*
Hospital	*bimârestân,*
	marizkhâneh
Dentist	*dandânsâz*
Chemist	*farmasi, dârusâzi*

Medication	*dâru, davâ*	Eighty	*hashtâd*
Diarrhoea	*es-hâl*	Ninety	*navad*
Cold	*zokâm*	One hundred	*sad*
Fever	*tab*	Two hundred	*divist*
Flu	*enfluanzâ, grip*	Two hundred	
		and thirty-one	*divist o si o yek*
NUMBERS		Thousand	*hezâr*
One	*yek*	Two thousand	*do hezâr*
Two	*do*		
Three	*seh*	**IN TOWN**	
Four	*chahâr*	Mosque	*masjed*
Five	*panj*	Bank	*bânk*
Six	*shesh*	Police Station	*kalântari*
Seven	*haft*	Town hall	*shahrdâri*
Eight	*hasht*	Museum	*muzeh*
Nine	*noh*	Bridge	*pol*
Ten	*dah*	Avenue, street	*khiâbân*
Eleven	*yâzdah*	Side street	*kucheh*
Twelve	*davâzdah*	Motorway	*bozorgrâh,*
Twenty	*bist*		*otobân*
Twenty-one	*bist o yek*	Square	*meidân*
Thirty	*si*	Port	*bandar*
Forty	*chehel*	Church	*kelisâ*
Fifty	*panjâh*	Consulate	*konsulgari*
Sixty	*shast*	Centre	*markaz*
Seventy	*haftâd*	River	*rud, rud khâneh*

CLIMATE

The climate of Irân is characterized by large differences in temperature from one season to another and between the north and south of the country. In general, winters are cold, except in the Persian Gulf, and summers very hot, with temperatures regularly reaching over 40° C (100° F). Winters in the mountainous regions are harsh and some areas are cut off by snow for weeks on end. In Azerbaijân and Kordestân (Kurdistan) in particular, temperatures fall well below 0° C (32° F) between December and February. In summer, however, these regions are less scorchingly hot than the plateau and the plains, where the temperature climbs steadily from spring onwards to reach between 45° C and 50° C (110°–120° F) in summer, most notably in Khuzestân and the central deserts. Khuzestân, which borders on the Persian Gulf, is also extremely humid and travelling there in summer can be an unpleasant experience. Winters, however, are comfortably warm.

The coastal zone between the Caspian Sea and the Alborz Range has a high rainfall all year round as the mountains form a natural barrier which prevents clouds from moving inland. Temperatures vary between 7° C (45° F) in winter and 26° C (75° F) in summer, sometimes with high humidity. However, the summer heat is less extreme than further south and many popular resorts have sprung up along the coast.

Spring (April to May) and autumn (mid-September to mid-November) are the most pleasant seasons to visit Irân. The inland regions are generally dry then and comfortably warm, although nights are cool. Showers and storms may occur until June in the mountains in the west and in Tehrân, and in the northwest, snow often lies in the mountains until April or May.

TOUR OPERATORS

Most Western tourists travelling to Irân today choose to go on an organized tour, either one proposed by a foreign tour operator, or a trip organized directly with an Irânian agency (see below for addresses). Although individual travel is less common than it was fifteen years ago, it is nevertheless perfectly possible and is likely to increase considerably in the years to come. A few foreign travellers have visited Irân with their own car or motorbike; the frontier with Afghânistân has now been reopened after the recent civil war and a new highway opened to Herât, but motorists are still more likely to use the routes from Turkey or Pakistan (although petrol is exceedingly cheap in Irân, no unleaded petrol is as yet available). The frontier posts on the Turkish border are located at Bâzargân and Seto, in Azerbaijân. The

Pakistani border can be crossed at Mirjâve, near Zahedân, in Sistân and Baluchestân Province. Rail links also exist between Tehrân and Ankara, between Zâhedân and the Pakistani border, and between Mashhad and the Republic of Turkmenistan.

FOREIGN TOUR OPERATORS

US OPERATORS:

Mir Corporation, 85 S. Washington St., Suite 210 Seattle, WA 98104
Tel: 206-624-7289 / 800-424-7289; fax: 206-624-7360; website www.mircorp.com
email: info@mircorp.com

Cyrus Travel, 9454 Wilshire Blvd., Suite M-20, Beverly Hills, CA 90212
Tel: 800 992 9787, 310 888 8810; fax: 310 888 8812
website: www.cyrustravel.com; email: info@cyrustravel.com

Geographic Expeditions, 1008 General Kennedy Avenue
PO Box 29902, San Francisco, CA 94129-0902
Tel: 415 922 0448, 800 777 8183; website: www.geoex.com; email: info@geoex.com

Distant Horizons, 350 Elm Avenue, Long Beach, CA 90802
Tel: 800 333 1240, 562 983 8828; fax: 562 983 8833
website: www.distant-horizons.com; email: amandab@distant-horizons.com

CANADA OPERATORS:

Silk Road Tours, 300–1497 Marine Drive, West Vancouver B.C, V7T 1B8
Tel: (604) 925-3831; fax: (604) 925-6269; website: www.silkroadtours.com
email: canada@silkroadtours.com

UK OPERATORS:

Eastern Approaches, 5 Mill Road, Stow, Selkirkshire TD1 2SD, Scotland. Tel: 01578
730361; fax: 01578 730 714; website: www.easternapproaches.freeuk.com

LTP (Link To Persia), Suite 312, 3rd Floor, Crown House, 72 Hammersmith Road,
Kensington Olympia, London, W14 8TH; Tel 020 7559 9600; fax 020 7559 9601;
email: LTP@altp.freeserve.co.uk

Steppes East, 51 Castle Street, Cirencester, GL7 1QD; Tel: 01285 651010
Fax: 01285 885888; website: www.steppeseast.co.uk
email: sales@steppeseast.co.uk

Martin Randall Travel Ltd, Voysey House, Barley Mow Passage, London W4 4GF
Tel: 020 8742 3355; fax: 020 8742 7766; website: www.martinrandall.co.uk
email: info@martinrandall.co.uk

Persian Voyages, 12d Rothes Road, Dorking, Surrey, RH4 1JN, Tel: 01306 885894
website: www.persianvoyages.com; email: info@persianvoyages.com

Silk Road Tours, 371 Kensington High Street, London W14 8QZ; Tel: 020 7603 1246; website: www.silkroadtours.co.uk; email sales@silkroadtours.co.uk

For those interested in bird watching and nature:

Birdquest Ltd, Two Jays, Kemple End, Birdy Brow, Stonyhurst, Lancs BB7 9QY
Tel: 01254 826317; fax 01254 826780
website: www.birdquest.co.uk; email:birders@birdquest.co.uk

AUSTRALIAN OPERATORS:

Sundowners Travel, Suite 15, Lonsdale Court, 600 Lonsdale Street Melbourne 3000; Tel: (03) 9672 5300; fax: (03) 9672 5311
website: www.sundownerstravel.com

LOCAL TOURIST AGENCIES

Certain Irânian tourist agencies can organize tours for one or several people lasting from a few hours to several weeks (which include all accommodation, transport, and an English-speaking guide). This is a useful solution for those who wish to visit specific sites which may not necessarily be included on more general tours, or for business men who have one or more free days in which to do some sightseeing.

Pasargad Tours, 146 Africa Avenue, Tehrân 19156. Tel: (021) 2058866
website: www.pasargad-tours.com; email: info@pasargad-tours.com

Iran Tourist Co, 257 khiabân-e Motahari, Tehrân 15868. Tel: (021) 8732008, 8739819, 8733050; fax: (021) 8736158

Iran Doostan Co. (Ltd.), 885 Valiasr Avenue, Tehrân 13149, PO Box 14185–454
Fax: (021) 899766

Pardisan Tour & Travel Agency. General Manager Mr. Mostafa Shafiei Shakib
57 Shahara St. Tehrân 14565/115. Tel: (021) 6439570–1; fax: (021) 6427470–2, email: info@pardisantour.com

Treasures of Persia Tour Agency, 3rd Floor, No 241, Motahari Ave., Tehrân
Tel: (021)8731200; fax: (021) 8503343; website: www.toptourism.com
email: info@toptourism.com

VISAS

Despite the increase in foreign applications for tourist visas, obtaining a visa can still be a long and complicated business. There are several types of visas: transit visas, valid for one or two weeks; pilgrimage visas; and tourist visas, valid up to a month (it is possible to get an extension once you are in Irân by applying at provincial capital visa offices). Almost all foreign nationals need a visa before they can enter the country; at the moment only Turkish nationals are exempt from this rule. American nationals may find it particularly difficult to get a visa unless they have family in Irân. Whatever your nationality, your passport should not contain an Israeli visa.

The visa request must go through one of the embassies of the Islamic Republic of Irân, but the embassy will only be able to issue the visa once it has received an authorization number from the Ministry of Foreign Affairs in Tehrân. Apply a good month before your departure date, even if you have joined an organized tour (in which case the travel agency will probably apply for the visa for you. However, you will still have to hand in your passport a month in advance). Passports must be valid for at least six months after the date you leave Irân. If you organize a tour with an Irânian agency, the agency will apply for your visa directly to Tehrân; you will have to send your passport to the Irânian embassy in your country once the embassy has received the authorization number from Tehrân.

Tourists travelling with a group generally have little trouble obtaining a visa, but individual travellers have occasionally been known to encounter some difficulties.

The following are the addresses of some Irânian embassies and consulates:

Australia, 14 Torres St, Red Hill, Manuka, Canberra. Tel: (06) 295 2544

Canada, 411, Roosevelt Avenue, 4th floor, Ottawa K2A 3X9. Tel: 7290 902

Turkey, Tahran Caddesi 10, Ankara. Tel: 1274 320, fax: 1682 823

    Consulates: Ankara Caddesi 1–2, Istanbul. Tel: 5138 230; Cumhuriyet Caddesi, Kuksay Sitesi 23/25, Erzerum. Tel: 13 876

United Kingdom, 27 Prince's Gate, London SW7 1PX. Tel: 0207 584 8101

    Consulate: 50 Kensington Court, London W8 5DD. Tel: 0207 937 5225

United States: An Irân special interest section is maintained at the Embassy of Pakistan, 2209 Wisconsin Ave, N.W., Washington DC 20007. See www.daftar.org/eng/default.asp; the Embassy in Canada may also be approached.

GETTING THERE

Incoming flights from Europe land at Tehrân's Mehrâbâd airport. The other international airports in Irân (Shirâz, Bandar Abbâs, Mashhad, and Esfahân) only take flights from the Middle East and Pakistan. The number of flights from Europe has greatly increased in the past two or three years, and several companies have now resumed direct flights to Tehrân: British Airways (from London), Lufthansa (Frankfurt), Alitalia, Air France, KLM (Amsterdam), SWISS (Zürich) and Austrian Airlines. The national company, Irân Air, also has direct flights from London, Frankfurt, Geneva, Rome, Paris and Vienna. Note that alcoholic beverages are not served on Irân Air, and that Islamic dress rules are enforced once in the aeroplane.

Irân Air flights also exist between Tehrân and Damascus, Dubai, Sharjah, Karachi and Istanbul. Other connections are possible between the United Arab Emirates and Shirâz, Esfahân, Mashhad and Bandar Abbâs.

CUSTOMS

It is strictly forbidden to import alcohol, drugs and pornographic material into Irân. Be careful with foreign journals and newspapers which may be confiscated, particularly if they contain pictures of women wearing makeup or without a headscarf. A reasonable amount of jewellery for personal use, a camera and five rolls of film, a pair of binoculars and a walkman can be taken into the country without any problem as long as you leave with them again. The exact number of films taken in per person is rarely checked but be aware that there is an official limit of five rolls.

Most of the souvenirs bought in Irân may be exported, except for carpets, antiques, gold and silver, precious stones, and food products. In the case of the latter, the rule is rarely enforced although caviar and large quantities of pistachios can be difficult to get past customs. The export of carpets and antiques, on the other hand, is very strictly controlled and can be done only if you are in possession of the right documents. It is recommended to buy these items in shops that have an export licence and can take care of shipping them abroad.

GETTING AROUND

BY AIR

Irân has a surface area almost seven times that of the UK and distances between towns are often very great. The quickest way of getting around is by plane. Irân Air operates scheduled flights between all the major towns; they are generally cheaper than flights of the same distance in Europe, although prices have recently increased and future increases are likely. Flying is a popular means of transport with Irânians and tickets are difficult to buy unless you make a reservation well in advance. It is essential to bear in mind when working out your itinerary that flights are frequently delayed and even cancelled. Reservations can be made in Irân Air offices in all the major cities.

By Train

Trains are a comfortable and relatively quick way of getting around, but the railway system is rather limited; there are no railway lines, for example, to Shirâz or Hamadân. The east–west line goes from Tabriz (and Turkey) to Mashhad, via Zanjân, Tehrân and Semnân. A smaller line links Tehrân with the Caspian coast and passes through Sâri and Gorgân. The second main line leaves Tehrân for the south, splitting at Qom into two separate lines, one running south–east to Yazd and Kermân, and the other south–west to Ahvâz and the port of Abâdân. There are three classes of seats and berths in the overnight trains. Tickets have to be bought at the station except in Esfahân, where there is a ticket office in town at Enqelâb-e Eslâmi Square.

By Coach

The inter-city coach system covers the entire country. The various bus companies have been organized into cooperatives, each one identified by a different number, such as Cooperative Bus Company No 1, also known as Irân Peima 1, No 2, or No 5. The main towns have several coach stations, some of which are shared between companies, while others belong to a single company. Seats on the buses are numbered and it is wise to buy one's ticket ahead of time.

BY BUS AND TAXI

For getting round within a city, there are both buses and taxis. Unless you can speak and read a minimum of Fârsi, the bus system can turn out to be extremely complicated as stops are not always well indicated and the number of the bus as well as its destination are written in Fârsi only. Taxis are either collectively owned or belong to agencies; they can be hired from the hotels for short excursions or ones lasting up to a whole day.

MAPS, BOOKS AND NEWSPAPERS

The best places to find maps of Irân, city maps and books about the country in foreign languages are the bookshops in the hotels Esteqlâl and Azâdi Grand in Tehrân, and opposite the Abbâsi Hotel in Esfahân. As yet, few hotels have shops in them, so it is best to buy maps, postcards and dictionaries at the beginning of your trip before you leave Tehrân.

Foreign language books are also on sale in some bookshops in Tehrân (try on khiâbân-e Enqelâb, near the University), and in Esfahân (opposite the Abbâsi Hotel).

Two English-language daily newspapers are published in Tehrân, the *Tehrân Times* and the *Keyhan*, both of which are available in the big hotels and are occasionally sold in the streets in the main cities (outside Tehrân they are usually a day or so out of date).

TOURIST OFFICES

The governmental tourist information service is run by the Ministry of Culture and Islamic Guidance and the tourist offices in the main towns are generally to be found in the ministry building (ask for the Edâre Ershâd Eslâmiye). All provincial capitals have tourist offices, which can probably provide you with town maps and a few practical tips. These offices vary considerably in helpfulness from town to town and do not all have English-speaking staff. The offices are closed Thursday afternoons and Fridays and are open on other days from 8 am till 2 pm.

The main offices are the following:

Tehrân, Department of Tourism and Pilgrimages, 5th floor, 11 khiâbân-e Dameshq, khiâbân-e Vali-e Asr. Tel: (021) 892 212, extn 29

Esfahân, corner of khiâbân-e Shâhid Madani and khiâbân-e Chahâr Bâgh, opposite the Abbâsi Hotel. Tel: (031) 21555

Before a marriage, Qom, 2004

Mashhad, Ministry of Culture and Islamic Guidance, 2nd floor, Eslâmi Road, khiâbân-e Bahâr. Tel: (051) 48288
Kermân, khiâbân-e Ershâd, khiâbân-e Ferdosi. Tel: (0341) 25098

CLOTHING

Irân is an Islamic republic and *hejâb*, or Islamic dress, is compulsory for all—both men and women. For women, a *châdor* need not necessarily be worn, but one's head and neck should at least be covered with a scarf, and a long dark coat (preferably calf-length and loose fitting) can conceal the legs and arms. Feet and any part of the legs left showing should also be covered (with socks or thick tights), even when wearing sandals. Do not wear lots of jewellery; try to keep to plain rings and discreet makeup.

Hejâb must be worn in all public places (even in restaurants and regardless of the temperature!). In practice, this means that the only time it can be taken off is in the privacy of your hotel room. But do not forget to put your coat and scarf back on when you go to answer the door! Some state hotels are very strict about *hejâb* in the lobby and may ask women to readjust their scarves if a few locks of hair have managed to escape.

The problem of packing for a trip to Irân is simplified for women by the rules concerning clothing: unless it is likely that you are to be invited into private society gatherings, do not bother taking along your best dresses for the evenings as no one will see them. On the other hand, a selection of scarves and a change of coat will come in handy. Scarves as well as long coats in a surprising variety of colours can be bought quite cheaply in Irân. Be careful when buying cloth in the bazaars as most of it is synthetic and very uncomfortable in hot weather. Trousers (jeans are perfectly acceptable) and long skirts or dresses are the most practical way of dressing. Be aware that wearing hejâb can be difficult in hot weather, particularly if you are overdressed; loose and light cotton clothing is best of all.

In certain holy places, such as the mausoleums of the descendants of the Emâms, women must wear a *châdor*, but these can usually be borrowed at the entrance gate. There is no need to buy one for the purpose. Be careful not to tread on the ends of your *châdor*: walking with a *châdor* on is not always as easy as it looks, especially if it is slightly too long!

The rules concerning clothing for men are much simpler: shorts should not be worn and arms should be covered, particularly when visiting holy shrines. Note that all these rules are more strictly observed during the months of Ramazân (Ramadan) and Moharram.

Even if these rules concerning clothing seem restrictive, it is very strongly advised that you stick to them (remember that, travelling in a group, you may simply be sharply reprimanded for improper dress, but it could be an entirely different matter later for your Irânian guide). If you are not prepared to obey these rules, then it is probably better not to visit Irân at the moment.

Given the great temperature swings between day and night, as well as differences in altitude (when travelling by car in the Zagros, for example, it is quite possible to go from the central plateau at a height of 1,000 metres [3,280 feet] above sea level to a mountain pass at 2,500 metres [8,202 feet] several times in one day!) it is important to have several layers of clothing handy that can be taken off or put on as need be. In winter, warm clothes are essential except along the Persian Gulf.

PHOTOGRAPHY

Although the Irânians themselves enjoy taking photos of their families, many are not yet used to the sophisticated photographic equipment that foreign tourists like to deploy, and may well regard some of it as highly suspicious, especially zoom

lenses. Groups of tourists descending from a bus with their cameras at the ready
and shooting off in all directions make policemen particularly nervous. Be careful
where you point your camera and avoid taking pictures of policemen and soldiers. It
is strongly recommended that you do not take pictures in or around airports,
military installations of any kind, barracks, frontiers and any other sensitive area. If
in doubt, ask your guide (policemen have been known to forbid pictures being
taken in the street, especially in small towns). When taking photos of people,
particularly of women, ask their permission beforehand—be courteous, and limit
intrusiveness.

Photography is permitted at most historic sites and even in some museums
(without flash) but not around certain holy shrines such as Mashhad and Qom. In
emāmzādeh (mausoleums of the descendants of Emāms) check first with a guardian
to make sure that photos are allowed.

HEALTH

There are no compulsory vaccinations for entering Irân but it is a good idea to be vaccinated against tetanus and typhoid. Malaria is present in some areas, such as Sistân and Baluchestân, southern Fârs and Khuzestân, particularly in summer. Check with your doctor about which anti-malarial drugs to take, and make sure you have insect repellent with you.

Take a small medical kit with the usual basic items (such as plasters, aspirin, anti-diaorrhea pills) as well as any particular medicine you might need.

The tap water can be drunk almost everywhere; if in doubt, take water purifying tablets with you. In many of the smaller towns, the water comes directly from the *qanât*, which are fed by melt water and is therefore relatively safe. However, in out-of-the-way places and in the heat of summer it is better to take proper precautions.

ACCOMMODATION

Hotels (*mehmânkhâneh* or *hotel*) in Irân are classified in categories from one to five stars, and guesthouses (*mosâferkhâneh*) in superior, first and second class. The *mosâferkhâneh* offer rudimentary services, particularly second class ones, but are very cheap and can often be paid in riâl, whereas most hotels now ask foreigners to pay in US dollars. The star system for the hotels bears little relation to the systems in use in the West, and the quality of hotel within any one class can vary quite considerably. In general, a five-star room is a 'deluxe' one with private bathroom. Do not expect the words ex-Hilton or ex-International to indicate the equivalent of those hotels in Europe. Most hotels were built in the 1970s and are now somewhat run down, although generally perfectly acceptable. In many hotels, even in the four-star category, the bedroom toilets may be of the squat variety rather than a Western-style one.

The names of hotels are liable to change when the owner changes. It is worth enquiring about previous names of a hotel if you can, and making sure that you have as exact an address as possible (street names frequently change too).

Theoretically, only married couples may share a hotel room. This rule is strictly applied in the case of Irânians but hotel staff may be more lenient towards foreigners, especially those in a group. However, be aware that the rule exists and do not assume that it will be waived just for you.

For a list of the main hotels, see p. 401.

MONEY

The basic monetary unit in Irân is the riâl. While written prices are usually given in Riâl, it is very frequent when giving a price orally to do so in tomân (one tomân is equal to 10 Riâl, 100 tomian are 1,000 riâl). In March 2005, 1 US$ was worth 8800 Riâls at the official rate of exchange; the black market offers better rates. The current trend is a slow decline in the value of the Riâl against the US dollar.

US dollars, cash, and traveller's cheques in dollars and in some foreign currencies (yen, euros, pounds sterling, Swiss francs) are generally accepted, but outside the major cities it is best to have dollars in cash. Credit cards (American Express and Visa) are sometimes accepted in the big hotels in Tehrân and Esfahân, but do not rely on them as your only method of payment.

The best place to change money is at the bank, although a thriving black market now exists. Branches of the major banks can be found at Tehrân airport and in most of the big hotels. If you want to change your Riâl back when you leave the country, make sure you have kept the bank exchange certificates and your customs declaration form. Banks are usually open from 9 am to 4 pm or 4.30 pm from Saturday to Wednesday, and are closed on Thursday afternoons and Friday.

Do not change too much money when you first arrive; US$50 go a long way, particularly if you are travelling with a group. If you are travelling alone, remember that most hotels will ask to be paid cash in dollars. Food and transport within the country are very cheap, and hotels will probably be your biggest expense.

SHOPPING

Irânian arts and crafts are extremely varied and, in most cases, have a very long tradition behind them. They include carpets, kilims (*gelim*), printed cloth, brocade, inlaid wood, miniatures, and copper and brassware, to name just a few. Unfortunately, these crafts have been declining in quality for a many years and the hotel and airport shops—when they exist—offer only a limited choice, which is soon repetitive. The bazaars have a much wider choice, but do not forget to bargain for anything you buy there, particularly in Esfahân. The bazaar is the best place to buy gold jewellery (in small quantities if you want to avoid trouble when you leave the country), textiles or a *châdor*.

Persian carpets are still of very high quality; as well as the traditional motifs there are now a variety of modern ones, including the portrait of Emâm Khomeini, some of which are of foreign inspiration. Because of the strict rules governing the

Carpet seller, Qom

export of carpets, it is best to buy them at a shop which has an exporting licence and which will take care of sending them to you, in your home country, against a down payment. If a carpet seller assures you that the laws on exporting carpets have just changed, check with your guide or at the hotel before buying. The same precautions are valid for antiques. Be careful with recent antiques, cloisonné fresh out of Chinese workshops and miniatures painted on ivory, bone or even plastic.

Caviar can be bought in Irân at extremely low prices, particularly along the Caspian, although the industry has been greatly affected by pollution. Theoretically, its export is forbidden unless it has been bought at the airport shop located after customs, where, although more expensive, it is still considerably cheaper than the prices on the European market.

TELECOMMUNICATIONS

Hotels are by far the most convenient place from which to telephone abroad and long-distance calls are relatively cheap. From Tehrân hotels, the connection is usually quite quick, but it may be necessary to wait an hour or two when calling from smaller towns as all calls abroad have to go through a receptionist.

It is also possible to send telegrams and telexes within the country or abroad from post offices in the larger towns. These services are also available in the bigger hotels. Email facilities at internet cafes are now increasingly available in Irânian cities.

TIME ZONE

Tehrân time is GMT plus three and a half hours. Irân has now introduced daylight saving time (the clocks change by an hour in March and September) so that for a few weeks there may be an extra hour's difference with Continental Europe.

OPENING TIMES

Friday is the day of prayer in Irân and most shops, businesses and offices close then. Thursday is half-closing day for many shops and offices. On other days, opening hours can vary quite considerably from one region to another. In general, shops close for an hour or two at lunchtime and stay open until 8 pm, whereas government offices are only open from 8 am to 2 pm.

MOSQUES, MUSEUMS AND HISTORICAL SITES

There is generally no problem for non-Muslims to visit mosques in Irân, except perhaps during Friday prayer. Shoes can be worn inside the mosques but should be taken off where carpets have been laid down, usually in front of the *mehrâb*. However, in the *emâmzâdeh* (mausoleums of the descendants of Emâms), it is necessary to take one's shoes off before entering the building. Remember to ask permission to take photographs inside the *emâmzâdeh* even if there are no signs expressly forbidding it. In some *emâmzâdeh*, such as Abdol Azim's in Rey, women must wear a *châdor*, which can be hired at the entrance.

At Qom and Mashhad, the most important pilgrimage centres in Irân, entrance to the holy shrine is forbidden to non-Muslims (with the exception of certain areas in Mashhad, see p. 214–5).

The opening times and days of museums and historical sites is often one of the most frustrating problems for the tourist in Irân. Most museums have fixed opening times, with one closing day a week, usually a Monday. Unfortunately, these times can change suddenly and those tourists with itineraries fixed in advance may have to cancel some visits or replace them.

At the most important sites, such as Persepolis, Pasargadae, or Susa, tickets are sold at the entrance, but some sites, particularly those away from the major towns, are unfenced and do not even have a guardian. Occasionally, it will be necessary to find the guardian and get him to unlock the gate. Should he be absent, you may even have to come back later or the next day. It is therefore recommended to have as flexible an itinerary as possible if you are determined to see a particular place, or to telephone in advance to be sure of getting in. Sites well away from large cities are often impossible or extremely difficult to get to by public transport; for these, it is best to hire a car and a driver if you are not travelling with an organized tour.

CALENDAR

There are three different calendars in use in Irân. There is a solar calendar, introduced by Rezâ Shâh, using the Zoroastrian month names of pre-Islamic Persia. The year is of of 365 days divided into 12 months of 30 or 31 days each. Despite its apparent resemblance to the Gregorian calendar, it differs on several important points: the first six months of the year have 31 days, the next five have 30 days and the last month 29 days, or 30 days in leap years. New Year's Day corresponds to the first day of spring, the 21st of March, which is the time of the great festival of Noruz. These years are counted from the first day of spring of the Muslim Hegira (622 AD). It is this solar calendar which is the most widely used in Irân today. For a quick conversion, add 621 to the Irânian year for the approximate date in the Christian calendar.

The names of the months are as follows: Farvardin (21 March–20 April); Ordibehesht (21 April–21 May); Khordâd (22 May–21 June); Tir (22 June–22 July); Mordâd (23 July–22 August); Shâhrivar (23 August–22 September); Mehr (23 September–22 October); Abân (23 October–21 November); Azar (22 November–21 December); Dey (22 December–20 January); Bahman (21 January–19 February); and Esfand (20 February–20 March).

There is also the Islamic lunar calendar used in all Muslim countries, and which serves to fix the religious festivals and ceremonies. With this system, the year is also divided into twelve months, but is only 354 days long. For this reason, the gap between the solar and lunar years is constantly growing (33 lunar years are equal to 32 solar years), and there is now roughly a forty-year difference between the Islamic and Persian calendars although both start with the year of the Hegira. Because the first month of the Islamic year, Moharram, can begin at any time in the

Gregorian calendar depending on the actual or official sighting of the new moon, it is very difficult to calculate the exact equivalent of an Islamic date, and conversion tables have been worked out for this purpose.

The Gregorian calendar is also used in Irân and appears, for example, on the newspapers alongside the other two calendars; thus the newspaper published on the 5th of October 1992 was also dated 13th Mehr 1371 (Persian solar calendar) and seventh Rabi-ol-sani 1413 (lunar calendar).

FESTIVALS AND HOLIDAYS

RELIGIOUS HOLIDAYS

These days are determined according to the Islamic lunar calendar. As the equivalents in the Gregorian calendar vary from year to year, only the Muslim dates are given below, in the order in which they appear in the Islamic calendar:

9 Moharram Tâsuâ	Eve of the martyrdom of Emâm Hosein
10 Moharram Ashurâ	Anniversary of the martyrdom of Emâm Hosein, killed at Kerbalâ
20 Safar Arba'in	40th day after the death of Emâm Hosein
28 Safar	Anniversary of the death of the Prophet and of the martyrdom of Emâm Hasan
17 Rabi-ol-avval	Anniversary of the birth of the Prophet and of Emâm Ja'far Sadeq
13 Rajab	Anniversary of the birth of Emâm Ali
27 Rajab Eid-e mab'as	Day when the Prophet began preaching
3 Sha'bân	Anniversary of the birth of Emâm Hosein
15 Sha'bân	Anniversary of the birth of the Twelfth Emâm
1 Ramazân	Beginning of the month of fasting
21 Ramazân	Anniversary of the martyrdom of Emâm Ali
1 Shavvâl Eid-e fetr	Festival to mark the end of the month of fasting
25 Shavvâl	Anniversary of the death of Emâm Ja'far Sadeq
11 Ziqa'deh	Anniversary of the birth of the Eighth Emâm, Emâm Rezâ
10 Zihajje Eid-e qorbân	Day of sacrifice to the pilgrims at Mecca
18 Zihajje Eid-e qadir	Anniversary of the naming of Ali as successor to the Prophet

NATIONAL HOLIDAYS

These holidays are calculated according to the Persian solar calendar and rarely vary in date in the Gregorian calendar:

1–4 Farvardin (21–24 March)	Noruz, the Irānian New Year
12 Farvardin (1st April)	Islamic Republic Day
13 Farvardin (2 April)	Sizdah bedar, the 13th day of the New Year
14 Khordâd (4 June)	Anniversary of the death of Emâm Khomeini in 1989
15 Khordâd (5 June)	Anniversary of the popular uprising in 1963, which followed news of the arrest of Emâm Khomeini
17 Shahrivar (8 September)	Day of the Martyrs of the Revolution
22 Bahman (11 February)	Victory of the Islamic Revolution (1979)
29 Esfand (20 March)	Oil Nationalization Day (1951)

Spice sellers, Regent's Bazaar, Kermān

FOOD IN IRÂN   —*Bruce Wannell*

Irân has had one of the world's great culinary traditions, based on a once-vigorous nomad pastoralism in the semi-arid steppes and a rich agriculture in the few well-watered areas of oases, rivers and the mountain valleys of the Alborz and Zagros ranges and the coastal areas along the Caspian Sea and the Persian Gulf. Irânians remain hospitable and courteous, and good food, though harder to find, is still there when the doors of hospitality open to travellers: the traditions of Irânian *javânmardi* (generous and chivalric behaviour) and of Islamic hospitality survive in spite of social and economic pressures. The discriminating and persevering traveller will find his/her way beyond impoverished modernity to a still-living tradition of fine eating and generous entertaining.

However these traditions have been severely endangered, if not quite destroyed, by the galloping industrialisation, pollution, destruction of the natural and social environment as well as the population explosion of the last 30 years—leading to uncontrolled growth of towns and cities engulfing limited agricultural land, contaminating water, decaying traditional extended family structures and increasing reliance on imported food and standardised supermarket and restaurant culture.

The Esfahân oasis has lost the life-giving water of the Zâyandeh Rud to a hare-brained project in the deserts of Yazd, with a resulting death of upwards of 50 kilometers of orchards and rice-paddies upstream; the Caspian coast has been parcelled up into tiny plots for holiday villas, where once productive agricultural land is sold off for building, while the valleys and forests of the Alborz slopes no longer offer a livelihood to shepherds, instead the trees are felled to make lavatory paper in Sâri; the semi-deserts have been turned into motorways and factories, and nomads no longer drive their flocks across the landscape; tax-concessions encourage most villages to house small and inefficient factories which pollute the atmosphere, while the last 25 years have seen the traditional mud-brick vernacular architecture of even the remotest areas swept away almost without trace, to be replaced with ugly concrete and steel-girder boxes.

The death of the single-storey courtyard house, open to the sky and housing the extended family around the courtyard and its central pool, means not only a loss of traditional identity and of a varied local architecture suited to the climate, but also, importantly for food in Irân, the loss of the mutually-supportive workforce that traditionally ensured the regular, labour-intensive preparation of delicious Irânian cuisine. Now as often as not the harassed lone woman of the nuclear family has to take a paid job outside the home and returns to the bleakness of a small flat with strip lighting and synthetic moquette and blaring television, too exhausted to go through alone the once-communal rituals of traditional cooking and eating.

American-style convenience food, with its attendant evils of flatulent obesity, is all the rage. In Tehrân, there are some reasonable restaurants serving an approximation of the varied traditional domestic cuisine, but even there the fashion is for greasy hamburgers or dimly-lit preparations that might pass as Mexican. The situation is little short of a catastrophe.

The lone traveller may be fortunate enough to be invited to Irânian homes where traditional food is still prepared, as Irânians continue to be gracious and hospitable. The tourist in a group will have to rely on his/her guide negotiating with the hotel chef to produce something a little better than the usual carelessly repetitive one-night-stand fodder. Group tourism alas, like factory farming, seldom if ever encourages gastronomic excellence!

One of the problems is that non-elite public eating in Irân derives from the bazaar cook-shop tradition, which never was intended to give a complete diet, only to provide essential protein and carbohydrates to the workforce: hence the endless kebâbs and flat-bread or rice, with barely a sprinkling of sour red sumâc seed or strained yoghurt with mountain garlic "*mâst o musir*" to enliven them, let alone a relish of pickled vegetables "*torshi*" (home-made they can be superb, especially matured garlic pickle often 20 years old: the quality of the vinegar is crucial—much factory-made pickle, as in England, is inedible because of the cheap chemical vinegar used). Kebâb is still regarded as the main form of public eating, so vegetarians will have a hard time of it! Even carnivores will tire of the over-use of chemical tenderiser on low-grade over-refrigerated meat smothered in passe-partout saffron—at home or for picnics, the freshly-slaughtered local lamb or mutton is marinaded overnight in onion and lime juice or in yoghurt and garlic before being roasted on skewers "*sikh*" over a charcoal fire—and the result is delicious. In Ramazân, a meat and wheat porridge called "*halim*" is served in the market at dusk; a thick broth "*âsh*" is traditionally served on Thursday evenings, based on grain and pulses, with herbs and dried whey

Kebâb seller, Tehrân

"*kashk*" and fried onions with dried mint; a traditional workman's breakfast is "*kalleh-pâcheh*" boiled sheep's head and feet, too strong for the uninitiated, and a delicious lunch "*âb gusht*" cooked and served in stone pots "*dizi*": a liquid stew of mutton, onions, chick peas and dried limes, eaten with bread, accompanied by a raw onion, and a fresh yoghurt drink "*dugh*"—the pre-bottled variety almost always tastes of preservative, so is best avoided, as also the sickeningly sweet fizzy drinks that are routinely offered; bottled water is fairly safe and at least doesn't interfere with the taste of the meal.

Irânian fruits and fresh herbs can be superb, with intense flavours that shame the watery productions offered for sale in English supermarkets. A favourite ending to a meal is a dish of fresh herbs, including tarragon, lemon basil, chives, mint, etc, served with white sheep's cheese and thin flat bread to wrap the selection in small rolls or triangles, very cleansing to the palate. There are a variety of flat breads baked in the "*tanur*" communal clay-oven —whose origins go back to ancient Mesopotamia—thin "*lavâsh*" and the standard "*nân*", with sesame or black-onion seeds, slapped onto the clay walls of the "*tanur*"; "*sangak*" oven-baked on a bed of pebbles; "*barbari*", crisp and ridged; very fine breads baked on convex metal plates by nomads like the Qashqâi, while shepherds in the mountains make a thick crusty bread under the ashes of the big log fires that keep them warm and the wolves at bay. Snacks of white feta-like cheese and flat bread are served with water-melon or with fresh grapes and walnuts in the autumn. Another snack sometimes served at lunch is a stiff herb and spinach omlette "*sabzi kuku*" fried on both sides, served with bread and plain yoghurt; another end-product of milk is "*kashk*", a slightly acrid residue of boiled-down and dried whey or yoghurt, added as a souring agent to soups and stews, and notably to fried aubergine "*kashk bâdenjân*"; grated cucumber and chopped fresh mint is used in "*mâst o khiâr*", and lightly boiled strained spinach with a little chopped garlic for the other yoghurt classic "*burâni esfinâj*"; yoghurt side dishes are also made with steamed, peeled and sliced red beetroot— which gives a beautiful intense purple, or with peeled and fried courgettes, or even with a large de-thorned thistle "*kangar*". Fresh dates in their own syrup "*rotâb*", pale golden-yellow from Shahdâd or Jahrom, darker from Bam, are served with plain yoghurt as a breakfast snack or desert, as is sesame-halva. Dried and salted melon seeds and the excellent pistacchios form an ever ready snack, or appetizer during the long wait before dinner, when conversation meanders and the host/ess peels little cucumbers and other fruits for the guests before the meal is served at the end of the evening.

Sweet and sour is a recurring feature of Irânian cooking—the refreshing taste helps cut the heaviness of the favourite fat lamb or mutton, and quenches thirst in a dry climate. Pomegranates are one of the marvels of Irân—translucent seeds varying from pale to darkest ruby, they are delicious simply as they are, providing you don't mind the woody inner seed, or as a fresh juice, or as a concentrated "*robb*" used as a souring agent in cooking —especially together with ground walnuts to make the classic festive dish "*khoresh fesenjân*", a stew of wild duck or pheasant or even chicken: the restaurant version is too often totally inadequate—the battery-chicken separately boiled in water with just a dribble of the pomegranate and walnut sauce splashed over it, eked out with lemon juice and sugar—whereas it should all be stewed long and slow together to form a rich sauce that is not cloyingly sweet; served with a plain "chelo" of the finest white rice, it is at its best unbeatable. Another pomegranate and walnut preparation, also originating from the Caspian coast, is the preserved olive, "*zeitun parvardeh*" which has recently gained currency throughout Irân. Another souring agent for stews is the aromatic dried lime "*limu 'ammâni*" cooked with herbs, red beans and fried mutton in the classic "*qormeh sabzi*". Other lamb stews soured with rhubarb "*khoresh rivâs*" or with quinces "*khoresh beh*" are typical of the north-east. Small sour grapes are sometimes added to the aubergine stew "*khoresh bâdenjân*", and sour grape verjuice "*ghureh*" is also used as a souring agent. All these stews are served with "*chelo*", plain long-grained white rice which is rinsed and soaked before boiling, then drained, sealed and steamed for up to an hour, so that each grain is separate and light: an additional refinement is to line the pot with thinly sliced potatoes and oil before steaming, which results in a crisp crust "*tah-dig*". This complex preparation indicates the prestige status of rice in Irân: this style of cooking rice became prevalent under the Safavid Shâh Abbâs (d.1629) as recorded by his chef Ustâd Nurullâh; since the oil-boom of the 1960's rice-consumption has become generalised throughout Irânian society, even in the poorest classes.

The other main form of rice preparation is "*polo*" also known as "*pilav*", similar to the first stages of "*chelo*" until the steaming stage, when various enrichments are added: sour cherries "*âlbâlu*" or barberries "*zereshk*"—both of these are also used to make delicious refreshing sherbets. The greatest of the polo rice dishes is "*bâqâli polo*" where peeled fresh broad beans and quantities of fresh chopped dill and chunks of lamb marinaded in turmeric and cumin and fried in its own fat are added for the final steaming, with a scattering of rice grains perfumed with saffron added on serving. A plain yoghurt is the only relish needed. A Shirâzi speciality is "*kalam polo*" with cabbage and herbs shredded in the rice, which is served with meatballs. The most famous meatballs, giant in size and built around apricots or plums with a forcemeat of chopped lamb and crushed chickpeas is the "*kufteh tabrizi*". The other great festive *polo* is made with slivers of blanched bitter-orange peel, pistachios and saffron "*shirin polo*" also known as "*nârenj polo*", with chicken stewed separately and incorporated at the last stage. Bitter oranges are also used to squeeze on to fried fish or grilled kebabs, when they are in season.

Irânian sweets are also varied and delicious, if properly made with good ingredients: among the best known are the toffee-like "*sohân*" from Qom made with the sweet flour of germinated wheat, clarified butter, saffron, pistachios etc; the fine layered pastry stuffed with almond and cardamom paste drenched in rose-water syrup "*bâqlavâ*"; the crumbly biscuits of roasted chickpea flour "*nun nakhodchi*"; the lozenges of saffron almond paste "*lozineh*" from Jolfâ Esfahân; the nougat with tamarisk manna "*gazangebin*" better known as "*gaz*" from Esfahân; an Armenian speciality is "*shirovharz*", a lokoum of grape-juice and walnuts and spices sun-dried to the consistency of a stiff jelly; and the rose-water and saffron rice-pudding "*sholeh zard*" is offered in the street on feast days.

The repertoire of Irânian food is greater than what has been sketched here, and its influence reaches into the Caucasus, Mesopotamia, Central Asia and even India, areas with which Irân shares much history and many traditions—even the Spanish and South American dish "*escabeche*" has a distant Irânian origin via Abbâsid Baghdâd and the Arab advance across North Africa to Andalusia. All food is not only a necessity but also a luxury, its study is a prism for studying the health and history of a nation, its cultural and agricultural imports and exports through time. The Irânian tradition of food is a great tradition, but now beleaguered and endangered, threatened by a tragic loss of quality and authenticity, which in turn threatens the health and even the identity of the nation.

A young girl carries home some freshly baked nân *bread.*

GEOGRAPHY
THE PLATEAU AND THE MOUNTAINS

Irân, which has a surface area of some 1,648,000 square kilometres (636,000 square miles equivalent to Britian, Germany, France, Italy, Australia and Switzerland combined), is an elevated plateau with an average height of over 1,000 metres (3,300 feet) above sea level, set between two depressions, the Caspian Sea to the north and the Persian Gulf to the south. The central desert plateau is surrounded by tall chains of mountains. In the north, the Alborz Range creates a formidable but narrow barrier between the plateau and the fertile coastal plains along the Caspian. The physical differences on either side of the mountains are striking: from the heat and dust of Tehrân (1,100 metres, 3,600 feet) the road climbs quickly up to the mountain passes before descending again to the humidity and luxuriant vegetation of the coast situated at an average of 40 metres (130 feet) below sea level. While the annual rainfall in Tehrân is only 210 millimetres, it is as high as 1,224 millimetres at Rasht, by the sea. It is in this coastal area that rice, tea and various citrus fruits are grown.

The Alborz Chain includes several peaks over 4,000 metres (13,000 feet) in height, including the Alam Kuh (4,840 metres, 15,875 feet) and Mount Damâvand (5,671 metres, 18,600 feet), an extinct volcano which dominates the skyline of Tehrân. The chain stretches east into Khorâsân Province but is lower there than further west and cut by fertile valleys. This region is one of the few areas giving easy access onto the Irânian Plateau and has been used for centuries by nomads and invaders from Central Asia.

To the west of the plateau, the Zagros Chain stretches south from Lake Van in Turkey to the Persian Gulf, and also reaches over 4,000 metres (13,000 feet) in height in places. The mountain ridges, which lie in regular folds running from the northwest to the southeast, are cut by transverse valleys. The remains of what were once vast oak, pistachio, almond and walnut forests are visible on the mountainsides, now occupied mainly by grazing herds of sheep and goats. In the valleys, wheat, cotton, tobacco and barley are grown.

To the southeast of the plateau, the Makrân Chain forms a barrier between the sea of Oman and the central plateau, while along the frontier with Pakistan is yet another chain. Its highest point is Mount Taftân (4,042 metres, 13,260 feet), a still active volcano, near the town of Zâhedân.

The plateau itself has an average height of 1,000 metres (3,300 feet) above sea level. In the centre of it are two areas of desert: the Dasht-e Kavir, the salt desert in the north, and the Dasht-e Lut, the sand desert in the south. These are among the most arid areas in the world. While the Dasht-e Kavir does have some oases in it, the Dasht-e Lut cannot support any form of life at all. The zones of human settlement are therefore to be found mostly along the edges of the plateau and in the oases.

To the southwest of the Zagros lie the plains of Khuzestân, a sort of enclave of the Mesopotamian plain through which flow the Arvand-rud (better known as the Shatt el-Arab) and the Kârun. The coastal area of the Persian Gulf, which stretches for some 800 kilometres (497 miles) from the Iraqi frontier to the Straits of Hormuz, is arid with only very little natural vegetation and a few palm groves. The main source of income in the region is oil, first drilled for here in 1908. To the east, near Bandar Abbâs, are several offshore islands which belong to Irân, including Qeshm, Kish, Kharg and Hormuz.

Like the neighbouring states around the Caspian Sea, Irân is located in an active earthquake zone and tremors are a frequent phenomenon, sometimes occurring very violently. The area around Tabriz, Qazvin and the Caspian has suffered considerably from earthquakes over the centuries, most recently in June 1990 when an earthquake hit the towns of Rudbâr and Rasht in Gilân Province, leaving 48,000 people dead. Other regions of the country are also prone to earthquakes, particularly in the south, from Fârs Province east to Baluchestân. Bam, in the southeastern province of Kermân, was the most recent major settlement to suffer in this area, being devastated by an earthquake at the end of 2003 (see p. 390–5).

THE WATER PROBLEM

Irân has only one navigable waterway, the 850 kilometre (528 mile)-long Kârun, which originates in the Zagros Mountains and joins the Arvand-rud at Khoram Shahr before flowing into the Persian Gulf. Most Irânian rivers, however, are not permanent and never reach the sea. The Zâyandeh-rud, for example, which flows through the city of Esfahân, ends up in the Ghavkhâneh marshes nearby, now dried out.

Irân's largest lake is Lake Orumieh (4,368 square metres, 47,016 square feet) in Azerbaijân. Like most of the other lakes, such as the Salt Lake (daryâcheh-ye Namak) near Qom and Lake Bakhtegân near Shirâz, it has a high salt content. Several fresh water lakes are to be found in the east, in Sistân, including the largest one, the Hâmun-e Sâberi, fed by the Hirmand from Afghânistân (this river is known as the Helmand on the Afghân side of the border). Since the construction of a dam on the river, however, the volume of water in the lakes has considerably decreased.

(Following pages) The Dasht-e Kavir desert between Tehrân and Qom

The problem of obtaining water is a serious one in Irân and has existed since antiquity. South of the Alborz in particular, rain is rare and tends to fall mainly between November and April. Under these conditions, agriculture is only possible if combined with irrigation. The mountains, however, serve to collect the winter precipitation in the form of ice and snow and release it slowly during the drier spring and summer months. But a dry winter is often a sign of drought for the following summer.

One solution to the problem which is particularly well adapted to the country is the *qanât*, an underground channel which captures the water directly from the water tables in the foothills of the mountains and carries it onto the plains. The *qanât* system was first devised by the Medes and Persians and has remained essentially unchanged ever since. The series of small depressions that can often be seen crossing the desert reveal the presence of a *qanât* below the ground: they are the vertical wells dug at regular intervals to provide fresh air and light for the workers below, to allow the rubble to be cleared and maintenance work carried out. Some *qanât* are tens of kilometres long and may be dug 300 metres (984 feet) below the surface. Many oases are entirely dependent on *qanât* for their survival rather than on well or spring water.

Dams also appeared very early on in Irân. The first bridges with sluice gates were built by the Sasanians in the third century AD to irrigate the plains of Khuzestân. The Khâju Bridge at Esfahân is based on the same principle and serves not only for irrigation purposes, but also to control the volume of water in the river. In the 20th century, several dams and mountain reservoirs have been built, particularly in the Alborz, in order to increase the surface area of arable land available and to satisfy the demand for water from Tehrân and the large industrial centres (there are dams, for example on the Sefid Rud near Rudbâr, and in Khuzestân Province, near Dezful).

FLORA AND FAUNA

The vegetation in Irân is remarkably varied from one area to another. Irân is situated at the junction of four different phyto-geographic regions (the Irâno-Turanian, Euro-Siberian, Saharo-Arabian and Sudanian) and has over 8,000 species of plants, of which about 20 per cent are endemic. These endemic species are now to be found mostly in isolated spots, on the peaks of the Zagros and Alborz, on a few mountains of the central plateau and on the ridges south of Kâshân and Yazd and north of Kermân. Although 60 per cent of the land is classified as arid or semi-arid, these

areas are not entirely barren and can sustain a sparse vegetation, adapted to the dry-
ness and salinity of the soil (*Acacia, Ziziphus, Heliotropium, Astragalus, Artemisia*).

The natural vegetation of the Zagros is one of oak forests up to 2,200 metres
(7,220 feet), and above that of mixed forests of oak and juniper. The slopes of the
Alborz which face the plateau were also originally covered in juniper forests but on
the north side facing the Caspian Sea the forests are very dense and of great
botanical complexity; there are even species there representative of Tertiary flora
which have survived the ice age. The forests here are mainly composed of
deciduous trees (elm, oak and beech) with box, elder and vine. Along the Shatt
el-Arab are marshes, now heavily polluted and partly dried out, and off the coast
where the Persian Gulf meets the Indian Ocean, some of the islands such as Qeshm
are surrounded by mangroves.

Irân is also at the junction of different faunal regions (the Palearctic, Oriental
and Ethiopian), and its great climatic and geographic diversity has led to the
establishment of an extremely rich and varied fauna (jungle cat, brown bear, wild
boar, mouflon, ibex, goitred and Dorcas gazelles, crested porcupine). Until the
1940s, tigers, lions, panthers and leopards were hunted in Irân, but today only the
panthers and leopards still survive. Irân is one of the most important regions in the
whole Middle East for bird migration, particularly in the Ansali marshes, the salt
lakes of Orumieh (Azerbaijân) and Bakhtegân (Fârs), the Shadegân marshes
(Khuzestân), lakes Parishân and Arjân (Fârs) and the Persian Gulf. Over 500
species of bird have been recorded in Irân, of which 325 breed there. Among the
more interesting species are the Irânian bee-eater, the grey-necked bunting, the
crowned and black-bellied sandgrouse, the great rock nuthatch, the houbara
bustard, the white-throated robin, and the Socotra cormorant.

Unfortunately, centuries of tree felling, grazing herds of sheep and goats, cultivation, as well as modern pollution and urbanization have had a serious impact on
the environment. The vast stretches of primary forest have been seriously depleted
and a large part of the Zagros, now covered in grasses and bushes, is suitable for
grazing but no longer supports trees. In the past 25 years or so, the Irân–Iraq war,
and atmospheric and maritime pollution brought about by the burning of the
Kuwaiti oil fields during the Gulf War, have also had an effect on the Irânian
environment. The Shadegân marshes and the Khor al-Amaya and Khor Musa tidal
mudflats, for example, have been contaminated, probably by Iraqi chemical
weapons. The draining of marshland and its conversion into arable land has led to
the disappearance of numerous species of birds, frogs and insects. Twenty years ago,
more than 12 million birds migrated regularly through the Irânian marshes; today

Turkoman Steppe landscape, Qal'eh Tapeh Sheikh, Māzanderān Province

there are just over one million. Although hunting and pollution have contributed to this decline, the main factor behind it is the loss of the birds' natural habitat. This draining of the marshes is sometimes linked to irrigation projects: the Hâmun-e Sâberi Lake in Sistân was practically dry during the winter of 1976 because of the construction of a dam on the Hirmand in Afghânistân.

Natural reserves have existed in Irân since 1927. In 1974, four categories of protected area were established (national parks, wildlife refuges, protected areas and national natural monuments). In addition to these, there are forest parks, protected rivers and coastal areas, as well as Râmsar sites (named after the town in which a convention was signed in 1975) for the protection of wetlands. Today, Irân has over 70 of these reserves of various types, scattered throughout the country and with a total surface area of just over 10 million hectares (25 million acres) in 1991. Among the most accessible and interesting parks and reserves are the Kavir National Park in the desert southeast of Tehrân (Dorcas gazelles, ibex, bustards, sandgrouse, desert larks), the Golestân National Park near Gorgân and the Caspian Sea (goitred gazelles, wild boar, Isabelline shrike, grey-necked buntings, wheatears), the Miân Kaleh wildlife refuge, also on the Caspian coast (a wetland park), and the Arjân protected area near Shirâz (waterbirds, sombre tit, masked shrike).

AGRICULTURE, ANIMAL HUSBANDRY AND FISHING

Irân remains today a mainly agricultural country although less than half the population still lives in the countryside and only a third of the arable land is systematically irrigated. Wheat accounts for just over 50 per cent of Irân's agricultural production, followed by barley (17 per cent) and fodder crops (6.5 per cent).

In mountainous areas, the valley floors offer relatively sheltered and easily irrigable land for growing wheat, barley and various fruits and nuts (grapes, apricots, peaches, pistachios). On the plateau, sugar beet and potatoes are also grown, while in more arid areas one can find plantations of dates, jujubes and tamarisks.

In the coastal provinces of Gilân and Mâzanderân which have high rainfall, rice can be cultivated (approximately four per cent of the country's agricultural production). Gilân used to be known for its silk, especially at the end of the 17th century, but the province's main crop is now tea, a relatively new plant in the area which was introduced at the beginning of the 20th century. Cotton, tobacco and citrus fruit are also grown along the coast.

Animal husbandry is mainly practised by the nomadic or semi-nomadic tribes over vast areas of now poor pasture. At present, there are some 35 million sheep, 19 million goats and five million cows in Irân. A few horses are raised in the north and in the Zagros. The herds winter in the valley bottoms and move slowly to higher pastures in spring. This seasonal migration was traditionally done on foot, although now it has become partly mechanized and many animals are transported by lorry.

Fish has traditionally been a major element of the diet of the people living along the Caspian Sea and Persian Gulf, and because of the demographic increase in the country as a whole, fish is gradually gaining in importance for the inland urban populations too. But the seas and lakes are still badly exploited and the catches are consequently relatively small. Because of irregular fishing, there is some concern over the long-term survival of shrimp beds in the Persian Gulf. There is heavy sea pollution in the Gulf as well as in the Caspian. Since the breakup of the Soviet Union, there has been an increase in industrial waste dumped in the Caspian, a situation which is seriously endangering the reproduction of the sturgeon and thus threatening one of the region's main luxury products, caviar.

Sturgeon are fished in the mouths of the rivers that flow into the sea. Caviar is one of Irân's best-known export products. From 1888 to 1927, the exploitation rights to caviar on the north coast of Irân were held by a Russian firm, Lianosov, and almost the entire production was exported to Russia. In 1928, the Irânian government granted the monopoly to a mixed Irânian and Soviet firm, and the fisheries were modernized. In 1953, the caviar industry in Irân was nationalized. Present production is about 50 tons a year. The sturgeon, which generally weigh between 40 and 300 kilos according to the species (but which can weigh up to 600 kilos [1,323 pounds]) are also an important source of meat (about 1,500 tons a year).

INDUSTRY

Irân's main industry is of course oil, followed by mining, textiles (wool and cotton) and food. Apart from oil, the Irânian soil contains large amounts of coal and many minerals (iron, copper, lead, zinc, manganese, chromium) which are mined mostly for domestic use.

Oil was first discovered in Irân in 1908 at Masjed-e Soleimân, near Dezful, in Khuzestân Province. The following year, the Anglo-Persian Oil Company bought the concession and in 1913 was granted the right to prospect for, exploit, refine and export all Irânian oil. This British control lead to a political crisis in 1951 when the

Irânian Prime Minister Mosaddeq decided to nationalize the oil industry. After 1954 and the signing of a series of agreements, the control of the industry passed into the hands of an international consortium which paid part of the proceeds over to the Irânian National Oil Society. Production, which was of 31 million barrels in 1950, quickly increased to 80 million barrels in 1964 and reached 300 million barrels at the end of the 1970s.

During the Pahlavi dynasty, Irân's industrial sector, financed mostly by revenues from the oil industry, developed very fast. Under Rezâ Shâh, emphasis was placed on light industry (sugar refineries, textile mills, canning factories) but in the 1960s this trend was reversed in favour of heavy industry, particularly petrochemicals, steelworks and coal mining. This industrial expansion increased after 1973 when petrodollars started pouring in, while other sectors of the economy, particularly agriculture and light industry, were neglected. The revolution and the war with Iraq interrupted most of the large-scale industrial projects that were underway. Oil refineries, especially those in the Persian Gulf, became prime targets for Iraqi attacks. The Abâdân refinery, the largest in the world at the time, and the refinery at Kermânshâh, were completely destroyed. Faced during the war with a critical economic situation, the government did everything it could to ensure a constant flow of petrol to foreign countries. Today, oil-based products are still Irân's main source of revenue and account for 80 per cent of export earnings.

The economy now has a chance to recover from the war years, largely due to the adoption of Five-Year Plans aimed at encouraging economic growth, but several sectors still need urgent development, especially the road and rail networks, as well as port facilities. The 4,500 kilometres (2,796 miles) of railway lines in Irân, for example, are completely inadequate for the country's needs and do not even extend as far as certain provincial capitals such as Shirâz or Hamadân. By 2004, Irân had embarked on an ambitious programme of rebuilding and extending the rail infra-structure, at a rate of 1000 miles of track built every year. A very large proportion of goods transported around the country is done so by lorry and as a result the roads are overused and overcrowded. The construction of sections of motorway between Tehrân and Qom, Tehrân and Qazvin, and by-passing Kâshân to Esfahân, as well as the widening of some of the other major roads has helped to ease the traffic somewhat, although a long-term solution to the problem has still to be found. The unlimited output of the car factories is leading to increased private car use thoughout the country, with consequent ecological devastation. This is compounded by the understandable but misguided policy of giving tax concessions for factories outside the main cities; while this may have had a very slight impact on the unwanted rural migration to the big cities, it has created immense pollution throughout rural areas as well as destroying the very limited available farmland. For example, the Marvdasht/Zarghân area now hosts over 100 small factories, which are responsible for covering Persepolis in a brown smog.

POPULATION

Since the beginning of this century, the population of Irân has increased at a very rapid rate. In 1875, it was estimated at six million people; in 1956, the first official census recorded over 18 million. At the time of the last census (1976) this figure had grown to 49.4 million people. The present population is estimated to be 70 million, and is expected to double within the next thirty years.

One of the main features of the population distribution in Irân during the second half of the 20th century has been the rural exodus towards the large urban centres, particularly Tehrân, Mashhad, Tabriz and Shirâz. This movement, at its strongest during the 1960s and '70s, has now slowed down somewhat although it is still noticeable. A few figures are revealing: at the end of the World War II, 75 per cent of the work force was engaged in agriculture, whereas in 1976 this had decreased to 34 per cent. In 1986, over 54 per cent of the total population lived in urban areas, and Tehrân on its own accounted for 16 per cent of it. Between 1986 to 1996, it is believed that at least 283,000 people left the rural districts annually, and the trend of urban growth in recent years has not at all been staunched; latest figures (2004) suggest that the population of Tehrân has increased to 7.5 million.

ETHNIC GROUPS IN IRÂN

The numerous migrations of peoples who have passed through Irân, sometimes settling there, have created an ethnically diverse population. The biggest influence has come from Central Asia, first the Indo-European tribes that arrived on the plateau in the second and first millennia BC. Small communities of Jews and Greeks settled in Irân as mercenaries, traders, doctors etc, which had little impact until the invasion of Alexander, whilst the Arab invasions on the mid 7th century massively restrcutured the whole region. Arab garrison towns were founded; Arab nomad pastoralists occupied large tracts of land; the Irânian nobility were dispossessed and only found a toe-hold in the new dispensation as clients of Arab patrons; and descendants of the Arab Prophet (Seyyed descendants of the Emâms) became the new hereditary elite of the Islamic cities of Irân. Intermarriage and the cultural prestige of the defeated Sasanian empire led to the adoption of the Persian language by most of these settlers. The same held true for the Turkish and Mongol tribes, who migrated to Irân between the 10th and 14th centuries AD, though the considerably greater numbers involved led to the turkicisation of considerable areas of Azerbaijân and Khorâsân, and a genreralised bi-lingualism.

Traditionally, there has always existed a close link in Irân between the ruling dynasty and the domination of one particular tribe or ethnic group (Saljuq, Zand, Qâjâr). In the 20th century, some governments have attempted to carry out national integration of this heterogenous population, in the hope that tribal and cultural distinctions would disappear with the economic and political development of the country. Under Rezâ Shâh in particular, the Persianisation of the population was carried out by vigorous methods, including a policy of enforced settlement of the nomadic tribes. Today, cultural pluralism is officially admitted but the changes that have occurred since the beginning of the century are in most cases irreversible. The traditional way of life of the nomad groups has been drastically altered by their settlement in villages and by the agricultural reforms of 1962, which were accompanied by land redistribution. Traditional pastures are shrinking under pressure from agriculturalists and large-scale nomadism was reduced by the sealing of the political frontiers with the former USSR in the north-east.

The main ethnic minorities live in the mountain regions along the edge of the central plateau; several provinces, such as Baluchestân and Kordestân (Kurdistan), take their names from the dominant group living in them). There are no precise or recent official figures concerning ethnic minorities; however, Irânian minorities (groups speaking Irânian languages other than Fârsi, i.e. Kurds, Baluch, and speakers of Caspian dialects such as Gilaki) are estimated at about 30 per cent of the total population of the country and Turkish-speaking groups at 25 per cent. About 1.5 million Arabic-speakers live in Khuzestân on the borders of Iraq.

The main Irânian minorities are the Kurds, the Lurs, the Bakhtiâri, the Baluch and a few groups along the Caspian Sea such as the Gilâni, Mâzanderâni and Tâleshi. The **Kurds** are descendants of the Indo-European tribes that arrived in Irân in the first millennium BC, and they regard themselves as the descendants of the Medes. Today, the Kurds are to be found mainly in Iraq, Irân, Turkey and Syria. Almost nine per cent of the population of Irân is Kurdish, about 5.5 million, living mostly in Azerbaijân, Kermânshâh, Ilâm and Kordestân provinces. The Kurds speak Kurdish, a west Irânian language, and are for the most part Sunni Muslims.

The **Lurs** live mainly in Kermânshâh and Lurestân, south of Kordestân. They speak Luri, a language related to Pahlavi (Middle Persian) and are currently estimated to number 2.5 million. Like the Kurds, the Lurs were once a sedentary nation that made only short pastoral migrations. Their way of life was radically changed with the arrival of the Turks and Mongols whose armies devastated the countryside, forcing many of the sedentary villagers to take up a nomadic lifestyle.

The **Bakhtiâri** live in the Zagros Mountains to the west of Esfahân, around Shahr-e Kord, moving in winter to the warmer plains around Dezful, Susa and Râmhormoz. They are divided into two main groups, the Haft-Lang and the Chahâr-Lang, sub-divided in turn into several tribes and sub-tribes, or *taifeh*. Most Bakhtiâri speak Fârsi or a Luri dialect, although part of the population, concentrated in the towns and villages in the south, speaks Arabic. The total number of Bakhtiâri is currently estimated today at about 900,000.

The **Baluch** live in the far southeast of Irân, in the Makrân costal area of Baluchestân, but they originated much further north, in Khorâsân, which they were compelled to leave in the 12th and 13th centuries by the invading Turkish armies. In Baluchestân they mingled with the local population, which included several very ancient tribes. Among these are a very few **Brahui**, who speak a Dravidian language. In this extremely arid and inhospitable area, the Baluch adopted a nomadic way of life, spending summer in the inland mountains and descending to the coast in winter. Agricultural reforms and forced settlement have driven them to find work in urban centres such as Zâhedân. The Baluch population is estimated at 1.2 million.

The origins of the Turkish-speaking minorities in Irân date back to the invasions and migrations that occurred between the tenth and fourteenth centuries AD, in the area contained within Irân's current political boundaries. However, the area of earlier Irânian empires, especially Transoxiana, witnessed Turkish penetration already in the late Sasanian period. The Afghân frontiers of India were penetrated by Turkish Khalaj already before the Ghazanvids and mutated into the Pushtun tribes of the Ghilzai. The **Azeris** are by far the most important ethno-linguistic minority in Irân, with a population of over six million living in the two provinces of Azerbaijân and Zanjân. The settlement of this part of Irân by Turkish tribes in the Saljuq and Mongol period led to an ethnic fusion with the original Persian-speaking Azeri population, which to this day speaks an Irânised Turkish dialect. The Azeris' conversion to Shi'ism during the 14th and 15th centuries under the charismatic Sufi Shaykhs of Ardabil assured their integral role in the Irânian polity established in the 16th century by the Safavid ruler Shah Ismâ'il .

The **Turkoman** who live in Khorâsân in northeast Irân also arrived very early on, in the 11th century. Traditionally they are nomads and extremely proud of their warrior past: until recently, they were greatly feared around Gorgân and Dâmghân

CONGRATULATIONS FOR A GIRL?

I was born on New Year's Day in Iran, Norooz, the twenty-first of March, the first day of spring. In Iran Norooz is a major celebration. People prepare months in advance. They spring-clean, buy new clothes, decorate and prepare delicacies. Having survived the harsh winter they celebrate, everything is cleaned and freshened, people wear their new clothes. If adults can't afford them somehow they manage for the children. They have to. Everyone tries to wear something new. People start visiting to wish each other Happy New Year, the senior members of the family first, grandparents, great uncles and aunts, senior members, who give presents to the young ones. Children receive coins from aunts and uncles, and coloured eggs and sweets from friends. Young married women receive a trayful of goodies from their parents and brothers-sweets, cakes, coloured eggs, a scarf, bits of jewellery maybe, and a piece of material for a dress, usually, or a châdor, and this is called pi, a share, signifying that the women still play parts in their lives, that they have not been forgotten. Women who live far away receive their presents a few days before.

I was born early in the morning at about five o'clock. The news of my birth was taken to my father who stayed in a nearby house as was the custom in the village. 'Congratulations, it's a girl,' the messenger shouted.

'Congratulations for a girl?' my father asked. The woman expected this response. She wasn't dismayed. The news had to be taken. She'd done her duty. 'It would have been better if a child had brought the news,' she thought, but it was too late. Had it been a boy it would have been totally different. The women would have arrived breathless with running. 'You have a boy.' 'Wonderful,' he would laugh. 'Here.' And he would place a coin in her hand. He would go out and treat everyone in the neighborhood to fruit and sweets. Everyone in the village would know that he had a boy. He would hold his head high, proud. In some cases, fathers of daughters would not return home

for a while, or not speak to their wives for a time. What does a wife expect, giving birth to a girl? It wasn't too bad in my case, since luckily my father already had a son ... Ali, the eldest, the first male, was always given special treatment. He was given the best of the soup, the best of everything. He was the family's hope, because he was male, the first son, the eldest. The first son was always regarded as the family's future security. He would carry the family burden, look after his parents in their old age. He was the life line of the generations. Daughters left home when married but sons stayed, even after they had married. The eldest son always stayed with the parents, and eventually took over the running of the household. There was great prestige in giving birth to a male child first. It was even more wonderful if the second and third were also male, just in case something happened to the first son. The parents would register the birth of a son late, thus their age was given as a few years younger on the birth certificate and the parents could benefit from having their son stay with them longer before he had to leave to do national service. On the other hand daughters were registered as a few years older than they actually were so they could be married off early. The legal age for marriage was fifteen so, a girl would often, in fact, be married at twelve. National service for boys was at eighteen but they often went at twenty-one or twenty-two.

Gohar Kordi, An Iranian Odyssey, *1991*

Gohar Kordi was born in a small Kurdish village in Irân. At the age of four, she became blind. She writes of her growing up in a working-class family in the country, the family's move to Tehrân and her personal struggle to obtain an education and become the first blind woman student at the university.

for the ferocity with which they swept down to pillage caravans and villages. The Turkoman were traditionally divided into two groups whose lifestyle was governed by their geographic environment. The Sarwa, nomad herders, lived in the steppes of Khorāsān and the present Republic of Turkmenistan, moving each year with their herds across vast distances in regions unsuitable for agriculture. The Somir, on the other hand, were semi-nomadic agriculturalists who lived between Gorgān and the forests of the Alborz, in Māzanderān Province, where they grew mainly wheat. While the Somir would strive to better their social status and become nomadic herders, it was not uncommon for financially ruined Sarwa families to settle down and become farmers, or even to make for the Caspian coast and work as fishermen. The closure of the frontier with Soviet Russia in 1928 suddenly cut off the traditional migration routes and profoundly modified the way of life of the Sarwa. Today, the Turkoman are mostly sedentary and have become agriculturalists and fishermen. Unlike the other Turkic groups, they are Sunni.

The **Shāhsevan**, who live in the northeast of Irān, in the province of East Azerbaijān, differ from most other groups in that their formation was the result of a political decision and not a spontaneous movement on the part of the nomads themselves. In the 17th century, Shāh Abbās I created a militia from tribes of diverse origins, most of them Turkish-speaking, that would serve to put down the rebellions of other nomadic groups. The Shāhsevan tribal confederation survived the fall of the Safavid dynasty. Like the Turkoman, their traditional territory has been divided in half by the closure of the frontier with the former USSR.

A major ethno-linguistic group in Fārs Province are the **Qashqāi**, Shi'a Turkish-speakers organized into a confederation composed of five main tribes and a few smaller ones. Traditionally, the Qashqāi wintered on pastures in the foothills of the Zagros to the south and west of Shirāz, near the Persian Gulf, and moved north to the mountains in the spring. The Qashqāi confederation was sufficiently powerful in the 19th and early 20th centuries to play an important role regionally, and at times even nationally, as the provincial authorities frequently relied on the tribal leaders to maintain law and order in rural areas. In the 1960s, Mohammed Rezā Shāh attempted to reduce their power by disarming them and nationalizing their pastures. Since then, many Qashqāi have been forced to settle or to become semi-nomads. In the 1950s they were estimated at about 400,000 but there are considerably fewer now who follow a traditional lifestyle; de-tribalisation by migration to the cities accounts for this demographic oddity.

Fārs Province also includes a rival confederation, the **Khamseh**, formed in the middle of the 19th century by a rich merchant family from Shirāz who wanted to protect their caravans on the way to the Persian Gulf. The **Khamseh** are a confederation of five tribes (*khamseh* means five in Arabic), of Persian, Arabic and Turkish origin.

The **Afshâr** arrived on the Irânian Plateau in two waves, first of all in the 11th century under the Saljuqs, and then in the 13th century with the Mongols. They served the Safavid rulers and were given posts all over the empire. As a result, the Afshâr were split into several groups. Today, the main groups are to be found in Azerbaijân, between Lake Orumieh and Qazvin and Hamadân, and in an area between Kermân and Bandar Abbâs, in the south of Irân. Traditionally, the Afshâr are pastoral nomads but many have now settled down and become farmers.

In addition to these various ethnic groups, there are also a number of religious minorities living in Irân. Zoroastrians, Jews and Christians are recognized as minorities by Article 13 of the constitution, which guarantees them freedom of religion. The Baha'i are not recognized as a valid religious minority, and have suffered not inconsiderable persecution. The **Zoroastrians** still practice the ancient pre-Islamic religion, whose origins go back to the beliefs of the Indo-European immigrants of the first millennium BC and which was confirmed as the state religion under the Sasanians. After the Arab conquest and the arrival of Islam, the Zoroastrians were tolerated as a disarmed and defeated poulus paying heavy taxes. Christians and Jews, as People of the Book, or *ahl al-kitab*, were also made to pay the poll tax as a protected minority, *ahl al-dhimma*. The Arab policy of religious tolerance towards non-Muslims living in the conquered territories provides them with a legal status within the Muslim community. This status was determined by a pact, or *dhimma*, said to exist between the two communities. According to this pact, non-Muslims accepted a subordinate position with certain social restrictions and the payment of tribute, in return for which they were guaranteed physical protection against their enemies, freedom of worship and a limited autonomy in the running of their community. Despite conversions and emigration, there are currently about 30,000 Zoroastrians still living in Irân, mainly around Esfahân, Yazd and Kermân.

The history of **Christianity** in Irân is closely linked to that of the Syriac and Armenian communities there. From the second century AD onwards, Christianity spread from Antioch to Armenia, Upper Mesopotamia and the Adiabene in the north of present Iraq, where several communities established themselves. Out of these Syriac Christian communities the Church of the East (the so-called Nestorians) and the miaphysite Syriac-Orthododox Church (also called Jacobites) emerged by the 5th century. The mass deportation of Christian prisoners of war by Shâpur I (241–272) and by Shâpur II (309–379) brought from the Eastern Roman

Empire tens of thousands Christians into Irân, who eventually were integrated into the Church of the East; Baptists also spread to the Sasanian realm. Armenia converted to Christianity during the reign of its king Tiridates III (AD 294–324). After the Arab conquest, Christians were recognized as *ahl al-dhimma*, and the Church of the East even went through a period of great expansion in Central Asia and Mongolia where it remained active until the fall of the Mongol Yuan dynasty in China in AD 1368. An important Armenian Christian community settled in Esfahân in 1603 when Shâh Abbâs forcibly moved families of Armenian merchants there from Jolfâ in Azerbaijân. Today, Christians form the largest religious minority in Irân with a population estimated at around 200,000, most of whom are Armenian and live in Tehrân.

The presence of a **Jewish** community in Irân dates back to the period of the first Achaemenian conquests and the capture of Babylon by Cyrus the Great in 539 BC. Cyrus freed the Jews who had been deported to Babylon by Nebuchadnezzar and gave them permission to return to Jerusalem and rebuild their temple. At that time, Jerusalem was placed under Persian administration. During the Islamic period, the Jews were also considered as *ahl al-dhimma* and were thus able to continue living and working on Persian soil. While about 75,000 Jews lived in Irân under the Pahlavi dynasty, more than half of them left the country after 1979. The exact number of Jews now living in Irân is unclear but is thought to be very slight.

Turkoman farmer with scythe, Qal'eh Tapeh Sheikh, Mâzanderân Province

ISLAMIC ART AND ARCHITECTURE

In any discussion of Islamic art it must always be remembered that the artistic tradition of the Muslim faith developed not only over a long period of time beginning with the Hegira in AD 622, but also over a very wide geographical area extending from Spain and Morocco to Central Asia, India and Indonesia. Given these conditions, it would have been surprising for a single, homogenous artistic tradition to emerge. Indeed, the very richness and variety of Islamic art is due in part to the appearance of regional trends within the Islamic world, particularly once the Abbâsid Caliphate began to weaken in the tenth and 11th centuries, thus allowing the formation of local political powers. The ethnic diversity of the Muslim world—which includes Arabs, Irânians, Turks, Indians, Berbers and more—the variety of pre-Islamic traditions that existed in the newly-conquered territories, and the continued presence of non-Muslim communities in those areas, all contributed to the creation of an art with strongly marked regional characteristics.

And yet, despite this tendency towards specific regional characteristics, other forces were at work which tended towards the development of a universal and unified art. The main force was of course Islam itself, the basis of the whole civilization. Along with faith came an entire way of life, as well as certain attitudes and a vision of the world which were common to all regions concerned. The proper functioning of the mosque required only a few elements (*mehrâb,* or niche in the wall facing Mecca; *membar,* or pulpit; prayer carpet) and none of the ritual or liturgical paraphernalia present in temples of other faiths. The decorative motifs used in the mosques were by no means limited to a strictly religious context but could equally well serve as secular ornament, on a wide range of media. The major public art, calligraphy, was the natural vehicle for the divine message transmitted by the Prophet, plays an important role in mosques but also is largely used on ceramics, textiles and in handicrafts in general. The almost complete absence of sculpture, with a few rare exceptions, is another universal characteristic of Islamic art, influenced partly by the rejection in the *Hadith* (Traditions) of human representation. It should be noted, however, that despite this disapproval, humans and animals have frequently been depicted on ceramics and are in miniature painting. Book illustration, a private art, had been one of the most creative art forms in Persia, Turkey and Moghul India.

A second unifying factor in Islamic art has been the great mobility of people within the Muslim world, either as individuals or in groups. There have been numerous cases, particularly in Irân, of rulers who were foreign to the region or the

country they governed. It is no coincidence that these mixed courts were often the ones in which the arts flourished the most, a direct result of the interaction between the local, traditional styles and those brought by the newcomer. Artists, architects and poets travelled over great distances in their search for generous patrons. Other migrations were not undertaken voluntarily: large numbers of refugees and conscripts have, at various times, been compelled to start a new life in new lands. But it was particularly trade along the maritime and overland caravan routes that was behind the widest artistic exchanges. As a result, artists came into contact with new decorative motifs and new techniques which were quickly absorbed into the local artistic repertoire.

ISLAMIC ARCHITECTURE IN IRÂN

MOSQUES

The centre of Islamic religious life is the mosque, or *masjed* in Arabic, literally the 'place of prostration'. The first mosque, which served as a prototype, was the house of the Prophet himself in Medina. It was composed of a central courtyard with a portico of palm trunks along one wall supporting a roof of palm fronds. This wall, or *qebleh* wall, indicated the direction of Mecca and of the Ka'beh. According to some sources, the Prophet delivered his addresses from a pulpit, known as *membar*, resembling a tall chair with three steps. These basic elements, the assembly area, the portico, the *qebleh* wall and the *membar*, were all to be adopted in later mosques, along with the *mehrâb*, a niche set in the centre of the *qebleh* wall.

The Umayyad caliphs of Damascus (661–750) decided at an early stage to build monuments to the Islamic faith capable of rivalling the imposing Christian basilicas which existed in their newly conquered lands. In some towns, churches were converted into mosques, and the original orientation to the east was replaced by an orientation towards Mecca, to the south. In other places, however, entirely new monuments were built. These first mosques, including those of Basra and Kufa in Iraq, have almost completely disappeared, having been incorporated into later buildings or entirely rebuilt, but they appear to have been simple in shape, with a square, central area and a deep portico along the *qebleh* wall. The oldest Muslim building still standing today is the Dome of the Rock in Jerusalem (built between 687 and 692), a holy place of Islam associated with the Prophet's miraculous night-time journey to Heaven.

The development of Umayyad mosques lead to the recreation of the hypostyle mosque (a building with a roof held up by columns) by extending the use of the

Royal Mosque, Esfahân

portico to the other three sides of the central courtyard. Two new elements also appeared at this period: the maqsureh, an enclosure reserved for the prince in the *qebleh* wall of the larger mosques, and the minaret.

The development of the mosque under the Abbâsid caliphs (750–950) is still unclear. In Irân, there was a period of adaptation and experimentation of Islamic forms which lasted until the beginning of the 11th century, and which was influenced to some extent by the older native architectural forms. Square domed buildings with plans reminiscent of the Sasanian fire temples (*chahâr tâq*) seem to have been added to certain mosques, probably to serve as maqsureh. When found on their own, usually in villages, these buildings are termed kiosk mosques. Lacking a courtyard, they were inadequate for large congregations. Among the oldest mosques in Irân are those of Susa and Dâmghân (eighth century), Fahraj (ninth century) and Nâ'in (tenth century), all of them hypostyle, and occasionally domed, mosques.

From around 1086 on, during the Saljuq dynasty (1038–1157), a remarkable series of mosques were built along the edge of the central desert, particularly in Esfahân, Ardestân, Zavâreh and Qazvin. The main novelty was the integration of a domed pavilion with the central courtyard (*sahn*) surrounded by arcades. In the centre of each side of the court was an *eivân* (or iwan, a barrel-vaulted room open on one side); the *eivân* in the *qebleh* wall gave directly onto the *mehrâb*, itself set at the back of a domed room. This combination of domed chamber and *eivân* had already appeared in Irân in the earlier Sasanian palaces. The oldest Islamic example of this is in Zavâreh (1136), although the most remarkable example is undoubtedly the Friday Mosque in Esfahân, which was built in several phases.

Once the plan of a courtyard with four *eivân* had been established, it changed very little through the centuries, and most later developments concern decoration, and the relative proportions of decorated and plain surfaces. The culmination of nearly six hundred years' development of the four-*eivân* mosque is, as Arthur Upham Pope observed, the superb Royal Mosque in Esfahân, built in the reign of Shâh Abbâs (built 1611–1638).

MAUSOLEUMS

The mausoleum is another major type of Islamic construction in Irân. A number of commemorative monuments were built over important burial places, particularly those of Shi'a saints, around the ninth and tenth centuries. In Irân and Central Asia, further constructions commemorated local rulers, Biblical figures, Companions of the Prophet, scholars and popular heroes.

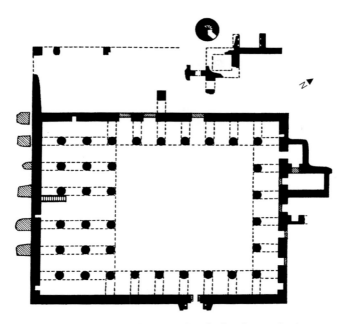

Plan of a hypostyle mosque (Târik Khâneh, Dâmghân)

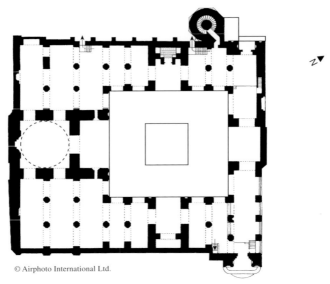

© Airphoto International Ltd.

Plan of a four-eivân mosque (Zavâreh)

The first extant Irânian mausoleums, which date back to the tenth century, are represented today by two types, the canopy tomb and the tower tomb. Canopy tombs are square buildings with openings on all four sides. The best examples can be seen in outer Irân, in particular the tombs of Ismâ'il the Samanid at Bukhara (914–943) and of Arab-Ata at Tim, near Samarqand (977). Of the tower mausoleums, the most spectacular is without doubt the Gonbad-e Qâbus built in 1006 near Gorgân, in northeast Irân. This conical tower, star-shaped on the outside but circular inside, is 51 metres tall and shows great purity of line and a masterly use of brick.

These two forms of mausoleum were to undergo great diversification from the 11th century onward. The tower-shaped tomb adopted a circular plan, seen in Dâmghân (1027 and 1056), and at the Gonbad-e Ali at Abarkuh (1056), all of which are much shorter than the Gonbad-e Qâbus. The canopy tomb can be square, hexagonal, or octagonal, such as those at Damâvand and Kharaqân. Unlike the tower tombs, of which only the upper sections are decorated, the entire surface of the canopy tombs' outer wall is decorated with geometric brick motifs.

A third very important style at this period, which appears mostly in the northwest, in Azerbaijân, seems to incorporate elements from both the above styles. A good example is the Gonbad-e Kabud at Marâgheh, a domed tower with corner columns, entirely decorated outside. This type of mausoleum, which appears in a variety of shapes (square, circular or polygonal) continued to be built for several centuries.

The tomb of Sultan Oljaitu Khodâbandeh at Soltânieh, near Zanjân, built in 1306, is another form of mausoleum reminiscent of the earlier monuments in eastern Persia such as the tomb of Sultan Sanjar at Merv (c. 1152) or the Gonbad-e Hâruniyeh at Tus, in Khorâsân (early 14th century). These mosque-mausoleums are characterized by their great height, the elevation of the dome itself and the presence of a gallery around the base of the dome.

In addition to these isolated tombs, which are generally built for sultans or local rulers, there are other infinitely larger and more complex mausoleums in Irân which commemorate the Shi'a Emâms or their descendants and which have become important pilgrimage destinations. Two of the main mausoleums of the Shi'a faith, those of Ali and Hosein, are actually located outside the borders of modern Irân, at Kerbalâ and Najaf, in Iraq. Among the most popular in Irân itself are the tombs of Fatima, at Qom, of her brother the Emâm Rezâ, at Mashhad. In these holy cities, the tombs are part of vast complexes which include a large four-*eivân* mosque and

Classes in the madraseh *are often held in the open air* (Madraseh *of the Shah's Mother, Esfahân*)

sometimes one or more *madraseh*. While the sites of these tombs are generally quite old, the buildings themselves are often more recent. At Qom, for instance, the sanctuary of Shâh Ismâ'il (1503–1524) is located among Qâjâr and Pahlavi buildings, while at Mashhad the main mosque was built onto a tenth-century sanctuary between 1405 and 1417. A more recent example is that of the tomb complex of the Âyatollâh Khomeini near Behesht-e Zahrâ, Tehrân.

THE MADRASEH

The *madraseh* is a place of higher religious education. At first privately run and of modest size, the first real *madraseh* were founded in the 11th century, when they became political institutions under state control and served to fix the Sunni orthodoxy—the first Shi'a *madraseh* was founded around 1050 at Najaf, in Iraq, by the Shi'a scholar Tusi. Among the most famous *madraseh* of the period were those founded by the great Saljuq vizir Nezâm ol-Molk (and therefore called *nezâmiyeh*), most notably those in Baghdad, Neishâpur and Esfahân. Almost nothing remains today of the early Irânian *madraseh*, probably built during the Ghaznavid dynasty (962–1186), and very little of the Saljuq buildings. According to some scholars, these *madraseh* probably consisted of four-*eivân* courtyards similar to those of mosques, a plan which was adopted again later for *madraseh*, particularly under the Safavids. The *eivân* of the *madraseh* served as classrooms; the students lived in the small rooms behind the double arcades surrounding the courtyard.

THE DOME

With the importance that the dome and the vault rapidly gained in Islamic architecture, it soon became necessary to devise a solution to the problem of the transition zone between the square chamber and the dome above it, namely from a square plan to a circular one. The basic solution depended on the squinch, an arch set at an angle across each corner of the building. In the 11th and 12th centuries, the corner squinches were generally variants on the following scheme: centred; set over the corner; a small barrel-vaulted squinch flanked on either side by a quarter dome with the whole composition enclosed within a larger broken arch. Between each of these corner squinches, centred above each side of the square chamber, is a similar lobed arch. In this way, an octagon is created over the base of the chamber. Above these squinches a row of smaller arches, set over the angles of the octagon, thus form a sixteen-sided polygon. This so-called *muqarnas* system appeared in a simple form at the end of the tenth century at Tim, in Central Asia, and then at Yazd, in the Davâzdah Emâm Mosque, built in 1037. It reappears frequently afterwards, particularly at Ardestân and at Esfahân in the Friday Mosque.

The small triangular squinch was to have multiple applications, even covering, in superimposed rows, the entire interior surface of *eivân* domes. Each row is shifted sideways in relation to the ones below, and each squinch becomes gradually narrower towards the apex of the arch. Under the Safavids, each row was shifted slightly forwards so that it jutted out over the one below it, forming a network of cells, or hanging stalactites.

Another important building technique was the use of a double-shelled dome to lighten and strengthen the structure. In Irân, the oldest examples of this technique appear in the Kharaqân tombs, in Zanjân Province, built at the beginning of the 11th century. This technique enabled the inside and outside of the dome to be designed in different shapes. Good examples are the spectacular Timurid and Safavid domes, such as those of the Gur Emir Mosque at Samarqand (1434) and of the Shaykh Lotfollah and Royal mosques in Esfahân (1598 and 1611).

DECORATION

BRICK AND STUCCO

Colour did not play a major decorative role in the earliest mosques. Instead, much emphasis was placed on using the building materials themselves, most commonly brick, to create a decorative effect. In its simplest form, this technique consisted of placing the bricks alternately on their short or long sides to create zigzag motifs. At Marâgheh and Kharaqân, a more sophisticated use of bricks of different sizes, some of with a solely decorative function, gives extremely successful and more complex results.

A second very widespread, decorative method was carved stucco, or gach. This was either applied to entire walls, or restricted to a particular architectural feature, such as the mehrâb, a gate, or niches (Nâ'in, Ardestân, Dâmghân). Stucco had the advantage of being a relatively cheap and abundant material, easy to work and long-lasting. Examples of decorative stucco have been found that date back to the Parthian and Sasanian dynasties, but the most complex and the most beautiful stucco work was executed in the Islamic period, between the 11th and the 14th centuries. The mehrâb of Sultan Oljaitu in the Friday Mosque in Esfahân (see picture, p. 307) is one of the best preserved pieces; its decoration is of extraordinary intricacy, resembling in places the finest of lacework.

TILEWORK

During the Saljuq period (1038–1157), the use of coloured tiles on buildings gradually became more common, although at the outset they served mainly to accentuate certain elements of the interlaced geometric designs created in brick. It has been suggested that the early development of colour was an attempt to make the Koranic inscriptions on the exterior of mosques more legible. The usually turquoise tiles appeared sparingly in the 11th century on funerary towers at Dâmghân and Kharaqân. Within a century, this use had increased dramatically: on the Gonbad-e Kabud in Marâgheh (Azerbaijân, 1196) the entire upper section of the tower, that is to say the niches, the band of interlaced inscription, the stalactite cornice and the pyramidal roof, is decorated with glazed tiles.

The mausoleum of Sultan Oljaitu Khodâbandeh at Soltânieh, near Zanjân, built in the first decade of the 14th century, marks a turning point in architectural tile-work: the exterior of the dome, as well as the stalactite cornice, was entirely covered in turquoise tiles, while the entire interior surface of the walls of the great hall and of the dome were originally decorated with tiles and stucco. Up to the Safavid period, this type of ornamentation increased until it covered the entire

visible surface area, inside as well as out. The range of colours also increased, first by the addition of white and two different blues, a turquoise and an ultramarine, followed by ochre, olive green and brown (these colours were used in the Blue Mosque at Tabriz, built in 1465, which is often considered the greatest example of glazed tilework decoration in Irân).

During the reign of the Safavid ruler Shâh Abbâs I (1587–1629), decorative tile-work underwent a major technical change. In the midst of an ambitious building programme, and finding the traditional methods too time-consuming and laborious, Shâh Abbâs approved the adoption of a previously elaborated technique, that of polychrome tile painting, or *haft rangi*, or 'seven colours'.

The earlier method involved the creation of a cut faïence mosaic, requiring great patience, skill and precision to carry out. First a full-scale drawing of the final design was made on paper, which was placed over a layer of plaster. The lines of the design were pricked out with a needle and covered with a coloured powder to transfer it to the plaster beneath. The different elements of the mosaic were then carved and fitted to the plaster mould. The pieces of paper from the original stencil were stuck onto a glazed sheet of the desired colour. Once these tile sections were cut out and filed down, they were placed, glazed side down, into the corresponding holes in the plaster mould. When all the pieces were in place, a layer of mortar was poured over the whole as a fixative. The panel was then set against the wall in its final position, leaving a small gap between it and the wall into which more mortar was poured to hold it firmly in place.

(Above) *Glazed tile mosaic design: the edges of each piece of the mosaic are clearly visible, modern period, tomb of Kemâl ol-Molk, Neishâpur*

With the new *haft rangi* technique, the motif was no longer created by mosaic but painted directly onto the tile. There was therefore no longer any need to cut out the elements of the design and assemble them, but just to place the tiles side by side on the wall (dome exteriors were covered with glazed bricks, never with these painted tiles, which were too fragile). Unfortunately, this method is shorter-lived than the older one and the tiles, fixed to the wall with plaster, easily become detached.

After Shâh Abbâs' reign, the palette of colours changed once again and reds, yellows and even oranges were added to the earlier blue harmony. At the beginning of the 18th century, the reds disappeared and a golden yellow appeared which was often used together with blues. A very fine example of this is the west *eivân* of the Friday Mosque in Esfahân, redecorated during the reign of Shâh Soltân Hosein (1694–1722). But glazed ceramics gradually declined in quality, continuing a process which had already begun after the reign of Shâh Abbâs.

Zand and Qâjâr tilework shows a completely new departure from that of the Safavid period. For the first time, representations of people and animals form the main subject matter: there are hunting scenes, illustrations of the battles of Rostam,

the hero of the national epic, the *Shâhnâmeh*, soldiers, officials, scenes of contemporary life and even copies of European illustrations and photographs. The figures are usually shown against a white background, sometimes set within a floral medallion. Large panels of still life fruit and flowers, with rather dominant yellows and pinks, were another favorite motif. Shirâz, followed by Qazvin and Tehrân, became the centres of this new style which was used in the decoration not only of mosques and *madraseh* but also of administrative buildings and royal palaces.

Haft rangi tilework, Royal Mosque, Esfahân

HANDICRAFTS

PERSIAN CARPETS

Carpet weaving is by far the most widespread handicraft in Irân; it is also the best-known abroad. The origins of the carpet date back to antiquity: texts and carvings tell us that the ancient Sumerians and Egyptians owned carpets, as did the Achaemenians in Persia. The oldest known knotted carpet was found at Pazyryk in the Altai (Siberia) and is thought to have been made by Irânian nomads around the fifth century BC. Despite the existence of this ancient example, little is known about the subsequent history of carpet-making in Irân until the 16th century. The nomadic tribes' herds of sheep and goats provided them with high-quality, durable wool. The sale of this wool, either untreated or in the form of textiles and carpets, was for a long time one of the major sources of income for the nomad communities.

The manufacture of rural and nomad carpets was carried out on a relatively small scale by geographically dispersed groups, but as royal manufacturers and independent workshops opened up in the large urban centres from at least the Timurid period in the 15th century, carpet-making grew into a national industry. Carpets began to figure among Persian export products to Europe, India and even the Ottoman Empire. Under the influence of contemporary miniature painting and Chinese designs, new motifs were created. Gradually, hunting scenes, animals, flowers and figures were added to the older, purely abstract or stylized designs.

In addition to the carpets produced in the urban workshops, there existed an important production of tribal carpets, often less well known abroad. Qashqâi, Turkomans—in particular the Yomut and Tekke tribes—Afshâr, Shâhsevan and Bakhtiâr each had their own motifs and styles. Certain designs, transmitted from generation to generation, are very old; they are reproduced from memory without the use of a model or a design cartoon. Carpet weaving was one of the most important tasks for nomadic women and was taught to girls at a very young age. The carpet held such economic importance for the group that a woman's ability to weave was a major criterion in the choice of a wife.

Tribal carpets are frequently made on small, horizontal looms which are easy to dismantle and to transport. The size of the loom determines that of the finished product, and many tribal carpets are therefore traditionally narrower than those made in urban workshops where there is room for the larger vertical looms.

Persian carpet makers use two types of knot, the Turkish knot and the Persian knot (both these knots are used over a wide geographical area and these terms do not necessarily imply a connection with linguistic or ethnic boundaries). The

Turkish knot, also called the symmetrical knot, is tied with a hook and produces a rigid carpet; the back, however, appears less uniform and coarser than a carpet made with the Persian knot. The latter, also known as the asymmetrical knot, is hand-tied and produces more flexible, softer carpets with a flat and uniform back. The tighter and closer together the knots, the clearer and more focused the designs; most Persian carpets have between 120 and 180 knots per square inch, but the finer ones may have between 600 and 800.

TEXTILE PRINTING

The technique of cloth printing using carved blocks (*qalam kâr*), also known in India, was already well established in Persia in the Sasanian period when it was used for the decoration of woollen, silk and linen cloth. Later it was used for cotton, and today Esfahân is still famous for its printed textiles. The cloth used for this technique is usually a light beige calico decorated with four colours, black, red, blue, and yellow, applied in that order. A wooden block, carved with the motif in reverse, corresponds to each colour. The black colour serves to fix the outline of the design. A fifth colour, green, is sometimes added as well.

WOODWORKING AND INLAY

There is a very long-standing tradition of woodworking in Irân. The forests of Mâzanderân, once provided an abundant supply of a great variety of different trees. Although few examples of antique woodwork exist in the market today, many of the handicrafts still produced attest to their long heritage, particularly carved beggars' bowls (*kashkul*), latticework panels used as doors and windows, and textile printing blocks.

One of the traditional handicrafts that the visitor to Irân cannot fail to come across is marquetry (*khâtam*), a delicate decorative technique that requires great precision and a steady hand. The oldest known examples of wood inlay date back to the Timurid period (15th century); later, *khâtam* was so highly esteemed at the Safavid court that certain royal princes were taught it in the same way that they were taught music or painting. In the 18th and 19th centuries, marquetry went through a period of decline but was revived by Rezâ Shâh (1925–1941) who founded several specialized schools for handicrafts in Tehrân, Esfahân and Shirâz.

As harmonious colour combination is vital to the overall effect of *khâtam*, the craftsman selects a variety of different types of wood (jujube, orange, ebony, teak, rosewood), metals (brass or even gold and silver) and bone or ivory. Very fine strips of wood or bone are filed into triangular lengths two to six millimetres wide. These pieces are assembled and glued together in strict sequence to form a cylinder, which provides the basic decorative unit; a six-pointed star set within a hexagon. The cylinder is cut into sections, which are then stuck close together between two fine strips of wood. Once this has dried, it is cut in half lengthways revealing a design formed by a repeat of the basic unit. These are applied to the surface of the object to be decorated. Rezâ Shâh had entire pieces of furniture from the Marble Palace in Tehrân covered in this way (now on show in the Museum of Decorative Arts), although *khâtam* is more commonly used in the decoration of picture and mirror frames, boxes, musical instruments and lecterns.

METALWORK

The use of metal in Irânian decorative art dates back to well before the Islamic period; some of the most beautiful examples of metalware are gilded silver cups and dishes, decorated with royal hunting scenes, of the Sasanian dynasty. From the seventh century, many everyday objects were made of metal, such as serving dishes and trays, candlesticks and incense burners. Over the centuries, the shapes and decorative motifs of these objects have been copied by craftsmen in the bazaars for a much wider clientele, and today every bazaar still has an alley for coppersmiths, tinsmiths and engravers. The techniques used vary from simple hammering of copper or tin sheets to nielloed, embossed or engraved designs.

The manufacture of jewellery was traditionally an important occupation of the silver or goldsmith. Although the heavy pieces of jewellery inlaid with semi-

precious stones of the Turkoman and Qashqâi tribes are rarely on sale, the buying and selling of gold and gold jewellery still flourishes in the bazaar.

(Left) *Tehrân Bazaar*
(Right) *Metalware shop, Esfahân*

MUSIC IN IRÂN
—Bruce Wannell

Music in Irân has an ancient history, though much of the evidence for it has disappeared.

A bronze trumpet in the Persepolis museum hints at the ceremonial fanfares which accompanied court ritual at the spring capital from the 5th to 3rd centuries BC. A distant descendant of these trumpet and kettle-drum fanfares, known as "*naqqâreh*" in the Islamic period, are the itinerant folk musicians playing the cylindrical double-headed drum and shawm "*dohol*" and "*surnâi*" to be found wandering the countryside playing for outdoor wedding festivities or accompanying the Bakhtiâri tribal stave-dance—further afield the same ensemble can be found marking the goals and victories in polo matches from Chitral to Ladakh.

The early 7th century AD hunting bas-reliefs at Tâq-e Bustân show harpists in boats accompanying with their music the bloody exploits of the Sasanian king Khusro II in his paradise hunting grounds. From the same period, silver dishes and carved plaster roundels show the harpist concubine Âzâdeh seated behind the king Bahrâm "Gur" on his camel, as he shoots stags and hinds with almost demonic skill. Other examples show the dancing maidens of the goddess Anâhitâ playing the short-necked lute and various wind instruments. The literature of the period before the Islamic Arab conquest, preserved for the most part in post-Conquest recensions such as "*Vis o Râmin*" and the "*Shâhnâmeh*", speaks of the courtly feasts that followed war, "*bazm*" after "*razm*", where musicians were an essential part of royal entertainment. Bârbad was the most famous of these musicians, credited with the composition of the 7 royal songs "*khosrovâni sorud*". A later survival of this tradition is the blind Zoroastrian poet and harpist Rudaki (d. AD 941) whose suggestive art was able to persuade a Sâmânid amir to return to Bokhârâ after a 3-year absence. Music and minstrelsy belonged to oral rather than written tradition, so it is difficult to reconstruct what its characteristic sounds and techniques might have been.

With the elaboration of Islamic courtly and scientific culture in Baghdâd from the 9th century AD, largely on the basis of translations from Greek texts as well as on the traditions of Irânian musicians and artists, music enters the written record as a self-conscious intellectual discipline—though often the theory was divorced from actual practice. Music theory in the middle ages was allied to mathematics, astronomy and medicine, and philosopher-physicians such as Fârâbi (d.950) and Ibn Sinâ (d. 1038) included sections on musical proportion, intervals, modes and ethos in their larger works on medicine etc, though there was still no effective convention of accurate musical notation. Meanwhile the artistic mind-set of the Muslim world was increasingly impregnated and formed by the subtle disciplines (emphatically distinguished from music) of Qur'ân chanting and calligraphy, and their secular equivalents in Arabic and Persian poetry and its performance, often in the context of courtly celebrations as well as the emotionally charged Sufi "khânegâh" rituals. It must be noted that the legal status of music was always a matter of controversy among Muslim legalists, largely because of its association in pre-Islamic Arabia with dancing girls, leading too often to drunken and disorderly behaviour—hence the primacy given to the recited word, ornamented with virtuosity, and the avoidance of large-scale public music except for royal or military fanfares: like painting, music in Irân remained an essentially private art, rarely going beyond the range of chamber music.

In the Mongol and Timurid periods, the most important writers on music were Safiuddin Urmavi (d. 1293), Qutbuddin Shirâzi (d. 1311) and Abdul Qâder Marâghi (d. 1435) who was a practising musician of high calibre. From the 15th century countless miniature book-illustrations show small groups of musicians performing in courtly or sufi contexts, the main foci for the development of art music allied to poetry, free of legalistic strictures. Some of the most frequently illustrated musical instruments have since disappeared from the mainstream Irânian repertoire: notably the harp "chang" and the short-necked lute "barbat". Music in Irân shared essential theoretical and practical characteristics (oral transmission, improvisation on the basis of a recognised progression of melodic and modal elements, etc) with the neighbouring musics of the Arabs, Turks, Armenians—especially until the early 18th century when the Afghân destruction of Safavid court culture and the ensuing political and social chaos led to a dissolution of Irânian cultural norms. It is interesting that while there is a continuum of musical culture from Irân to the Caucasus, Central Asia, Mesopotamia and Anatolia, the Indian world is musically very distinct, especially in its modes and musical structures, in spite of some historical influences from the Irânian and Islamic worlds, eg in literature Amir Khusro Dehlavi, etc. The Afghâns, at least the Pushtuns of the south-east, belong by taste and tradition to the Indian rather than the Irânian musical world.

The re-establishment of a centralised state under the Qâjârs with the capital at Tehrân from 1786 led to a new cultural and musical synthesis influenced by Azerbaijân, largely on the basis of folk tunes, which became de-localised as they provided the new modal frame-work for courtly classical music, together with what had been salvaged by musicians such as the Armenian bard Sayat Nova who had worked in Shirâz at the court of Karim Khân Zand (d.1779). Classical "*asil*" music in Irân today is the direct descendant of the new Qâjâr synthesis of the early 19th century with its characteristic instruments, the hour-glass shaped lute "*târ*" and the "*santur*" dulcimer struck with light hammers "*mezrâb*", both of which developed at that time. The great mid-19th century "*târ*" master Ali Akbar Farâhâni (d. 1860) founded a dynasty of performers and teachers who were still active in the late 1980's. The end-blown reed-flute "*ney*", the small frame-drum "*daff*" and spike-fiddle "*kamâncheh*" survive from the earlier tradition, while the goblet-drum "*zarb*" has developed into a virtuoso instrument in the last half-century—it is also known onomatopaeically as "*tombak*" from the characteristic "*tom*" of the deeper note struck in the centre of the taut skin and the lighter "*bak*" struck on or near the wooden frame; the slender long-necked lute also survives from before the debacle and is known as "*seh-târ*", meaning 3-strings, (the greatest master of this intimate instrument was the sufi Mushtâq Ali Shâh murdered by legalists in 1792)—though varieties from 1 to 4 strings are known in the regional repertoires, all with moveable frets to adapt to the different intervals of the modes—7 "*dastgâh*" and 5 "*âvâz*" with their constituent melodic fragments "*gusheh*"—many of which sound initially strange to western ears as they use micro-intervals between the whole-tone and semi-tone, like the expanded 2nd.

Various popular traditions, with strong regional flavour—Baluchi, Kurdish, Azeri, Turkoman, coastal Arab, with characteristic instruments ranging from the shawm "*surnai*", bagpipes "*ney hambân*" to skull-shaped fiddle "*saruz*", occupy a notable place in the spectrum of Irânian popular music, and even affect the traditions of art-music: a recent example is the penetration of the large and loud Kurdish sufi frame-drum "*dâireh*" into art music since the Islamic Revolution of 1979, often to accompany monodic chants of military nature celebrating the martyrs of the Irân-Iraq war. Music was condemned to silence at the beginning of the Revolution, with Revolutionary Guards carrying out search and destroy operations against musical instruments, until in 1989 on the brink of the grave, the Âyatollâh Khomeini issued a fatwâ in its favour—as long it was serious, traditionally Irânian and not likely to lead to lascivious dancing! The Fajr Festival of Revolutionary Chants has been held annually since this time, expanding to include regional and traditional music of Irân and the Muslim world. Classical western music had also, though with less success, been defended by early ideologues of the Revolution such as Dr. Ali Shari'ati. The official endorsement of traditional Irânian music has led to a boom in broadcasting it in public places—gardens and parks, galleries and restaurants, wall to wall, so much so that the music itself is devalued, and there is even a reaction against it among many young Irânians—who express opposition to the status quo by performing or listening to "rock" music and other forms of electronic popular music from the decadent West. Western cultural influence "gharb-zadegi" had of course already been penetrating Irân since the early 20th century, including the musical sphere, notably with the introduction of orchestras for light music and the growth of radio and film music—this mass-media music does indeed threaten to overwhelm the quiet elite traditions of the genuine "asil" music of Irân, which is nevertheless also at risk of putrefying and petrifying into a fixed museum-piece culture under close official supervision and control.

It is worth listening to recordings by the 20th century masters: in singing: Banân, Marsiyeh, Shajariân, Parisâ and the younger artists Shahrâm Nâzeri and Seyyed Abdul Husein Mokhtâbâd; for "zarb" Husein Tehrâni, Jamshid Shemirâni; for "ney" Kasâ'i, Muhammad Musavi; for "kamâncheh" Asghar Bahâri; for "santur" Farâmarz Pâyvar, Majid Kiâni; for "târ" Muhammad Rezâ Lotfi, Dâriush Talâ'i. These are available either as solos, duos or in small groups of performers, not normally exceeding 5—singer, percussion, plucked or bowed stringed instrument, and woodwind. Between the 1940s and early 70s, monodic orchestral accompaniments in the semi-classical style were favoured by recording studios, along with incontinent use of the echo-chamber, which gave a heavy, dragging feel to the music—whereas the ideal of the small ensemble is perfect concord and effortlessly rapid echo and uptake by the instrumentalists of the subtlest nuances of the singer. A measured instrumental prelude will be followed by performance of poetry in unmeasured recitative style, with moments of greater intensity marked by "tahrir" or "chah-chah" virtuoso ornamentation, interspersed with instrumental echoes and melismas growing out of the silence, and finally a faster rhythmic ensemble in lighter style. There are occasional concert performances, especially in Tehrân at the Tâlâr Vahdat (ex-Rudaki) or Farhangsaray Niâvarân, and increasingly on the western concert circuit as well: however it should be noted that the real spirit of Irânian traditional music is best communicated and appreciated in a small private gathering without any artificial amplification.

RELIGION

IRÂNIAN PRE-ISLAMIC RELIGIONS

In the second and first millennia BC, the native population of Irân adopted the cults of the Indo-European tribes who had recently arrived on the plateau. These cults, known generically by the term Mazdaism, were to develop along separate lines in different regions but most of them recognized a god called Ahura Mazda (or Ormazd). Very little information is available about this ancient past, which predates the Achaemenian period, and our present knowledge of these cults is based largely on the study and comparison of ancient Irânian and Indian oral traditions which much later were crystalised in oral form. Because of their common Aryan heritage, the Irânian cults show a close relationship with the ancient Indo-Aryan religion as it appears in the Vedas, particularly in the names and functions of the gods, and the division of society into three classes: priest, warrior and pastoralist-agriculturalist.

The Aryan religion was a polytheistic one which recognized a principal god, Ahura Mazda (Varuna in India), who was surrounded by a group of divinities known as the Amesa Spenta. The worship of these gods centred around two essential elements, fire and *haoma*. Fire, by nature sacred and purifying, remained a central element of Zoroastrianism, and is so today. *Haoma* is the equivalent of the Indian *soma*, an inebriating drink, honoured as an equal of the gods, which was used during sacrificial rites. The sacrifice of animals, usually of bulls, was one of the main rites associated with the worship of the gods in Mithraism.

ZOROASTRIANISM

Zoroastrianism is the religion which developed from the reforms of the old cults carried out by Zarathustra (or Zoroaster in its Hellenized form). Numerous legends exist about Zarathustra's life and it is often difficult to distinguish the fact from the fiction. The present consensus gives Zarathustra's place of birth as somewhere in eastern Irân; he is thought to have been born between 1000 and 600 BC and would therefore have lived slightly before the great Achaemenian kings. The main events of his life are known in part thanks to the hymns, or *gâthâs*, which are attributed to him and which form part of the *Avesta*, the holy book of the Zoroastrians.

Zarathustra appears originally to have been a priest who was expelled from his country for his strong heterodox views. He succeeded in converting Vishtaspa, the ruler of a Bactrian tribe, who became his protector and helped him spread his new doctrine. This was often done through the use of force. This doctrine inevitably aroused strong reactions when placed in oppositon to the traditional beliefs, and Zarathustra is said to have been mercilessly killed while at prayer in a temple.

Of the old Indo-Irânian pantheon, Zarathustra retained only Ahura Mazda, a beneficent god from whom all things originate. Subordinate to Ahura Mazda were the two twin spirits, Spenta Mainyu (the Holy Spirit) and Angra Mainyu (the Spirit of Evil), better known as Ahriman, personifications of the battle between Good and Evil, and Light and Darkness. This dualism is fundamental to Zoroastrianism: man is blessed with free will, and the choice of the road he takes in life is thus entirely his own. The supreme virtue of Ahura Mazda is Goodness, and one whose deeds, thoughts and words have been good during his lifetime, and who will thus have lived in accordance with God, will be rewarded after death by a place in His kingdom.

One of Zarathustra's greatest reforms was to introduce the idea of monotheism into Mazdaism. The supreme god Ahura Mazda does not take part in the cosmic battle between Ahriman and Spenta Mainyu; the dualism represented by these two spirits is only temporary and will end with the final victory of Good over Evil. At the appointed time for the Last Judgement, a great trial by fire and molten metal, presided over by Ahura Mazda, will punish the evil and reward the good with spiritual resurrection.

Zarathustra appears as a strong opponent of some of the practices of the Aryan religion, in particular of bloody sacrifices and the use of haoma. For Zarathustra, the suffering and death of a bull were incompatible with the doctrine of goodness and wisdom associated with the god to whom the animal is sacrificed. As for haoma, its intoxicating effects lead men astray.

The spread of Zarathustra's doctrine did not entirely supersede traditional Mazdaism and a certain syncretism occurred under the Achaemenians, most notably by the incorporation into Zoroastrianism of some of the practices of the Magi. The Magi had for centuries formed a priestly cast with hereditary politico-religious functions in the Median Empire. After the conquest of Media by the Achaemenians, they became the priesthood of the new dynasty. Fundamentally conservative, they did not always adopt the radical ideas of Zarathustra, and animal sacrifice was therefore maintained and the use of haoma reintroduced.

Under the influence of the Magi, several of the old Indo-Irânian gods were reinstated into the pantheon, particularly Anâhitâ (a fusion of the Old Irânian water goddess with the Babylonian Ishtar, the love goddess and warrior), associated originally with water and rivers, and Mithra, associated with the sun. A rock

The Faravahar, *or symbol of the Zoroastrian faith,*
from a relief at Persepolis, Iran (4th century BC)

inscription dated to the reign of the Achaemenian king Artaxerxes II (404–359 BC) invokes for the first time, and together, Mithra, Anâhitâ and Ahura Mazda, signalling a change from the practice of earlier reigns when only Ahura Mazda was called upon. Mithra was also the god of war, and presided over the bull sacrifices and the haoma rituals. His cult, known as Mithraism, spread throughout the Classical world, and was particularly popular in the Roman army.

Under the Sasanians, who were themselves descendants of a high priest of Anâhitâ, Zoroastrianism became a state religion organized around the Magi. At the beginning of the Sasanian period, there still existed a variety of Mazdaian doctrines, but orthodoxy developed under the influence of the priest Kartir, who held from c. AD 240 until 294 different functions of increasing importance under six different shâhs from Ardeshir I (224–241) till Narses (293–302). Kartir commissioned a series of inscriptions in which he described the main events of his career. Kartir was not alone in having built fire temples throughout the empire or in destroying pagan places of worship, but he was much more aggressive than his predecessors. He reorganized the priesthood and openly attacked the followers of non-Zoroastrian doctrines, particularly Manichaeans, Buddhists, Jews and Christians; the latter were seen as pro-Roman fifth columnists. The compilation at this period of a canon, the Avesta, from oral traditions of various origins, contributed to fix the orthodoxy of this state Zoroastrianism.

ZURVANISM

By the time of the Parthian dynasty, another branch of Mazdaism had developed which was particularly popular in Media: Zurvanism. Its name was derived from that of its supreme god, Zervân, who represents unlimited time. Once again, a cosmic battle between Good and Evil is represented, but unlike Zoroastrianism, it is Ormazd (Ahura Mazda) himself who battles with Ahriman and not Spenta Mainyu. According to Zurvanism, the history of the world will last a span of 9,000 years (some texts say 12,000), divided into cycles of 3,000 years. The first two periods, those of the reigns of Ormazd and Ahriman, represent an alternation of the reigns of Good and Evil, a concept which is completely absent from Zoroastrianism. In the final period, Light and Darkness battle with each other, creating a mingling of Good and Evil, until the final victory of Light. In this battle, Mithra plays the role of arbiter and mediator.

MANICHAEISM

In the third century AD, during the Sasanian dynasty, a prophet by the name of Mani preached a new, syncretic doctrine in Irân, influenced by Zoroastrianism, Christianity and Buddhism. Born around AD 216, Mani was brought up in a Gnostic Baptist sect in Babylonia. At the age of 24, a few years after having received his first revelation from God, he left the community and set off on a long journey through Irân as far as the Indus Valley. On his return, King Shâpur I invited him to court to expound his doctrine, and gave him permission to preach throughout the empire. But Manichaeism suffered badly from the religious persecutions of the period directed by the high priest Kartir. In 274 or 276, during the reign of Bahrâm I, Mani was imprisoned and executed.

The belief in the two opposite principles of Light and Darkness appears once more in connection with Manichaeism. Here again, events unfold over three periods; in the first one, the two principles are separate, each in its own kingdom, until Darkness invades the world of Light. Then begins the middle period, that of the mingling of the principles. Primordial Man, an emanation of God, is defeated by the demons who take away his armour (Light). The particles of Light thus captured are mixed with Darkness and Matter. While some particles are recovered by the Living Spirit to create the Moon, the Sun and the Stars, the more defiled ones remain captive. At this point, the Archons, demons bound by the Living Spirit and who beget the plants and the animals in which the particles of Light are incorporated, intervene. The human species was created by Concupiscence in the hope that as he multiplied, Man would scatter the particles and prevent their return to their own kingdom. To frustrate this plan, the Saviour communicates to the First Man, Adam, the Gnosis, or total knowledge about his origin and his vocation: although his body was engendered by demons, his soul is capable of freeing itself and returning to the Light. In the last period, when all the particles have returned, Light and Darkness will once again be separated and the demons and the damned enclosed for eternity in the world of Obscurity.

The death of Mani and subsequent religious persecution led to an exodus of Manichaeans to the ends of the Sasanian Empire. Many fled to Egypt, and even to Chinese Turkestan, where their faith survived at least until the 13th century. In the Chinese south-eastern province of Fujian, Manichaean communities flourished even till the late 16th century. But in Muslim as well as in Christian territory, the Manichaeans were considered heretics and a political threat. The persecutions continued and, at the beginning of the tenth century, the Manichaean Church left its native region for Central Asia.

MAZDAKISM

At the end of the fifth century, there appeared in Irân a movement called Mazdakism, named after its founder, Mazdak, whose religious teachings incorporated the dualism and Gnosis of Manichaeism. But Mazdakism is better known as an economic and social movement than for its religious doctrines. At a period of serious social unrest, the message of Mazdak, who defended the lower classes and preached the sharing in common of lands and women, captured the attention of the very poor. For Mazdak, all men were born equal, and the evil in the world stemmed from hate and social differences. Like Manichaeans, Mazdakites were persecuted and the movement lost its religious character and became more revolutionary. As a result of excesses committed by adherents, such as the capture and sacking of castles and kidnapping, the ruler Kavadh I (488–531) was faced with the prospect of serious social upheaval. In 528 he ordered the massacre of the Mazdakites. The sect went underground and was still in existence during the Islamic period.

Shi'ism

The two main branches of Islam are the Sunni, which includes the majority of Muslims, and the Shi'a, who account for slightly over ten per cent of the world Muslim community, living mostly in Irân, Iraq, Lebanon, the Arab Peninsula, Afghânistân, Pakistan and India. The split between Sunni and Shi'a dates back to the period of the first caliphs elected after the death of the Prophet in 634. Ali, a cousin and son-in-law of the Prophet and a popular candidate, was passed over and had to wait until 656 before his election. The reign of Ali is considered by the Shi'as as a Golden Age, although it did not last long. A first rebellion lead by Aisha, the Prophet's widow, intent on avenging the assassination of the third caliph Osman, was successfully defeated at the Battle of the Camel, near Basra, but was followed by a second revolt lead by the governor of Syria, Mo'awiya, a cousin of Osman. His army and Ali's met at Siffin, in Iraq (658). As the outcome of the battle seemed uncertain, the two sides agreed to an arbitration which turned in favour Mo'awiya. Having lost the caliphate, Ali also had to face a further rebellion, that of the Khareji who refused to accept a human arbitration for such an essential question as the succession to the head of the Muslim community, believing that this decision should be left to God alone. Ali defeated the Khareji but was assassinated by one of them at Kufa in 661.

According to Shi'a tradition, a movement rapidly formed aimed at restoring Ali's line to the caliphate. It soon became a full-scale opposition movement to the Umayyad dynasty founded by Mo'awiya, which it considered as having usurped power. The adjective Shi'a is derived from the name of this movement, the *shi'at 'Ali* or 'party of Ali'. In 680, after the death of his brother Hasan, Ali's second son, Hosein, took over the leadership of a rebellion against caliph Yazid. On the way to Kufa, they were forced to camp at Kerbalâ, an oasis in the desert. On the tenth day of the month of Moharram, the caliph's army attacked them and massacred Hosein and his followers. The list of Shi'a martyrs, headed by Ali, grew. Hosein became the principal symbol of Shi'a resistance and of the Shi'a struggle for justice.

Sunnis and Shi'as share certain religious obligations (prayer, charity, fasting, pilgrimage and the *jehâd*, or holy war) as well as certain fundamental beliefs: belief in *tohid*, or the oneness of God ('There is no God but God'), in *nobovvat*, or belief in the mission of the prophets whose duty it is to transmit the will of God and of whom Mahommed was the last in a series; and in *ma'âd*, the belief in a Judgement Day. In addition to these principles, the Shi'as believe in *'adl*, the concept of divine justice, and *emâmat*, the principle according to which Ali and his descendants represent the only legitimate authority on Earth until Judgement Day. Only these descendants, the Emâms, are empowered to interpret the Qur'ân as they alone retain the secret knowledge revealed to Ali by the Prophet and transmitted from one Emâm to the next. The majority of Shi'as, or Twelver Shi'as, recognize twelve Emâms; the last one, Mohammed al-Muntazar, disappeared around 873, leaving the visible world. His triumphant return will herald the end of tyranny and restoration of justice and peace on Earth. This messianic Emâm, known as the Mahdi or 'well directed', remains even in his absence as the sole legitimate head of the community, and the temporal governments that succeed one another can only act in his name, preferably in consultation with the *mujtahid*, theologians who, after long years of study, are considered authorities in matters of judicial and religious interpretation.

As legitimate successor to the Prophet, Ali is considered to be the First Emâm. In principle, the Emâm designated his heir during his lifetime and transmitted to him the secrets revealed by the Prophet; in practice, the role of Emâm has always passed from father to son, with one exception, that of Hosein, the Third Emâm, who succeeded his brother Hassan. For the Twelver Shi'as, the succession of Emâms continued until the Twelfth, but several branches of Shi'ism do not recognize this. The first to detach themselves were the Zaidis who supported as heir to the Fourth Emâm a half-brother of Mohammed al-Bâqer, who became the Fifth Emâm. The Zaidis ruled in Yemen until 1962. A second, more important, division occurred at the succession to the Sixth Emâm, Ja'far al-Sâdeq, who died in 765. He had designated as heir his son Ismâ'il, but the latter died before his father. After Emâm Ja'far's death, Musa, a son of Ja'far and a slave, was chosen to succeed him, but part of the community still considered Ismâ'il the legitimate heir and refused this choice. They became the Ismâ'ilis who recognize only seven Emâms, the last of whom, Ismâ'il, also disappeared in the same manner as the Twelfth Emâm (see special topic on the Assassins, page 232).

For centuries, in the absence of a Shi'a government, the survival of Shi'ism remained precarious. Dispersed Shi'a communities had settled in centres such as Qom, or Najaf in Iraq where the *madraseh* taught in accordance with emâmi beliefs. But persecutions lead the Shi'as to adopt the practice of *taqiya*, or dissimulation, which allowed them to hide their faith in order to ensure their own survival and that of their beliefs. Under the Safavid dynasty, in the 16th century, Shi'ism under-went a renaissance, although Shi'a knowledge had declined to such an extent that

Mausoleum of Shâh Cherâgh, Shirâz

Shâh Ismâ'il had to invite mullahs from Lebanon. From then on, Shi'ism remained the religion of the majority of Irânians although it has faced further difficulties in modern times, particularly under the Pahlavi dynasty, which tried to reduce the power of the clergy. This rivalry between political and religious power theoretically came to an end in 1979 with the establishment of the *velâyat-e faqih* system according to which political power lies in the hands of the religious authorities, and more specifically of the *faqih*, or *mujtahid*, specialists trained in jurisprudence.

MOHARRAM AND ASHURA

The lunar month of Moharram with which the Islamic year begins has a particular significance in the Shi'a religious calendar: it is a month of mourning, the time to commemorate the martyrdom of Emâm Hosein, killed at Kerbalâ. The two days known as Tâsuâ (the day preceding the martyrdom) and Ashurâ (the day of the martyrdom itself), the ninth and tenth of Moharram, are marked throughout Irân by great celebrations accompanied by processions of the faithful, beating them- selves on the chest with their hands or on their backs with chain, laments, and banners. In the villages there are representations of *ta'ziyeh*, the popular religious theatre. The plays put on enact various episodes of the life and death of Hosein and are performed on open-air stages among a weeping public, carried along by the intense, almost tangible emotion which increases inexorably until the final, inevitable drama, repeated year after year. In other processions, costumed figures represent the various protagonists: Hosein himself and Caliph Yazid; Abbâs, Hosein's brother, whose hands were cut off by one of the caliph's soldiers while fetching water from a well to quench his companions' thirst; Shemr, who advanced at the head of the soldiers and attacked Hosein; Zeynab, the Emâm's sister; and Ali, his son, the sole survivors of the massacre.

MODERN CINEMA IN IRÂN   —*Bruce Wannell*

Photography and film reached Irân shortly after they were invented in Europe: the monarch Nâsereddin Shâh (d. 1896) was himself a keen photographer, and also sponsored photographers through the Dâr al-Fonun college that had been founded in the mid-19th century on the initiative of his progressive minister Amir Kabir. Photographs of the period are now on display in the Golestân Palace in Tehrân. His successor Mozaffareddin Shâh (d. 1907) had a chief photographer Ibrahim Khân who first used a cine-camera in 1900 to film the monarch's tour of Belgium. In 1904 Sheikh Fazlollâh Nuri caused the first public cinema in Tehrân to be closed down. The first films date back to the 1920–30's period, when foreign visitors made anthropological and travel films like Merian Cooper's 1924 *Grass* about the Bakhtiâri tribal migrations across the Zagros mountains, and the Citroen team of *La Croisiere Jaune* filmed their car odyssey across Asia; local (Armenian) talent made the first silent film in 1930 and in 1933 Ardeshir Irâni made the first Irânian film with talking sound track, *Dokhtar-e Lor*, using a studio in Bombay. It was not until 1948 that the first film with Persian soundtrack was produced in Irân, which remained a minor centre of film production, heavily dependent on Indian movies for content and style, and for the next 60 years catered to low popular taste, based on violent action and on cabaret theatre with suggestive dance sequences: Mas'ud Kimiâ'i's 1969 *Qeisar* epitomises this genre of "lumpen-machismo" melodrama known as *"film-e fârsi"*.

The increasing international sophistication of the court and the elite led to the sponsoring of serious art cinema in the late 1960's, which culminated in 1969 with the appearance of Dâriush Mehrjui's experimental *Gâv* based on the playwright Gholâm Hosein Sâ'edi's powerful short story treating a man's obsession with his cow and hallucinatory self-identification with the animal. Sohrâb Shahid Sâles's 1973 quiet and intellectual chef d'oeuvre *Yek Ettefâq-e Sâdeh* forms, with *Gav*, the basis of subsequent Irânian art cinema. Mehrjui's 1978 *Dâyereh-ye Minâ* portrayed the corruption of rural migrants in the urban jungle of Tehrân, in the story of a boy turning into a blood-purchaser at the behest of a whisky-drinking dealer, and therefore missing his own father's funeral. Unfortunately most pre-Revolutionary films have been suspended from circulation, even in video or cassette or CD format—so are unavailable in Irân, though western cinematheques have copies. Among the intellectuals involved in the launching of serious Irânian cinema in the 1960's were the poetess Forugh Farrokhzâd who in 1962 made a short film about a leper-colony *Khâneh Siyâh Ast*, as well as the polymath Bahrâm Beizâ'i, who writes as much for theatre as for film and has produced historical studies of popular entertainment in Irân as well as of Irânian myths and legends that are still studied in Irânian universities—his films are characterised by an intellectual and declamatory style which show their origin in theatre. In spite of official patronage, modern art cinema was actually a focus of protest against and subversion of the Pahlavi regime, while looking to other international art cinema, such as that of the Soviet Armenian Paradjanov, the Japanese Kurosawa etc.

Most films actually screened in Irân before the 1978 Islamic Revolution were foreign imports, from Bollywood and Hollywood, and were widely seen as part of the colonisation of the mind against which opponents of the Shâh's regime were protesting. So it was not altogether surprising that cinemas were among the first objects of pent-up revolutionary aggression which marked the explosion of the late 1970's: whatever the manifold objective and subjective, conscious and unconscious reasons for the Revolution, it was certainly given focus by a renewed Islamic ideology and spearheaded by the Shi'a clergy under the charismatic exiled Âyatollâh Ruhollah Khomeini. Hostility to graven images had of course been part of Semitic religion since the laws of Moses, iconoclasm featured repeatedly in Christian history, but Islam was throughout, consistently and uninterruptedly, hostile to representations of living beings—initially in the context of opposition to pagan worship of idols, whether statues or paintings, but in 1978 it was part of the widespread rejection of the Shâh's arrogant imposition of western-ising modernism on the American capitalist model. The burning of the Cinema Rex in the oil town of Abâdân, which caused several hundred deaths, and the arson attacks on other cinemas throughout the provinces marked the boiling point of the incipient Revolution in 1978.

The exercise of power by the new revolutionary cadres immediately led to a desire to co-opt and control mass-media, notably television and cinema, as well as posters and large-scale wall-paintings of Islamic political leaders living and dead: this entailed a revision of the traditionally hostile Islamic attitude towards the visual arts, especially towards the medium of cinema itself. New directors emerged, notably Mohsen Makhmalbâf, born from a temporary marriage in the slums of south Tehrân, who cut his cinematic teeth filming forced political confessions for the new regime, and rapidly emerged as a brilliant angry young cineaste, with the frightening autobiographical *Bâykot* of 1985 and the grim allegory *Dast-forush* of 1986 representing the unregenerate slum-dwellers of south Tehrân. His 1991 film *Naseroddin Shâh Aktor-e Sinemâ* is a loving tribute to and selection from the history of Irânian film making which he had previously attacked. All these early films were based on his own theatre plays or screenplays. Operating within the constraints of post-revolutionary cinema, his work gradually descended into mawkishness as in his 1995 *Gabbeh* or patronising pretentiousness as in his 2001 *Safar-e Qandahâr*, though both still significant within the Irânian context—e.g. *Gabbeh* concentrates on beauty and love in a tribal context, at a time when the state was notable for eschewing beauty, espousing ugliness, eliminating the tribes, and leaving many widows and girls of marriageable age economically stranded and sexually frustrated by the large number of casualties from the Iraq war as well as the mass executions of prisoners in the late 1980's. The racist stereotyping of the Afghâns in *Safar-e Qandahâr* is typical of the egocentrism of Tehrân, but the film contains scenes of surreal visual impact, notably the parachuting of false limbs in the desert. Sources of funding can also have a strong influence on message and style: the recent feminist productions of the Makhmalbâf daughters and entourage are said to respond to the agendas of the arts funding they receive from the European Union; it is notable that they also concentrate on the ethnic periphery of Irân—Kurdish and Afghân, e.g. *Takhteh Siyâh* and *Zamâni barâ-ye Masti-ye Asbhâ* and *Usâma*.

There is a danger of sentimentality in the repeated treatment of a rural life that in reality has all-but vanished, as in the concentration on children as carriers of stories that are not allowed to be overtly critical or sexual. This is even the case—despite the powerful and authentic performances of non-professional child and youth actors—in the charming and well-crafted films such as Ja'far Panâhi's 1995 *Bâdkonak-e Sefid* and Majid Majidi's 1997

Bacheh-hā-ye Āsmān, which use largely the same location and similar story lines, of brave children facing material poverty. Majidi went on to produce the visually ravishing *Rang-e Khodā* about a blind boy in the forest landscape above the Caspian coast in 1999 and *Bārān* about an Afghan child refugee labourer in Tehrān in 2001. Panāhi produced *Dāyereh* about the plight of women subjected to restrictions on their movements and subjected to discrimination and sexual harassment by the new authorities. Realistic treatment of social issues and the darker side of urban low-life, using largely non-professional actors, became a feature of the new Irānian cinema, especially in the work of the documentary film maker Rakhshān Bani-E'temād, who produced powerful feature films featuring women in the capital, in her 1994 *Rusari-ye Abi* and her 2000 *Zir-e Pust-e Shahr*.

Filmmakers from immediately before the Revolution started to come back into production as national cinema blossomed in the absence of competition from imported films after the Revolution. Amir Nāderi's 1982/6 *Davandeh* showed a boy from Ahvāz running away from the destruction wreaked on his home by the Iraq war. Bahrām Baizā'i continued, in spite of some official disfavour due to his status as a secular intellectual and his Baha'i origins, to produce remarkable and demanding films, like the story of the Arab boy refugee from the war with Iraq who ends up working for a Gilaki-speaking woman whose husband is away at the front in the 1988 *Bashu Gharibeh-ye Kuchek*, and his elegant bourgeois drama *Mosāferān* of 1992 with its poignant mixing of preparations for marriage and sudden bereavement. Abbās Kiā-Rostami had emerged in the early 1970's from the Institute of Educational Cinema for Children, making short films until well after the Revolution. In 1987 he produced one of his best films *"Khāneh-ye Dust Kojast?"* again with boys as the main protagonists, one losing and the other searching to return a school exercise book; in 1992 *Zendegi va Digar Hich* renamed *Zendegi Edāmeh Darad*, a return after a destructive earthquake to the village where he had filmed in 1987, to witness life going on in spite of catastrophe; then in 1994 *Zir-e Derakhtān-e Zeitun* a slow contemplative love affair hinted at through the olive trees; and in 1997 *Ta'm-e Gilās* broaching the religiously taboo subject of suicide, with a Tehrāni intellectual driving around the slum outskirts to find a grave-digger to bury him after he commits suicide—his approaches verge on the sexual, are indignantly repulsed by a variety of Irânian workmen, until a young Afghân refugee, the epitome of the social outcast, accepts with quiet dignity—before the illusion of the whole is shown as the camera recedes to reveal the film crew and actors staging the drama in the bare landscape. A later film *Ta'ziyeh* 2002 shares the same agonisingly slow pace and concentration on the dignified faces of the poor—here, as they get absorbed in watching the re-enactment of the Kerbalâ tragedy.

A recent success, until it was banned once its subversive sub-text became apparent—Tehrân audiences were standing up in the cinema and cheering—was the rumbustious comedy *Mârmulak* of 2004 by Kamâl Tabrizi, where a burglar known as the lizard escapes prison disguised in a mulla's robes, and has a hilarious train journey impersonating the clerical manner. Subversive humour is an enduring feature of Irânian popular culture, just as oblique indirectness characterises Irânian high culture.

The progressive attitudes of Âyatollâh Khâtami from 1982 at the *Farhang o Ershâd* when he functioned as censor allowed serious art cinema to be developed, under certain conditions—avoidance of overt sex and direct political criticism, with a concentration on Irânian themes, social issues often seen through children's eyes, and a slow almost anthropological rhythm. While these constraints operated at best to produce films that are powerful and many-layered and as these productions were successful on the international circuit of film festivals, modern art cinema was seen as a welcome avenue for positive propaganda for Irân in the West, as well as being an essential channel for Irânian creativity, stifled in so many other areas. The string of prize-winning films produced in Irân in the last 30 years is impressive, though the drift into a style favoured by and aimed at the juries of international film festivals has been criticised as "*khâreji-pasand*"— as having lost its appeal to an Irânian mass audience—but that is perhaps the fate of most art cinema: it is only rarely that films of the power of Pontecorvo's 1965 *Battaglia di Algeri* can be made. Certainly the quality of the best Irânian films of the last decades show an encounter with modernity that has not, for once, falsified the Irânian identity, and has allowed Irânian visual culture to be reinvented with freshness and authenticity.

(Following pages) *Tehrân Bazaar*

THE CITY AND PROVINCE OF TEHRÂN

The tourist who arrives for the first time in Tehrân hoping to catch a glimpse of the splendour of ancient Persia will quickly be disappointed: Tehrân has been a capital for only two centuries and has undergone constant recontruction during that time. As a result, the only traces of the long and tumultuous history of the country are hidden behind the walls of the museums. The modern city is a huge, polluted agglomeration, hot and dusty in summer and beset with seemingly insurmountable traffic problems. It has brought together nearly 20 per cent of the entire population of Irân and has expanded chaotically and too fast. Nevertheless it is well worth spending a couple of days in Tehrân, if only to see some of the priceless treasures that are on show in its museums.

In addition to being the political, economic and intellectual centre of Irân, Tehrân is also a provincial capital. The province of Tehrân extends from the southern slopes of the Alborz Mountains into the Dasht-e Kavir desert and includes several mountain resorts popular with the Tehrânis, who are eager to escape the heat and pollution of downtown Tehrân. Karâj, 42 kilometres west of Tehrân, has become popular for its watersports since the building of a dam nearby. To the east of Tehrân, looms the unmistakable shape of Mount Damâvand (5,671 metres, 18,600 feet), an extinct volcano which provides good skiing, mountain climbing and walking. The road which skirts round the eastern flank of the volcano, following the upper Harâz Valley, from Ab-Ali through the villages of Polur and Reyneh and on to Amol and the coast, offers particularly good views of the mountain. It is from these villages that climbers usually set out for the summit.

HISTORY

Although present-day Tehrân is a modern city, the region surrounding it has a long history. Remains of Neolithic settlements have been discovered at the small town of Shahr-e Rey, about ten kilometres south of Tehrân. During the Achaemenian dynasty, Rey—then called Ragâ, or Rhages by the Greeks—was an important settlement. It was rebuilt by the Seleucids and remained the main city of Media under the Parthians and the Sasanians.

Partly destroyed after the Arab invasion, Rey was again rebuilt by the Abbâsid caliphs and was the birthplace of Hârun al-Rashid (766–809). Very early on, an important Shi'a community settled there, as well as in the towns of Qom and

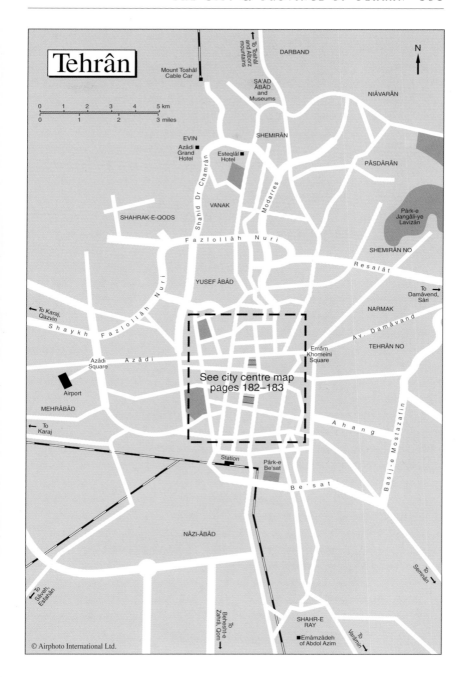

Tehrân

0 1 2 3 4 5 km
0 1 2 3 miles

N

To Toshâl and Alborz mountains

Mount Toshâl Cable Car

DARBAND

SA'AD ÂBÂD and Museums

NIÂVARÂN

SHEMIRÂN

EVIN

Azâdi Grand Hotel

Esteqlâl Hotel

PÂSDÂRÂN

Shahid Dr Chamran

VANAK

Modarres

SHAHRAK-E-QODS

Pârk-e Jangâli-ye Lavizân

Fazlollâh Nuri

SHEMIRÂN NO

Resalât

YUSEF ÂBÂD

To Damâvend, Sâri

Nuri

NARMAK

To Karaj, Qazvin

Shaykh Fazlollâh

Âv. Damâvand

TEHRÂN NO

Azâdi

Emâm Khomeini Square

Azâdi Square

See city centre map pages 182–183

Airport

MEHRÂBÂD

Ahang

Basij-e Mostazafin

To Karaj

Station

Pârk-e Be'sat

Be'sat

NÂZI-ÂBÂD

To Semnân

To Saveh, Estahâh

SHAHR-E RAY

Emâmzâdeh of Abdol Azim

To Beheshti-e Zahra, Qom

To Varamin

© Airphoto International Ltd.

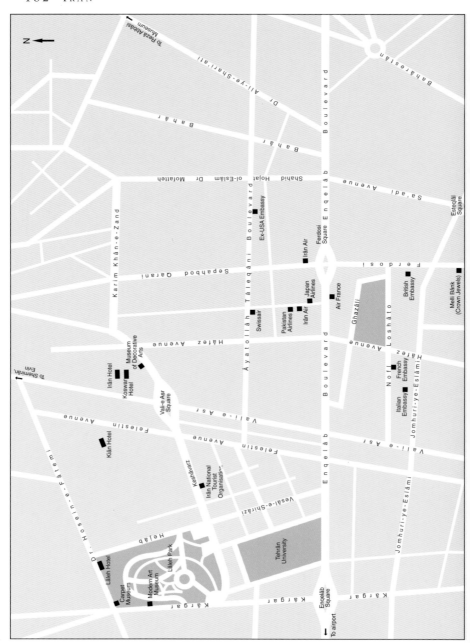

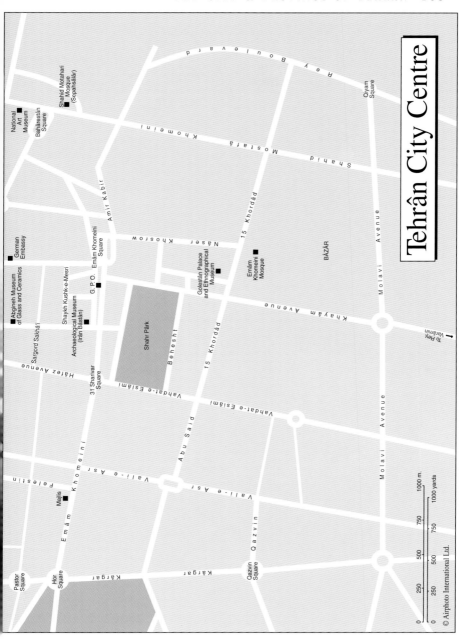

Tehrân City Centre

National Art Museum
Bahârestân Square
Shahid Motahari Mosque (Sepahsâlâr)
Rey Boulevard
Oyam Square
Khomeini
Mostafa
Shahid
Amir Kabir
German Embassy
Emâm Khomeini Square
Naser Khosrow
15 Khordâd
Molavi Avenue
Âbgineh Museum of Glass and Ceramics
Shaykh Kushk-e-Mesri
G.P.O.
Golestân Palace and Ethnographical Museum
Emâm Khomeini Mosque
BÂZÂR
Sârgord Sakhâï
Archaeological Museum (Irân Bâstân)
Shatr Park
Beheshti
Khayâm Avenue
To Rey, Varâmin
Hâfez Avenue
31 Shahrivar Square
15 Khordâd
Vahdat-e Estâmi
Felestin
Emâm Khomeini
Valî-e Asr
Vahdat-e Estâmi
Abu Said
Molavi Avenue
Majlis
Valî-e Asr
Qazvin
Pastor Square
Hôr Square
Kargar
Kargar
Qazvin Square

0   250   500   750   1000 m.
0   250   500   750   1000 yards

© Airphoto International Ltd.

Kâshân. In the tenth and 11th centuries, Rey was governed in turn by the Sâmânids, Ziyârids, Buyids and Ghaznavids, before falling into the hands of the Saljuq Turks in 1038. During the Mongol invasion 1220, Rey was sacked and never recovered its former importance. A new town developed gradually in its place, Tehrân.

The date of the founding of Tehrân is unclear but probably occurred sometime in the 11th century. Descriptions from foreign travellers in the 15th century mention the existence of a well-established town, but it was not until the reign of the Safavid ruler Shâh Tahmâsp I (1524–1576) that it was protected by a fortified wall. Shâh Tahmâsp rebuilt the bazaar and added a citadel, or arg, in the centre. Tehrân became a capital only in 1789, under Qâjâr rule, replacing Shirâz in that function, and in 1796, Aghâ Mohammed Khân was enthroned there. His successor, Fath Ali Shâh (1797–1833), continued the transformation of the town and had the Shâh's Mosque built, while Nâsereddin (1848–1896) enlarged the walls and commissioned the Sepahsâlâr Mosque.

During the 19th century, the centre of the city remained focused around the palace and the bazaar, in other words around the arg, the old Safavid centre. But during the reign of Rezâ Shâh (1925–1941), who preferred to live in his palaces to the west of town or in those at Sa'ad Âbâd, ten kilometres to the north, the urban plan of Tehrân underwent drastic changes. Large avenues were cut to link these different areas together, avenues which still feature among the main roads of the modern town. This was the beginning of the development of the vertical north–south axis which is so characteristic of Tehrân. The old walls of Nâsereddin, as well as the monumental tiled gates, were destroyed to make room for large boulevards. An attempt was being made at creating a modern city on a Western model, with large avenues lined with trees and based on a grid plan.

During the 1950s and '60s, Tehrân went through intense urban development. At the beginning of the Pahlavi reign (1925), the town had only 210,000 inhabitants, but its population doubled in the next twenty years, reaching 2.7 million in 1966. The railway station, built in the south of the town, prevented much planned urban development in that direction, and it was there that the poor and the peasants who had just arrived from the country lived in hastily erected, overcrowded shanty towns. To the north, between Tehrân and the higher ground around Shemirân, in the areas known as Takht-e Jamshid and Abbâs Âbâd, residential and business quarters were built for the middle classes and government employees. As empty land between Shemirân and the downtown area gradually filled up, the zones to the east and west of the old vertical axis were also developed. Towards the end of the

1970s, the population had grown to 4.5 million. To satisfy the increased demand for housing, more and more new blocks of flats were built in the empty areas which still remained between the older districts.

Tehrân today is the product of these decades of uncontrolled urban growth, carried out without any overall, long-term plan. The city now extends over a radius of 30 kilometres (19 miles) from the centre. The most coveted residential areas, where the air is less polluted and a bit cooler in summer, are located in the north, about ten kilometres from the centre of town, and even further from the poor quarters. Tehrân faces a number of serious problems, including overcrowding (the present population is estimated at ten million), severe air pollution and massive traffic jams, which have caused the local authorities to restrict access to the city centre to private cars on weekday mornings. A metro underground network has been built and is being further expanded.

One peculiarity of Tehrân remains to be mentioned: the *jub* or open-air canals, lined with plane trees, which run along the main streets. The *jub* network originally served to distribute the drinking water brought into town from the mountains by the *qanâts*. While the water is certainly fresh when it starts its journey through the city in the northern suburbs around Shemirân, it is much less so by the time it reaches the poorer areas at the foot of the hills! After spring storms, the *jub* can become veritable torrents; be careful when getting in and out of cars or crossing the road.

CITY TOUR OF TEHRÂN

Tehrân's most famous monument is probably the **Azâdi Tower**, a triumphal arch in white stone, standing 45 metres (148 feet) high, and composed of a large central block set on four splayed feet. Designed by a young Irânian architect, the tower was finished in 1971 for the celebrations of the 2,500th anniversary of the monarchy. Once called Shâhyâd, or 'souvenir of the Shâh', it has been rebaptized Azâdi or 'Freedom'. The tower is located to the west of Tehrân, at the junction of the roads from the airport and Qazvin, and acts as a grandiose gateway to the capital. A lift (when it is working) takes the visitor up to the top of the tower from where (smog permitting) there is a panoramic view of the sprawl of modern Tehrân.

Beneath the tower, is a cultural centre with a library, a museum and art galleries, which put on exhibitions of contemporary artists. Open every day except Saturdays from 9 am to 12 am and from 2.30 pm to 5.30 pm (tel 6058191–2).

Azâdi Monument, Tehrân

THE CITY CENTRE
THE ARG AND THE BAZAAR

The area round the *arg* (or citadel), the old royal quarter, forms, with the bazaar, the primitive heart of Tehrân as it was designed by Shâh Tahmâsp in the 16th century. Nothing is left of the Safavid arg, located between the present Nâser Khusro and Khayyâm avenues and the 15th Khordâd Avenue (ex-Buzardjomehri), but its site is marked by the **Golestân Palace** and gardens, which date back to the Qâjâr dynasty.

This palace, the Rose Garden Palace, was once the residence of the Qâjâr kings before being used, under the Pahlavi, for specific ceremonies, such as the coronation of the last Shâh in 1967. The first floor was at one time made into a museum; the famous Peacock Throne which was on show there can now be seen with the royal jewels in the vaults of the Melli Bânk (see page 189). The gardens and the main buildings of the palace have recently been restored and are now fully open to the public, including the marble throne room, the gallery of 19th century paintings, the photography gallery, and the ethnographic museum. The Golestân Palace Library houses the important royal collection of illuminated manuscripts, normally only open to scholars.

One of the garden pavilions, which houses the **Ethnographical Museum** (muzeh-ye Mardom Shenâsi, entrance on 15th Khordâd Avenue), is open to the public. This museum contains an interesting collection of everyday objects from all regions of the country from the Qâjâr period onward, including wax models, a variety of household implements, weapons and jewellery. On the first floor are some models of shops, as well as a display of the accessories used during the religious processions of Ashurâ, during the month of Moharram, including a large nakhl or ceremonial catafalque. Open from 8 am to 2.30 pm, closed Thursdays and Fridays. Tel 3110653.

The **bazaar** and the **Emâm Khomeini Mosque** (ex-Shâh's Mosque) are situated just to the south of the Golestân. The mosque, which was begun early in the 19th century and finished in 1830, is now one of the oldest buildings in Tehrân. Its main entrance is on 15th Khordâd Avenue but other doors lead directly into the bazaar: to the east they join the tinsmith's alley, and to the west the Great Bazaar (bâzâr-e Bozorg) and the gold and silversmiths' quarter. This mosque's proximity to the bazaar makes it one of the liveliest places in Tehrân.

The bazaar has always played a very important role in the economy and social life of Irân. In the broadest sense of the term, the bazaar is an organized system, grouped into guilds. It tends to be rather conservative, and controls almost three-quarters of the country's internal trade, whether it be agricultural, craft, or even industrial products. The bazaar acts as an interface between the town and the country, and has close links with the clergy. It is no coincidence that the Friday Mosques are so often located next to or in the bazaar. The bazaar is an economic power which is not to be under-estimated, as has been demonstrated on several occasions. When it senses that its interests are threatened, by the state, for example, or by a foreign monopoly (such as during the events that led up to the

Tehrân Bazaar

nationalization of oil in 1951), the bazaar can close down completely, a move which may have dire economic consequences.

In an Irânian bazaar, the shops are usually grouped by profession; thus one alley may be occupied by carpet sellers, another by goldsmiths and yet another by coppersmiths. In Tehrân, the bazaar is particularly lively with the constant coming and going of men loading and unloading an amazing variety of goods. The best way of visiting the bazaar is to go in by the 15th Khordâd Avenue entrance and to follow one of the two main alleys, the bâzâr-e Bozorg or the bâzâr-e Kaffâshhâ from which one can easily branch out into the maze of small side streets leading to the Friday and Emâm Khomeini mosques.

THE ADMINISTRATIVE AND BANKING QUARTERS

The ministries and other government offices, main branches of the large banks, the central post office and some of the foreign embassies (British, French, Italian and German) are located in an area to the north of the Golestân Palace and of Emâm Khomeini Avenue, around Ferdosi and Jomhuri-ye Eslâmi avenues.

The **Archaeological Museum** (muzeh-ye Irân Bâstân), which houses one of the most important collections of objects from both the pre-Islamic and Islamic periods, is located on Shâhid Yarjani Street, parallel to Khomeini Avenue. (Two other important collections are to be found in the Rezâ Abbâsi and Abgineh museums, see below). The museum was built in a style termed neo-Sasanian by the French architect André Godard, director of the Irânian Archeaological Service for nearly thirty years until 1960.

Begin your visit of the museum with the room to the right of the entrance in order to keep to the chronological order of the exhibits. The ground floor presents the pre-Islamic history of Irân, from the neolithic period to the Sasanian dynasty; it includes some very fine Neolithic pottery found at Tappeh-ye Sialk (fifth to first millennia BC); vases from Marlik, Susa, Choqâ Zanbil and Turang Tappeh; a copy of the famous Code of Hammurabi, dating from the second millennium BC, which was brought back from Babylon to Susa by an Elamite king (the original is in the Louvre Museum in Paris); Elamite vases made of tar from Susa (second millennium BC); Achaemenian bas-reliefs from Persepolis; a stone statue of the Achaemenian ruler Darius I, which was made in Egypt and brought back by his son Xerxes (end of the sixth century BC), found in Susa in 1972 ; a remarkable little lapis lazuli head of an Achaemenian prince; a bronze statue of a Parthian prince found at Shami (first or second century AD); a bas-relief of the Parthian king Artabanus V (beginning of the third century AD); and Sasanian mosaics from Bishapur, in Fârs (third century). Also in the collection of the museum is the treasury of Achaemenid and Sasanian gold and silver, which is not normally on public display.

Adjacent to this is the new building devoted to Islamic art; this contains some magnificent *mehrâb* decorations (carved stucco from Dâmghân, Rey and Esfahân from the 10th and 11th centuries, a marble *mehrâb* from Abarkuh, glazed tiles from Qom and Esfahân), carved wooden doors, a very fine membar from Fârs (14th century), as well as textiles, miniatures and illuminated manuscripts. There is also a model of the Tarik Khâneh Mosque in Dâmghân.

The museum is open Saturdays to Thursdays from 9 am to 12 pm and from 1 pm to 4 pm; on Fridays and holidays it is open from 8.30 am to 11 am only (tel 672016–6).

After leaving the Archeaological Museum, turn right along Si-e Tir Street towards Jomhuri-ye Eslâmi Avenue to get to the **Abgineh Museum of Glass and Ceramics** (at the corner of Jomhuri Avenue and Si-e Tir Street). Despite its small size, this museum is without doubt one of the best presented in Irân. If you have only a short amount of time in Tehrân, this is one place you should not miss. The building itself dates from the Qâjâr period; in the 1950s, it housed the Egyptian Embassy and was later bought by the Bank of Commerce before being turned into a museum in 1976 (it opened in 1980). The Abgineh Museum is interesting not just for the objects in it, which are of exceptional quality, but also for the general presentation of the pieces. The layout of the interior was designed by Italian museologists in a very modern style. In many rooms, each object is presented individually in a column-shaped case. It is a remarkable experiment, although some visitors may find that the modern presentation clashes with the turn of the century ceilings and floors, and with the fine spiral staircase in the hall.

The museum collections include some very fine glass, ceramic and crystal objects from the Achaemenian period to the 19th century, finds from excavations all over the country. In particular, there is a superb Achaemenian glass bowl on the ground floor and some very fine Kâshân ceramics on the first floor. Books, slides and postcards are on sale at the shop by the entrance. Open from 9 am to 5 pm every day except Mondays (tel 6456930).

Still in the same area, on Ferdosi Avenue, stands the large building of the main offices of the Melli Bânk. In its vaults are the **Irânian Crown Jewels** (muzeh-ye Javâherât), a vast collection of jewellery and precious and semi-precious stones of incalculable value, the result of centuries of war booty, inheritances and gifts, which were collected by the new Qâjâr dynasty from the 1790s onwards (see Literary Excerpt on page 113). The most famous of these jewels is undoubtedly the Dariâ-e Nur (Sea of Light), a 182-carat pink diamond, seen by the French jeweller Tavernier in the 17th century, and brought back from Delhi by Nâder Shâh in the 18th century. Another large diamond, the Koh-e Nur, Mountain of Light, was acquired by the British, severely cut down, and is now in the Tower of London.

The Mughal Peacock throne was also brought back from Delhi by Nâder Shâh, and was later broken up for its jewels; it is not the one on show in the Bânk Melli currently, which was ordered in the 18th century for one of Fath Ali Shah's wives, Tavus (Peacock). Among the myriad other treasures on show here are the Pahlavi Crown, made in 1924 by a jeweller from Bukhârâ and set with 3,380 diamonds, five emeralds, two sapphires, and 368 pearls on a red background; a gold belt with a 175 carat emerald; a globe weighing 40 kilos (88 pounds) and set with 51,000 precious stones; and cases full of stones, aigrettes, tiaras and brooches. If you have never seen what a handful of uncut diamonds looks like, this is the place to go.

Open for visits daily except Fridays and holidays, from 2 pm to 4.30 pm (tel 3110102–9). Needless to say, photography is not permitted inside the vault. Children under 15 are not allowed to enter.

To the east of Emâm Khomeini Avenue, near Vali-e Asr Avenue and Felestin Street, is the **Majlis** (Parliament) building, which used to house the Senate, and the **Marble Palace** (Takht-e Marmar), the residence of the last Shâh, now closed to the public.

Bahârestân Square, to the east of Emâm Khomeini Avenue, was once the site of a Qâjâr Palace but is now overlooked on the north side by the Ministry of Islamic Guidance and the **National Museum of Art** (muzeh-ye Honarhâ-ye Melli, entrance on Kemâl ol-Molk Street) which houses a very complete collection of Irânian art and handicrafts: marquetry (khâtam), miniatures, brocades, ceramics and mosaics. Open from 8 am to 3.30 pm, closed Thursdays and Fridays (tel 3116329).

To the east of the square is the **Shâhid Motahari Mosque** (ex-Sepahsâlâr Mosque).

Originally a *madraseh*, it was built between 1878 and 1890 and is one of the most successful examples of late Qâjâr architecture. Today, the building once again serves as a *madraseh* and is therefore closed to the public, but one may still see the tile-work decoration of the exterior walls with its floral motifs and figures so characteristic of Qâjâr art.

NORTH OF ENQELÂB AVENUE

At its westernmost end, Enqelâb-e Eslâmi Avenue (Avenue of the Revolution, ex-Shâh Rezâ) crosses the university quarter. Here it is lined with bookshops, some of which sell books in foreign languages. When the University of Tehrân was first built in 1930 on this avenue, it marked the northern limit of the city.

Directly behind the university, on the other side of Keshâvarz Boulevard, is the large Lâleh Park (Tulip Park) which includes within its grounds the Museum of Modern Art and the Carpet Museum. The **Museum of Modern Art** (muzeh-ye Honarhâ-ye Mo'âser, entrance on Kârgar Avenue, tel 655664), easily recognizable by the sculptures standing in the park, holds temporary exhibitions of contemporary Irânian and foreign artists. Open from 9 am to 12 pm and from 1 pm to 6 pm

every day. The **Carpet Museum** (muzeh-ye Farsh, at the corner of Kârgar and Dr Fâtemi avenues) houses a fine collection of carpets and kilim from all regions of Irân dating mostly from the 19th and 20th centuries, with a few older pieces. Open from 9 am to 5 pm, closed Tuesdays (tel 653027, 657707).

To the east of Keshâvarz Boulevard is Vali-ye Asr Square and the **Museum of Decorative Arts** (muzeh-ye Honarhâ-ye Tazini, 337 Karim Khân-e Zand Boulevard) which houses a collection of craft products from the 19th and 20th centuries (textiles, brocades, lacquerware, miniatures, carved woodwork) including inlaid furniture originally made for the Marble Palace in Tehrân. Open from 9 am to 5 pm, closed Mondays (tel 894380–4).

In the quarter known as Abbâs Âbâd, between the centre of town and Shemirân, is the **Rezâ Abbâsi Museum** (927 Dr Shari'ati Avenue, near the Resâlat Highway) which houses an astonishing collection of cultural objects dating back to Neolithic times. If you only have a single day in Tehrân, this is the museum to visit, due to the exceptional quality and variety of the objects on show—beware, however, that there are some fakes. Begin your visit on the third floor and work your way down if you want to keep to the chronological order of the exhibits. On the top floor are Neolithic pottery, Luristân bronzes from the ninth and tenth centuries BC, some superb Median and Achaemenian gold vases and jewellery, Parthian statuettes and Sasanian gold rhytons—drinking cups often in the form of an animal's head. Unfortunately, most of the labels are written in Persian only. The second floor is devoted to Islamic arts (bronzes, ceramics, tiles) with some particularly fine minâi from Kâshân and plates from Neishâpur. The first floor has a very good exhibition of miniatures and illuminated manuscripts, including illustrations from the *Shâhnâmeh*. Open from 9 am to 12 pm and 1 pm to 4 pm, closed Mondays (tel 863001–3).

Shemirân and the North of Tehrân

The northern suburbs of Tehrân, set on the mountain slopes some 800 metres (2,625 feet) above the centre of town—which at times is harly visible under its brown haze—have always been a much coveted residential area, the symbol of a social as well as a physical climb. Throughout its history, Tehrân's urban development has gradually progressed from south to north, from the plain to the higher slopes. Once a village completely separate from Tehrân, Shemirân is now a suburb, linked to the downtown area by the avenues built under Rezâ Shâh and by two new highways. It has a calm and rather select feel to it, far removed from the bustle of

'APPROACH TO TEHERAN'

The city itself was not visible, though we knew we could not be more than twenty miles distant, once we had come round the elbow of the hills at Karaj, and saw Demavend before us, the smooth white mountain, the beacon, soaring into the sky. Teheran must lie there, somewhere, in the dip. To the right glimmered a golden dome, far away; the mosque of Shah Abdul Azim, said someone, and little heaps of stones appeared like mole-heaps by the road, for in Persia, where you first catch sight of your place of pilgrimage, you must raise a heap of stones to the fufilment of your vow. I felt inclined to add my heap to the others, for it seemed to me incredible that I should at last be within walking distance of Teheran. But where was that city? A patch of green trees away to the left, a faint haze of blue smoke; otherwise nothing, only the open country, the mountains, the desert, and little streams in flood pouring at intervals across the road. It all seemed as forlorn and uninhabited as the loneliest stretches of Kurdistan. Yet there stood a gate, suddenly, barring the way; a gate of coloured tiles, a wide ditch, and a mud rampart, and a sentry stopping us, notebook in hand. Persian towns do surely spring upon one unawares, rising in their compact, walled circle out of the desert. But this, no doubt about it, was Teheran...

This country through which I have been hurled for four days has become stationary at last; instead of rushing past me, it has slowed down and finally stopped; the hills stand still, they allow me to observe them; I no longer catch but a passing glimpse of them in a certain light, but may watch their changes during any hour of the day; I may walk over them and see their stones lying quiet, may become acquainted with the small life of their insects and lichens; I am no longer a traveller, but an inhabitant. I have my own house, dogs, and servants; my luggage has at last been unpacked. The ice-box is in the kitchen, the gramophone on the table, and my books are on the shelves. It is spring; long avenues of judas trees have come into flower along the roads, the valleys are full of peach-blossom, the snow is beginning to melt on the Elburz. The air, at this altitude of nearly four thousand feet, is as pure as the note of a violin. There is everywhere a sense of oneness and of being at a great height; that sense of grime and over-population, never wholly absent in European countries, is wholly absent here; it is like being lifted up and set above the world on a great, wide roof—the plateau of Iran.

Vita Sackville-West, Passenger to Teheran, 1926

Vita Sackville-West, 1892–1962, was a British writer and gardener. *Passenger to Teheran* is dedicated to her husband Sir Harold Nicolson, a diplomat, politican and writer, with whom she travelled to Persia. This passage is of historical interest as a contrast to the polluted megapolis that Tehrân has become today.

the town centre. It is here that one finds the gardens of some of the foreign embassies, private parks, the International Trade Fair compound, the Pârk-e Mellat (Park of the Nation), which has become a popular meeting place for young people, and the large international hotels built in the 1970s, such as the Esteqlâl Hotel (ex-Hilton) and the Azâdi Grand Hotel (ex-Hyatt).

At the north end of Shemirân is the old Pahlavi royal residence, Sa'ad Âbâd, (majmue-ye Farhangi-ye Sa'ad Âbâd, entrance to the north of Tajrish Square, on Alborz Kuh Street) now turned into museums. Open to the public every day from 8 am to 4 pm, closed on national mourning days such as Ashura. The 18 palaces and residences of Sa'ad Âbâd, all dating from the 1930s, are scattered in a vast park of some 120 hectares (297 acres), landscaped in a Western style.

The **White Palace**, or Palace of the Nation, is the Shâh's old Summer Palace where he lived for three months of the year. Built by Rezâ Shâh in a style which was to become characteristic of his reign, it resembles more an administrative building than a palace. Fortunately, the tall columns of the front porch restore a certain regal air to it. However, the treasure-filled interior, belies the austerity of the exterior. The Persian carpets are the most exceptional quality, the best to be produced in the first half of the 20th century: woven specially for the palaces and to the exact measurements of each room, some have a surface area of over 100 square metres (1,076 square feet). The palace is tastefully decorated, without deliberate ostentation, so that the furniture and carpets can be fully appreciated. The last Shâh developed a taste for French culture and entrusted the interior decoration of the palace to a French designer. The curtains and much of the furniture are therefore French; the china comes from France and Germany, while the glass and crystalware are from Bohemia. Outside the palace, at the foot of the steps, stands an enormous pair of bronze boots, the only remains of a statue of Rezâ Shâh destroyed during the revolution.

The second palace open to the public is that of the Shâh's mother, known today as the **Palace of Admonition and Reversion**. The furnishings are similar to those in the Shâh's Palace, but the interior design of the building is entirely different: all three floors give directly onto a central well which forms the main hall. Here again, carpets, furniture, and china have been carefully selected.

A third palace has been turned into a **Military Museum**. Outside the building, in the park, stand various large modern war machines, including fighter planes. Inside, on the ground floor, is an exhibition of life-size model soldiers wearing uniforms from each dynasty since Achaemenian times, as well as several rooms of armour and weaponry from different periods, including some fine Safavid armour. The 20th century is well represented by a variety of guns and pistols, ranging from the Winchester to the Uzi.

Other buildings in the park open to the public are the Rajeat and Ibrat Palace, the Museum of Fine Arts (water colours, furniture), the Natural History Museum and the Ethnological Research Museum.

The park and museums of Sa'ad Âbâd are open from 8 am to 5 pm every day, (tel 282031–9). Cameras, handbags and shopping bags are not allowed inside the park and have to be left at the entrance.

The area known as **Niâvarân**, where the old summer residence of Fath Ali Shâh was located, is to the east of Sa'ad Âbâd on the edge of the city. Open to the public from 8 am to 4 pm, closed Thursdays and Fridays.

For those who wish to get away from the noise and heat of town, a short trip into the mountains around Tehrân is recommended. From the northern suburbs it is very easy to get into the Alborz. The simplest way is to take the cable car to **Mount Toshâl** (telekâbin-e Toshâl, tel 272733, leaves from Velenjak, north of Evin). The trip to the top takes about half an hour, with several stops on the way. Several paths lead from the top station, including one to the summit of Toshal (3,933 metres, 12,900 feet). Remember that whatever the temperature down in Tehrân, it is always much chillier at 3,000 metres, even in mid-summer. Other walks are also possible from Darband, behind Sa'ad Âbâd, where numerous little tea houses line the streams that flow down the mountainside.

EXCURSIONS FROM TEHRÂN

For those who have a bit more time in Tehrân, there are several interesting visits that can be made in the southern suburbs. The closest is to **Shahr-e Rey**, which was an important centre under the Achaemenians and remained so until the Mongol invasion in 1220. Only a single monument remains in Rey of this period, the funerary tower of Toghril Beg, built in 1139. Today, Rey is an industrial suburb with a lively bazaar in the centre of town. Next to it is the *emâmzâdeh* **of Abdol Azim**, a great-grandson of the Second Emâm, Emâm Hosein. The sanctuary, with its golden dome, is a very popular pilgrimage site. A second tomb in the same complex is that of Hamze, brother of Emâm Rezâ. Women must wear a *châdor* inside the compound (these can be hired at the entrance). The mausoleum of Rezâ Shâh, the first Pahlavi ruler, used to stand beside the *emâmzâdeh*, but was pulled down after the revolution and replaced with a public lavatory.

Inner courtyard of the câravânsarai of Deir-e Gachin founded by the Sasanians, and later restored by the Saljuqs and Safavids

Hazrat-e Masumeh Mosque, Qom

Near the edge of town, on a rock overlooking the spring of Cheshmeh Ali, are several carvings dating from the reign of the Qâjâr ruler Nâsereddin Shâh. They represent, in one case, the ruler sitting among his courtiers and, in another case, the king holding a falcon. It was here that the carpets of Tehrân used to be washed, as the water of the stream was renowned for its purity. Today, the stream still runs but its banks have been cemented over and the site has lost much of its former charm.

On the right hand side of the road from Rey to Varâmin are the ruins of a **Sasanian fire temple**, built on the top of a hill known as Tappeh Mil. Part of the surrounding walls and two of the arches of the temple are still standing, as well as a long tunnel which ran under the temple. The site has not yet been systematically excavated although there is talk of doing so in the near future.

About forty kilometres south of Tehrân is the small town of **Varâmin**. After the destruction of Rey by the Mongols, Varâmin became the regional centre until the 16th century when Tehrân superseded it. The **Friday Mosque** (masjed-e Jomeh) was built between 1322 and 1326, during the reign of the Il-Khân sultan Abu Said, son of Sultan Oljaitu Khodâbandeh whose mausoleum can be seen at Soltânieh. The mosque has been partially destroyed, and the west side has disappeared, but the original plan of a four-*eivân* courtyard can still be made out. The decoration is part brick, part glazed tiles. The complex brick motifs on the porch and on the dome of the *mehrâb* are particularly fine.

In the centre of town stands a Mongol funerary tower (finished in 1289) known as the tower of Ala od-Din. The only decoration of this circular brick tower is a Kufic inscription around the base of the dome (open mornings only, closed Thursdays).

Leaving Tehrân by the main road southeast towards Qom, one cannot fail to notice an imposing golden dome flanked by tall minarets near the cemetery of Behesht-e Zahrâ in the middle of the desert: this is the **tomb of Emâm Khomeini** (*haram-e motahar*). The mausoleum complex is now completed but there are plans not only to extend the new metro out here, but also to build a town around it, and also to open the much-discussed new international airport. At night, the whole compound is lit up by powerful projectors and can be seen for miles around. The interior is a vast hall measuring 100 metres long, with a carpeted marble floor; in the middle stands the tomb itself surrounded by grills. The size of the building easily absorbs the crowds that come here to pray, mostly people from the poorer areas of Tehrân or from the countryside. The atmosphere here is very different, however, from that of the *haram* at Qom or Mashhad: the children are free to run around and slide on the marble and families on a day's outing sit down to picnic quietly in a corner.

Between Rey and Qom stands **Deir-e Gachin**, one of the oldest and largest câravânsarais of Irân. Its ground plan forms a perfect square with each outer wall measuring 135 m; each corner is fortified with a round tower. Entering from the south through an 8 m high gate, the merchants would come into the huge inner courtyard with four *eivâns*. Around the courtyard stood 40 guestrooms, behind them 66 stables. The câravânsarai was built in the early Sasanian period, when a branch of the Silk Road linked Merv in today's Turkmenistan with Ctesiphon near present Baghdâd. It was restored under the Saljuqs and the Safavids.

About 300 m to the north-east of the câravânsarai stand the quite dilapidated ruins of another complex whose mud walls measure 250 x 100 m. Its original function is unclear, but since the name Deir-e Gachin means "Monastery of Chalk", it could have well been a Nestorian monastery. A rectangular room located in the east of the complex ends on its eastern side with a larger central apses and two smaller lateral ones. Pilasters and niches located along both longer walls strengthen the impression that this was a sacral room, possibly a church. But only excavations could prove that Deir-e Gachin was once a Christian monastery.

The holy town of **Qom** is only 154 kilometres (96 miles) south of Tehrân, on the road to Kâshân and Esfahân. Qom is not part of the Province of Tehrân but of Ostân-e Markazi, the central province, with its capital at Arâk. The early history of Qom is hazy but from the seventh century onwards, it became an important Shi'a centre, along with Rey and Kâshân. After the death in 816 of Fatima, the sister of Emâm Rezâ (the Eighth Emâm is buried in Mashhad), it became a pilgrimage site. The sacred precinct with its golden dome is located in the centre of town near the river. The entrance to the shrine is to be found in a small square, dominated by minarets and the main gateway. Non-Muslims are not permitted to go further than this gate and signs in both Persian and English remind one that photography is forbidden. The Safavid Friday Mosque (masjed-e Jomeh) nearby is also forbidden to non-Muslims. As a holy town and a theological centre, Qom has a high population of mullahs, and almost all the women in the streets wear a *châdor* rather than a simple scarf around their heads. It is very strongly recommended that foreign visitors act in as discreet and respectful a manner as possible. Even if the main monuments are out of bounds, a stroll in the streets of Qom can be very interesting. In particular, try the local speciality, called *sohân*, a flat, sweet biscuit made of germinated wheat flavoured with saffron and pistachios. One remarkable feature about Qom is the number of sweet shops, which appear to have almost overtaken the shops selling religious souvenirs.

Hazrat-e Masumeh Mosque, Qom

ISLAMIC CALLIGRAPHY

Calligraphy occupies a privileged place in Islamic culture. From the moment it reproduced and transmitted the Word of God in the Qur'ān, it acquired a sacred function. But very rapidly it was also employed for decorative ends in all social contexts. Metal bowls and vases, for example, are often decorated with a combination of floral scrolls and inscriptions which quote the verses of a well-known poet, express wishes of happiness and prosperity or list the titles of a ruler.

The Arabic system of writing, derived ultimately from the Syriac and the Nabatean, is characterized by a contrast between vertical lines and the horizontal base line formed by the links between the letters. The aesthetic potential of this system was exploited very early on and a large range of different scripts has evolved over the centuries. New styles are created by altering the proportions of each letter, either by extending or shortening the base line, by varying the slope of the vertical strokes, or by changing the curve of the loops which descend below the horizontal line. But calligraphers are not entirely free to play around as they wish with these elements and are restrained by very strict stylistic rules.

Among the numerous calligraphic styles which have developed, some are more common than others. A first very important category covers the so-called Kufic scripts, which are very angular and are used mainly in religious contexts, such as for reproductions of the Koran and for inscriptions in mosques. Among the different variants are Floriated Kufic, in which the vertical elements end in floral motifs, and square Kufic, which avoids all curved lines and is often made of different-coloured glazed brick ends.

The non-Kufic scripts are called 'cursive'. Naskh, which has a very regular and balanced appearance, has been widely used as an everyday writing style for reproducing texts. Thulth, on the other hand, has majestically extended and rounded letters, and may be written in lines so close to one another that elements of the letters intersect. This is a difficult style to master and requires a great deal of practice. From the 11th century, calligraphers developed a new cursive style known as Ta'liq, which joined together letters normally kept separate in the naskh style. A variant of this style called Nasta'liq (Naskh + Ta'liq) was created, and by the 15th century, and became the quintessentally Persian style, characterised by a perfect balance between horizontal, vertical and rounded elements. The elegance and lightness of the words on the page make it an ideal complement to a poem or book illustration.

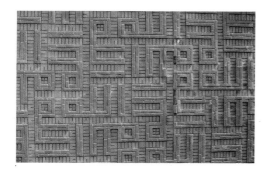

The Banâ'i Kufic style, composed only of straight lines. The blue tiles repeat the name of God to infinity. (Emâmzâdeh Mahruq, Neishâpur)

A form of Shikastah Ta'liq, a style designed for rapid writing which was mostly used in the Persian administration and gradually replaced Nasta'liq.
(Mausoleum of Omar Khayyâm, Neishâpur)

Thulth is frequently used in the decoration of mosques; the best examples are those of the Safavid calligrapher Ali Reza Abbassi, which can be seen in Isfahan and Mashhad.
(Emâmzâdeh Mahruq, Neishâpur)

© Airphoto International

THE NORTHEAST: THE PROVINCES OF SEMNÂN AND KHORÂSÂN

SEMNÂN PROVINCE

Despite the size of the province, the population of Semnân is very heavily concentrated in the north, along the Tehrân–Mashhad road. To the south of this road lies the Dasht-e Kavir, the salt desert, where the extremely hot and arid climate prevents much permanent human settlement. The capital of the province, **Semnân** (200 kilometres (124 miles) from Tehrân, was once an important stop along the trade route between eastern and western Persia which enabled caravans to skirt round the desert in relative safety. Due to its favourable location, Semnân has always made a quick recovery from the numerous invasions and raids that have swept through it. Today, Semnân has the appearance of a rather small provincial town. Its most interesting monument is the **Friday Mosque**, built in 1425, which still contains an attractive carved stucco *mehrâb*. Next to the mosque is an 11th- or 12th-century Saljuq minaret. The **Emâm Khomeini Mosque** nearby is a much more recent. Built by Fath Ali Shâh in the early 19th century, it is one of the more successful examples of Qâjâr architecture. Its tiled entrance *pishtâq* and *mehrâb* with stalactites are particularly fine.

About a hundred kilometres (62 miles) from Semnân, on the road to Mashhad, is the small town of **Dâmghân**, famous for its early examples of Islamic architecture, dating from the Abbâsid and Saljuq periods. Dâmghân was first settled in the prehistoric period and important excavations have been carried out a few kilometres out of town at Tappeh-ye Hissar (fourth millennium BC). Dâmghân is very probably the site of the Hellenistic town of Hecatompylos, the 'City of a Hundred Gates', first a Seleucid centre and then the capital of the Arsacid Parthians under Tiridates I (around 200 BC). Hecatompylos was located on one of the main trade routes linking Central Asia to the Mediterranean ports, and which passed through Merv and Ecbatana (Hamadân), a location which ensured the prosperity of the town. Like Semnân, Dâmghân was also repeatedly destroyed during the Turkish and Mongol invasions, and has suffered from a number of devastating earthquakes. Despite this, several interesting ancient buildings still remain in the centre of town.

The first of these is the **Tarik Khâneh Mosque**, one of only a handful of early Abbâsid buildings in Irân. It was built between 750 and 789 and thus predates the mosque at Nâ'in, which has a similar plan to that of the Tarik Khâneh but was built at the same time as the first Friday Mosque at Esfahân. The Tarik Khâneh is a hypostyle mosque: its central courtyard is surrounded by single arcades on three sides, and by a portico of three rows of six columns along the *qebleh* wall (a model of the mosque can be seen in the Archaeological Museum in Tehrân). The columns are massive structures made of baked brick. The arcades are of particular interest to the specialist as their shape is reminiscent of Sasanian architecture. In fact, the building techniques used in this mosque and those seen in a Sasanian building excavated nearby at Tappeh-ye Hissar have many common factors. The Tarik Khâneh is therefore considered to be representative of the transition period between pre-Islamic and Islamic architecture in Irân. The mosque has been renovated several times, most notably during the Saljuq dynasty (11th century), but it has kept its original simple form and has remained undecorated. Near the mosque stands a minaret, built in the middle of the 11th century and entirely decorated in geometric and calligraphic brick motifs. In 1991 and 1992, the mosque was closed to the public while restoration work was being carried out, but is now open to the public every day.

The Saljuq period is also represented in Dâmghân by two funerary towers. The first, the **Pir-e Alamdâr**, was built in 1026, while the second, the **Chehel Dokhtar** (Forty Daughters), was built in 1054. Both are circular brick towers of similar shape. Only the upper part of each tower is decorated with geometric motifs and calligraphic inscriptions in brick.

In the small town of **Bastâm**, near Shâhrud, where a secondary road from Gorgân and the Caspian coast joins the main road to Mashhad, stands the mausoleum complex of **Shaykh Bâyezid Bastâmi**, a well-known ninth-century mystic. The present buildings, covered in blue glazed tiles, were restored during the reigns of the Mongol Il-khân sultans Ghâzân (1296–1303) and Oljaitu (1303–1316). The mausoleum, recognizable by its conical turquoise roof, is built next to a mosque which contains a fine *mehrâb* from Ghâzân's reign. The minaret, which predates the restorations, is a good example of Saljuq art (1120). The complex also includes a second funerary tower, the *emâmzâdeh* Muhammad, similar in shape to the first one.

RUMI

Bliss—
The instant
spent seated
on the terrace,
me next to you
two forms and
two faces
with just one soul,
me and you

The chatter of birds
The garden's murmur
flowing
like a fountain of youth
as we stroll
through roses,
me and you
The stars of the firmament, bent low to look over us
Let's eclipse them, shine like the moon,
me and you

Me and you join,
beyond Me
beyond you
in joy
happy, released from delire and delusion
Me and you, laughing like this,
reach dimensions where celestial birds suck sugary cubes
Magical! me and you, here,
in our corner of the earth,
but wafting on airs of Iraq and Khorasan,
me and you
In one form here on earth
in other forms in paradise,
eternal, sunk in fields of sugar,
me and you

Jalâl od-Din Rumi (1207–1273), translated by Franklin Lewis, from Rumi,
Past and Present, East and West, *published by Oneworld, Oxford, 2000*

KHORÂSÂN PROVINCE

Khorâsân is the largest Irânian province and has a surface area of some 300,000 square kilometres (115,830 square miles), but its population totals only just over five million, of which half live in the Mashhad and Neishâpur area. Khorâsân used to be the easternmost province of Persia—its name means 'land of the rising sun'—and included Afghânistân and Bactria as far the Amu Darya river. It was through this province that the numerous invasions from the Central Asian steppes reached the Irânian plateau. Not surprisingly, Khorâsân's history has been dogged by frequent changes of ruler. With the weakening of Abbâsid power in Baghdâd, several local dynasties established themselves in Khorâsân (the Tahirids, Saffârids and Sâmânids) before the Saljuq Turks succeeded in uniting the region and settled in Neishâpur. In the 11th century, Khorâsân became the centre of intellectual life in Irân, but after the breakup of the Saljuq Empire, it was overrun by Khwarazm, a Central Asian Turkish state. In 1221, Khwarazm was defeated by Genghis Khân and was to remain under Mongol control until 1337 when another local dynasty, the Sardebarians, proclaimed their independence in the northwest of the province. This dynasty lasted only a short period of time and, in 1380, Tamerlane conquered the entire region. Khorâsân benefitted greatly from Timurid rule, particularly during the reign of Shâh Rokh (1405–1447), a keen patron of the arts, whose wife Gohâr Shâd commissioned the superb mosque in Mashhad that bears her name. Timurid rule in Khorâsân was replaced by that of the Safavids at the beginning of the 16th century. After its incorporation into the large Safavid Empire, the history of the province follows closely that of Irân as a whole.

The main road which crosses Khorâsân from east to west and links Tehrân with Mashhad passes through the towns of Sabzevâr and Neishâpur. Near the former, a solitary minaret, built around 1112, stands out in the plain. It marks the location of the ancient city of Khosrogerd, destroyed by the Mongols in 1220. Sabzevâr, very close to Khosrogerd, was rebuilt after the invasion and briefly became the capital of the local Shi'a Sardebarian dynasty (1337–1381).

Today, **Neishâpur** is a small provincial town containing only a few historical monuments, but it was once one of the most glorious centres of all Persia. Founded in the third century AD under the Sasanians, it was the seat of the Arab governors of the region at the beginning of the Islamic period. Built at the foot of the Binalud Hills on the caravan route between Central Asia and the Irânian Plateau, it quickly became a flourishing trading town and, in the 11th century under the Saljuqs, one of the intellectual centres of Sunni Islam. It was renowned in particular for its Sufi masters and its *nezâmiyeh*, one of a series of *madraseh* founded by the great vizir Nezâm ol-Molk. One of the most famous of the teachers of the *nezâmiyeh* was the theologian al-Ghazâli (1058–1111), known for his attempt to integrate Sufism into orthodox Islam.

However, this glorious period in Neishâpur's history was short-lived and the city fell rapidly into decline in the 12th century after a series of disasters befell it: invasions by Turkish tribes, internal wars, earthquakes and finally the catastrophic arrival of Mongol troops in 1221 and the massacre of the city's entire population. Neishâpur was later rebuilt but it never regained its former position and was supplanted by Mashhad.

The great majority of Neishâpur's ancient buildings have been destroyed. Only a handful of mausoleums remain in the outskirts of the modern town, near which more recent commemorative monuments have been erected. The most famous of these is undoubtedly **Omar Khayyâm's tomb**, built in 1934 in the gardens of the *emâmzâdeh* Mahruq, a few kilometres southeast of town. In the West, Omar Khayyâm (1048–c.1125) is best known as a poet, due to Edward Fitzgerald's translations of his works published in the 19th century, but in Irân, Khayyâm is remembered foremost as an astronomer and mathematician. Born in Neishâpur, he served at the court of Sultan Malek Shâh (1072–1092) and worked, along with other mathematicians, at the revision of the calender and the construction of an observatory. His celebrity as a mathematician is due to his treatise on algebra in which he demonstrated how to solve cubic equations by both algebraic and geometric methods. Khayyâm was a contemporary of the great vizir Nezâm ol-Molk, but the legend that these two men were students with Hasan Sabbâh, the founder of the Assassins (see page 232) seems to have no historical basis. Nezâm ol-Molk (died 1092) was some thirty years older than Khayyâm and no record suggests that Khayyâm and Hasan Sabbâh ever met.

Khayyâm's poetry is highly controversial, and although several hundred *rubâ'iyat* have traditionally been attributed to him, it is very difficult to determine exactly which were indeed written by him. The first mention of Khayyâm as a poet dates from half a century after his death and there is little reason to believe that he ever collected his poems into a divan (poetry anthology) during his lifetime. The Mongol destruction of the great Islamic centres of learning in Khorâsân, and in particular of the libraries, has undeniably contributed to the loss of a large part of pre-13th-century Persian literature, and perhaps also of poems written by Khayyâm.

It is the subject matter of the works attributed to Khayyâm which attracted strong criticism from orthodox thinkers, especially from the numerous opponents of 'Greek thought', first and foremost the famous philosopher al-Ghazâli. Khayyâm, a disciple of Avicenna, was considered too materialistic and incapable of following Sufi spiritual paths, to the extent that the poet Farid od-Din Attâr (see below) tells of a vision he had in which a shamed and confused Khayyâm is refused entry to heaven because he lacks the spiritual qualities needed to appear before God. Two themes running through Khayyâm's work are pessimism and scepticism, in particular a profound doubt in resurrection and life after death, a fundamental belief of orthodox Islam.

Khayyâm's mausoleum is a modern structure said to resemble the shape of an inverted wine cup. Wine, which gives Man temporary respite from his doubts, and the cup, a fragile and ephemeral creation of Man, are two further themes which appear constantly in Khayyâm's poems. The inside walls of the mausoleum are decorated with a mosaic work of floral designs, while couplets by Khayyâm are reproduced on the outside.

Near Khayyâm's tomb, in the same garden, is the *emâmzâdeh* **Mohammad Mahruq**, a 17th century Safavid building commemorating one of the Prophet's descendants who died as a martyr.

In a small park nearby stands the tomb of **Farid od-Din Attâr**, one of the greatest Irânian Sufi poets, who was born in Neishâpur a decade or so after Omar Khayyâm's death, and who died around 1220, possibly during the Mongol invasion. Attâr is known principally for his *masnavi*, long, imaginative mystical poems written in a simple style, such as *Ilahi-nâmeh* (The Book of God) and *Mantiq al-Tair* (The Conference of the Birds). This last work describes in allegorical form the journey of the birds in search of the Simurgh, a mythical beast which represents God. Attâr is also the author of an important work of prose, *Tadhkirat al-Auliya* (The Memorials of the Saints), a collection of biographies of sufi shaykhs.

The mausoleum itself is an octagonal building with a domed roof and a tall drum. Next to it is a second mausoleum, decorated with floral mosaics, built in memory of a modern painter, **Kemâl ol-Molk** (died in 1938). The architect, who also designed Omar Khayyâm's tomb, has reinterpreted the traditional *eivân* in a very creative manner by placing four *eivân* back to back with arches connecting above the tomb.

About 30 kilometres (19 miles) from Neishâpur, on the road to Mashhad, is the small town of **Qadamgâh** (the Place of the Footstep), where one can visit a sanctuary set in a charming garden, built around a stone bearing the footprints of Emâm Rezâ. (Since attempts by some over-enthusiastic pilgrims to take the stone away, it has been set into a wall inside the building.) The sanctuary, built during the Safavid period in the 17th century and later restored, is decorated with *haft rangi* tiles of high quality, particularly the relief calligraphy inside, and with paintings on the walls and ceiling. Beside the mausoleum is an old câravânsarai built by Shâh Abbâs and still very well preserved. The large, elevated arched niches around the central courtyard served as rooms for travellers while their animals filled the yard. Behind the arcades, a covered corridor with similar arches were used as winter quarters.

Nearer Mashhad, at **Sangbast**, stands the mausoleum of Arslân Jâzeb, built in the 11th century. This is a domed building with geometric and calligraphic brick designs inside; note in particular the simplicity of the squinch arches here which allow for a smooth transition from a square plan to a circular one.

MASHHAD

Mashhad is Irân's holiest city, visited each year by more than 14 million pilgrims. Its history is closely linked to that of its main shrine, the tomb of the Eighth Emâm of the Shi'a tradition, Emâm Rezâ. Before his death in 809, the Caliph Hârun al-Rashid divided the Abbâsid Empire into two, giving half to each of his two sons. In 816, Caliph Ma'mun, ruler of the eastern region, wanted to make the Eighth Emâm his heir and invited him to travel to the capital, Merv (near present-day Mary, in the Republic of Turkmenistan). The Emâm was at first wary but eventually accepted the invitation and made his way to Khorâsân. While resting in the village of Sanâbâd, he died suddenly after eating some grapes (or pomegranates, depending on the version of the story). Caliph Ma'mun had the Emâm buried in Sanâbâd beside the tomb of his own father, Hârun al-Rashid. Word spread that the Emâm had been poisoned by the caliph, and his tomb, known as *mashhad* or 'place of martyrdom', soon became a Shi'a pilgrimage site. In 994, the tomb was destroyed by Saboktagin, founder of the Ghaznavid dynasty and a devout Sunni, but was rebuilt by his son Mahmud in 1009. In the 13th century, both town and mausoleum were damaged during raids of nomad Ghuzz Turks but Mashhad soon recovered and continued to prosper, finally becoming the capital of Khorâsân in the 15th century. Shâh Rokh (1405–1447), the son of Tamerlane, enlarged the mausoleum, and his wife Gohâr Shâd commissioned the building of a mosque next to it (built between 1405–1417).

During the Shi'a Safavid dynasty, Mashhad became one of the most important Shi'a pilgrimage centres as the holy cities of Mecca, Kerbalâ and Najaf were in enemy territory under Ottoman Sunni domination. In the 17th and 18th centuries,

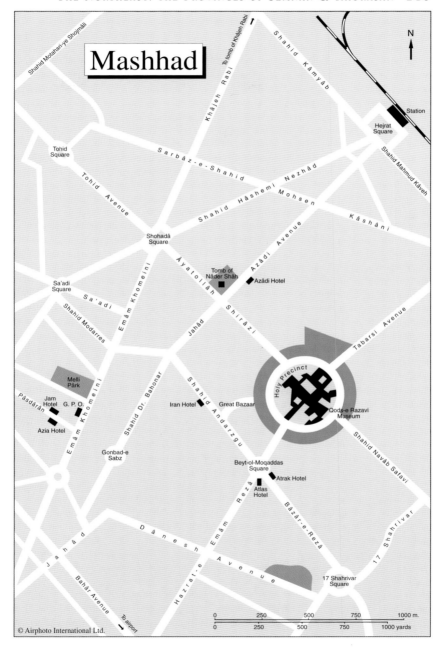

Mashhad

© Airphoto International Ltd.

Mashhad was attacked several times by Uzbek and Afghân troops, although the shrine was never damaged. In 1736, Nâder Shâh established his capital at Mashhad and, although a Sunni himself, he made generous donations to the town and to the mausoleum.

Under Rezâ Shâh, Mashhad was modernized and several wide avenues were built in the old quarter as well as a circular boulevard around the holy precinct. In the past twenty years, the population of the town has grown considerably, from half a million to over two million inhabitants, including a large community of Afghân refugees—some of whom are slowly returning to Afghânistân, although many will undoubtedly remain now that they have made themselves a living in Irân. Mashhad is currently the second biggest industrial centre in the country, and this economic importance is reflected in the bustling activity that is so characteristic of its streets; it is an atmosphere very different from the quieter, more provincial religious centre of Qom.

The goal of the thousands of pilgrims who arrive each day, and indeed the main attraction in Mashhad, is the tomb of Emâm Rezâ, in the centre of town, not far from the station, at the junction of Tabarsi and Âyatollâh Shirâzi avenues. The holy precinct, the *haram-e motahar*, is set inside a vast circular boulevard. The various constructions on the outside of this boulevard are soon to be pulled down and will be replaced by public buildings such as hospitals, and hostels for the pilgrims.

THE HOLY PRECINCT (HARAM-E MOTAHAR)

The tomb of Emâm Rezâ and the buildings that are connected to it (including mosques, *madraseh*, libraries, museums and administrative offices) form the only complex of its kind in Irân. A visit to the compound, especially at night when it is lit by projectors, is an unforgettable experience. However, non-Muslim tourists, particularly in groups, are allowed only limited access to the area and are not permitted to enter many of the buildings and inner courtyards. During religious festivals and important pilgrimages, visits for non-Muslims may be curtailed or temporarily suspended. Photography is discouraged inside the precinct and women must wear a *châdor*.

Entering the precinct from the west, along Avenue Âyatollâh Shirâzi, one arrives at the **sahn-e Atiq**, the 'old court', paved in black stone. In the centre of it stands the Golden Fountain (saqqâkhâne-ye Zarin) built in the reign of Nâder Shâh. In the north and south façades of the court are two large *eivân*; the north one, built by Shâh Abbâs in the 17th century, supports an older minaret, dating from the reign of

Shâh Tahmâsp (16th century). The south *eivân*, or *eivân* Talâ-ye Ali Shir Navâ'i, named after the Timurid vizir and Uzbek poet who built it in the 15th century, was restored under Nâder Shâh when it was given its present golden, mirrored frontage.

To the southeast of the courtyard are three *madraseh*, the *madraseh* Parizâd, Do Dar and Bâlâsar; next to the latter stands a mosque of the same name. The Nava'i *eivân* leads to the Tohidkhâneh, the 'Place of the Unification', and then to the holiest site of all, the **tomb of Emâm Rezâ**, which can be seen from the courtyard through a grille (entry to the shrine is strictly forbidden to non-Muslims). The oldest parts of the tomb are said to date back to the 12th century, but there have been numerous restorations and renovations and the present building is an amalgam of different styles: the tombstone itself dates from the reign of Shâh Abbâs while the solid gold chandelier was a gift from Shâh Rokh (1418). The shrine is covered by a large golden dome, rebuilt under Shâh Tahmâsp in 1675.

To the south of the mausoleum is **Gohâr Shâd's Mosque**, by far the most beautiful building in the entire precinct. It was built between 1405 and 1418 by the Shirâzi architect Qavâm od-Din for Gohâr Shâd, the wife of Shâh Rokh (1405–1447). This is the best preserved of all the buildings that Gohâr Shâd commissioned, most of which were in the Timurid capital, Herat. It has a classic plan, with a square courtyard surrounded by four *eivân* and arcades entirely decorated with blue tiles. The south *eivân*, flanked by two minarets, has a turquoise dome with yellow inscriptions. According to Shi'a tradition, the membar next to the *mehrâb* is the one on which the Mahdi will sit when he returns for the Judgement. The decoration of the mosque is characterized by the extraordinarily high quality of the workmanship. The finesse of the motifs, the elegance of the calligraphy, the alternate use of matt and glazed bricks and particularly the harmony of the whole, reflect the genius of the architect. But the most successful feature is perhaps the decoration of the interior of the south *eivân* and the *mehrâb*, where complex but extraordinarily fine floral designs set on a light ground form a striking contrast to the blue exterior.

To the east of the mausoleum a street leads to the **sahn-e Jadid** or New Courtyard, built by Fath Ali Shâh around 1818 with a very attractive *eivân* in the west façade (*eivân* Talâ-ye Fath Ali Shâh).

The **Qods-e Razavi Museum** (the entrance is on the circular boulevard near Avenue Shâhid Navab Safavi) contains objects of various origins, most of which were gifts made to the shrine, including some magnificent carpets, ceramics, Safavid weapons, Koran lecterns and the old gilt doors of the shrine.

(Following pages) *The golden dome above the tomb of Emâm Rezâ, Mashhad, 17th century.*

There are several other interesting buildings to visit in Mashhad outside the holy precinct, some of which are located just out of the town centre. To the southeast of the circular boulevard is the **Great Bazaar**, the *bâzâr-e Bozorg*; on the first floor are the shops of the turquoise dealers. The area around Mashhad and Neishâpur is known for the quality of its turquoise and turquoise mining has been a major industry here for centuries. In the bazaar, you can watch the stones being cut and polished. If you are buying, be careful to distinguish between synthetic and real turquoise, and remember that, despite what you will be told, turquoise is not cheaper in Mashhad than on the European market. The entrance *pishtâq* and minaret of the old **Mosque of the 72 Martyrs** (previously the Shâh's Mosque), built in the 14th or 15th century, is also to be found in the bazaar. Today it houses the offices of the Pasdaran organization and is therefore closed to the public.

A bit further west, on Avenue Shâhid Dr Bahonar, in the middle of a square, stands the **Gonbad-e Sabz**, or Green Dome, a Safavid mausoleum (partially rebuilt later) which contains the body of a Sufi shaykh, Mohammad Hakim Mo'men.

Further north along the same avenue (now Avenue Azâdi), at the junction with Avenue Âyatollâh Shirâzi, is a small park and the **tomb of Nâder Shâh** (1736–1747), a modern 20th-century building with a small adjoining museum of weapons and other 18th-century objects. The tomb is easily spotted by its large statue of the ruler on horseback.

On the other side of the holy precinct, on Boulevard Mosallâ, is a *mosallâ*, an open-air gathering place consisting only of a *mehrâb* chamber and an *eivân*, without a courtyard and side walls. The *mosallâ* is dated to 1677 and is still decorated with the original tilework on the outer wall. It is currently under repair and is closed to the public.

EXCURSIONS FROM MASHHAD

A few kilometres north of Mashhad is the **mausoleum of Khâjeh Rabi**, one of the first Shi'a saints, a disciple of Emâm Ali, whose tomb was built between 1617 and 1622 by Shâh Abbâs. Its shape is similar to that of the Hasht Behesht Palace in Esfahân, built about fifty years later: here the four deep *eivân* lead to a central domed room decorated with tiles and paintings which still retain their rich colours. The tile designs are close to those at Qadamgâh (see above). The very fine inscriptions are the work of Ali Rezâ Abbâsi, one of the most famous Persian calligraphers of the Safavid period. The park around the mausoleum has now become a cemetery for the martyrs of the Irân–Iraq war.

The small town of **Tus**, about 30 kilometres (19 miles) north of Mashhad, was once the capital of the region before it was superseded by Mashhad. The Turkish and Mongol invasions, as well as its proximity to the great city of Mashhad, contributed to its decline and today Tus is mostly known for being the native town of Ferdosi, the author of the Irânian national epic, the *Shâhnâmeh*, and of Nezâm ol-Molk, the great Saljuq vizir. **Ferdosi's tomb** is a modern construction built in the second half of the 20th century and composed of various architectural elements borrowed from the Achaemenian period. The overall shape of the tomb is reminiscent of Cyrus the Great's mausoleum at Pasargadae; to this the architect has added capitals from Persepolis and the winged symbol of Ahura Mazda. In a room dug underneath the tomb a series of modern bas-reliefs illustrate a few episodes of the *Shâhnâmeh*.

Just south of Tus stands another tomb, **boq'eh-ye Hâruniye**, which is attributed, according to local tradition, to the Caliph Hârun al-Rashid who died here in 809. The shape of the building, however, suggests a rather later date, perhaps 14th century.

From Mashhad, it is possible to continue by road either to the north, and on to the Caspian coast, or south along the Afghân border into Sistân and Baluchestân. Those taking the first of these routes can make a short detour to the village of **Râdkân** (before reaching Quchân, turn right off the main road at Seyyed Âbâd), to see a 13th-century Mongol funerary tower. It is 25 metres (82 feet) tall, and decorated on the outside with brick and tile designs.

Driving on the ancient trading route linking Mashhad and Neishâpur with Merv in the direction of Sarakhs, the border town with Turkmenistan, one arrives after 70 km at the **câravânsarai of Robat-e Mahi** which is visible on the left side of the road. To reach it, cross the railway line and walk for about 10 min. Floral elements and calligraphy made out of chalk mixed with sand decorate its brick walls. A 1.5 to 2 m high pile of rubble indicates that the câravânsarai has never been excavated.

Another 60 km (40 miles) to the east, turn at the village of Shurlaq to the right and after 6 km (4 miles) one reaches the huge **câravânsarai of Robat-e Sharaf** which was founded in 1114 by Sultan Sanjar's minister Sharaf od-Din Vadjih ol-Molk on the ruins of an older câravânsarai. The total complex measures 110 x 75 m and is surrounded by 6 m high brick walls fortified with 6 round towers. It consists of two parts: the forecourt with three small mosques and the quarters for average travellers and the larger, square quarter with three cisterns and the restrooms for the more wealthy merchants. These latter rooms and the mosques are lavishly decorated with stucco ornaments. The place is currently being excavated and restored.

NORTHWEST IRÂN

0   50   100 Kilometres

0   50   100 Miles

TURKMENISTAN

C a s p i a n   S e a

Bandar-e Anzali
Kiyâshahr
Rasht
Lahijân
Rudsar
Râmsar
Tonekâbon
Châlus
Nur
Mahmud Âbâd
Kenâr Daryâ
Bâbol Sar
Behshahr
Kord Kuy
Gomishân
Bandar-e-Torkaman
Pol
Gonbad-e Qâbus
dbâr
owshân
Qazvin
Tâkestân
hâvand
Estehârd
Karâj
Eslâmshahr
TEHRÂN
Shahr-e Rey
Varâmin
Firuzkuh
Bâbol
Âmol
Pol-e-Sefid
Sâri
Qâ'emshahr
Emâmrud
Qosheh
Semnân
Sorkheh
Sâveh
fresh
Qom
Salafchegân
Namak Lake
Arak
Delijân
Kâshân
D A S H T - E - K A V I R

A L B O R Z   M O U N T A I N S

International Ltd.

THE CASPIAN COAST

The two coastal provinces of Gilân and Mâzanderân in the north of the country present an astonishing contrast to the vast desert lands slightly further south. The Alborz Mountains which separate the plateau from the coast, and which rise to over 3,658 metres (12,000 feet), act as a barrier preventing the moisture from the Caspian from entering inland. Although Tehrân is only 115 kilometres (71 miles) away from the sea, it receives on average six times less rainfall than the coastal towns. As a result, while the southern flanks of the Alborz are almost entirely bare of vegetation, its northern slopes are covered in thick forests, which are being cut down, and rice paddies, which are being built on. The hot, humid climate of the coast generates thick mists which cling to the hills almost all year round.

The Irânian coast of the Caspian stretches for 630 kilometres (391 miles) from Astârâ in the west, on the border with the Republic of Azerbaijân, to the Bandar-e Torkman region in the east, near the Republic of Turkmenistan. Over such a distance, the vegetation and crops, as well as the ethnic groups, are naturally far from homogenous. The western province, Gilân, is mountainous and its population is concentrated in the plain of the Sefid Rud delta, around the provincial capital of Rasht. Gilân has remained relatively isolated through the centuries and its inhabitants have developed their own customs and their own dialect, known as Gilaki. Mâzanderân is much larger and geographically more varied than Gilân. A large part of the province is taken up by the Alborz Range, leaving only a narrow coastal strip in the west, which is being developed with wall-to-wall holiday chalets. Around Bâbol and Sâri, however, this widens to become a plain which eventually joins the vast Turkoman Steppes in the region of Gonbad-e Qâbus. Unlike Gilân, this eastern region has been more open to influences from Central Asia. It is the land of the Turkoman, a now mainly sedentary nation, but one which is proud of its nomadic past and which has kept its old traditions alive, particularly the breeding of horses and the manufacture of carpets.

GILÂN PROVINCE

One of the more interesting trips to be done in Irân from the geographical point of view is to cross the Alborz Range by foot or by car, from the plateau to the coast. In addition to often spectacular scenery, the most striking feature of the drive is the speed with which the transition from a desert climate to an almost sub-tropical one occurs. From Tehrân, the road to Gilân passes through Qazvin and Rudbâr from where it follows the course of the Sefid Rud to Rasht. From Rudbâr, the vegetation, which until then is sparse, suddenly becomes much denser. As one progresses towards the coast, the olive groves give way to terraced rice paddies and then to tea plantations.

The close proximity of Russia has had a strong influence on the history of Gilân, and Rasht, the provincial capital, has been occupied on several occasions by the Russian army, the last time at the end of World War II. In the 17th century, the town was destroyed by a Cossack leader. At the beginning of the 19th century, when fishing rights off the south coast of the Caspian were granted to Russia, an important Russian trade centre was set up at Bandar-e Anzali, the main port north of Rasht.

Rasht has become an important industrial centre, particularly for the processing of agricultural products. Until the 20th century, the town was known for its silk, but this activity has almost completely disappeared. Today, thanks to the road link with Tehrân, Rasht has become one of the favourite weekend resorts of the Tehrânis. However, it has few attractions for the sightseer other than the museum which contains a collection of local archaeological finds.

The small town of **Lâhijân**, set at the foot of the mountains and famous for its tea, is much more interesting. It has succeeded in preserving some of the old wooden houses with their open-work galleries and sloping tiled roofs. The **Chahâr Olyâ Mosque** (Mosque of the Four Guardians), more correctly a mausoleum, is built in the same style as the local houses. Just outside town stands a small but attractive mausoleum, built in 1419 for Shaykh Zâhed. Its unusual pyramid-shaped roof, decorated with turquoise and yellow tiles, is visible from the road.

MÂZANDERÂN PROVINCE

In its western part, Mâzanderân Province is geographically quite similar to Gilân, but the climate becomes gradually drier further east—although still receiving two or three times the rainfall of Tehrân—and the crops consequently change, with orchards of fruit trees replacing the tea plantations. In western Mâzanderân are two popular resorts: Râmsar, with a luxury hotel built in the Shâh's time, and Châlus, where the Hotel Enqelab, probably the best hotel in the country at present, is located. A mountain expressway leads directly from Châlus to Tehrân (202 kilometres, 125 miles).

The small town of **Amol**, set slightly inland west of Sâri, the ninth century capital of the province of Tabarestân, a province which corresponded more or less to present-day Mâzanderân. Amol declined after the Mongol conquests and has little to show today of its past. Its main monument is the mashhad-e Mir-e Bozorg, the founder of the Mar'asahi Seyyed Dynasty, built at the order of Shâh Abbâs I (1587–1629) and which has been restored as offices for the *miras farhangi* (Cultural Heritage organisation). This sanctuary is covered by a red brick dome, once decorated with blue tiles. Nearby is the small tomb tower of the 14th century Shi'a theosopher Seyyed Heidar Amoli.

A few kilometres from Amol is the town of **Bâbol**, once an important river port linked to Bâbolsar, the main trading outlet on the coast. In Bâbol is a 15th-century funerary tower built for Sultan Mohammad Tâher in a style similar to that of the towers in Sâri.

Sâri, the capital of Mâzanderân Province, is also connected by road to Tehrân but is much less developed than Rasht, with fewer tourists. Sâri has a long history and is said to have been the capital of Sasanian Tabarestân before the Arab conquest. Important finds in the area of Sasanian gold and silver artefacts support this theory.

Turkomans water their horses, Qal'eh Tapeh Sheikh, Mâzanderân Province

The Caspian Coast, near Bandar-e Torkman

The main sites in Sâri are two 15th-century funerary towers in the town centre, near the bazaar. The first, the *emâmzâdeh* Yahyâ, is a somewhat austere circular building with a conical roof, a shape characteristic of the region. The second, the borj-e Soltân Zein al-Abedin, is a square construction still bearing a few traces of the original blue decorative tilework. Outside town, to the east, stands another tower, built around 1491, known as the *emâmzâdeh* Abbâs, which commemorates a nephew of Emâm Hosein.

Halfway between Sâri and Bandar-e Torkman, in the small town of **Behshahr**, are the remains of a Safavid palace built by Shâh Abbâs in 1612 for his mother, which formed part of a palatial complex set in large landscaped gardens. The whole complex was severely damaged by the Turkish invasions and only this one building, known as the Safiâbâd Palace, located on the crest of a hill, still remains. It is smaller and much simpler than the contemporary palaces in Esfahân. Unfortunately, the building can no longer be visited, as a military base has been set up on the hill.

From the Bay of Gorgân and Bandar-e Torkman lies a vast fertile plain, caught between the mountains in the south and the Turkoman desert (*Torkaman-e sahrâ*) to the north. Further east, begin the steppes which stretch into Central Asia, the land of the Turkomans. The town of **Gorgân**, once known as Astarâbâd, occupies a key position in this border region between the settled fertile coastal plains and the steppes. Set at the foot of the Alborz Range, Gorgân became an important caravan post and the main market town for the nomadic Turkomans, a meeting point of two completely opposed ways of life. But because of its proximity to the steppes, it was also raided on numerous occasions by the nomads, particularly in the 19th century. Today, Gorgân is a busy provincial town with a lively and colourful bazaar.

In the centre of Gorgân, in the bazaar, is the Friday Mosque (*masjed-e Jomeh*), which has been rebuilt several times and is currently being restored. Its short and stocky minaret, decorated with brick designs, is topped by a wooden roof. Inside, are an interesting tiled *mehrâb* and a 15th-century membar. Near this mosque is the *emâmzâdeh* Nur, a 14th- or 15th-century funerary tower.

Unlike Gorgân, **Gonbad-e Qâbus**, set further inland, is essentially a Turkoman town: in the streets the black châdor gives way to the traditional long colourful shawls (which are now imported from Turkmenistan) and Turkoman is spoken as readily as Persian in the shops. Gonbad-e Qâbus, the 'tower of Qâbus', owes its name to its most famous building, a 51-metre (167-foot)-tall mausoleum which is perhaps the most impressive of all the funerary towers in Irân. Built in 1006–07 by Qâbus, a local prince of the Ziyârid dynasty, also associated with the masterpiece of early persian prose, the *Qâbus-nâmeh*. it dominates the entire plain from its artificial platform. Circular inside, it is shaped like a ten-pointed star outside and has a conical roof about 12 metres (39 foot) high. The tower, built entirely of brick, is almost completely plain except for two bands of calligraphy around the foot and the top. The artistic origins of this building are unclear although it has been suggested that it is related to some form of Mazdean commemorative monument. Nevertheless, the uncompromising severity of its lines, its size and its remarkable state of preservation cannot fail to impress the visitor.

About 30 kilometres (18.5 miles) north of Gonbad-e Qâbus, on the way to the frontier of Turkmenistan, are the remains of an ancient wall known as the **Sadd-e Eskandar**, or Alexander's Wall. According to popular belief, this wall was built by Alexander the Great although it is more likely that it is of late Sasanian date and was designed to protect the Gorgân Plain from nomad raids. The remains stretch over some 70 kilometres (43 miles), from Gonbad-e Qâbus to the sea, but they have suffered such severe erosion that in many places there is little more than the odd mound left to see. Because of the proximity of the border, it is necessary to get a permit to visit the wall.

From Gorgân, the main road continues east into the province of Khorâsân, passing first through tobacco and cotton fields and then through the mountains and the **Golestân National Park**. This park, opened in 1957, covers some 92,000 hectares (227,337 acres) and is one of the most interesting in the country from the point of view of wildlife and plants. It is unusual in that it stretches over two very different climatic zones and therefore includes both, thick deciduous forests—beautiful in their autumn colours—and semi-arid steppes. There is still an abundant animal life here and it is relatively easy to see wild boar, deer, gazelles and ibex; it is also a paradise for birds of prey. The Caspian tiger that used to live here, however, has not been seen since the 1960s.

THE NORTHWEST: ZANJÂN AND AZERBAIJÂN

ZANJÂN PROVINCE

For the sightseer, the most interesting town in the province of Zanjân is **Qazvin**, 125 kilometres (78 miles) west of Tehrân, at the junction of the roads leading north to Rasht and the Caspian Sea, northwest to Tabriz and Turkey, and southwest to Hamadân and—until recently—Baghdâd. Qazvin was probably founded by the Sasanian ruler Shâpur I in the third century AD. It was for a short time capital of the Safavid dynasty when Tahmâsp I (1524–1576) transferred his court, after the previous capital Tabriz had been sacked by the Ottomans in 1517. The Safavids remained in Qazvin until 1598 when, in the reign of Shâh Abbâs I, the capital was once again moved, this time to Esfahân.

Today Qazvin is a medium-sized town of some 300,000 inhabitants. Despite the numerous earthquakes which have plagued its history, it still has something to show of its former glory. The oldest sections of the **Friday Mosque** (masjed-e Jomeh) date from the beginning of the Islamic period, although the mosque was largely rebuilt during the reign of the Saljuq ruler Malek Shâh (1072–1092). The very simple decoration of the arches surrounding the central court is particularly fine, though it is largely obscured by recent additions of concrete hangers for awnings. The south *eivân* and the prayer room with its marble *mehrâb* date to the 12th century. Various sections of the mosque have been restored at different periods, including the eastern *eivân* (Safavid) and the minarets (Qâjâr).

The *Haidariye madraseh*, just east of the town centre, was originally a 12th century Saljuq mosque. During the Qâjâr dynasty, it was incorporated into a madreseh, but the very attractive though much-damaged original Saljuq *mehrâb* can still be seen. The Saljuq mosque was a kiosk mosque, a square-domed chamber (now no longer visible) facing towards Mecca. The decoration on the walls (stucco inscriptions and floral designs) are very fine and in places well preserved; the carved stucco decoration of the *mehrâb* is one of the richest examples of this period to be seen in Irân.

Little is left in Qazvin of the Safavid period other than a small palace, the **Chehel Sotun**, located in a park in the centre of town, Azâdi Square (Sabz-e Meidân). It is a two-storeyed building, restored by the Qâjârs in the 19th century, and the interior has recently been restored as a museum. Inside, fragments of paintings on the walls and ceiling are still visible. In places, one can clearly see several layers of paint, the result of a common feature of Irânian interior decoration which was to plaster and then paint over existing designs without removing them. On the first floor is the regional museum which displays a very extensive collection of calligraphy.

Behind Azâdi Square, at the other end of the avenue leading to the Friday Mosque, is another Safavid building, the **Âli Qâpu Palace**, of which only the entrance gate is left and which is now occupied by the police.

In the east of town is a small funerary tower, of late Mongol date (14th century) built for the Persian geographer and scholar

Conic roof of the funerary tower of historian Hamdollâh Mostofi (1281–1350)

Hamdollâh Mostofi, minister to Sultan Oljaitu. The square building has a conical roof decorated with turquoise tiles.

The *emâmzâdeh* **Hosein**, on Boulevard Jomhuri-ye Eslâmi near the Friday Mosque was founded in the 16th century by Shâh Tahmâsp, and restored during the Qâjâr dynasty. The entrance gate, in front of which is a small park, is typically Qâjâr, decorated with geometric tile motifs; it supports six narrow minarets with floral designs. Behind this gate is the mausoleum itself with its turquoise dome. The outer façade of the sanctuary, at the back of the terrace, is entirely covered in small, shining mirrors.

There are two more Qâjâr constructions in Qazvin, both monumental gateways. The first, the **darb-e Kushk**, in the north of town on Avenue Hâfez, was built in 1917. It is richly decorated in blue, yellow and white tilework; above the central arch is the old emblem of Irân, the lion and the sun (the crowns of the lions have now been removed). The second gateway, known as the **Gateway to Tehrân** (*darvâzeh Qalem-e Tehrân*), can be seen at the eastern exit of town, on the road to Tehrân. It was restored in the 1960s.

The Friday Mosque of Qazvin, rebuilt by the Saljuq Malek Shâh (1072–1092)

THE ISMÂ'ILIS AND THE ASSASSINS

The term 'assassin', used in Europe from the 13th century to describe a hired killer, is said to be derived from the Arabic *hashishiyun*, or 'hashish eater'. This expression, probably a pejorative one from the very beginning, was used to denigrate the Ismâ'ilis who were said by their enemies to intoxicate themselves with hashish before their politically or religiously motivated murders. The Assassins were feared as much in the Muslim world as in the Christian one for their daring practice of unexpectedly attacking even the most prominent men despite the protection that might surround them.

The Ismâ'ilis emerged from the scism which occurred in the Shi'a community on the death of the Sixth Emâm, in 765 (see page 94). They refused to accept as successor a younger son of the Emâm and recognized as legitimate heir his elder half-brother Ismâ'il. Like the Twelver Shi'as, the Ismâ'ilis believe in the return of the Mahdi, the messianic Emâm. In order to prepare for his return, the *dâ'i*, or propagandists, were entrusted with the duty of preaching to the faithful. Pursued for their beliefs as much by the Sunnis as by other Shi'i, the *dâ'i* were frequently compelled to carry out their task in hiding.

Taking advantage of the reduced personal power of the Abbâsid caliphs in Baghdâd towards the end of the ninth century, Ismâ'ili missions were sent out to the Yemen, India, and North Africa. Their success was such that in 909, the hidden Emâm proclaimed himself caliph and founded the Fatimid dynasty. In 937, after the conquest of Egypt, the Fatimid Caliphate built the new city of Cairo as their captial. This first Ismâ'ili state, after repeated attacks from Sunni armies, finally fell to the Kurdish leader Saladin who restored the Abbâsid caliphate in Egypt in 1171.

During the 11th century, the Ismâ'ili community was shaken by a deep ideological crisis. In 1017, the Druze proclaimed the divine nature of the Fatimid caliph al-Hâkim, an unacceptable promotion in the eyes of other Ismâ'ilis. Many intellectuals were led to re-examine the very foundations of their own beliefs.

In this climate of political and moral uncertainty, one man, possessed of a very strong personality and determined to defend his Ismâ'ili faith against the aggression of the Sunni Saljuq rulers, came to the fore: Hasan Sabbâh. Born towards the middle of the 11th century in Qom, Hasan Sabbâh was brought up in Rey in the Shi'a faith. Having converted to Ismâ'ilism, he spent several years in Egypt before returning to Iran. There he joined the Nizaris and militated against the Saljuqs first in the Dâmghân area and then later around Qazvin where he gathered together a band of dedicated followers. In September of 1090, his men captured the castle of Alamut through trickery. An isolated and practically inaccessible fortress, it was to become the headquarters of the Ismâ'ilis. Until his death in May 1124, Hasan Sabbâh never left Alamut again, and directed all his operations against the Saljuq Empire from there. The capture of Alamut was followed by the seizure of a series of other castles, first of all nearby in the Rudbâr, an area which had long been a Shi'a stronghold, and then further afield near Dâmghân, Esfahân and in the mountains of Kuhestân, near present-day Afghânistân.

In 1092, the Saljuq sultan Malek Shâh attacked the Ismâ'ili fortresses at Alamut and in Kuhestân. Faced by an enemy far superior in number, Hasan Sabbâh decided to remain entrenched, relying on his most fearsome weapon: assassination. It was at Alamut that the first *fidâ'i*, or 'those who devote themselves', were formed. After a very strict doctrinal and military training, the *fidâ'i* were prepared to sacrifice their own lives to carry out any task they might be given, in the belief that their actions would grant them entry to Paradise. Then began a series of carefully executed attacks against high-ranking or prominent men—princes, governors, generals, theologians—all of whom had condemned Ismâ'ilism. One of the first victims was the vizir of Sultan Malek Shâh, Nezâm ol-Molk, killed in 1092.

Ismâ'ili missions which had been set up outside Iran adopted the same methods as their fellow believers, and with great success, most notably in Syria where their armies for the first time faced the Crusaders. The assassination of Conrad de Montferrat, the king of Jerusalem, caused a great stir throughout the Christian world.

The heir to Hasan Sabbâh at Alamut, Bozorg-Omid (ruled 1124–1138), succeeded in maintaining the strength of the Ismâ'ilis, but their power declined after his death, particularly after the appearance of the Mongols at the beginning of the 13th century. The final blow was delivered by Hulagu, Genghis Khân's grandson, who in 1256 launched a series of attacks against the Ismâ'ili castles in the Rudbâr and Kuhestân. In order to obtain the best possible conditions for surrender from Hulagu, the Ismâ'ili Emâm Rokn od-Din ordered his fortresses to give themselves up without a fight. Most of them obeyed, although Alamut and Lamassar refused. In December 1256, Alamut finally surrendered and the once proud castle was burned down. Its library, was destroyed, and only a few fragments were saved from the flames.

THE CASTLES OF THE ASSASSINS

Several roads from Qazvin lead into the Alborz Mountains, and more specifically into the Rudbâr, Alamut and Dailam massifs which separate Zanjân from the Caspian coast. By the Sasanian period, the inhabitants of these isolated and harsh regions had a reputation as tough and independent-minded fighters, and a series of strong fortresses were built in the hills to keep them at bay. From the ninth century, the Dailam area became a Shi'a refuge, particularly for the Zaidi, a sect which recognized a separate lineage of Emâms from the Twelver Shi'a majority. A local dynasty, the Buyids (945–1055), which originally came from Dailam, succeeded in extending its domination over much of Irân, reaching as far as Baghdad. Dailamite domination ended with the arrival of the Saljuqs in the 11th century but the region remained open to Shi'ism. When Hasan Sabbâh undertook, around 1090, to establish the headquarters of his Ismâ'ili followers (known in the West as the Assassins) in the area, he was faced with only limited opposition. The most famous of the Rudbâr castles is that of Alamut above Gâzor Khân village, which Hasan Sabbâh occupied, but others have been identified in the region, among them Lamassar, above Râzmiân and Meimundez, above Shams Kelâyeh which were the last to surrender to the Mongols after the fall of Alamut in 1256. The ruins of Alamut (which today consist only of a few piles of stones) are perched at 1,800 metres (5,905 feet) above sea-level, on top of a rocky outcrop dominating the village of Gazor Khân, in a fertile but narrow valley. According to a local legend, a ruler of Dailam out hunting saw his trained eagle on top of the rock and realised the strategic value of the location.

Although the trip to **Alamut** is slightly less arduous today than it was 20 years ago, when it took several days on horseback to reach the castle, it is still difficult. It is a full-day's excursion from Qazvin, and requires an early start, particularly in autumn when the sun sets early, in order to allow sufficient time at the castle itself and to avoid negotiating the mountain roads in the dark. The pass which leads to the valley below the castle is generally closed by snow until May. The road from the pass is now in good condition; it winds first through Mo'allem Kalâye and then goes on to the village of Gâzor Khân from where a steep path leads up to the rock itself (a good half-hour's walk up).

In cloudy or very windy weather it is worth thinking twice about whether you really want to go up the last stretch: the path is very narrow and the clouds may block the view off completely. In good weather, however, the trip is well worth the effort and allows one to glimpse a rural mountain life that would otherwise remain hidden.

Remains of the fortress of Alamut

Qazvin is linked directly by road to Hamadân, 234 kilometres (145 miles) to the southwest, one of the oldest towns in Irân. Near the border between the provinces of Zanjân and Hamadân, in the district of Avaj, are two brick funerary towers, known as the **towers of Kharaqân**. Built in 1067 and 1093 by an architect from Zanjân, Mohammed ibn Makki, they are similar in shape and very sophisticated decoration to the tomb of Ismâ'il the Sâmânid at Bokhârâ (built 914–943). Built on an octagonal plan with eight corner pillars (one of which contains an internal staircase) they are the oldest dated monuments to possess double-shelled domes and among the first to have been decorated with coloured glazed tiles.

The road from Qazvin to Tabriz goes through the town of **Zanjân** (180 kilometres or 112 miles), the provincial capital, the provincial capital, famous for manufacturing penknives, which has no monuments of particular interest except for a Safavid bridge. However, about 40 kilometres (25 miles) before Zanjân, a large blue dome stands out at the foot of the hills. This is **Soltânieh**, once the capital of the il-Khân Mongols and now a small village. The dome is that of the mausoleum of Sultan Oljaitu Khodâbandeh.

In 1306, Sultan Oljaitu (1304–1316)—who had originally been baptized as Nicolas by the Nestorian Patriarch Mar Yahballaha III, before turning to Buddhism, Sunni Islam and finally around 1309/10 Shi'ism—began the construction of his new city, Soltânieh, to replace Tabriz as the imperial capital of the il-khâns. It would appear that the building of his own mausoleum started at around the same time. Having converted to Shi'ism, Oljaitu decided to alter the building so that it could house the bodies of the Emâms Ali and Hosein, buried in Kerbalâ and Najaf, in Iraq. But both towns refused to part with the Emâms, and the mausoleum was used for the sultan himself. Traces of other buildings linked to the mausoleum have been found recently as well as the base of the walls with semi-circular bastions, now partly restored, that surrounded it. These are made from the green stone from Tâsh Kasan, where there is also a famous carved Buddhist dragon.

The mausoleum is an octagonal domed construction, built of brick. This spectacular construction became for centuries the prototype for princely Mongol tombs, down to the Taj Mahal in India. In shape it is more reminiscent of certain mausoleums in Central Asia, such as the tomb of Sultan Sanjar at Merv (1157), than of buildings in nearby Azerbaijan. When the decision was made to turn it into a mausoleum for the Emâms, a *mehrâb* was added to the south-western side and a funerary chapel to the north-west. This gives the impression from the outside that the building was either left unfinished or has been partly destroyed. A vaulted gallery runs around the top of the building and opens into a series of triple arcades; above this is a *muqarnas* cornice. The remains of eight minarets are visible around the dome, one at each corner. The latter, completely covered in turquoise glazed tiles, is 52 metres (171 feet) tall and very elegant with its rather pointed shape. The minarets and the dome, currently being restored, were originally decorated in blue and black tiles, while the vaults of the gallery still bear the very fine painted mouldings executed during the period after Oljaitu's conversion to Shi'ism (the gallery is now open to the public). The decorative design on the walls and vaults of the galleries are strikingly similar to contemporary book illuminations. The latter

The mausoleum of Sultan Oljaitu (1304–1316), Soltânieh

Gallery vault in Oljaitu's mausoleum, Soltânieh

acted most likely as a source of inspiration for the former. In the galleries we also find so-called cloud collars, four- or eight-lobed patterns, which motif stems from China and was probably derived from Central Asian or Mongolian costumes. Beneath the gallery the brick of the exterior walls was left plain except on the south-west side, facing towards Mecca, where there are still traces of glazed decoration. The interior of the mausoleum was also originally richly decorated in tilework, which was plastered over at a later date, either when Oljaitu decided to turn the building into his own mausoleum or as part of Safavid restoration work.

On the outskirts of Soltânieh, the il-Khânid mausoleum for the Sufi master Baraq Baba built in 1310, the adjacent hospice for Sufis, dating from 1333, and the Safavid mausoleum for Mullah Hasan Kashi, dating from 1595, are all worth a visit.

THE PROVINCES OF AZERBAIJÂN

Irânian Azerbaijân is now divided into two separate provinces (ostân), a Western and an Eastern one, which occupy the northwest corner of the country. The frontier with the Republic of Azerbaijân follows the course of the Aras (or Araxes) River; in the east, the Turkish frontier runs through the Zaki Mountains. Geographically, this region is very varied as it contains a succession of mountain massifs and basins, the largest of which contains Lake Orumieh. The mountain ranges are of volcanic origin and have an average height of about 2,500 metres (8,200 feet); the Sahand, between Tabriz and Marâgheh, reaches 3,710 metres (12,170 feet) and the Sabalân, to the west of Ardabil, culminates at 4,811 metres (15,780 feet). The climate of Azerbaijân is very dry and most of the basins are sheltered from rainfall by the surrounding mountains. The plains of the Aras and Tabriz, as well as the Orumieh Basin, only receive an average of 200 to 300 millimetres of rainfall a year, hardly more than Tehrân. As a result, crops can only be grown on the sides of the hills, except where the land is irrigated too. Azerbaijân is much colder than the Irânian Plateau, with average temperatures around 27° C (80° F) in summer (21° C, 68° F at Ardabil, closer to the Caspian Sea), and -2° C (30° F) in winter (-20° C in Ardabil).

Once inhabited by mountain peoples of Indo-European origin, Azerbaijân has undergone a slow but thorough ethno-linguistic change since the arrival of Turkish tribes from Central Asia. This process, which may have begun in the seventh century, increased considerably in the 11th and 12th centuries after the Saljuq rulers sent Turkish tribes to Azerbaijân to defend it against the Christian state of Georgia and the Byzantine Greeks of Trebizond. The Turks settled for the most part in the north and in Anatolia, and in somewhat smaller numbers around Tabriz and Marâgheh. The adoption of Shi'ism by the Safavids was followed by the return to Irân from Anatolia of many of these Shi'a Turks, fleeing the Sunni Ottoman Empire. The decision by Shâh Abbâs (1571–1629) to form the Shâhsevan confederation from several different Turkish tribes also attracted a large number of nomads to the region, and Azeri, a Turkish dialect, became widely used, spreading as far as Qazvin. Today, Azeri is spoken by around 9.5 million people in Irân, mostly in the two Azerbaijâns, as well as in parts of Zanjân and Gilan.

The geographic and climatic conditions prevalent in Azerbaijân are ideal for a nomadic lifestyle, and the Turkish tribes who settled there had little trouble adapting to their new home. However, in the past hundred years, this traditional way of life

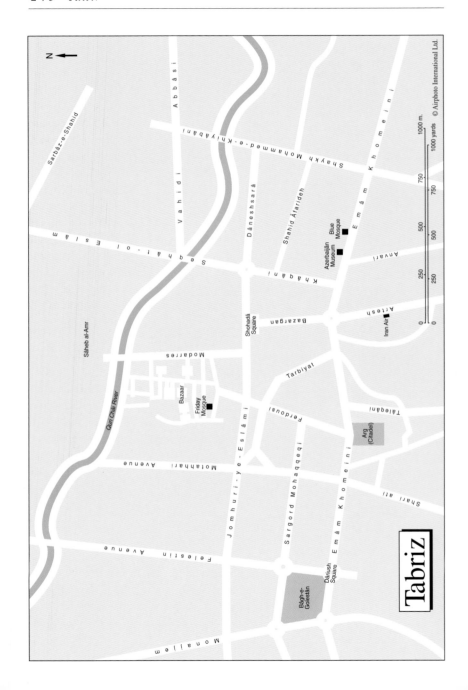

Tabriz

has been profoundly modified. The closure of the frontier with Russia in 1886 cut off the Shâhsevan in East Azerbaijân from their winter pastures in the Araxes Plain, and the policies of Shâh Rezâ in the 1930s led to the enforced settlement of many nomads in villages. Today, although there still exists a semi-nomadic population in Azerbaijân, large-scale nomadism has completely disappeared.

TABRIZ

Tabriz, the capital of East Azerbaijân, is set in a valley at the foot of the Sahand Mountains, 294 kilometres (183 miles) northwest of Zanjân. The second biggest town in Irân, it has a population at present of almost one million and has become an important industrial and trade centre for business between Tehrân and Turkey. Tabriz is said to have been founded in Sasanian times, and by the tenth century was by all accounts a major centre. It was promoted to the rank of capital by the Mongol Il-khân ruler Ghâzân Khân (1295–1304) and retained that status almost without interruption until the 16th century, when the Safavids transferred the court first to Qazvin and then to Esfahân, which was less prone to attack from Ottoman forces. Tabriz suffered in the wars between the Safavid and Ottoman empires, as well as from the clashes with Russian troops which began in the 18th century, and was occupied several times by foreign armies. Earthquakes and epidemics also took their toll, to such an extent that at the beginning of the 19th century the population of the town was reduced to one third of what it had been a hundred years earlier. Today only a few historical monuments remain in Tabriz.

The most important of these is the *Blue Mosque* (masjed-e Kabud), once considered a masterpiece of Irânian decorative tilework. Built towards the end of the reign of the Timurid ruler Jahân Shâh (1436–1467), it was seriously damaged by an earthquake; today only a few pillars, parts of the outer wall and the main gate, and sections of the vaulted ceiling and a dome remain. The mosque plan is a variant on the usual Irânian four-*eivân* courtyard style: the courtyard has been replaced by a large domed chamber with an entrance on each of the four sides. The *mehrâb* is in a smaller room, also domed. On three sides of the main chamber are further vaulted rooms. This rather original plan may be a result of local adaptation to cope with the colder, harsher climate of Azerbaijân.

The decoration of this mosque is justly renowned for the exceptional quality of the work, the finesse of the designs and the harmony of the overall composition. The range of colours used is more varied than previously, with the addition of an olive green, an ochre and a brown to the more usual blues and whites. The best

Ruins of the Blue Mosque in Tabriz, 1881

examples are to be found on the gateway, especially on the inside walls of the porch where the magnificent mosaics really do warrant closer inspection. Inside the mosque, the decoration has been less well preserved but is equally rich and reproduces the same designs as outside (medallions, flower arabesques and inscriptions).

Apart from the mosque, there are few other buildings to visit in Tabriz. The **Azerbaijân Museum**, next door to the mosque (Emâm Khomeini Avenue), has a rather mixed collection of archaeological and ethnographical objects. Further west along the same avenue are the remains—two solid towers and a wall—of the **citadel**, or *Arg*, which dates back to the Mongol occupation at the beginning of the 14th century.

The covered **bazaar** and the **Friday Mosque** are to be found in the old quarter between Jomhuri-ye Eslâmi Avenue and the Quri Châi River. On the other side of the river is a more modern mosque, the **masjed-e Sâheb ol-Amr**, surrounded by a wall, and surmounted by a low dome set on a tall drum. The mosque was turned in 2000 into the **Museum for ancient Qur'âns**. It contains precious calligraphies in Kufic script, in Naskh and in Ta'liq.

Tabriz has for many centuries played host to an Armenian community which still possesses four churches. The most important is the episcopal seat, **St. Sergius Cathedral**, (Kelisâ-ye Sarkis-e Moghaddas), built in 1905. Much older is **St. Mary's Church** (Kelisâ-ya Maryam) located near the bazaar, which was mentioned by Marco Polo who visited it on his return trip from China in 1294. However, it was completely rebuilt in the early 20th century. The other two churches are close to the cathedral.

From Tabriz it is possible to make day excursions (some of which will be long days) to visit other major sites in both provinces of Azerbaijân. The road that goes to Astârâ and the Caspian Sea passes through the old town of **Ardabil** (235 kilometres, 146 miles), once an important Sufi centre and famous for being the place of origin of the Safavid rulers. The mausoleum of Shaykh Safi al-Din (1252–1334), an ancestor of Shâh Ismâ'il, the founder of the Safavid dynasty in the 16th century, is located here. Shâh Ismâ'il himself is also buried in the same tomb. The mausoleum is a domed circular tower decorated with large glazed brick designs (those around the door were added after the construction of the building). At the base of the dome is a short Kufic inscription. Inside, behind a silver grille, are the tombs of the Shaykh and his two sons. The walls are richly decorated in tilework, with stalactite niches and fretwork panelling, similar in style to that of the Âli Qâpu Palace in Esfahân. The mosque beside the mausoleum has been rather badly preserved but its stalactite gateway is still very fine.

(Following pages) *The Armenian monastery of Saint Stephanos near Jolfâ*

A one or two days' excursion to the ancient Armenian **Church of Saint Stephanos** (Kelisâ Darre Shâm) is most rewarding. A good road leads from Tabriz for 137 km northwards to the small town of Jolfâ, where simple yet clean accommodation can be found. It is from here that Shâh Abbâs I deported, after 1598, thousands of Armenian craftsmen with their families to Esfahân in order to rebuild his new capital. The mountain road leading north-westwards to St. Stephanos is 18 km long and closely follows the river Aras which marks the border between Irân and the enclave of Nakhichevan belonging to the Republic of Azerbaijân. While it is usually easy to pass the inner-Irânian checkpoint after Jolfâ, it is advisable neither to stop on the way nor to photograph the tightly guarded border. About midway one sees across the river on the Azerbaijâni side thousands of tightly arranged stone slabs commemorating a massacre of Armenian fugitives committed by Turkish irregulars during World War I.

The monastery lies in a setting of spectacular scenery close to the confluence of the rivers Aras and Âgh Chây. According to legend, it was founded in AD 62 by the Apostle Bartholomew. While another tradition attributes its foundation to the Armenian King Ashot around the end of the 9th century, the oldest extant parts date from the 14th, but much of the rest of it from the 16th century. The monastery's early decline in the 17th century was caused by Shâh Abbâs' deportations which deprived it of its community. A last revival occurred around 1820 when Crown Prince Abbâs Mirza bequeathed a whole village to it which generated a secure tax income. The Turkish massacres of Armenians after 1915 forced the remaining monks to flee. The abandoned monastery is today a popular weekend excursion for Christians and Muslims alike. It is an interesting experience on Fridays to hear Persian and Arabic songs from Muslim tourists' tape recorders and Armenian songs sung by Christian visitors side by side.

The monastery consists of two rectangular parts which are surrounded by a strong stone wall of around 60m by 80 m in length fortified with six round towers. The upper part housed the monks' cells and is in a bad state of repair. However, reconstruction has started with the intention of opening a restaurant and a small hotel. The cruciform stone church stands in the centre of the lower part and has been recently restored. Its outer walls are decorated with many fine carvings featuring Christ, the angels, the stoning of Saint Stephen, Armenian crosses and inscriptions.

Another very interesting Armenian church is the **Church of Saint Thaddaeus** (Kelisâ-ye Tâdî or Gharra Kelisâ, the Black Church) located north-west of Mâku near the Irânian-Turkish border. Mâku lies 240 km to the north-west of Tabriz, and

150 km from Jolfâ by road (which is 137 km north-west of Tabriz). From Mâku, three roads lead to Saint Thaddaeus: The middle one, at 55 km in length, is the shortest in terms of distance yet the longest in terms of time, being a steep mountain road climbing to 2350 m above sea level with some non-tarmaced sections. The southern one, although 74 km long, is the fastest while the northern one (100 km) has the benefit of a spectacular view over snow-covered Mount Ararat (5137 m above sea level).

The early history of the church is unknown. It is said that in the 5th century a hermit found in its vicinity the bones of Saint Thaddaeus who is supposed to have suffered martyrdom between AD 62 and 66. The hermit then built a chapel and buried the mortal remains of the saint in a niche near the altar. From the oldest church on the site only the chevet remains; the rest was destroyed by an earthquake in 1319. The church was rebuilt between 1319 and 1329 using mostly black stone which gave it the present local name of the Black Church. The remains of this period of construction can still be seen around the altar, the baptistery and the eastern part of the nave covered by the black dome. In 1490 the church and the surrounding monastery were restored and enclosed by a wall 6 m high and 5 m thick into which the monks' cells, the refectory and the store rooms were integrated. Following a substantial donation by Crown Prince Abbâs Mirzâ, the size of the church was doubled between 1810 and 1820 by the construction of a westwards extension. In contrast to the old church, this extension was built using white and yellowish stones. It is decorated with finely carved friezes and large figures featuring not only apostles, saints, two and four winged angels but also scenes taken from daily life and from Ferdosi's *Shâhnâmeh* as well as mythical animals like monstrous fishes and dragons. Like at St. Stephanos, the Turkish massacres of 1915–1917 forced the monks to flee.

Today, service is only celebrated once a year on the occasion of the feast day of St. Thaddaeus in late June or early July when thousands of pilgrims gather to celebrate. Otherwise the church remains generally off the beaten track of tourists. About 25 km to the north-east stands near the village of **Baron** the tiny Armenian chapel dedicated to the Holy Virgin, locally known as Zor Zor. It dates from the 14th or 15th century and stands above a recently constructed artificial lake; the chapel originally stood in the area now flooded, and had to be dismantled and rebuilt in its present place.

About 90 km (56 miles) south of Mâku on the road to Khoy lies the tiny village of **Bastam**, 6 km (4 miles) to the west of Qareh Zeyâ od-Din. The huge Urartian fortress called Rusai-Uru Tur sits on the northern side of a steep mountain ridge, whose southern edge falls almost vertically into the river Âgh Chây. The citadel was

built in terraces and consisted of three fortifications: the lower fortress with the quarters of the military commander, the middle one with a temple dedicated to the main Urartian god Khaldi and the upper fortress where the town's archives written in cuneiform were discovered. From here the visitor gains a good view over the fertile valleys of the Âgh Chây and its large tobacco and sunflower fields.

The fortress was built by King Rusai II between 685 and 645 BC and was destroyed in the 6th century BC by the Medes. Later, between the 9th and 13th century AD, the upper citadel was reoccupied by a mixed Armenian and Muslim population. Since the fortress was utterly destroyed and its ruins looted by the villagers of Bastam to build their own houses, a visit here is mainly rewarding for historians and archaeologists who can "rebuild" the city in their imagination based on the easily recognizable pattern of ground walls.

Due to a favourable location in a fertile plain, near the roads linking the Irânian Plateau, Turkey and Armenia, **Marâgheh** (143 kilometres, 89 miles, from Tabriz) became an important city, first under Arab and then under Kurdish domination. During the reign of Hulagu (1256–1265), it was briefly made the capital of the Il-Khân Mongols. This period was its heyday and Hulagu's policy of religious tolerance encouraged the settlement there of large numbers of foreigners, including Nestorian Christians and Buddhists. Today, very little is left of Marâgheh's early history: Hulagu's famous observatory and the old Friday Mosque are in ruins, and only a series of remarkably well preserved mausoleums, dating back to the 12th century, remain.

(Left) *The Armenian Saint Thaddaeus Church. The apse end, built with dark stone, dates from the 14th century, whilst the larger part built in white stone was added in the early 19th century.* (Above) *Figure of a saint, southern wall, Saint Thaddaeus Church, early 19th century*

The oldest of these, built in 1147, is the **Gonbad-e Sorkh**, or Red Tomb, which owes its name to the deep red colour of its bricks. It is a square building with a conical, eight-sided roof and a stalactite ceiling. The decoration of the exterior walls is limited to Kufic inscriptions above the door and in a niche, geometric brick designs and some discreet touches of turquoise tilework, particularly on the half-columns set at each corner.

This mausoleum was one of the earliest in Irân to use glazed tiles in its decoration, a technique which had advanced greatly by the time of the second circular mausoleum was built nearby in 1167. Here the geometric patterns and the Kufic inscriptions formed by the red bricks are enhanced with turquoise tiles.

The octagonal **Gonbad-e Kabud** (1197) is the most ornate of the Marâgheh mausoleums. Each side of the building is decorated as if it were a *mehrâb*, with a *muqarnas* arch above it. Only the stone base is left plain. The flat panels, and the half-columns at the corners, are decorated with an interlaced polygon pattern made of bricks. The arches above the panels, Kufic inscriptions, stalactite cornice and roof were all once entirely decorated with turquoise tiles of which a few traces still remain.

The **Gonbad-e Khafariyeh** is the mausoleum of a Mamluk emir, Shams od-din Karasunkur, viceroy of Egypt and then of Syria, who fled to Irân in 1311. Sultan Oljaitu Khodâbandeh (whose own mausoleum can be seen at Soltânieh) gave Marâgheh to the emir where he lived until he died. His mausoleum, completed in 1328, is also built of red brick but is decorated with black, blue and white tiles, colours which also appear at Soltânieh, built a few years earlier. The fifth mausoleum at Marâgheh, known as Khoi Burj and which was probably a Timurid building, collapsed in 1938.

Lake Orumieh, very near to Marâgheh, is Irân's largest lake. Its average surface area is some 4,500 square kilometres (1,737 square miles), and may expand to 6,100 square kilometres (2,355 square miles) in particularly wet years. Because of its high salt content there is only a very limited marine life and flora, but its waters are famous for their therapeutic value, especially in easing rheumatisms, and several spas have been built along the shores of the lake. **Orumieh** (1,300 metres, 427 feet), set in a very fertile plain on the west side of the lake, is the main city of West Azerbaijân. Its inhabitants are a mixed population of Kurds, Azeris, and a relatively large Christian community of Armenians, Nestorians, Chaldean Catholics, Roman Catholics, Protestants and a few Russian Orthodox (see the section on the Christians in Orumieh). The **Friday Mosque**, built in the Saljuq period (12–13th century) has been restored several times but the *mehrâb* still retains its very fine original carved stucco decoration. The **Se Gonbad** (Three Towers), located in the southern quarter of town, is a circular funerary tower similar to those at Marâgheh. Built in the late 12th century, it is another attractive example of Saljuq decorative art.

Just south of Lake Orumieh, near Naqadeh and Mohammad Yâr, is the archaeological site of **Hasanlu**. According to Assyrian administrative documents, the region south of Lake Orumieh was known as 'Mannai' in the ninth century BC and the remains of a fortified citadel at Hasanlu have thus been attributed to the Manneans, an Irânian people who formed a small principality in the area. Surrounded by powerful neighbours, (Assyrians, Urarteans and Medes), the Manneans took part in the changing political and military alliances struck between these nations, finally becoming vassals of the Scythians. At Hasanlu, the administrative town and the temples were located within the citadel, protected by walls nine metres (30 feet) high. Excavations have yielded a number of gold and silver objects, including the famous Hasanlu gold cup, now in the Archaeological Museum of Tehrân, decorated with engraved mythological scenes, tentatively identified as representations of the Hurrian god Kummabi. Around 800 BC, the town was completely destroyed by invading Urartians who had settled near Lake Van.

The site of Hasanlu provides us not only with important information on Mannean culture, still very poorly understood, but also on the early development of architecture in Irân and particularly of the hypostyle hall. Although limited in size—the largest room has two rows of four columns—the halls at Hasanlu do appear to represent an early stage in the evolution of the Achaemenian âpâdânâs of Susa and Persepolis.

TAKHT-E SOLEIMÂN—SASANIAN SHRINE AND MONGOL PALACE

In the south of Azerbaijân is one of the most important archaeological sites of Irân, the **Takht-e Soleimân** (Solomon's Throne). The site has, of course, nothing to do with the Solomon of scripture; nevertheless, locals throughout the Middle East often name their majestic places after this king who is also respected by Muslims. In the ancient Pahlavi language this great Sasanian religious centre was named 'Ganzak' or 'Ganjeh', while the Romans called it 'Gazka' and the Arabs 'Shiz'. The site is located at an altitude of 2070m above sea level 42 km (25 miles) to the northeast of Takab which lies on the Miyândoab-Bijâr road. The ruins lie on top of a 25 m high oval shaped plateau of 330 x 250 m formed out of calcareous sinter stemming from the small lake at the centre of the site which has a very high mineral content. This tiny, yet 60 m deep lake is fed by an underground source. Just 3 km (2 miles) to the north-west of Ganjeh another 110 m high conical mountain

The Zoroastrian shrine and later Mongol palace of Takht-e Soleimān and Zendān-e Soleimān in the background on the left

also formed out of calcareous sinter rises into the sky. Named Zendân-e Soleimân (Soloman's Prison), its crater has a diameter of 70 m and is more than 100 m deep. In Sasanian times a Zoroastrian shrine was build along its steep outer slopes which was converted in the 7th century AD into a fortified settlement. Not far from Takht-e Soleimân are the remains of the quite dilapidated Sasanian fortress called "**Fort of Bilquis**", the legendary queen of Sheba who supposedly visited King Solomon.

In Ganjeh, the main Zoroastrian temple was dedicated to Adur Gushnasp, the fire of the king and the warriors, which was one of the three most important fires in Zoroastrianism. It was built in the late 5th century AD on top of the remains of Parthian buildings which themselves had been constructed on top of older dwellings dating from the first millennium BC. In Sasanian times a stone wall up to 8 m high was built, strengthened by round towers of which 38 remain. The site was a favourite residence of Queen Shirin, the Christian wife of King Khusro II (590–628), for it is said that she kept here the so-called True Cross her husband had captured in 614 from Jerusalem. The decline of the royal shrine started in 624 when it was looted and destroyed by an invading Roman army.

In the later 13th century the site experienced a renaissance when il-Khân Abaqa (1265–1282) choose it as one of his summer capitals which was called Sughurlukh (meaning 'place abounding with marmots') and ordered a huge palace to be built in the southern part of the site around the lake. Since the Sasanian ruins were also included in the new complex, parts of them like the huge northern *eivân* were rebuilt. The palace's ruins are the only remains of il-Khânid courtly architecture kept in Irân. Abaqa's selection of Ganjeh as one of his seasonal capitals was not a hazard, but followed the strategy designed by the powerful brothers Shams od-Din Mohammed Juvaini (died 1284) who was sâhib-e diwân (chief minister) and 'Ata Malek Juvaini (1226–1283), governor of Baghdâd and southern Iraq. The Juvaini brothers subscribed to the concept of "Irânshar", glorifying and reviving the pre-Islamic culture of Irân. The belief of the Mongol il-Khânid rulers and their ministers in the idea of Irânian cultural independence brought Abaqa to choose Ganjeh, where in pre-Islamic times royal coronation ceremonies had taken place, as one of the capitals. The political symbolism of this choice was further enhanced by the fact that the palace's frieze tiles were decorated with quotations taken from Ferdosi's national epic, the *Shâhnâmeh*, glorifying the pre-Islamic heroic times. Thus it was implied that the Mongol il-Khânid rulers were the legitimate successors of the Sasanian shâhs and Irân's legendary figures. The site was abandoned in the 17th century.

Today's entry to the ruins is through the southern gate built by the Mongols; the second main entry, that of the Sasanians, was in the north. This is consistent with the Mongols' custom of orienting buildings, the entries to camps and tents towards the south. While the southern *eivân* in front of the lake has disappeared, there remain several ruins of the il-Khânid palace along its eastern and western shores. Archaeologists found here numerous tiles decorated with mythical animals popular in China such as dragons and phoenixes which highlight the artistic influence from China during the il-Khânid Dynasty (1256–1335). At least during the first il-Khânid period which ended with Ghâzân's (1295–1304) conversion to Islam, Irân was culturally and politically more oriented towards Central and Eastern Asia than towards its Muslim neighbours in the West. At the north-western edge stand the ruins of the western and the northern *eivân*, the latter being supported by iron scaffolding to prevent its collapse. The northern *eivân* led to two octagonal buildings which may have served as princely private quarters. Their unusual shape is in line with the Mongol preference for polygonal buildings reflecting the design of the Mongol round tent, the *ger*.

Passing through the northern *eivân*, one enters the Sasanian part of Takht-e Soleimân. Following the central axis from south to north the visitor passes first the coronation gallery, then the cruciform Adur Gushnasp fire temple ending in a court-yard. In this context it has to be stressed that the Zoroastrians did not venerate the fire as such but those dimensions it symbolized: goodness, purity and purifying energy. These values were the basis for the Zoroastrian commandment that mankind should observe the "purity of thought, speech and action."

Adjacent to the eastern side of the temple the everlasting fire was kept in another cruciform room, as it is described in the *Avesta*. To the north of this room stood the shrine dedicated to Anâhitâ, the composite ancient Irânian deity of domestic animals, fertility and water. When the Achaemenian king Xerxes I (486–465 BC) forbade the veneration of Babylonian deities, several aspects of the Babylonian goddess Ishtâr were transferred to Anâhitâ whereby she also became the goddess of love and war.

While the central and eastern parts of the Sasanian complex had religious functions, the western part served profane purposes. Here we find going from south to north and then westwards the royal dining hall, the hypostyle hall, the festivity hall and finally the reception hall.

In spite of its dilapidated state, Takht-e Soleimân is very much worth a visit. The 15 minutes climb of a hill to the south-east of the site offers a fantastic view of Takht-e Soleimân as well as Zendân-e Soleimân in the background.

ORUMIEH—A STRONGHOLD OF THE CHURCH OF THE EAST —Christoph Baumer

THE EARLY CHURCH OF THE EAST UNDER PARTHIAN AND SASANIAN RULE

In the 2nd century, Christianity crossed the Euphrates, originally the political divide between Sasanian Iran and the Roman Empire and which became after AD 424 the religious divide between the Church of the East and the Western Churches. It first reached Edessa (today's Urfa in south-eastern Turkey). According to the Book of the Laws of Countries, which contains the writings of the Syriac philosopher and theologian Bardeisan (154–222), it seems that Edessa's King Abgar VIII (c. 177–212) was a Christian; if this is correct, it would make him the world's first Christian ruler and Edessa the first Christian state in history—more than a century earlier than Emperor Constantine of Rome who converted to Christianity in 312.

The Gospel spread in northern Mesopotamia probably at the same time as it set foot in Edessa. First in the region of Adiabene in northern Iraq whose large Jewish communities offered an excellent initial ground for missionary work. From here Christianity spread rapidly southwards along the shores of the river Tigris until it reached the Persian Gulf and from there the Iranian island of Kharg, which was located on the maritime Silk Road. According to Bardeisan, the Gospel had crossed by the second decade of the 3rd century also into the territory of present Iran—mainly into Azerbaijân, Media and Khuzestân, as well as the region of Gilân south of the Caspian Sea, and even the Kushan Empire whose western part corresponded to Transoxiana. Hence, the Church of the East already stretched from the Euphrates to the Hindu Kush following one of the main routes of the Silk Road linking Imperial China with the Roman Empire.

While the ideological indifference of the Parthians represented an ideal opportunity for the spread of Christianity, the situation changed after 224 with the seizure of power by the Sasanians. The new rulers wanted to associate themselves with the glory of the Achaemenians; as a part of this, they revitalized Zoroastrianism by elevating it to state religion—a policy which limited the tolerance Christianity had so far enjoyed. At the same time, the Sasanian rulers adopted a forward policy against the Roman Empire contrasting with the merely defensive strategy of the Parthians. Several victorious campaigns into Roman territory brought as a side-effect an influx of Christian prisoners of war, for example when Shâpur I sacked Antioch in 260 and deported ten thousands of Antiochians including bishop Demetrius. Most of the deportees were settled in Iranian Khuzestân.

Like all other non-Zoroastrian religions, the Christians came soon to suffer from the uncompromising zeal of the Zoroastrian priest Kartir who served over a period of more than half a century (240/41–294) six different shâhs. He organized the hierarchy of the Zoroastrian clergy, controlled the orthodoxy of the Zoroastrian faith and proclaimed in numerous stone-inscriptions the principles of the new state religion. In 274 or 276 he succeeded in defeating his rival Mani (216–274/76) by convincing King Bahrâm I (273–276) that the pessimistic asceticism of Mani, who condemned all earthly matters as evil, could threaten the social order and functioning of the state. He ordered a systematic persecution of Manichaeans and of Buddhists, which he extended in 287 to Christians; in the eyes of Zoroastrians, who perceived earthly life as positive, there was no major difference between Christians and Manichaeans whose religious elites withdrew from earthly matters and rejected procreation as evil. Kartir became the "Grand Inquisitor" of Zoroastrianism, which was in its heart neither tolerant nor pacifistic. Since Zoroaster himself required that people endorse the forces of Good and fight the forces of Evil, this order translated for the Sasanian state that it must promote Zoroastrianism and suppress its rival religions. Within this context, apostasy from Zoroastrianism meant *ipso facto* high treason and the death penalty. But since there were only few Zoroastrians in Mesopotamia, Christianity could continue to progress there while it remained a small minority in the Zoroastrian heartland of Fârs. This first persecution of Christians stopped under King Narses (293–302); it later proved to have been a mere mild prelude compared to those occurring in the 4th and 5th centuries.

As long as the Sasanians' arch-enemy Rome was persecuting Christians, Eastern Christianity in Iran had been only a religious problem. Yet, after the Emperor Constantine's conversion in 312, his Edict of Tolerance of Milan in 313, and his overbearing and patronizing letter sent in 315 to King Shâpur II (309–379), the situation worsened. With Rome adopting Christianity as its state religion, Sasanian Iran turned anti-Christian. From now on Iranian Christians were suspected of representing a Roman "Fifth Column". In the first Great Persecution from 339 till 383 they suffered about 200,000 causalities, among them dozens of bishops. The martyrs were decapitated, crucified or slowly tortured to death. But, in spite of these persecutions, the Church of the East continued to grow. At the council of 410 it reconstituted its hierarchy which had been decimated by the persecutions, appointed the bishop of the capital Seleucia-Ctesiphon as its Catholicos-Patriarch, adopted the Creed of Nicaea from 325 and established new rules confirmed by the signature of 36 bishops.

In 424 the Church of the East became, for political reasons, an auto-cephalous Church independent of any western institution. The core resolution of the council states: "The oriental bishops may not appeal to the western patriarchs against their [own] patriarch anymore. Any litigation in which he is involved and which does not find its solution will be kept for Christ's Throne of Judgement. He [the patriarch] shall judge all his subjects while Christ will judge him for He has elected, elevated and placed him at the head of His church." The Patriarch can only be judged by Christ, not by his subordinates, the bishops. It has to be stressed that this declaration of hierarchic independence was no schism, for the Creed of Nicaea formed the common ground with the western patriarchates. According to this oriental vision, the universal church does not consist of one single worldwide hierarchy but of an ecumenical community of independent churches sharing a common faith and creed.

At that time, the Church of the East was in no way "Nestorian" for Nestorius (d. 451) was then only an obscure Byzantine monk who was later patriarch of Constantinople from 428 till 431. The gradual theological antagonism between the so-called Nestorian Church of the East and the western churches resulted from political calculations and from the continued condemnation by western councils of the two Greek bishops Diodor of Tarsus (d. 392) and Theodorus of Mopsuestia (352–428) on whose theology and christology the scriptural exegesis of the Church of the East and of Nestorius were based. The main characteristic of this christology lies in its emphasis of the human dimension of Christ while the western Churches, especially the miaphysite (monophysite) ones such as the Jacobites or the Copts, stress rather his divine nature.

The intellectual power of the Church was further stimulated in the 5th century by the influx of Greek theologians from the West following the anti-Nestorian riots in Edessa in 457 and the Byzantine Emperor Zeno's closure of its famous School of the Persians in 489. Teachers and students fled to Nisibis (south-eastern Turkey), which had belonged since Shâpur II's victory over the Roman Emperor Julianus Apostata in 363 to Iran. The University of Nisibis was for a century the most famous university of the Church until it was challenged by those of Baghdâd and Gondeshâpur in Khuzestân, called Beit Lapat by the Christians. Here, in Gondeshâpur, the most famous Nestorian university came into being where the subjects taught spread over an

Armenian cross and inscription at the outer wall of the Saint Stephanos Church, Jolfâ

encyclopaedic width. Besides core religious subjects like theology, scriptural exegesis, rhetoric and grammar, others such as Greek and Indian medicine, mathematics, astronomy, astrology, Greek philosophy and logic were also taught. Later Khusro I (ruled 531–579) enlarged this Nestorian university to become the first state university where law, finance, administration and agriculture were also taught. In order to link the theoretical teaching to practice, a hospital and an observatory were attached to the university. This expansion of a Nestorian institution to a state university indicates that the relations between the Sasanian state and the increasingly numerous Christian minority were quite relaxed under Khusro I.

The fate of Gondeshâpur's neighbour Susa was also tightly bound with that of the Nestorians. The first example of this was its destruction by Shâpur II after 341, allegedly on account of a Christian rebellion. Similar catastrophes befell it in 420 when Bishop Abdas' refused to rebuild a Zoroastrian temple destroyed by one of his priests which provoked further persecutions, and also in 551 when the Christian son of Khusro I, Nushizad, unsuccessfully tried to overthrow his father. Although the local Christians were involved in the coup and were risking the wrath of the Shâh, he appointed the Nestorian Patriarch Mar Aba I (540–552) to convince the Nestorians to abandon the rebellion.

Only very few Nestorian architectural relics from the Sasanian time in Iran have survived, apart from those around Orumieh which is described below. The ruin of a Nestorian church founded at the end of the 4th century may have been identified in Merv, Khorâsân, which belongs today to Turkmenistan. Another possible Nestorian relic is Deir-e Gachin, situated 80 km (50 miles) south of Rey, a bishopric since the late 4th or early 5th century (see p. 200). On the island of Kharg in the upper Persian Gulf north-west of Bandar-e Bushehr, Christian tombstones as old as the 3rd century and ruins of a large Nestorian monastery built in the 5th century have been found. The Church of the East experienced stormy times under Shâh Khusro II (591–628). The ups and downs in the Church's history of those days were mainly as the result of the whims of Shirin, the king's favourite wife. Since she was a Nestorian, Khusro initially supported them. But the favourable climate deteriorated when the influential Nestorian physician Gabriel of Singar, who had apparently enabled Shirin to become pregnant with a son, quarrelled with Patriarch Sabrisho over a question of divorce. The angered Gabriel switched his allegiance to the Jacobites who had in the 6th century rapidly grown in numbers due to their persecution in the Byzantine Empire and the subsequent flight to Iran. Shirin followed her physician into the Jacobite Church and convinced her husband to now favour the Jacobites to the detriment of the Nestorians. After the Nestorian bishops tricked the Shâh in an election to the patriarchate, he forbade the position from being filled when it next fell vacant, and the Church remained leaderless from 608 to 628.

UNDER ARAB RULE

The Christians of Iraq and Iran met the invading Arabs with at least indifference, or even welcomed them as liberators; they had no reason to regret their former Sasanian oppressors. And had Mohammed not accepted the Christians and the Jews as People of the Book? At that time, the Christians were at the verge of becoming the religious majority of the Sasanian Empire, for they probably accounted for 40% of the total population. The Nestorians formed the bulk of the Christians with a share of about 75%, while the Jacobites accounted for 15 to 20% and the other Christians for 5% to 10%. The higher clergy of the Church of the East numbered at that time one patriarch, nine metropolitan bishops and 96 ordinary bishops: 106 bishops in total. The community was organized since the early Sasanian times as a semi-autonomous theocracy (later called millet), placed under the authority of their patriarch. He was responsible for the good behaviour of the members of his community, over whom he held judicial power and the right to gather the required taxes. His election had to be confirmed after 410 by the ruler, the Sasanian shâh or later the Muslim caliph. In that sense he was a state employee; in fact under the Abbâsid dynasty he became one of the highest dignitaries of the empire. Later the authority of Patriarch Timothy I (780–823) was expanded over all the Christians of the Caliphate, a jurisdiction which was formally confirmed on behalf of Patriarch Odisho II (1074–1090).

The status of the Christians was defined in the so-called Covenants of Omar. While these documents guaranteed life and property of the Christians and the integrity of the existing churches, they imposed many discriminatory burdens on the subject communities: Christians had to pay double taxation, they were prohibited from testifying in court against Muslims, the conversion of Muslims to Christianity was prohibited, and any conversion to Islam was seen as irreversible. The construction of new churches and the repair of existing ones was prohibited. The protected status of so-called dhimmis was equivalent to a socio-political ghetto which was further highlighted by public humiliations such as the obligation for Christians and Jews to wear a special belt or a yellow or red patch on the front and back of their clothing. In spite of these discriminations, the early Abbâsid time was a period of intellectual fertility. It was the Period of Translation, when Christian scholars translated philosophic and scientific texts from Greek to Syriac and then to Arabic. But under the Caliph al-Mutawakkil (847–861) the tide turned against the Nestorians, the discriminatory regulation were reinforced and many churches were either destroyed or changed into mosques.

A LAST RENAISSANCE UNDER MONGOL RULE

The 13th century brought dramatic changes. The Mongols, advancing from Central Asia, first devastated Khorâsân and destroyed cities with strong Nestorian minorities such as Merv, Nishâpur and Herât. Later, Hulagu (1256–1265), the grandson of Genghis Khân, conquered Baghdâd in 1258 and ended the Abbâsid Caliphate. Since the new rulers treated all religions as equal as long as their members obeyed the orders of the Mongol rulers, the Nestorians were now on an equal footing with Muslims. Their position was further improved by the fact that several il-Khâns had Nestorian mothers or wives who had within Mongolian society considerable influence: for example Hulagu's mother, Sorqoqtani; his chief wife Dokuz Khatun, who prompted her husband to build many churches, and another wife named Toquiti Khatun.

The Nestorians also participated in the diplomatic efforts of the il-Khâns to win military support from Christian powers against the Muslim Mamluks who had defeated the Mongolian Nestorian general Kid Buka in 1260 at Ain Jalut near Nazareth. Of the several envoys sent to Europe, the Uighur Nestorian Visitor-General Rabban Sauma (d. 1294) is the most famous. Patriarch Mar Yahballahah III (1281–1317) who was a native Mongol Ongüt was later personally involved when he wrote in 1302 to Pope Boniface VIII to endorse the credentials of Ghâzân Khân's envoy. The Muslim Ghâzân Khân (1295–1304) was so keen to obtain a military alliance from a European power against Egypt that he even offered to become Christian. But Ghâzân was not to become a Mongol Constantine. The Crusades had ended in disaster and Europe had lost interest in Palestine. Ghâzân remained Muslim and his successor, the Christian prince Nicholas converted to Islam under the name of Oljaitu (1304–1316). By this time, Irân and Iraq became irreversibly Muslim. Due to increased pressure, discrimination and the persecution by Tamerlane after 1380, a large share of the Nestorians either converted to Islam or left the cities and sought shelter in the mountainous regions of Kurdistan, Azerbaijân and in Hakkari (Eastern Turkey).

The Church of the East was not spared in its mountain refuge from the further blows of fate. In 1553, a major schism occurred when a part of its clergy under the leadership of Bishop John Sulaqa (d. 1555) entered into a union with the Catholic Church of Rome, from which the Chaldean Catholic Church arose with its present see in Baghdâd. After the 1840s the Muslim Kurds committed against the Nestorians—who now called themselves Assyrians—several massacres which culminated during World War I in the death of half of the Nestorian people and the assassination of their patriarch— a genocide proportional in size to the concurrent massacre of the Armenians. Lured by empty promises of an autonomous homeland, the Assyrians' irregular troops sided with the Russian troops operating in Azerbaijân and later fled to the British protectorate of Iraq. The Islamic revolution in 1979 and the first Gulf War in 1991 further accelerated the move into exile.

THE NESTORIANS IN THE ISLAMIC REPUBLIC OF IRÂN

Since 1979, half of Irân's 65,000 Nestorians have left the country. They now represent less than 0.05 % of Irân's population, and share with the 8,000 Chaldeans a parliamentary seat which is presently held by Mr. Yonathan Bet Kolia; the Armenians hold two seats. Although the constitution stipulates the equality of all Irânian citizens, there are many exceptions: 1. It remains strictly prohibited to convert Muslims to Christianity; the activity of conversion is in itself subject to punishment. On the other hand, conversions from Christianity to Islam are welcome and encouraged. 2. It is hardly possible for Assyrians to find public employment. 3. Professions commanding prestige or political power in the judiciary or politics are only open to Muslims. 4. The blood money to be paid for any Christian man killed was, until December 29th 2003, when the law was abrogated by the National Parliament, only 1/13th of the that for a Muslim man; for a Christian woman the figure was 1/26th.

On the other hand, the Christians are free to repair their churches or to build new ones should they be needed, which is not the case in other Muslim countries such as Egypt or Saudi Arabia. The head of the Irânian Bishopric is Cor-Episcopa Domara Benjamin who reports to Patriarch Mar Dinka IV (1976–), the former Bishop of Tehrân from 1962 till 1976. He is assisted by an archdeacon and five priests.

In Tehrân there are, besides the two main Nestorian Churches, also the Church of the Assyrian Pentecostals which numbers about 2000 followers, and a Church belonging to the Assyrian-Protestant community. Small Nestorian communities live in Tabriz, Esfahân, Hamadân and Ahvâz.

THE NESTORIAN CHURCHES OF ORUMIEH

After Tehrân, the second and traditional Nestorian stronghold in Irân is the region of Orumieh where about 10,000 Nestorians currently reside. It is a region rich not only with legends and lore—for example it is said that it is the birthplace of Zoroaster and that il-Khân Hulagu hid his treasures and found his last resting place on a tiny island in Lake Orumieh—but also with many ancient Nestorian churches. Within the western plain of Orumieh, which stretches from Salmas in the north to Kaleh Zeva in the south, about 100 Assyrian churches and chapels still exist. In most of them however mass is only celebrated at most only once a year at the respective saint's feast day. To visit the churches in the countryside it is recommended to hire a taxi driven by a Christian knowing the places and also where to fetch the key for entering the churches which are usually kept locked; the easiest is to ask for advice at the Virgin Mary Church in Orumieh city. The most interesting churches are:

First the Virgin Mary Church in downtown **Orumieh**, which is said to have been founded by St. Thomas on the spot where the Three Magi are said to have built a shrine having returned from Palestine. It is possible that the first chapel dates back to the 4th or 5th century. When Bishop Mar Yuhanan joined the Russian-Orthodox

The ancient (4th–5th century) Virgin Mary Church in the foreground,
and the modern Virgin Mary Church (1965) in the background, Orumieh

The Saints Sergius and Baccus Church in Bos Vatch. The ram standing in front will be sacrificed during a funeral service.

Church for political reasons in 1898 (he hoped Orumieh would become a Russian protectorate) St. Mary's was expanded in the Russian style. But this new church was destroyed by rampaging Kurds in 1918; today there are only a few Russian-Orthodox believers left in the region. The church was then rebuilt in the archaic style; it displays the typical ground plan of Nestorian churches. The entrance door is located at the southern side, which first leads to a crypt with the tombs of deacon Isha, brother of Patriarch Mar Shimun XIX murdered in 1918, and of a Russian missionary after which one enters the nave. As in all Syriac churches, access to the choir is restricted to the clergy only. Just next to this small church a new, much larger church has been constructed in 1965, which is also dedicated to the Virgin Mary. The Nestorians share it with the remaining Russian Orthodox Christians. Orumieh numbers more than 6000 Christians, of which half belongs to the Church of the East; the others are Protestants, Chaldeans and Russian Orthodox.

8 kilometres to the south-west of Orumieh stands the very old stone church dedicated to Saints Sergius and Baccus in the village of **Bos Vatch**. The old ritual of making sacrifices in front of the church is still performed on special occasions—for

example a ram at a funeral—and with its blood a cross is drawn on the arch above the entry. Another ancient, formerly widespread tradition is also maintained: people suffering from epilepsy or mental disorders are locked for a night in a pitch dark room below the crypt, where relics are kept walled in, whereupon they are supposedly healed. Not only Christians but Muslims also undergo this special form of therapy. Further down towards the centre of Bos Vatch one passes the tiny St. Mary's Chapel

The nave of the St. Sergius Church in Bos Vatch

which was built in 1995 after the Virgin allegedly appeared to Christians and Muslims alike.

Driving towards the mountain in the west one reaches after 20 km (12 miles) the village of **Dasgir** at an altitude of 1820 m above sea level. In the garden of a Kurdish farmer stands the incredibly tiny church dedicated to the famous Nestorian saint Rabban Hormizd. It is 2.5 m long, 1.8 m wide and 1.7 m high; to enter, one has to creep through the 60 cm low door. 14 km further to the north, the ancient

The Assyrian-Protestant Mar Thoma Church in Mushâbâd

Mar Thoma Church in **Balulan** is worth a visit. (The eastern Syriac word Mar is an honorific title attributed to saints and bishops.) Only another 5 km to the north stands the large Virgin Mary's Church in **Mawana**. Its ancient foundations built out of rough rocks remains up to 2 m high; the rest was rebuilt in 1879 with bricks.

The second excursion out of Orumieh to the north up to Salmas (around 80 km, 50 miles) follows the western side of the lake and will take a full day by taxi (about US$30 to 40). After 20 km (12 miles) one arrives first at the village of **Ada**. In its centre stands the large Mar Yuhanan Church built in 1901 out of red bricks. It belongs to the Church of the East, but is used by all Christian communities. Just outside of Ada stands the ancient Mar Daniel Church dating back to the late Sasanian period (6th/7th century). Ada has also two Nestorian cemeteries, of which the Holy Virgin cemetery at the hamlet of **Khamajieh** (Chamaki) is worth a visit. It numbers more than one hundred mostly engraved tombstones; unfortunately many of them have been broken by treasure hunters who have not recoiled even from opening tombs. Unfortunately, all unguarded churches and Christian cemeteries around Orumieh have been desecrated and even wilfully vandalized.

Only 4 km (2.5 miles) north of Ada the visitor arrives at the village of **Mushâbâd**, here stands the large Assyrian-Protestant Mar Thoma Church built in European style at the end of the 19th century. The church is surrounded by a 3 m high brick wall. It reminds one of the presence of the Protestant missions which were active from the 1830s until 1979, and which competed intensely among themselves and also with the Catholic Lazarist mission to "help" the Nestorians.

(Left) *The Nestorian Rabban Hormizd Chapel in Dasgir*

The Nestorian Mar Gewargis Church in Ardishai

While some missionaries honestly tried to support the Nestorians with religious books, schools, printing machines and medical services, others practised a policy of literally "buying souls". They rewarded the conversion to their own church with material goods like money, cattle or employment. Near Mushâbâd, the Virgin Mary Church is located in the village of **Yengija**, which was recently built in 1965. In those days more than 300 Nestorians lived here; now only two elderly people remain. All others went after 1979 either to Tehrân or else abroad. Just a couple of kilometres away, in **Supurghan**, the Assyrian Russian-Orthodox bishop Mar Yuhannan (1853–1911) is buried in the huge Mar Gewargis (George) Church built in a European late 19th century style out of red bricks.

From Mushâbâd it is a 28 km (17 miles) drive northwards to reach **Gawilan** which has two churches. The newer one is in the centre of the village while the very old Mar Yuhannan Chapel sits on a ridge overlooking the western shore of Lake Orumieh. Unfortunately, treasure-hunters have broken into the church and vandalized the choir. After a further 8 km (5 miles) northwards one reaches the village of **Govarchin** at the shore of the lake. The tiny peninsula called **Kazim Dashi** (fortress of Kazim) is one of the two islands where Hulagu is supposed to have hidden his treasures and found his last resting place. The famous historian Rashid od-Din (1247–1318) writes in his History of the Mongols of Persia: "Hulagu Khân had accumulated immense treasures taken from Baghdad. He ordered for a high fortress

The Nestorian Mar Gewargis Church in Khusro Âbâd was founded in 520 and destroyed in 1930 by an earthquake.

to be built on an island located in the Lake of Orumieh near Salmas. After all treasures were melted to ingots, they were hidden at that place." These treasures have never been found.

About another 30 km (20 miles) northwards, one arrives in the region of **Salmas**, called Delemon by the Christians, to the village of **Khusro Âbâd** (Khosrowa) whose bishop John of Persia allegedly attended the Council of Nicea in 325. Delemon and Khusro Âbâd were, with intervals, sees of the Chaldean Patriarchs from 1581 till 1672. According to the Syriac inscription located in the western entrance wall, the Mar Gewargis Church was founded in 520, an assertion which is not beyond the bounds of possibility. The earthquake of 1930 destroyed the building dating from the 11th century, which had been restored in 1845 by Catholic missionaries. Next to this church is the Mar Sargis (St. Sergios) Church. It was built by the Nestorians in the late 17th century and is now owned by the Armenians. Adjacent it stands the Church of the Sacred Heart, built in 1935, which is regularly used. Close to these churches is the large graveyard which is used by the Assyrian, Chaldean and Armenian communities jointly. Some of the 250 tomb-stones illustrate the profession of the deceased, and carry Syriac or Armenian inscriptions. The oldest tomb dates back to the 14th century. Besides some older tombs a large stone figure of a ram also stands; its significance is unclear. Are they a relic from the Mongol period or an adoption of the ancient Irânian veneration of

the ibex? Other tombs bear the names of Catholic French nuns and monks who worked here in the 19th century. The nearby (2 km, 1.25 miles) Nestorian Mar Jacub Church dating from the 13th century was on March 16th 1918 witness to tragic events, for it was here that the Nestorian Patriarch Benjamin Shimun XIX was perfidiously murdered by the Kurdish leader Aga Simko at the instigation of the governor of Tabriz.

The third excursion to the south-east of Orumieh takes about 4-5 hours by taxi. After a few kilometres one arrives at the village of **Göktepe** (Gugtapah), having passed a large cemetery with two small chapels next to the road. More than 700 Nestorian families lived here till 1979; today only nine are left; all the others have emigrated. While the Mar Zarya Church, dating from the 16th century and rebuilt in 1951, is well kept, the huge Mar Gewargis Church is a pathetic ruin; only the outer walls remains. The natural erosion of the building is being accelerated by the locals using bricks from the building for private construction. The large Nestorian cemetery, located on the top of a huge artificial mound behind the church which might have originally been a Zoroastrian sanctuary, has been desecrated like the graveyard of Khamajieh near Ada. Like at other Assyrian graveyards, large stone figures of a ram stand next to the tombs.

Only 3 km (2 miles) away from Göktepe is **Gülpashan**. Both churches built with red bricks at the end of the 19th century are either almost intact (the Virgin Mary Chuch) or in the process of being completely restored (the Mar Gewargis Church). The nearby Mar Sejun Church is a ruin abused as rubbish pit. About 15 km (10 miles) further south, close to the village of **Alqai**, is the Mar Addai (Thaddaeus) Church

The Nestorian Mar Jacub Church in Khusro Âbâd where Patriarch Mar Shimun XIX was murdered in March 1918.

The Nestorian cemetery of Göktepe located on an artificial hill,
probably a former Zoroastrian Shrine.

built in the 15th century. Although it lost its roof many decades ago, mass is still celebrated there every three or four years. A few minutes drive from Alqai is **Ardishai** where the Mar Gewargis Church, built out of red and yellow bricks, stands within a large orchard. This lonely church has also been robbed of all its contents and vandalized. A story preserved amongst the few remaining Christians relates a misfortune that befell a thief who wanted to steal the entrance door: having taken it off its hinges, he placed it on his shoulders, but suddenly was paralysed. Immediately, he dropped the door, put it back into its hinges, and fled.

PERSIAN POETRY

Poetry has always been one of the richest expressions of Persian creativity. Strongly influenced in its composition and vocabulary by Arabic poetry, Persian poetry is also the heir to a very ancient tradition of bardic verse. The first verses written in literary New Persian appear in the ninth century in Khorâsân; in the tenth century, the official encouragement of the use of Persian at the Sâmânid court, rather than Pahlavi (Middle Persian) or Arabic, stimulated the development of a written literature in that language. From that time on, the use of the Persian literary language spread to the entire plateau, gradually replacing the local dialects.

The official role played by poetry in the royal courts explains the appearance very early on of the panegyric *qasida* which proclaimed, according to well-defined models, the virtues and courage of the ruler or of a patron. Among the numerous poets of panegyric *qasida* were Anvari (died around 1187) and Khaqani (died in 1199), known for the subtlety of their images and themes.

A lyric form was developed from the *qasida*, the *ghazal*, a much shorter form used mainly to express love, both mystic and human. The *ghazal* flourished from the 12th century, and led to the uncontested masters of this form, Sa'adi (died around 1290) and Hâfez (died in 1389), whose use of language and subtlety of thought are unrivalled.

The *rubâ'i*, which became famous in Europe in the 19th century with Edward Fitzgerald's translation of Omar Khayyâm's poetry, and the *do-beiti* are both four-line poems which differ from one another in their rhythm. They deal with mystical, philosophical or romantic themes, and their form imparts the impression of both spontaneity and elegant precision. There are few Persian men of letters who have not written at least one *rubâ'i*, but the very number of these poems, which were rarely signed, makes it difficult to attribute them with any accuracy to a specific poet.

Apart from these short, precise poetic forms, there exists also a tradition of rhyming couplets, *masnavi*, used for narrative and epic poetry or for various forms of didactic works ranging from history to medicine. The epic dates back to the pre-Islamic period in Irân; Ferdosi himself was inspired by older epic works when he wrote his *Shâhnâmeh*. After Ferdosi, the epic poem was best developed by Nizami (1141–1209), the author of five long dramatic romantic epics, among which is *The Book of Alexander*, which tells of the feats and wisdom of the Macedonian conqueror, and Khusro and Shirin, which narrates the lifes and love of the Sasanian king and an Armenian princess. But the masnavi was also used with great success by Sufi poets, in particular by Farid od-Din Attâr (died around 1220) in his *Conference of the Birds*, which is considered one of the master-pieces of Persian literature, and by Jalâl od-Din Rumi (1207–1273) in his *Masnavi Manawi*.

WESTERN IRÂN

The western part of Irân, which covers the five modern provinces of Kordestân (Kurdistan), Kermânshâh, Hamadân, Ilâm and Lurestân, is dominated by the Zagros mountains with its deep valleys, its high cols and some surprisingly varied mountain scenery which is among the most beautiful in the country. Winters here are very cold with heavy snow falls, but summers are much more pleasant than on the plateau or near the Persian Gulf. At the beginning of this century, these provinces were still considered wild and dangerous, and even today they are under-developed, particularly Kordestân and Ilâm. There is no rail link, for example, between western Irân and the rest of the country except for one line that passes through southern Lurestân without even reaching the provincial capital. Despite this, the area has been one of vital strategic importance since antiquity because of its position between the Mesopotamian Basin and the Irânian Plateau. In the third millennium BC, the Kassites, Lullubi and Guti fought here against the Babylonian dynasties and the Akkadian Empire, causing the fall of the latter around 2200 BC. The Kassites, who had come from Lurestân, succeeded in establishing their own dynasty in Babylon between the 16th and 12th centuries BC. The Medes, who had settled in the modern province of Hamadân, fought for centuries against the Assyrian Empire, based in the Upper Tigris Basin, finally capturing its capital, Niniveh, in 612 BC. With the formation of the huge Achaemenian and Sasanian empires, western Irân retained strategic importance, located as it was between the imperial capitals (Babylon, Ctesiphon) and the Irânian Plateau.

The mountainous nature of the region and its cultural links with Mesopotamia lead to the development in this part of Irân of a very specific form of artistic expression, rock-carved bas-reliefs. Until the seventh century BC, these carvings were relatively few in number, but increased considerably once the Achaemenian rulers used them for political and religious reasons, combining figurative representations with inscriptions. This practice continued, with greater or lesser success depending on the period, during the Parthian, Seleucid and Sasanian dynasties. These carvings, often remarkably well preserved despite their age and the harshness of the climate, are historical documents of exceptional importance and form a large part of the cultural visits in the region. However, some of the sites require long detours by road and may therefore be difficult to include in a tour.

Today, western Irân is still the land of the Kurds and the Lurs, two of the main Irânian-speaking minorities. The precise identification of these ethnic groups through the centuries is difficult. It would appear that Kurdish mercenaries, known as Kardukoi, formed part of the army that attacked Xenophon's Ten Thousand in 400 BC. But the Arab geographers who later described the region used the term 'Kurd' for all the nomadic tribes in the area, regardless of their ethnic or cultural background. It was only after the Mongol invasions in the 13th century that the name 'Kordestân' was used to designate the whole northwestern zone of the Zagros. The central government of Irân never really had much direct administrative control over this region until 1865, during the Qâjâr dynasty, when the last Kurdish prince was dismissed from his post.

During the 1920s and 1930s, Kurdish demands for separatism, which were growing as much in Irân as in Turkey and Iraq, were suppressed by Rezâ Shâh. In 1946, however, taking advantage of the Russian occupation of northern Irân, the small Kurdish Republic of Mahâbâd was founded around Lake Orumieh. Isolated from other, more predominantly Kurdish areas further south, the republic lasted only a few months. Since then, the Kurdish question has been continually present in the political arena and has influenced many of the decisions taken by the central government. The problem of Irânian support for Kurdish autonomists in Iraq, for example, was one of the key points in the negotiations that lead to the signing, in 1975, of the Algiers Agreement between Irân and Iraq.

The Lurs live mainly in the provinces of Kermânshâh and Lurestân. The capital of the latter, **Khoram Âbâd**, has for centuries been identified with Lur regional power. It was here that the *atabek*, the Lur chieftains, built their citadel, the Dez-e Siâh or Black Fortress. For nearly four centuries, they controlled the region from this fortress and were only subdued when Shâh Abbâs stormed it at the beginning of the 17th century, putting the last *atabek* to death. The ruins of the fort, set atop a rocky outcrop, can still be visited today.

KERMÂNSHÂH

Kermânshâh (known for a brief period after the revolution as Bâkhtarân), is an important city of about half a million inhabitants. Less ancient than Hamadân, it is thought to have been founded during the reign of the Sasanian king Bahrâm IV, at the end of the fourth century AD. Because of its location on the main roads leading to Baghdâd and Kirkuk and its proximity to the Mesopotamian border, it has been repeatedly attacked during its history. It suffered badly during the wars between the Ottoman and Safavid empires (the last occupation of the town by the Turks was in 1915) and more recently in the war with Iraq. From September 1980, the border

Bas-relief showing the investiture of Ardeshir II, centre, receiving the sacred crown from the Ahura Mazda, Tâq-e Bustân, Kermânshâh

region around Qasr-e Shirin, Sar-e Pol-e Zahâb and Gilân-e Gharb (less than 200 kilometres, 125 miles, from Kermânshâh) became one of the two main fronts of the war, and Kermânshâh, with its large oil refinery, was a prime target for Iraqi shelling. As a result, much of the town has been rebuilt recently.

A few kilometres northeast of Kermânshâh, nestled at the foot of the Paru Mountains, is the Sasanian site of **Tâq-e Bustân** (the Arch of the Garden), where a series of bas-reliefs and grottoes have been carved into the cliff face. The first of these reliefs can be seen just after the entrance to the garden, before reaching the grottoes. It represents the investiture of Ardeshir II (379–383), with the king in the centre, standing over a Kushan soldier (or Ahriman, the god of Evil), and receiving the royal diadem from the hands of the god Ahura Mazda, on the right. Mithra is shown standing on the left, holding the sacred barsom twig-bundle.

The grottoes of Tâq-e Bustân are unique in Sasanian art. It is possible that three grottoes were originally intended, with two smaller ones flanking a larger, central one. The right-hand cave, the later of the two existing ones, is decorated on the back wall with representations of Shâpur III (383–388) and his grandfather, Shâpur II (310–379), shown leaning on their swords. Beside each of them is an inscription in Pahlavi which identifies them.

The left-hand grotto, the larger and most complex one, is generally dated either to the reign of Firuz (457–484) or to Khusro II (591–628). Unlike the previous grotto, there is no inscription here to identify the figures with certainty. The outer wall around the entrance is decorated with floral motifs, similar to the designs found on fragments of carved stucco from Sasanian palaces, and with two winged figures holding a royal diadem. The back wall is divided into two registers. The upper one shows another royal investiture with the king standing between the gods Ahura Mazda and the goddess Anâhitâ. Beneath this is a remarkable sculpture of a knight on horseback, dressed in full armour with jousting lance raised. This warrior is thought by some scholars to represent Khusro II and his horse Shabdiz. Close examination of the astonishing detail, particularly of the chain mail, will reveal the sculptor's skill. In the large hunting scenes on the side walls, the king is again shown as the principal figure, successfully shooting the game driven towards him by his beaters. The scene at the top of the left wall, which still bears some of the original paint, is a much later addition which dates to the reign of the Qâjâr ruler Fath Ali Shâh (1798–1834). Near the entrance to the site are several fragments of Sasanian columns and capitals which were found in the area.

The road which leaves Kermânshâh for the Iraqi border (and which used to continue to Baghdâd) goes through **Sar-e Pol-e Zahâb** (120 kilometres, 75 miles) where some of the earliest rock carvings in Irân may be seen. The most important one dates back to the end of the third millennium BC and shows the victorious king Annubanini of the Lullubi, a mountain people who controlled the trade routes between Babylon and the Irânian Plateau. The king is portrayed standing with one foot on a slain enemy while the goddess Inanna presents him with a royal ring. Beneath the figures, an inscription in Akkadian invokes the help of the gods against the enemy. It is this bas-relief, whose composition is said to have inspired the Achaemenian artists who carved Darius' bas-relief at Bisotun (see below).

BISOTUN

About 40 kilometres (25 miles) from Kermânshâh, in the direction of Hamadân, the road passes under a tall cliff which bears one of the most famous bas-reliefs in Irân. This is the site of **Bisotun** (or Behistun). In addition to the Achaemenian carving for which the site is best known, there are several later sculptures scattered around the foot of the cliff next to the road. Among these are two Parthian carvings accompanied by Greek inscriptions. The left one, unfortunately badly damaged by a 17th century Persian inscription, represents king Mithridates II (123–87 BC) receiving four dignitaries. This is the oldest known Parthian carving and still reflects the traditional Achaemenian manner of presenting figures in profile rather than face on. The right-hand carving commemorates the victory of Gotarzes II (AD 38–51) over his rival Meherdates and shows the king on horseback brandishing a spear and accompanied by a winged Victory. The style in this much later sculpture is closer to the Roman.

On the far right of the site, protected by a metal covering, is a Seleucid carving (148 BC) in high relief showing a reclining Heracles. Nearby, on an isolated block of stone, is a further Parthian carving showing a priest or a nobleman carrying out a ritual at an altar. The inscription accompanying it mentions the name of Vologases, the name of five Parthian kings who ruled between 51 and 228 AD.

The most famous carving at Bisotun is set about sixty metres above the road. It was sculpted by order of the Achaemenian king Darius I in 520 BC to commemorate his victory over the Magus Gaumata and the subsequent consolidation of his power. In 522 BC, it was claimed that Gaumata rebelled against Cambyses II and usurped the throne. He was executed a few months later by Darius who then proclaimed himself king. However, his legitimacy to the throne was contested by eight other pretenders who began a series of rebellions. In this relief, Darius is represented on the left, standing over the body of Gaumata. Facing him are the eight rebel chiefs chained together. The last figure, wearing a pointed hat, is Skunkha, king of the Scythians, whose portrait was added to the bas-relief at a later date after Darius' victory against the Scythians in 518 BC. Behind Darius, on the left, stand his allies, Gobryas and Artaphernes. Above the prisoners hangs the winged symbol of Ahura Mazda, the all-powerful god, in whose name the Achaemenian kings ruled. Although this relief of Darius is the first great art work of his reign, the representation of the figures surpasses that of the time of Cyrus the Great. The inspiration for this carving appears to have come from the Lullubi relief at Sar-e Pol-e Zahâb (see above): the composition is very similar and makes use of size to indicate the relative importance of the figures.

Around the relief are inscriptions in three languages, Elamite, Neo-Babylonian (or Akkadian) and Old Persian, which give the official version of Darius' fight for power and his final triumph. The importance of this text lies in the fact that it is the only one by an Achaemenian ruler to relate the historical events of his reign and those that preceded it. Darius recounts Gaumata's rebellion against Cambyses II in detail, followed by the rebellions of each of the eight provinces and their final defeats. He ends with an acknowledgement of Ahura Mazda's invaluable assistance in his struggle—thereby justifying the legitimacy of his claim to the throne—and appeals to future rulers to preserve the monument and spread his message. The Elamite text, which appears to have been carved first, is in two sections, one to the right of the relief and the other below, to the left. The Babylonian text is carved on the left, and the Old Persian text directly below, the figures. It was thanks to these inscriptions, which are comparable in value to the Rosetta stone, that a British officer, Henry Rawlinson, was able, in 1838, to decipher Old Persian cuneiform.

Darius' decision to carve his message to the world on the Bisotun cliff was hardly an arbitrary one: the cliff is directly above the road that lead from his summer capital, Ecbatana, to Babylon. The message itself was addressed as much to posterity as to his subjects. Indeed, the inscriptions are placed too high to be read from the road and access to them was deliberately rendered almost impossible, on the king's orders, by smoothing down the surface of the rock beneath them. But copies of the inscriptions—of which several fragments have been found—were sent to each province of the empire, including Babylon, thus ensuring that the king's message was made known to all.

Further along the same road is the small town of **Kangâvar**, about 90 kilometres (56 miles) from Hamadân. Excavations here have revealed the remains of a temple dedicated to Anâhitâ, the goddess of water and abundance, which dates back to Seleucid or Parthian

One of the trilingual inscriptions at Ganjnâmeh (Hamadân), carved by the Achaemenian kings Darius I and Xerxes

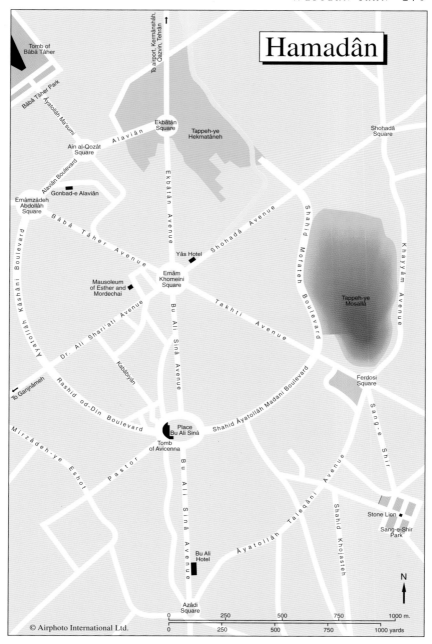

Hamadân

Tomb of
Bâbâ Tâher

Bâbâ Tâher Park

Âyatollâh Ma'sumi

To airport, Kermânshâh, Qazvin, Tehrân

Ekbâtân
Square

Tappeh-ye
Hekmatâneh

Shohadâ
Square

Ain al-Qozât
Square

Alaviân

Alaviân Boulevard

Gonbad-e Alaviân

Emâmzâdeh
Abdollâh
Square

Bâbâ Tâher Avenue

Ekbâtân Avenue

Shohadâ Avenue

Yâs Hotel

Emâm
Khomeini
Square

Mausoleum
of Esther and
Mordechai

Âyatollâh Kâshâni Boulevard

Dr. Ali Shari'ati Avenue

Bu Ali Sinâ Avenue

Takhti Avenue

Shahid Mofateh Boulevard

Tappeh-ye
Mosallâ

Khayyâm Avenue

To Ganjnâmeh

Rashid od-Din Boulevard

Kababiyân

Shahid Âyatollâh Madani Boulevard

Ferdosi
Square

Mirzâdeh-ye Eshot

Pastor

Place
Bu Ali Sinâ

Tomb
of Avicenna

Sang-e Shir

Bu Ali Sinâ Avenue

Âyatollâh Taleqâni Avenue

Shahid Khojasteh

Stone Lion

Sang-e-Shir
Park

Bu Ali Sinâ Avenue

Âyatollâh Taleqâni Avenue

Bu Ali
Hotel

N

Azâdi
Square

| 0 | 250 | 500 | 750 | 1000 m. |

| 0 | 250 | 500 | 750 | 1000 yards |

© Airphoto International Ltd.

times. The site was first described in 1840 by two Frenchmen, Eugène Flandin and Pascal Coste, although the presence of modern houses on the site at the time led to inaccuracies in the drawing of their temple plan. Excavations were carried out in the 1960s and 1970s, but have been interrupted since. Today, the main remains are the platform on which the temple was built and a large staircase on the south side leading up to it. The best preserved part of the temple is in the western corner where several sections of columns are visible (the best view of them is to be had from the side road parallel to that part of the temple). Fragments of columns and building blocks have been assembled in front of the staircase and, despite the work that has already been carried out, it is still rather difficult to imagine the overall layout of the temple complex.

HAMADÂN

The city of **Hamadân**, the provincial capital, is equidistant from Sanandaj, Kermânshâh and Arâk at the foot of the Alvand Mountains (3,565 metres, 11,696 feet) in the Zagros, at an altitude of 1,700 metres (5,577 feet). It occupies a key site on the road which, even in antiquity, linked Mesopotamia to the Irânian Plateau. It is here that the first Median capital, Ecbatana, was founded. The Medes, who formed a loose federation of warlike tribes of Indo-European origin, settled on the plateau around the ninth century BC. In 673 BC, the chieftain of one of these tribes, Phraortes, succeeded in unifying the various Median groups under his command and established his capital at Ecbatana, the 'Place of Assembly'. In 550 BC, Cyrus the Great defeated the last Median king, Astyages, and Ecbatana became the summer residence of the Achaemenian court, well away from the torrid heat of Susa. After Alexander the Great's conquest (331 BC), Ecbatana lost much of its former importance although it remained a staging post between the plateau and Mesopotamia. In the 12th century, Hamadân briefly became the capital of the Saljuq dynasty, but it was destroyed a century later during the Mongol invasion, and again by Tamerlane's armies in 1386. Because of its position, Hamadân was also severely hit by the wars between the Ottoman and Safavid empires—the Turks occupied the city from 1724 to 1730—to the extent that when the English writer James Morier visited it in 1813, he found little more than a mass of ruins.

These successive sackings have spared few of Hamadân's ancient monuments. In addition, part of the modern town around the small hill known as Tappeh-ye Hekmatâneh, near Ekbâtân Square, is built over the site of Ecbatana and no large-scale excavations have yet been carried out on the ancient Median capital. For the moment, almost the only visible remains of the pre-Islamic era is the **Sang-e Shir**, or Stone Lion, a statue tentatively dated to the Parthian dynasty which has been set up in a park in the southeast of town. With a little imagination one can just make out the form of a lion in the now shapeless rock, badly eroded by time and weather, and smoothed down by the thousands of women's hands which have patted it in the hope that their wishes would be fulfilled.

In the very centre of Hamadân is Emâm Khomeini Square (once Pahlavi Square), from which radiate six large avenues connected to each other by a ring road. The main monuments in town are to be found within or just outside this ring road. The oldest monument is undoubtedly the mausoleum of **Esther and Mordechai**, located in a small side street off Shari'ati Avenue, near Khomeini Square. This is an important Jewish pilgrimage site and Hamadân still has a small and elderly Jewish community, at present numbering 28. According to tradition, Esther, the Jewish concubine of the Achaemenian king Xerxes (485–465 BC), succeeded in securing royal protection for the followers of her faith and organized, with the help of her uncle Mordechai, the establishment of Jewish colonies throughout the Persian Empire. However, the tomb is also attributed to a Sasanian queen who died in the early fifth century AD. Inside, are two wooden cenotaphs draped with cloth; the bones have been buried in the crypt.

Near the ring road stands the **Gonbad-e Alaviân**, a 12th century Saljuq tomb (the original dome has disappeared, replaced by a modern roof). The *mehrâb*, as well as the walls inside and out, are decorated with geometric and floral designs in carved stucco. In the crypt, which can also be visited, is a tomb covered in various votive offerings. To get to the tomb, follow Bâbâ Tâher Avenue from Khomeini Square to *Emâmzâdeh* Abdollâh Square, and turn right onto Alaviân Boulevard. The tomb is located in the courtyard of a school (the entrance door is in a small street to the right of the boulevard).

The two other mausoleums in Hamadân are modern constructions which are reminiscent, each in their own way, of the tall Gonbad-e Qâbus in Mâzanderân Province, which dates back to the 11th century (see page 223). The first tomb is that of **Avicenna**, located south of Khomeini Square on Bu Ali Sinâ Avenue. Built in 1952, this tower is composed of a conical roof held up by twelve tall pillars around an empty central space. A small museum at the foot of the tower contains copies of Avicenna's works.

Born in Bokhârâ around 980, Abu Ali Hosein ibn Abdollâh ibn Sinâ, or Avicenna, was one of the most influential—and criticized—scholars both in the Islamic world and in the West. One hundred and fifty-seven works have been attributed to him on such diverse subjects as metaphysics, mechanics, acoustics, astronomy, and geometry. In Europe, Avicenna is best known for his *al-Qânum fit'tibb*, or 'Canon of Medicine', translated into Latin by Gerard of Cremona in the 12th century. This encyclopaedic work in five volumes is the sum total of Islamic medical knowledge at the time; its scope, clarity, layout and particularly its synthesis of ideas from Galen and Aristotle were to make it one of the most important texts in European medical faculties until the 17th century.

Avicenna took up Aristotle's ideas on logic and metaphysics, including the importance of scientific observation. But such peripatetic philosophy and logic were criticized by many schools of thought, and Avicenna's writings in particular were strongly attacked by the great Sufi scholar al-Ghazâli (1058–1111). Even in Europe, Avicenna did not escape criticism: in 1526, Paracelsus is said to have burnt a copy of the Canon at Basel University.

The second tomb is that of **Bâbâ Tâher**, built in the north of the town in a small park. Like Avicenna's tomb, it has twelve external pillars, but here the central space is filled by the tower itself. Very little is known about the life of Bâbâ Tâher, a famous Sufi poet who lived between the tenth and 13th centuries and who gained his reputation for his *do-bayti*, four-line poems of a simpler metre than the *rubâ'i*. In these poems, Bâbâ Tâher presents himself as a humble dervish, filled with passion and love for God yet deeply aware of Man's insignificance and loneliness. To resolve these problems, the poet seeks the way to absorption and annihilation within God.

A dozen kilometres southwest of town, in the Alvand Hills, is the site of **Ganjnâmeh**. At the end of a narrow valley, two Achaemenian inscriptions have been carved into the rock face, the first one by Darius I (522–486 BC) and the second by his son Xerxes (486–465 BC). Both are written in three languages, Old Persian, Neo-Elamite and Neo-Babylonian, and are practically identical in wording to one another, differing only in the name and genealogy of each ruler. The inscriptions begin by praising the god Ahura Mazda, creator of the world, of Paradise, of Man and of the Great King of the Achaemenians and end with the titles of the ruler, including that of King of Kings (*Shâhânshâh*), and with the name of his father.

KHUZESTÂN PROVINCE

The Khuzestân Plain which lies at the foot of the Zagros and Bakhtiâri mountains is a prolongation of the Mesopotamian Plain in Iraq, through which flow the Tigris and Euphrates rivers. The southeastern frontier of the province, near Abâdân and Khoram Shahr, is formed by the Shatt el-Arab (or Arvand-rud in Persian), the confluence of these two great rivers. The Khuzestân Plain, which has a surface area of some 40,000 square kilometres (15,444 square miles), is the largest expanse of low-level land in Irân, rising, at the foot of the mountains, to a height of only 170 metres (558 feet) above sea level. Just like Mesopotamia, Khuzestân is a fertile plain, particularly along its main rivers, the Dez, Karkheh and Kârun. Thanks to the construction, in the 1960s, of a large dam on the Karkheh, it has been possible to provide better irrigation for the plain. This in turn has lead to the wider cultivation of crops in the region, including the native sugar cane. Today, the province's wealth comes mainly from its oil deposits, concentrated in Lower Khuzestân (south of Ahvâz) where large-scale salination of the soil has rendered vast expanses of land completely sterile, preventing the agricultural development of the area.

The population of Khuzestân is ethnically very mixed and includes a high proportion of Arabs. The Safavid Dynasty had named the region Arabistân, recognizing the ethnic origin of the majority of its inhabitants. In the 17th and 18th centuries, Arabistân was claimed as much by Persia as by the Ottoman Empire. Local authority was in the hands of two Bedouin tribes, first the Bani Kaab and then the Bu Kassab who, in 1812, founded the emirate and town of Mohammara (now Khoram Shahr). Caught between two powerful empires, the emirs of Mohammara succeeded nevertheless, through careful politics, in keeping their autonomy. After 1908, the emirate even benefited from military assistance from the British, who were keen to protect the oil wells and refineries that they controlled in the area. However, the foundation of the Pahlavi Dynasty in 1925 marked the end of the emirate. The Persian army invaded Arabistân and captured the emir. Then began a movement to counter the strong Arab identity in the province: Arabistân was renamed Khuzestân (Country of Towers), Mohammara became Khoram Shahr, the Persian language replaced Arabic and the immigration of non-Arab families was encouraged. Spontaneous revolts, which became more and more organized, began and continued until the 1970s.

THE IRÂN–IRAQ WAR

Of all the Irânian provinces, Khuzestân suffered the most from the war between Irân and Iraq and was the scene of some of the bloodiest and hardest-fought battles. The Iraqi high command had hoped to cash in on the historical and cultural links between the populations living on either side of the Shatt el-Arab, Iraq's only access to the Persian Gulf, but the expected uprising against the Irânian government failed to materialize. The strategic and economic importance of the oil-rich lands in Irân directly to the east of the Shatt el-Arab explain in large part the Iraqi aggression and the concentration of their attacks on the urban centres of Ahvâz, Khoram Shahr and Abâdân. **Abâdân**, originally an island in the Arvand-rud with a population of a few hundred villagers, became, in 1913, the site of an oil refinery. It was chosen partly because of its proximity to the port of **Khoram Shahr**, the old emirate of Mohammara, located at the confluence of the Arvand-rud and the Kârun. The latter, which is navigable as far as Ahvâz, the capital of Khuzestân, 160 kilometres (99 miles) further north, allowed relatively easy communication with the hinterland. A town rapidly developed around the Abâdân

refinery, and, in the 1970s, had grown to over 300,000. In 1980, the refinery was the largest in the world and was therefore of vital economic importance to Irân.

All three towns have been largely rebuilt since the end of the war with Iraq. At one point Khoram Shahr became a ghost town and was all but razed to the ground. In May 1982, the Irânian army launched an offensive to recover Khoram Shahr, with the reported loss of some 50,000 lives. The shelling of the towns of Khuzestân, and particularly of Dezful in the north, lead to an exodus of the population, with nearly two million refugees forced to settle in camps set up well inland. Today, however, oil drilling and processing is well under way again and the port of Khoram Shahr is functional once more.

SUSA AND THE SUSIAN PLAIN

The province of Khuzestân can be divided into two separate zones, Upper and Lower Khuzestân. The former, which includes the Susian Plain, has a higher rainfall than Lower Khuzestân (south of Ahvâz). Thanks to this and a good

Fragments of columns at Susa, c. 1881

understanding of irrigation techniques, Susiana has been, at various times in its history, an extremely fertile plain. While the climate in winter is very pleasant, with temperatures rarely below 20° C (68° F), summers are scorching, and temperatures regularly reach over 50° C (120° F). It is this climate which drove the Achaemenian rulers to leave their administrative capital of Susa in summer for Ecbatana (Hamadân), situated more than 500 kilometres (311 miles) further north in the mountains.

The Susian Plain owes much of its historical importance to its geographic location, which resulted in the introduction of the Sumerian and Babylonian cultures into this part of Irân from the fourth millennium BC. This location also contributed to the development of Elamite civilization.

About 30 kilometres (19 miles) from Dezful, and 115 kilometres (71 miles) north of Ahvâz, is the small town of Shush, the site of the ancient city of **Susa** and a pilgrimage centre for the faithful who come to pray at the tomb of Daniel (see below). Despite the importance and long history of Susa, there is very little left of the monuments today, and the visitor will have to make quite a considerable effort to picture what this glorious city might have looked like at the different stages of its development.

PRE-ELAMITE SUSA

There are several distinct periods of human settlement at Susa. A first religious and administrative centre was built at the beginning of the fourth millennium BC. This very early period is not well understood, but the discovery of numerous seals and high quality vessels suggests links with Lurestân and the Irânian Plateau, not just with Mesopotamia. During the fourth millennium BC, Susa turned away from the Irânian world and drew closer to Sumer, centred around the city of Uruk in Mesopotamia. This swing between two civilizations, from Mesopotamia to Irân and back again, became a characteristic feature of Susian Plain history.

Gradually, a new culture with its own script, sometimes called proto-Elamite, developed around Susa. The city became an important trading centre, and the excavation of the stratigraphical layers of this epoch have revealed a large number of seals, inscribed tablets which deal mainly with accounts and small marble statues. This period appears to have ended rather abruptly for reasons that are still unclear, and Susa turned once again to Mesopotamia, becoming a medium-sized town of Sumerian type (c. 2800–2300 BC). Around 2300 BC, Susa was annexed by the Semite Akkad Empire and elevated to the rank of main city of one of the empire's administrative regions. After going through a period of peace and prosperity which ended with the fall of Akkad in 2150 BC, Susa was captured by the new, independent state of Elam, which had formed in the nearby mountains.

THE ELAMITE EMPIRE

It was as capital of the Elamite empire (2000–500 BC) that Susa was to know its period of greatest glory, particularly during the 12th century BC after the destruction of the Babylonian Kassite Empire by Elam. An impressive amount of treasure was brought back from Babylon to Susa, including the famous Code of Hammurabi (now in the Louvre Museum in Paris), victory statues of the kings of Akkad and royal charters. However, at the end of the 12th century, during the reign of Nebuchadnezzar I, Babylon took its revenge. Susa was sacked and burned to the ground.

Practically nothing is known about the four centuries following the destruction of Susa, but it would appear that the city was rebuilt and prospered once again. One date is certain, that of the sack of Susa in 645 BC by the Assyrian king Assurbanipal after the Elamites suffered a severe defeat in 659 BC. Elamite power was broken, but the Assyrian Empire was to last only a few more years itself, and Susa was integrated into the Persian Achaemenian Empire.

ACHAEMENIAN SUSA

Susa under Achaemenian rule produced another brilliant period in its history. In 521 or 520 BC, Darius I decided to make the city his administrative capital. Its geographical location halfway between Babylon and Pasargadae was very favourable. The reconstruction and embellishment of Susa continued throughout Darius' reign, and Artaxerxes II later added a new palace to the south. Unlike Persepolis, which appears not to have been known to the Greeks before Alexander the Great's conquest, Susa's reputation as a great city had already travelled far beyond the borders of the empire. But the breakup of Alexander's empire marked the end of Susa's role as capital. Under the Seleucids, the town was renamed Seleucia on the Eulaeos, and the objects found there from this period suggest a certain Hellenization of the town. During the Parthian period, Susa prospered but its population declined dramatically under the Sasanians. In the 13th century, the town developed again to some extent, due in part to the number of pilgrims visiting Daniel's tomb, but it then declined again thereafter.

It was not until the 19th century that the West rediscovered Susa; the first archaeological surveys were carried out in 1851 by a British mission, and were followed by excavations directed by William Loftus. From 1884 to 1896, Marcel and Jane Dieulafoy unearthed part of the Achaemenian palace and found the famous glazed brick lion and archer friezes which are now on show in the Louvre Museum in Paris. Several French archaeologists then worked at Susa from the late 19th century to the mid-1960s: Jacques de Morgan; Roger de Mecquenem; and finally Roman Ghirshman who spent twenty-one years there, working his way down the various stratigraphic levels. In the late 1960s and 1970s, the excavations were taken over by joint Irânian and American teams.

VISITING THE SITE
THE ACROPOLIS
The main remains at Susa date back to the Achaemenian period and are dispersed on two of the four hills of the site. The most imposing monument, and one which no visitor can fail to notice on arrival, is in fact a modern one: it is the castle, built at the end of the 19th century by the French director of excavations, Jacques de Morgan, as the team's headquarters. It is built on the tell of the acropolis and has the advantage of allowing the visitor to get his bearings as it is visible from a great distance in this plain whose small hills are otherwise devoid of other distinguishing marks. The acropolis was the site of the Elamite royal city, although excavations have also revealed stratigraphic layers dating back to the Neolithic, proto-Elamite, Achaemenian, Parthian and Sasanian periods. At present, there are few visible remains of the acropolis and any earth walls still surviving are rapidly being eroded by the elements.

THE ÂPÂDÂNÂ
The foundations of the palace of Darius I are to be seen on the tell of the âpâdânâ to the northeast of the acropolis. The palace was built on a partly artificial terrace; the only access to it was from the eastern side, by a ramp that led to Darius' Gate. The palace was composed of a series of courtyards aligned on the same axis and flanked by smaller chambers which probably served as apartments. To the north of the terrace was the âpâdânâ, a hypostyle room of 36 columns, each topped by a capital in the shape of animals set back to back. Three of the sides of the âpâdânâ opened out onto columned porticos.

Modern access to the hill is from the west, through the apartments surrounding the courtyards. The latter are still easily recognizable by their paved floors and the walls separating the various rooms have been partly rebuilt in brick and clay so that the overall plan of the palace is visible. The famous glazed brick lion frieze that Dieulafoy took back to Paris was found at the foot of the north wall in the east courtyard. In the âpâdânâ a few fragments of columns and capitals have been left on the ground.

OTHER VISITS
To the east of the âpâdânâ was the **royal city** with the residential quarters of the court and officials; this site was also occupied in the Parthian, Sasanian and Islamic periods. In the 1970s, a second palace, which is thought to date from the reign of

Artaxerxes II, was discovered on the other bank of the Shur behind Daniel's tomb. Near the entrance to the site of Susa, on the main road of the village, a small museum exhibits some of the objects found during the excavations (the opening hours here are rather erratic, particularly in the afternoon).

Near the museum is the **tomb of the prophet Daniel** (ârâmgâh-e Dânyâl), recognizable by its white sugar loaf dome, which still attracts large numbers of pilgrims every year. The honeycomb appearance of the 13th-century dome is characteristic of Khuzestân. The front of the tomb, with its central *eivân* flanked by two short minarets, is decorated in blue tiles. Men and women enter the building by separate doors (*châdors* must be worn by women and may be hired at the entrance) and remain apart during the entire visit. Like many mausoleums, this one is richly decorated inside with small mirrors.

CHOQÂ ZANBIL

Forty-five kilometres (28 miles) from Susa, on the road to Ahvâz, stand the ruins of the ziggurat of **Choqâ Zanbil**, by far the best preserved of the few Elamite monuments to have survived. The ziggurat, a pyramidal stepped temple, evolved from the early Sumerian temple platforms and became characteristic of Mesopotamia. Choqâ Zanbil, however, is so far a unique example of this form of architecture in Elam. Investigatory excavations were first carried out on the site in the 1930s by the Frenchman Roger de Mecquenem, and systematic excavations followed between 1951 and 1962, directed by Roman Ghirshman. These unearthed the earliest glazed tiles to be used in Irân for decorative purposes. Although still simple in shape and design, they are the precursors of the later Achaemenian murals from Susa.

In 1330 BC, a change of dynasty in the Elamite kingdom marked the beginning of a new period of territorial expansion. In the 13th century BC, the king Untash-Napirisha (or Untash-Gal according to the old method of transcription) founded a religious capital, Dur Untash, on the road from Susa to Anshân, the main city of Elam. The centre of this new town was the temple, dedicated to the god Inshushinak, which was surrounded by the walled religious city.

At this period, the temple consisted only a vast square courtyard enclosed within walls. The ziggurat was built later when the king decided to dedicate the temple not just to Inshushinak, the god of Susa, but also to Napirisha, the god of Anshân. The original construction became the ground floor of the ziggurat and the upper four storeys were built one inside the other (rather than one on top of the

The Elamite ziggurat of Choqâ Zanbil, c. 13th century BC.

other as was the case in Mesopotamia) until the entire surface of the old central courtyard was covered over. A small temple was erected at the summit. Today, the ziggurat stands only 25 metres (82 feet) tall but would have reached over 60 metres (197 feet) originally. Unlike the Mesopotamian ziggurats which are squatter and have three outer staircases, this has only a single covered staircase which is invisible from the outside.

On the northwest side of the ziggurat stood a group of temples dedicated to the secondary divinities (Ishnikarab and Kiririsha). An oval wall surrounded these temples and the ziggurat; a second larger wall enclosed yet more temples, and a third and final one protected the city of Al-Untash. It appears that houses were never actually built in the city, but a royal quarter has been identified in the south-east which included residential buildings and a funerary palace equipped with vaults to hold the royal ashes. A nearby temple was dedicated to Nusku, the fire god.

Al-Untash was abandoned in the 12th century BC when the Elamite kings moved to Susa, taking with them the treasures of Choqā Zanbil which were to decorate the newly-restored temples of Susa. In 640 BC, Al-Untash was completely destroyed by the Assyrian king Ashurbanipal a few years after his conquest of Susa.

Choqā Zanbil is still located within a military zone and it is necessary to get written permission from the Shush Archaeological Bureau to visit it. Photography is not allowed at the site.

The capital of Khuzestān, **Ahvāz**, is located almost in the centre of the province, 140 kilometres (87 miles) south of Shush and 130 kilometres (81 miles) north of Khoram Shahr. It is an industrial town, largely rebuilt after the war with Iraq, but is useful as a stopover for people visiting Susa and the region. Note that distances by road between Ahvāz and the major tourist sites outside the province, such as Shirāz or Hamadān, are quite considerable, and that at the moment there are few air links with other cities, except Tehrān.

For those with free time on their hands and who are particularly interested in the ancient history of Irân, there are several possible excursions to be made around Masjed-e Soleimān and Izeh (the roads are not always very good in this area, and distances are quite great, between 160 and 240 kilometres (99 and 149 miles) from Ahvāz). Near **Masjed-e Soleimān**, now a large industrial centre, are the remains of several terraces, thought to be of Achaemenian date and which may be the forerunners of the terraces at Pasargadae and Persepolis. About 25 kilometres (16 miles) north, at **Bard-e Neshandeh**, is yet another terrace. Parthian statues and carvings have been found here, although it appears that the site was occupied as early as the Achaemenian period.

Slightly further east, near **Izeh**, are a series of Elamite rock carvings. One of these, at Kuh-e Farah (eighth century BC), represents, in superimposed registers, long processions of worshippers and is believed to have influenced the composition of the Achaemenian bas-reliefs on the staircases at Persepolis. About 40 kilometres (25 miles) north of Izeh, in the Bakhtiāri Hills, is the site of **Shami** where the famous bronze statue of a Parthian prince, now on show in the Archaeological Museum in Tehrân, was found. The remains of a Seleucid and Parthian temple as well as a terrace are still visible at the site.

FARSI FOR SILK

I arrived in Osku with an effective Persian vocabulary of one word. I got out of the bus and said it. 'Abrisham'. Around me were scenes of mid-afternoon torpor. Old men lay sprawled about in the shade of a tree. Some sipped tea through sugar lumps held in their teeth. It was very hot. A few of the old men looked up, but no one answered me. I took a glass of tea from a ragged chai-khana boy, and slumped down against the bark. Now was no time for battling against language problems.

An hour later the sun had sunk a little lower and I tried again.

'Abrisham', I said.

The old man next to me shrugged his shoulders.

'Abrisham', I said again.

This time, for some reason, it worked.

'Abrisham'? said the Persian.

'Abrisham', I replied.

The old man muttered to his neighbor and a Chinese whisper passed around the tree. One of the younger old men on the far side of the trunk was deputed to guide me. The man got up, shook the dust from his flap cap, and led on through a maze of mud walls. I followed. After a few minutes we arrived at a small wicket gate set low in the wall. The old man knocked, waited, then knocked again. There was the sound of footsteps and the gate opened. A tall man in his late thirties came out. The old man rattled away in guttural dialect, pointed at me, shurgged his shoulders then grunted. The tall man smiled and extended his hand.

'How do you do'? he said. 'My name is Salim. I am the village schoolmaster. This old man says that you are a crazy foreigner who keeps repeating the same word over and over again. What do you want'?

'I am looking for the silk farm. The word I kept repeating was "Abrisham". Farsi for silk.'

'Oh I see. I am sorry. You see most people around Tabriz speak Turkish. No one here understands a word of Farsi'.

Salim took me to the silk farm. It was another backyard affair, although by necessity a silk loom was a more complicated machine than the simple carpet loom we had seen outside Sivas. It lay in a small semi-subterranean mud-brick hut, attached to a courtyard house in a distant part of the maze. The silk was already wound onto seven weighted spindle whorls which Salim said came from a village nearby. The silk was spun across the full five-foot width of the loom frame into a sheet of separate threads. At the far end a single man sat on a bench. He operated the entire machine. Two pedals alternately lifted and lowered two frames of tightly strung cross-threads. A chain shot a shuttle in between, across the width of the loom, carrying a line of silk alternately under and over the spread of silk threads. A comb then pulled the woven material towards the operator where it wound itself around a wooden roll.

The machine was completely unmotorized and apparently homemade. Its existence near Tabriz, where Polo talks of the weaving of 'many kinds of beautiful and valuable stuffs of silk and gold', again proves Polo's accuracy in all matters mercantile, although since the time of the Yule that has never really been in doubt. I was shown the finished dyed silks and to the inexpert eye they looked exceptionally fine.

I was on the verge of haggling for a piece but, looking at my watch, I saw the time and rushed back to the square to catch the next bus back into town.

William Dalrymple, In Xanadu, *1990*

William Dalrymple followed on foot the route of crusader Robert Curthose from Rouen to Jerusalem, and then in the footsteps of Marco Polo from there to Genghis Khân's palace of Xanadu in China. Guided by his explorer and historian predecessors, Dalrymple chronicles his journey in *In Xanadu*.

Andîmeshk
Dezful
Susa
Shush
Choqâ
Zanbil
River
Masjed-e Soleimân
Izeh
IRAQ
Haftkel
Ahvâz
Râmhormoz
Kârun
Khalaf Âbâd
Âghâjâri
Mâhshahr
Behbehân
Basra
Koram Shahr
Bandar-e-
Âbâdân
Emâm Khomeini
Dey
KUWAIT
KUWAIT
Gonâ
Persia
Hafar al Batin
SAUDI ARABIA

SOUTHWEST
IRÂN

0   50   100 Kilometres

0   50   100 Miles

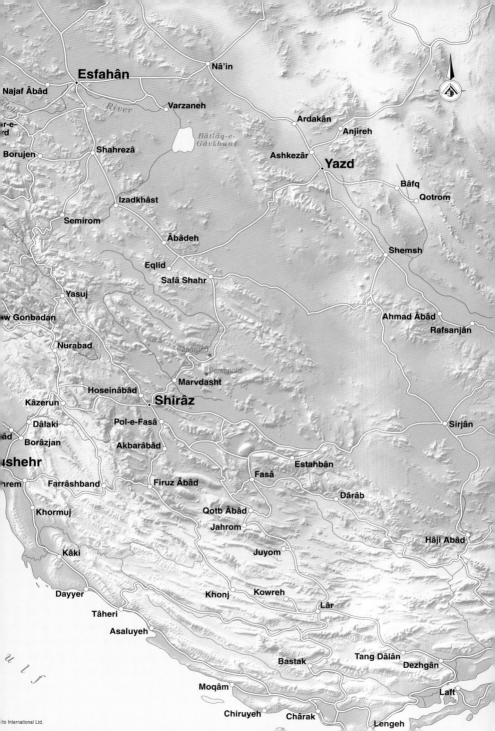

ESFAHÂN PROVINCE

The province of Esfahân is located almost in the centre of Irân between Tehrân and Fârs. It is mainly a province of mountains and desert with an arid climate, but despite this, it has quite a large population, living mostly in the numerous oases that were linked by the old caravan routes. These routes linked not only the north-west and southeast of Irân, but crossed the mountain cols to the south, towards Shirâz and the ports on the Persian Gulf. For most tourists, the main destination in this province is the city of Esfahân itself but it would be a shame to miss some of the smaller towns, many of which are still very traditional, and which can easily be visited from Esfahân or on the way to one of the neighbouring provinces.

KÂSHÂN

About 100 kilometres (62 miles) south of Qom on the secondary road to Esfahân, is the town of **Kâshân**, once one of the most prosperous oases in Irân. Known since Saljuq times for the quality of its ceramics (the Persian word *kâshi* for glazed tiles is derived from the name of the town), Kâshân was also, until the 19th century, an important centre for the manufacture of carpets, silk and other textiles. During the Safavid Dynasty, the town benefited greatly from the patronage of Shâh Abbâs I (1587–1629) who set out to embellish it further, notably by laying out a garden, the Bâgh-e Fin, and who even requested to be buried there. Given the grandiose construction projects that mark his reign, one might expect the **mausoleum of Shâh Abbâs** to be a sumptuous building, but it is in fact remarkably modest in size and appearance. It consists at present of a black tombstone, placed in the crypt of the *Emâmzâdeh* Habib ibn Musâ, now a mosque. This mosque (on Zeyârat Habib Street, off Emâm Khomeini Avenue, just north of Khomeini Square) is currently being entirely rebuilt but the tomb is still visible in a corner.

In the centre of Kâshân are the mosque and the *madraseh* **Âghâ Bozorg** (turn right off Fâzel-e Narâqi Avenue, towards Kemâl ol-Molk Square). The traditional plan of Irânian mosques has been adapted here and comprises only two large *eivân*, each flanked by two rows of arcades, one on the north side, by the entrance, and the other on the south side, in front of the *mehrâb*. The courtyard, surrounded by single arcades, contains a second, sunken court in the centre which has been turned into a garden with trees and a fountain. The south *eivân* with its two minarets gives onto the *mehrâb* chamber, which is covered with a brick dome (there is a good view from the entrance over the courtyard and this *eivân*). The decoration of the arcades and *eivân*, which is restricted to blue, red or yellow touches against a brick ground, is very simple but elegant.

Among the other mosques in Kâshân are the **Friday Mosque** (masjed-e Jomeh), built under the Saljuqs and restored several times since, and the Meidân-e Fays Mosque, built during the Timurid Dynasty (15th century). The bazaar, located between Bâbâ Afzal and Mohtasham avenues, is very interesting for the architecture of its old câravânsarais, with their domed roofs and painted walls.

Another recommended visit is the **Borujerdi House** (khâneh-ye Borujerdihâ; the entrance is on a street right off Alavi Avenue, in the southern part of town; open mornings only). This is an old private house, now open to the public, and which retains a very original six-sided wind tower, pierced with window-like openings which create a draft for cooling the house.

A few kilometres southwest of Kâshân, in the small village of Fin, is one of Irân's most famous gardens, the **Bâgh-e Fin** (or *Bâgh-e Shâh*, the King's Garden), which was designed for Shâh Abbâs. The original Safavid buildings have partly been replaced by Qâjâr ones, but the layout of the trees, canals and basins is still very close to the original. It is difficult to find a more pleasant spot to relax in the shade after a long trip through the sand and heat of the desert.

The road that goes out to Bâgh-e Fin (Amir Kebir Street) passes by an important prehistoric site, **Tappeh-ye Sialk**, one of the first and most rewarding sites ever excavated in Irân. Sialk was occupied almost continuously from the fourth millennium BC until the eighth century BC; it has yielded, layer by layer, a hoard of cultural artefacts, particularly painted pottery, from which it has been possible to work out in remarkable detail the chronology of the cultural development of this part of the Irânian Plateau. The objects excavated are now in the Louvre Museum in Paris and the Archaeological Museum in Tehrân. There are only a few very modest remains left to be seen today on the two badly eroded hills at Tappeh-ye Sialk, including the odd shard and the outline of a few houses. One of the side pavilions contains the national museum of Kâshân with fine collections of pottery and calligraphy.

On the other side of the road, about a kilometre in the direction of Kâshân, is the *emâmzâdeh* **Abu Lolo**, built during the Safavid Dynasty and recognizable by its pointed roof decorated with very fine turquoise and yellow tiles.

From Kâshân, the road to Esfahân goes to **Natanz** (80 kilometres or 50 miles from Kâshân), where one can visit the funerary complex of Abd al-Samad, including the Friday Mosque. Abd al-Samad came from Esfahân to Natanz and became a great Sufi teacher. One of his students became a vizir for the mongols and commissioned the buildings from a local architect. The building of the complex took several years. The oldest section is an octagonal Buyid pavilion which was turned into a four-*eivân* mosque between 1304 and 1309. The tomb itself is dated to 1307. It is a cruciform chamber with a pyramidal eight-sided roof, decorated outside with turquois and lapis blue ceramics. Inside is a superb *muqarnas* dome with an inscribed frieze. Between 1316 and 1317, a *khânehqâh*, or dervish monastery, was added to the southwest of the complex. Today, only its gateway still stands, richly decorated in blue ceramics.

From Natanz, it is possible to make a wide detour to the northeast along the Yazd road to pass through the towns of Ardestân and Nâ'in. Within a very short distance, one finds a remarkable concentration of some of the oldest mosques in the country, all of which have been spared destruction or rebuilding in later styles. These small and relatively simple buildings, completely devoid of colourful glazed tile decoration, will be of particular interest to the student of early Islamic architecture in Irân. Fifteen kilometres (9 miles) north of Ardestân is **Zavâreh**, a village which possesses the oldest dated mosque in Irân to have been built with four *eivân* around a central courtyard (the mosque was finished in 1136). It is this plan which became that most frequently used for Irânian mosques, replacing the older hypostyle mosque such as the one at Nâ'in (see below). The Zavâreh mosque is small and simple in structure. Its decoration is limited to a single Kufic inscription, even the *mehrâb* is plain. Zavâreh has a second mosque, the masjed-e Pamonar, built during the Saljuq period (11th century). It is in a bad state of preservation and only very little of the original stucco decoration remains.

(Left) *Bâgh-e Fin, Kâshân*
(Right) *Portrait of a cleric, Kâshân*

The Friday Mosque at **Ardestân** is another of the very earliest four-*eivân* mosques, but unlike Zavâreh it was built over an older hypostyle mosque. This small mosque is characterized by wide pillars and low vaults. The dome of the main *eivân* still bear traces of its very fine decoration, and the *mehrâb* are covered in carved stucco. The remains of a Saljuq madraseh can be seen in the northwest corner.

The small town of **Nâ'in**, located at the crossroads to Yazd (162 kilometres, 101 miles), Esfahân (145 kilometres, 90 miles), and Tehrân, was once famous for its carpets. The oldest sections of its Friday Mosque date from the Abbâsid period (tenth century); it is a hypostyle mosque, with a courtyard surrounded by porticos but with no *eivân*. The columns of the porticos are rather squat and set close together, but their rich stucco decoration, and that of the *mehrâb*, hides a certain structural heaviness. This tenth-century stucco decoration at Nâ'in is still in exceptional condition and is renowned for the great variety of its geometric and floral motifs as well as the quality of its calligraphic inscriptions. The wooden *membar* to the right of the *mehrâb* is 14th century.

At Nâ'in it is also possible to visit a private house of the Safavid period, built in a style once typical of town houses here but which has become only too rare today. The centre of the house is its rectangular courtyard, planted with trees and in which stands a water fountain. Around it, are two floors of vaulted chambers some of which (on the first floor) still bear the original painted decorations: panels with hunting scenes; miniature-style representations of garden parties with dancers and musicians; and star-shaped medallions of phoenixes and dragons. The latter are a good example of the way in which painting styles in Persia were modified after the Mongol invasion and the introduction of Chinese designs. The dragon and the phoenix are ancient motifs in China where they are frequently represented together, as they are here, with coiled bodies.

THE CITY OF ESFAHÂN

Esfahân nesf-e jahân, 'Esfahân is half the world': this well-known saying was originally coined to describe Esfahân in Safavid times, when the city was at the height of its glory. Even today, Esfahân's monuments can be ranked among the most splendid of the Islamic world. The atmosphere in town is a relaxed one: this is a place to wander in, to get to know slowly, with its gardens, its river side and its shopping streets. It is a town that contains a multitude of hidden treasures and a quick visit, even if it takes in the main monuments, will hardly do it justice.

However, many Irânians will tell you that its inhabitants are miserly; best to see for yourself and make up your own mind.

Shâh Abbâs the Great made the town his capital in 1598 and had it rebuilt according to a precise plan, with large avenues, magnificent gardens and a royal enclosure with palaces and gardens. Esfahân's history is considerably older than the Safavid Dynasty; some scholars have even identified it with the Achaemenian city of Gaba mentioned by Strabo. The remains of two Sasanian fire temples suggest that an important centre existed here at that time, a centre which may well have been the city of Jay. The earliest detailed information about Esfahân is from the beginning of the Islamic period. The town was then composed of two sections, one of which was the old city of Jay, called the *shahrestân*, that is the 'town' itself. Outside its walls was a Jewish colony, the Yahudiyeh, founded, most likely, in Sasanian times.

From 935, Esfahân was governed by the Buyid Dynasty, and after that, at the beginning of the 11th century, by a local dynasty, the Kakuyids. The urban development which had begun under the Buyids continued under the Saljuqs, in particular during the reigns of Alp Arslan and Malek Shâh, when Esfahân became the capital. It was at this period that the Friday Mosque assumed its present shape. In 1228, the town was captured by Genghis Khân's Mongol troops but seems not to have suffered much infrastructural damage. In 1398, however, at the time of Tamerlane's invasion, the inhabitants of the city rebelled rather than pay ransom money to the conqueror. As a result, the entire population was massacred.

The transfer of the Safavid capital to Esfahân by Shâh Abbâs in 1598 marks the beginning of the city's most glorious period. The decision to move the capital was a strategic one, prompted by fear for the safety of the old capitals, Tabriz and Qazvin, which were considered too close to the Ottoman Empire. Shâh Ismâ'il (1501–1524) had already begun work on several gardens and palaces in Esfahân, but it was during Shâh Abbâs' reign that the city finally took the form that it still partly visible today, centred around the Royal Square and Chahâr Bâgh Avenue. Concerned about developing trade in his new capital, Shâh Abbâs ordered the deportation of Armenian families from Jolfâ, in Azerbaijân, to the southern suburbs of Esfahân. Due to the presence at the Safavid court of a large number of foreigners—English and Dutch merchants from the East India Companies, European artists, and diplomats hoping to secure alliances against the common Ottoman enemy—Esfahân was opened up to the outside world, and became one of the most glorious cities of its time.

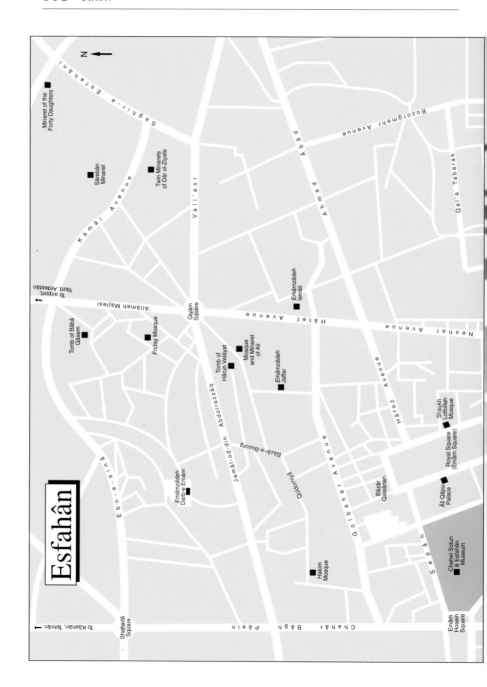

Esfahân

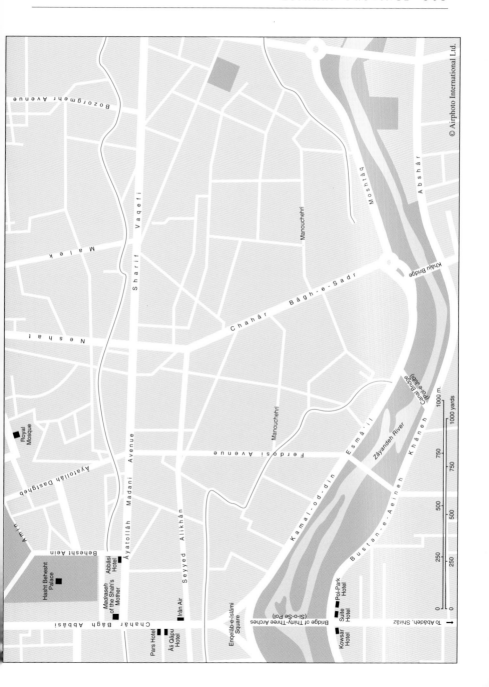

© Airphoto International Ltd.

This splendour and magnificence lasted only just over a century. Esfahân was ruined by the Afghân invasion at the beginning of the 18th century and by Nâder Shâh's decision to transfer the capital to Mashhad in 1736, a move which relegated the city to the role of a provincial town. During the 18th and 19th centuries, Esfahân had a half-abandoned look to it; when the French writer Pierre Loti visited it at the beginning of the 20th century, he wrote : 'Approaching, one is struck by the sad state of these buildings that promised such splendor from afar! ... Where they are exposed to the winter winds, the domes and minarets, all but stripped of their long-patient mosaics, seem eaten away by a grey leprosy.'

   Esfahân's main monuments are centred around the following areas: the Royal Square and Chahâr Bâgh Avenue, the Friday Mosque, and on the other bank of the river, New Jolfâ. Most of the buildings are from the Safavid period, although a few monuments still remain from the Saljuq dynasty (the Friday Mosque, the Sareban and Forty Daughters minarets, the Shahrestân Bridge) and the Mongol dynasty (the tomb of Bâbâ Qâsim, *emâmzâdeh* Jaffar).

NORTH OF THE BAZAAR: THE PRE-SAFAVID MONUMENTS

Just north of Qiyam Square, on Allâmeh Majlesi Avenue, is the **Friday Mosque** (masjed-e Jomeh), one of the most venerable and magnificent of all the buildings in Esfahân. Compared to the great Safavid mosques, this one is very sobre: its dome is of undecorated brick, and the interior vaulted halls around the central courtyard have also been left plain. But it is this austerity which is part of its beauty and which allows one to appreciate all the more the tilework decoration of the courtyard and *eivân*.

   From an architectural point of view, the mosque is extremely complex, both because of its size (it has 476 separate domes), and because of the number of different periods of construction it has known. Excavations carried out in 1977 have brought to light the remains of a very early mosque at this site which dates back to the eighth century (according to the historian Abu Nu'âim the mosque was founded in 771–772). Rebuilt around 841, it was, in the tenth century, a hypostyle mosque with porticos surrounding the central courtyard. Inscriptions dated to the 11th and early 12th centuries, and which correspond to the oldest sections of the present mosque, have shed some light on the various changes which occurred during the Saljuq period. A large dome was first built in front of the main *mehrâb* by the vizir Nezâm ol-Molk between 1072 and 1092 (the same dome in place today), and a second one, known as the Gonbad-e Khâki, was added in 1088 at the

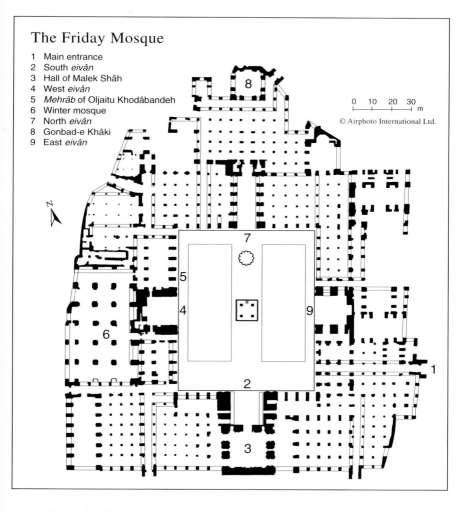

The Friday Mosque

1 Main entrance
2 South *eivân*
3 Hall of Malek Shâh
4 West *eivân*
5 *Mehrâb* of Oljaitu Khodâbandeh
6 Winter mosque
7 North *eivân*
8 Gonbad-e Khâki
9 East *eivân*

0 10 20 30
m

© Airphoto International Ltd.

northern end of the complex, opposite the main *mehrâb*, by Taj ol-Molk, Nezâm's sworn enemy. It is often said that the Gonbad-e Khâki was built by Taj ol-Molk in an attempt to outdo Nezâm ol-Molk's construction, but its exact function remains unclear: it has been suggested that it was a ceremonial chamber. It should be noted that the pavilion was originally free-standing and well-lit; subsequently, two sides were bricked up as also the oculus in the dome.

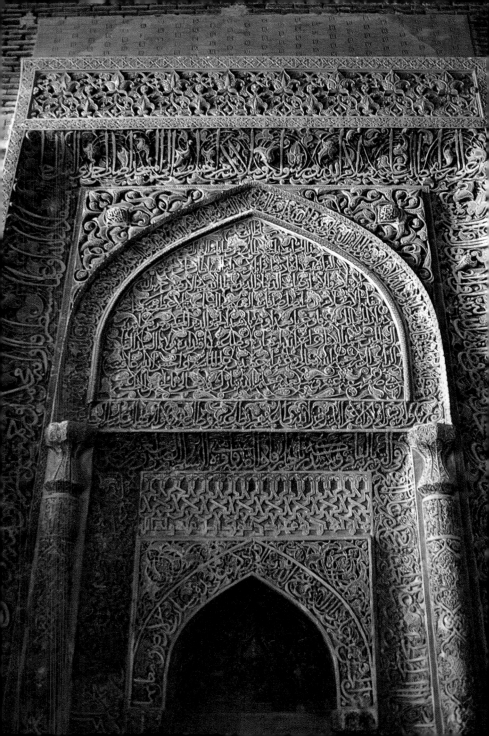

An inscription on a door in the northeast façade mentions the reconstruction of the mosque after a fire in 1121 which spared only the few sections described above. The complex that one visits today is therefore in large part a mosaic from different periods, the result of all the renovations and modifications carried out since the fire: a 14th century *mehrâb*; a winter hall which is probably Timurid; minarets built by the Black Sheep Turkoman; and interior decoration of the Safavid period.

The entrance to the mosque is through the southeast door by the ticket office which gives out onto one of the streets of the bazaar. This door, of Saljuq date, is very simply decorated with turquoise tilework. A corridor leads directly to the central courtyard; on the right, is an entrance to a madraseh. There is also an entrance next to the Gonbad-e Khâki in the north of the mosque.

The courtyard is a classical one with four *eivân* and a marble fountain in the centre. The façades of double arcades which join the *eivân* are entirely decorated with mosaic tilework, mostly from the 17th century. In the southwest *eivân*, which is flanked by two minarets and leads to the prayer chamber, there are very fine raised panels of Timurid geometric tile mosaics (15th century) and a maze-like Persian poem in angular script. The inscriptions on the outside, as well as the white and blue tiles of the arch, are somewhat later (16th and 17th centuries).

Behind the *eivân* is the *mehrâb* hall built under Malek Shâh at the order of Nezâm ol-Molk, one of the few sections of the old mosque to have survived the fire in 1121. This huge chamber, beautifully proportioned, is covered with a brick dome. The inscription at the base of the dome dates to the 11th century. The alabaster *mehrâb* is not original but was added in the 17th century.

The northeast *eivân*, built during the Saljuq period, has seen very little change since Safavid times and is characterized by its rather discreet decoration. It leads on to the Gonbad-e Khâki, the domed chamber built by Taj ol-Molk in 1088. Despite its small size (10 metres [33 feet] wide and 20 metres [66 feet] high) and its sobriety, this room is nevertheless one of the most perfect and most elegant examples of the transition from a square base to a circular dome in Persian architecture. The solution chosen here was to use a succession of arches ever decreasing in size, ending up with a circle of sixteen arches on which the dome is set. There is no tilework decoration and the pentagonal star patterns inside the dome are created by the brick alone.

The northwest *eivân*, recognizable by the small pavilion at its top and which is used for calling the faithful to prayer, is also a Saljuq construction. The original shape of the stalactites remains under the Safavid redecoration. The ochre and

Mehrâb of Sultan Oljaitu Khodâbandeh in the Friday Mosque, Esfahân

mustard colour scheme on the inside of the half-dome *eivān* is an exquisite piece of work for the harmony of its colours and forms: the entire surface is covered with large squinches decorated with very simple, dotted geometric motifs from the early 18th century in the reign of the last Safavid monarch, Shāh Soltān Hosein. To the right of the *eivān* are the *mehrāb* chamber of Sultan Oljaitu Khodābandeh and the winter mosque (these rooms are usually kept locked; ask one of the guardians to open them for you). This famous *mehrāb*, built in 1310 and remarkably well preserved, was made for the Mongol Sultan Oljaitu Khodābandeh, whose tomb is at Soltānieh. The floral motifs and the exquisite calligraphy in carved stucco of the *mehrāb* are unusually fine. The inlaid *membar* (14th century) to the right of the *mehrāb* is another work of great quality.

A door at the back leads to the winter mosque, a large bare low-ceilinged room with intersecting arches that run down from the ceiling to the floor as thick pillars. The lighting, which today is artificial, used to be limited to the glow that filtered through the translucent alabaster windows in the ceiling. This winter hall is thought to date from the rebuilding around 1447.

Mention must also be made of the remarkable vaulted rooms all around the central courtyard which are built entirely of brick and date from the 12th–14th centuries. Here again, there is no decoration other than that of the brick itself, but the result is never monotonous, and it is said that no two vaults in the entire mosque have exactly the same design.

Just to the north of the mosque is the **tomb of Bābā Qāsim** (ārāmgāh-e Bābā Qāsim), built in memory of a Persian theologian by one of his students, in 1340. Restored in the 17th century, it has an attractive stalactite gateway decorated in blue and white tiles. Next to the mausoleum stands the *madraseh*-ye Emāmi, also built in honour of Bābā Qāsim. Here again, the use of glazed tiles is relatively limited and the colour of the natural brick plays an important role in the decoration.

To the west of the Friday Mosque is the *emāmzādeh* **Darb-e Emām**. This monument, finished in 1453, was built over the tombs of two descendants of emāms, Ibrahim Batha and Zain al-Abedin. It is unusual in having two domes, but its fame is mainly due to the quality of the tile mosaic on the main *eivān*, considered a worthy rival of the Blue Mosque in Tabriz. The tilework on the exterior of the domes, also very fine, is later than that of the *eivān*. The dome over the main chamber was restored during the reign of Shāh Abbās (1642–1666) and the one over the *eivān* was added as part of modifications carried out (1670–1671) during the reign of Shāh Soleimān.

Several old minarets still remain in the quarters between Vali-e Asr and Sorush avenues. The first, the **twin minarets of Dâr ol-Ziyafeh**, were once part of the entrance gate to a Mongol *madraseh*. They are to be found just south of Kamâl Avenue. Slightly further north is the **Sâreban Minaret** (*menâr-e Sâreban*), or Minaret of the Camel Driver, perhaps the most beautiful of all Esfahân's surviving minarets with its decor in natural brick and its glazed stalactite cornices. It was built towards the end of the 12th century during the Saljuq period. The mosque to which it was originally attached has now disappeared. The **Minaret of the Forty Daughters** (*menâr-e Chehel Dokhtarân*) on Sorush Avenue is of the same period (1108) but is squatter and less slender than the former one. It has one unusual feature, a window set two-thirds of the way up which looks southwest in the direction of Mecca.

THE SAFAVID ROYAL CITY

The centre of Esfahân during the Saljuq period was the Friday Mosque and the Meidân-e Kohneh, to the north of the present Royal Square. In 1598, Shâh Abbâs decided to shift this centre and turned to the Naqsh-e Jahân (Image of the World), a vast palatial square and park expanded on the orders of Shâh Tahmâsp (1524–1576). The palace at the edge of the park was enlarged to become the Âli Qâpu Palace, and additional buildings were erected in other areas of the park. Between 1589 and 1606, work began on the square itself and on the buildings around it, as well as on a large avenue called Chahâr Bâgh which was to link the royal city to the river. The Allâhverdi Khân Bridge at the end of this avenue also dates from this period. Work was interrupted for a few years and only started again in 1611 with the construction of the Royal Mosque. At this time, the finishing touches were added to the other monuments around the Royal Square. Today, several of the gardens, pavilions and palaces from this early Safavid period have disappeared, in particular along the banks of the Zâyandeh-rud.

THE ROYAL SQUARE

The Royal Square of Esfahân was the symbolic centre of the Safavid dynasty and of its empire. Usually filled with a crowd of street-sellers and entertainers, the square was also used for a variety of celebrations and festivals, for polo matches—the stone goal posts are still visible at either end of the square—and for public executions. The Shâh and his court watched the festivities from the balcony of the Âli Qâpu Palace.

The square is surrounded on all four sides by long walls with double arcades, interrupted at intervals by the main monuments: the Royal Mosque in the south, the Mosque of Shaykh Lotfollah in the west, the Âli Qâpu Palace in the east, and the entrance to the Great Bazaar in the north. The centre of the Square has now been laid out in the suburban manner with fountains and water basins and recently planted with trees. It is a very popular spot on summer evenings when the Esfahânis settle down on carpets on the lawn and bring out their picnics and samovars. The shops under the arcades sell a variety of tourist souvenirs, textiles and handicrafts (compare prices and quality from shop to shop before buying and bargain hard).

At the end of the Royal Square is the huge gateway to the **Royal Mosque**, flanked by two turquoise minarets. Behind it and slightly to the right are the main *eivân* and the dome of the prayer hall. The construction of the mosque, commissioned by Shâh Abbâs, began in 1611. This monument is the largest of those attributed to Shâh Abbâs, and he considered it his masterpiece. In his impatience to see it finished, he hurried the pace of work by adopting a previously little-used method of glazed tilework decoration, known as *haft rangi* (see page 155). As a result, some sections of the mosque are decorated with the technique of tile mosaic and others with polychrome painted tiles.

The gateway to the mosque has a mainly ornamental role and serves to balance the entrance gate to the bazaar at the other end of the square. Finished in 1616, this is one of the largest *pishtâq* in Irân (about 27 metres [89 feet] high). It is also one of the most richly decorated with its triple-twisted columns around the arch and its half-dome covered on the inside with a cascade of stalactites. These stalactites are repeated in the niches to each side of the entrance. The large inscription around the arch is the work of the great Safavid calligrapher from Tabriz, Ali Rezâ Abbâsi, who joined the entourage of Shâh Abbâs around 1593. He quickly became one of the best-known court calligraphers and his work can be seen on all Shâh Abbâs' great monuments in Esfahân and Mashhad. His style is characterized by great clarity and a sharp sense of proportion and was often imitated by later artists. Here he used the technique of writing a text on two or more superimposed lines, a technique typical of the thulth script frequently used for the decoration of mosques and tombs during the Timurid and Safavid periods.

One of the peculiarities of this mosque is that it is not built on the same axis as the gateway which gives onto the square. Because of the necessity of orienting the *mehrâb* towards the southwest, i.e. Mecca, and of keeping the *pishtâq* aligned with the walls of the square, there is a 45° angle between the gate and the north *eivân*. Instead of being rectangular, the back of the north *eivân* is triangular. One of the sides of the triangle gives onto the domed vestibule which one enters on passing through the gate. From here, the visitor has a first glimpse of the vast central courtyard over an intervening bench wall. This aesthetic effect, one of the greatest architectural *'coups de theatre'* in Islamic archtiecture, has recently been severely impared by the erection of metal posts and brown awnings over the entire courtyard. To gain entrance, go round the *eivân*, either on the right or the left, along an angled corridor.

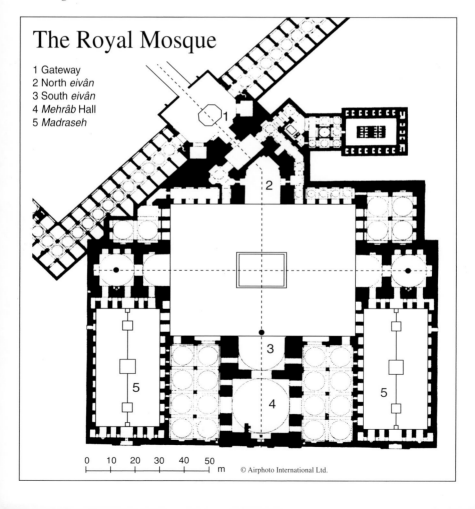

The Royal Mosque

1 Gateway
2 North *eivân*
3 South *eivân*
4 *Mehrâb* Hall
5 *Madraseh*

0 10 20 30 40 50
|—|—|—|—|—|—| m   © Airphoto International Ltd.

As soon as one enters the central court, attention is drawn by the south façade and its *eivân*, minarets and the dome of the prayer hall. The outer wall of the *eivân* is decorated with white and gold arabesques set on a blue ground, while the minarets are predominantly turquoise. The dome which rises up behind retains this turquoise colour in its very regular design of thin white and yellow scrolls. The outside of the dome rises to a height of 52 metres (171 feet), but the ceiling inside is only 38 metres (125 feet) tall, a discrepancy produced by the use of a double shell. This construction technique allows the architect to design a dome of entirely different shapes outside and in. Here, the outer dome is onion-shaped while the inner one is squat, with proportions adapted to the space of the prayer hall. Unlike the dome of the Mosque of Shaykh Lotfollah, where both shells are built parallel to one another and begin at the same level, here the shells start at different heights; thus the windows which, on the outside, are set in the drum, are to be found in the curve of the dome itself on the inside.

The decoration inside the dome is remarkably elegant and repeats with subtle variation the blue, white and gold shades seen outside. The *mehrâb* and the *membar* are both made of marble. On either side of the prayer hall is a rectangular room with two bays of wide vaults set on stone pillars. Except for the pillars, the entire surface of the vaults and the walls is covered in glazed designs. The floral motifs at the centre of each vault echo the design inside the dome.

The east and west walls of the central court are strictly symmetrical, with a prayer hall behind each *eivân*, and three arcades to either side of it, one of which opens onto a *madraseh*. These *madraseh* are composed of a central rectangular court with trees surrounded by rooms for the students. As in the main courtyard, the entire surface of the walls is decorated with glazed tiles; the motifs in the southeast court, in cobalt blue and bright yellow, are particularly fine.

Despite its more modest size, the **Mosque of Shaykh Lotfollah**, on the eastern side of the Royal Square, is nonetheless a worthy rival of the Royal Mosque. Probably begun for Shâh Abbâs in 1602, it was finished in 1619 and was named after a famous theologian who happened to be Shah Abbâs' father-in-law. Its dome has extremely fine arabesques and harmonious shades of colour: the exterior of the dome is decorated with blue and black flowers with white scrolls set against a creamy-coloured ground, while the drum is predominantly blue. The entrance gate is a rich mosaic of blue, yellow, white and green floral motifs with a particularly fine stalactite vault.

(Preceding pages) *The Royal Mosque, Esfahân*

From the square, one notices that the dome is not aligned with the entrance gate. Unlike the Royal Mosque, the reason for this here is not linked to the orientation of the *mehrâb* towards Mecca (this mosque has no courtyard so that the problem of orientation does not arise). Instead, it should be understood as an attempt to create increased security for the small building, which was the private royal chapel.

The asymmetry of the gate is not the only architectural peculiarity here. There is no four-*eivân* courtyard nor any minarets, only a single domed prayer room which is entered along a narrow corridor. At the end of this dark passageway is a sharp turn, and one emerges suddenly into a sumptuously decorated chamber so rich and so exuisitely ordered that visitors experience overwhelming beauty. The large panels of floral scrolls on the walls are surrounded by large and dense inscriptions by Ali Rezâ Abbâsi, the famous calligrapher of the reign of Shâh Abbâs. (See the literary excerpt below from Robert Byron's *The Road to Oxiana*).

The transition from a square to a circular plan in this room is one of the most successful that exists: the four corner squinches extend to the ground and alternate with four blind arches of the same size to form a regular octagon. Small faceted pendentives, each corresponding to one of the windows in the drum, form the transition to a sixteen-sided polygon.

Opposite the Mosque of Shaykh Lotfollah is the **Âli Qâpu Palace**, or 'Exalted Gateway'. Originally a small Timurid palace, it was enlarged by Shâh Abbâs to become the monumental entrance to the palaces and kiosks located in the huge park of the royal domain which extended as far as Chahâr Bâgh Avenue. It served also as a reception pavilion for foreign dignitaries and embassies. The *tâlâr* on the first floor which overlooks the square served in summer as a throne room from where the ruler could watch the polo matches below or review the troops (there is a magnificent view over the square and the town and the surrounding moutains).

The Âli Qâpu Palace has six floors which are reached via a series of small twisting staircases and low doors. The rooms are empty today but the walls and ceilings still bear some original fresco, beautifully restored, and glazed tile decoration. The painted wooden ceilings of the *tâlâr* and *eivân* are particularly fine. It would be impossible to give a detailed description here of the incredible variety of motifs in these rooms, but it is well worth taking a little time to discover them. Be sure to go as far as the top floor, to the music room, for the fretwork panelling on the walls and vaults cut into vase-shaped niches. The decoration on the inside of the dome in this room is also extremely fine.

Mosque of Shaykh Lotfollah, Esfahân

THE MOSQUE OF SHEIKH LOTFOLLAH

*T*he Mosque of Sheikh Lotfollah is Persian in the fabulous sense: the Omar Khayam brigade, to whom rational form is as much anathema as rational action, can wallow in it to their hearts' content... Colour and pattern are a commonplace in Persian architecture. But here they have a quality which most astonish the European, not because they infringe what he thought was his own monopoly, but because he can previously have had no idea that abstract pattern was capable of so profound a splendour.

As though to announce these principles as soon as possible, the outside of the mosque is careless of symmetry to a grotesque degree. Only the dome and portal are seen from the front. But owing to the discrepancy between the axis of the mosque and the Âli Gâpu opposite, the portal, instead of being immediately under the dome, is set slightly to one side of it. Yet such is the character of the dome, so unlike is it to any other dome in Persia or elsewhere, that this deformity is hardly noticeable. Round a flattened hemisphere made of tiny bricks and covered with prawn-coloured wash runs a bold branching rose-tree inlaid in black and white. Seen from close to, the design has a hint of William Morris, particularly in its thorns; but as a whole it is more formal than pre-raphaelite, more comparable to the design of a Genoese brocade immensely magnified. Here and there, at the junction of the branches or in the depths of the foliage, ornaments of ochre and dark blue mitigate the harshness of the black and white tracery, and bring it into harmony with the golden pink of the background: a process which is continued by a pervading under-foliage of faint light blue. But the genius of the effect is in the play of surfaces. The inlay is glazed. The stucco is not. Thus, the sun strikes the dome with a broken highlight whose intermittent flash, moving with the time of day, adds a third texture to its pattern, mobile and unseen.

If the outside is lyric, the inside is Augustan. Here a still shallower dome, about seventy feet in diameter, swims above a ring of sixteen windows. From the floor to the base of the windows rise eight main arches, four enclosing right-angles, four flat wall-space, so that the boundaries of

the floor form a square. The space between the tops of the arches is occupied by eight pendentives divided into planes like a bat's wing.

The dome is inset with a network of lemon-shaped compartments, which increase in size as they descend from a formalized peacock at the apex and are surrounded by plain bricks; each is filled with a foliage pattern inlaid on plain stucco. The walls, bordered by broad white inscriptions on dark blue, are similarly inlaid with twirling arabesques or baroque squares on deep ochre stucco. The colours of all this inlay are dark blue, light greenish blue, and a tint of indefinite wealth like wine. Each arch is framed in turquoise corkscrews. The mehrab in the west wall is enamelled with tiny flowers on a deep blue meadow.

Each part of the design, each plane, each repetition, each separate branch or blossom has its own sombre beauty. But the beauty of the whole comes as you move. Again, the highlights are broken by the play of glazed and unglazed surfaces; so that with every step they rearrange themselves in countless shining patterns; while even the pattern of light through the thick window traceries is inconstant, owing to outer traceries which are several feet away and double the variety of each varying silhouette.

I have never encountered splendour of this kind before. Other interiors came into my mind as I stood there, to compare with: Versailles, or the porcelain rooms at Schönbrunn, or the Doge's Palace, or St. Peter's. All are rich; but none so rich. Their richness is three-dimensional; it is attended by all the effort of shadow. In the mosque of Sheikh Lotfollah, it is a richness of light and surface, of pattern and colour only. The architectural form is unimportant. It is not smothered, as in rococo; it is simply the instrument of a spectacle, as earth is the instrument of a garden. And then I suddenly thought of that unfortunate species, modern interior decorators, who imagine that they can make a restaurant, or a cinema, or a plutocrat's drawing-room look rich if given money enough for gold leaf and looking-glass. They little know what amateurs they are. Nor, alas, do their clients.

From *The Road to Oxiana* (1933), by Robert Byron

The Bazaar and Old Quarters
to the north of The Royal Square

On the north side of the Royal Square is the *Bâzâr Qaisârieh* or Imperial Bazaar (also known as the Great Bazaar, *bâzâr-e Bozorg*), a grand entrance to the labyrinth of domed streets which stretches into the old town. The gateway to the bazaar, built in the reign of Shâh Abbâs, is decorated with tilework mosaic; its main motif represents Sagittarius, the town's astrological sign corresponding to the putative date of the town's foundation, shown here as a chimera, half-man and half-tiger. It was just to the west of this area that the trading posts of the English and Dutch East India Companies were located in the second half of the 17th century.

Inside the bazaar, past Golbahar Street, is the **Hakim Mosque**, founded in the 12th century and rebuilt in 1654. The royal physician, Hakim Dâoud, built the mosque with the money that he had sent back to his family from India. (India was the Eldorado that attracted generations of Irānians eager to make their fortunes, not unlike the 'brain-drain' of later centuries from Europe to America). The sober and subtle decoration of this four-*eivān* mosque is less lavishly dense than the royal foundations.

Further east in the bazaar, near Hāruniyeh Street, stands the *emāmzādeh* Ja'far. This small octagonal tower built in 1325 during the Mongol period is one in a series of tombs of Ja'far, a Companion of the Prophet. Its blue and white tilework mosaic was restored in the 1950s.

Further north towards Jamal ol-Din Abdolrazāq Avenue is the **Mosque of Ali**, whose minaret (menār-e masjed-e Ali) is said to be the oldest in Esfahān, built between 1131 and 1155. Now restored, it is 50 metres (164 feet) tall and has a plain brick decoration. The present mosque is later than the minaret and dates back to 1521.

Nearby is the tomb of **Hārun Velāyat**. Nothing is known about the person for whom this tomb was built in 1513, during Shāh Ismā'il's reign. The tile panelling on either side of the entrance into the tomb is one of the finest examples of early Safavid tile mosaic, with delicate scrolls and rich complex designs.

Just to the east of Hātef Avenue, which joins Qiyām Square and Neshāt Avenue, is the *emāmzādeh* Ismā'il, started in the reign of Shāh Abbās and finished in 1634. The entrance to the *emāmzādeh* is through a superb domed brick hall, now occupied by shops.

CHAHĀR BĀGH AVENUE

Chahār Bāgh Avenue once led from the Safavid city to Jolfā and the royal gardens at Hezār Jerib on the other bank of the Zāyandeh River. Shāh Abbās chose not to connect the avenue directly with the Royal Square, and it therefore began to the west of the palatial complex. It was planted with trees, and a canal ran down the centre of it in a series of little waterfalls. It was a favourite promenade of the people of Esfahān, and still is today: Chahār Bāgh has become one of the main shopping streets of the city with tea rooms, cinemas and fashionable clothes shops.

The main monuments around Chahār Bāgh were built in the reigns of Shāh Abbās' successors and are equally great works of art as the constructions of that great ruler. Unfortunately, all too often, the only remains we have today of the innumerable houses, palaces and pavilions of Safavid Esfahān are the descriptions left by 17th- and 18th-century travellers. Among the few buildings still standing is the **Chehel Sotun** (or Forty Columns), set in the old royal park between the Āli

Qâpu Palace and Chahâr Bâgh Avenue (the entrance is on Ostândâri Avenue, next to the Natural History Museum in a converted Timurid domed kiosk with an assortment of plaster dinosaurs in the courtyard). Used for official ceremonies and particularly for receiving foreign embassies, the palace was finished in 1647 during the reign of Shâh Abbâs II; it was later partly rebuilt after a fire in 1706. The palace opens out onto a spacious *talâr* with very tall, graceful wooden columns set on carved stone bases. The name of the palace—whose porch has only twenty columns—may be an allusion to their reflection in the water of the large pool in front of the *talâr*. One of the characteristic features of Safavid palatial architecture is the integration of buildings into a natural environment such as a park or a garden. Here, water plays a very important role in the spatial relationship between inside and out. In addition to the large ornamental pool at the Chehel Sotun, the architects laid out fountains in front of the throne and on the terrace, as well as canals linking the pools in the garden.

The *talâr* is covered with a flat wooden roof, whose ceiling and eaves are painted with very fine geometric motifs, while the walls of the *eivân* are decorated with floral frescoes. Stalactites set with mirrors and mirror stars on the ceiling remain in the *eivân* which gives onto the *talâr*, where the throne was placed.

This throne room leads into the great audience hall with its three domes, which now houses the **Esfahân Museum**. Here again, the ceiling is painted with sumptuous designs in blues, reds and golds. There are six large historical murals on the upper part of the walls: four from the mid 17th century Safavid period, and the two central ones added later in a crude style for Nâder Shâh Afshâr in the mid-18th century. The realistic representation of court life and military exploits of Safavid rulers are painted in a style which reflects a European influence, and are important as historical documents of material and social cuture. The ideological program underlying these representations the victory of Shâh Ismâ'il I (1501–1524) over the Uzbeks; the receptions by Shâh Abbâs I (1587–1629) and Shâh Abbâs II (1642–1666) in honour of fugitive rulers of Turkestan; the sumptuous banquet given by Shâh Tahmâsp I (1524–1576) for the Mughal prince Humayun who had fled from India show the Safavid court as a refuge and the dynasty as victorious protectors of neighbouring royalty. The clumsy additions by Nâder Shâh, on the other hand, are anti-Safavid propaganda showing their most notorious defeat by the artillery of the Ottoman Janisseries of Sultan Soleimân at the Battle of Châldirân (1517) and Nâder Shâh's personal victory over the Mughal Emperor of India at the battle of Panipat in 1739.

Beneath these great scenes are smaller paintings showing a world of langorous and flirtatious idylls, in the style of the great 17th century Esfahāni miniaturist Rezā Abbāsi. Covered in plaster during the Qājār period, they have recently been carefully restored. All around the room are a series of exhibits, mostly Safavid objects from the 17th and 18th centuries, including carpets, armour, porcelain, manuscripts and coins (the dates given in the cases are those of the Islamic calendar).

Just south of Emām Hosein Square is Pārk Shahid Rajâi (ex-Bâgh-e Bolbol) and the small Hasht Behesht Palace (Palace of the Eight Paradises). Built in 1699 by Shâh Soleimân, this pleasure pavilion was later renovated by the Qājār ruler Fath Ali Shâh around 1880, and again under the Pahlavis. It is a more or less octagonal building with a large central domed hall which gives onto a series of small chambers. Fragments of paintings survive on the walls; the stalactite ceilings are decorated both with small mirrors and with paintings, but particularly interesting are the spandrel tile decorations on the exterior showing pairs of often mythical hunting animals.

Just past the park, at the corner of Chahâr Bâgh Avenue and Shâhid Âyatollâh Madani Street, is the **madraseh of the Shâh's Mother** (*madraseh-ye Mâdar-e Shâh*, also known as *madraseh-ye Chahâr Bâgh*), built between 1706 and 1714 during the reign of the Safavid ruler, Shâh Soltân Hosein. It is an enormous complex which includes, in addition to the *madraseh* itself, a câravânsarai (*khân-e Mâdar-e Shâh*) of the same date, now turned into the luxury Abbâsi hotel. Today the *madraseh* functions as a theology school and visits are therefore limited to Thursdays and Fridays.

The entrance gate of the *madraseh*, on Chahâr Bâgh Avenue, stands out sharply from the rather austere arcaded façade of the building. The gate, which has a richly decorated stalactite vault, has superb doors covered in partly-gilded silver sheets decorated with floral motifs and inscriptions. Once past the gate, one enters a domed vestibule with a design of polished bricks and blue and white tiles.

Unlike the courtyards of the mosques which are large, empty areas, the central courtyard here resembles a garden with its tall plane trees and central canal (currently being repaired). Doors at each corner of the courtyard lead to smaller yards. All around are the rooms of the students, set on two floors, each one opening out onto a vaulted niche, sparingly decorated with black and blue lines. The outer surface of the walls around the court is covered in glazed tiles.

Madraseh of the Shâh's Mother, Esfahân

The north and east *eivân* of the court, decorated with scrolls and inscriptions, serve as classrooms. As is the case in mosques, the south *eivân* is the most ornate. It is flanked by two quite short minarets, very richly decorated, particularly on the balcony and stalactite cornices. Behind the *eivân* is the domed prayer hall. From the exterior, the dome is reminiscent of the dome on the Royal Mosque in the Royal Square, with a calligraphic inscription around the drum, broken at intervals by the windows, and a floral design on the dome itself. This elegant decoration has been executed and restored with a skill hardly equalled in any other building in the city, and there is no sign here of decadence, despite the late date of its construction. The inside of the dome is covered with a rich design of arabesques. Next to the *mehrâb* is a very fine *membar* carved out of a single block of marble.

The income from the câravânsarai next to the *madraseh* was intended to pay for the upkeep of the theological college. Built along classical lines with rooms giving out onto the central courtyard, the câravânsarai was turned into a luxury hotel (Hotel Abbâsi) under the last shâh. Even if you are not staying there, the garden is a very pleasant place for afternoon tea. In the street behind the câravânsarai is the Honar Bazaar (bâzâr-e Boland), which was also part of the income-generating complex of the *Madraseh*.

THE ZÂYANDEH-RUD AND ESFAHÂN'S BRIDGES

The bridges over the Zâyandeh-rud, the river that separates Esfahân from its southern suburbs, include some of the most important constructions in the city. The oldest bridge is the **pol-e Shahrestân**, which was probably built in the 12th century during the Saljuq period. Until recently, it was still located outside the town limits. This ten-arch bridge of stone and brick is the simplest of the old bridges and was originally defended on one side by a tower.

Further upstream is the **pol-e Khâju**, perhaps the most famous of Esfahân's bridges, and which has the unusual feature of serving as a sluice gate. In this desert climate, ensuring a sufficient and constant supply of water is of vital importance to the survival of a settlement. The problem was solved in various ways in Irân over the centuries, most notably by building the famous *qanât*. In Esfahân this sluice gate was devised to allow the accumulation, in times of changes in the level of the river, of reservoirs of water. The gates are set in the water channels which run between the pillars of the bridge.

The pol-e Khâju was built by Shâh Abbâs II in 1650 on the site of an older bridge. It has 24 arches and is 132 metres (433 feet) long. The rhythm of the arches is lightened by the presence of semi-octagonal pavilions on each side of the bridge. With its two storeys of arcades and its stone steps over which the water flows, the pol-e Khâju is certainly one of the most picturesque spots in the city.

The next bridge is the **pol-e Jubi**, or Aqueduct Bridge, 147 metres (482 feet) in length and formed of twenty-one arches, which was originally an aqueduct (now covered over) which supplied the gardens on the north bank of the river. Below this bridge is one of the most attractive tea houses in Esfahân.

Slightly further upstream, at the end of Chahâr Bâgh Avenue and Enqelâb-e Eslâm Square, is the Allâhverdi Khân Bridge, named after of Shâh Abbâs' Georgian general who was responsible for its construction. It is more commonly known as **Si-o-Se pol**, or Bridge of Thirty-Three Arches. Built around 1600 during the reign of Shâh Abbâs I, it linked Esfahân with the Armenian suburb of Jolfâ. At 295 metres (968 feet) long it is by far the longest bridge in town. It has two levels of arcades and resembles the pol-e Khâju without the pavilions. The small châikhâneh (tea house) under the bridge on the south is a fun place to have tea or an ice cream, or to smoke a *qaliân*.

The last of the old bridges is the *pol-e Mârnân* in the far west of town. It was partly destroyed by floods a few years ago and has been rebuilt recently.

ON THE SOUTH BANK: JOLFÂ

Jolfâ, also called New Jolfâ, the Armenian quarter of Esfahân, was established in 1603 on the south bank of the Zâyandeh and was linked to the Muslim town by Si-o-Se pol. As all the caravans that arrived from Shirâz and the south of the country passed through Jolfâ on their way to the Royal Square, it rapidly became a flourishing trading quarter. Shâh Abbâs had been counting on this prosperity when, despite strong opposition on their part, he imported Armenian families from the town of Jolfâ on the Aras River in Azerbaijân. During Shâh Abbâs' reign, Jolfâ was given complete religious freedom as well as a certain administrative autonomy, and was, for example, permitted to name an Armenian mayor. A cathedral, churches and even a convent were built and the Armenian community soon numbered some 30,000—and almost twice that figure according to some estimates. The first 100 years following the founding of the town were its most prosperous, and visiting European travellers have left us descriptions of luxurious houses whose beauty rivalled the Safavid palaces on the other bank of the river. Christian missionaries also settled at Jolfâ, first the Portuguese and then, from 1653, the Jesuits. But during the reigns of Shâh Abbâs' successors, life became more difficult for the Armenian community because of heavy taxation and, during Shâh Soltân Hosein's reign (1694–1722), persecutions and confiscations of property and belongings.

Today, Jolfâ is a rather quiet suburb, with none of the great bustle of activity which it once knew. Because of modern urban development and extensive reconstructions, it has lost much of its earlier character. To appreciate the importance of the Armenian community and what it has represented since its arrival in Esfahân at the beginning of the 17th century, a visit the **Cathedral of the Holy Saviour** (Kelisâ-ye Vânk) is recommended.

The entrance to the cathedral, indicated by a tilework plaque showing the cathedral and inscribed in Armenian, is in a small side street (Kelisâ Street) off Nazar-e Sharqi Avenue. In the inside courtyard, on the right, stands the belfry, a sort of square tower open on all sides. The cathedral itself is domed in the same manner as the mosques. Its outer walls, which are covered in protective bricks, have a very modern appearance. However, some of the original paintings, now badly damaged, can still be seen near the door.

Work on the cathedral began in 1606 but very soon it became obvious that the building would be too small for the needs of the rapidly-expanding Christian community, and it was rebuilt in 1655. If you have just visited one of Esfahân's mosques, the contrast upon entering this cathedral will be striking: there is none of

the brightness and tranquillity of the mosque with its vivid colours and purely geometric or floral designs. Here, the visitor encounters an interior space which is typical for a European 17th century construction in seeming smaller than suggested by the height of the dome. Around the base of the walls is a wide band of glazed tiles, many of which show large flowering plants of distinctly Mughal inspriation— not surprisingly given the importance of the Armenians as traders between Irân and India. Above this, the walls are covered murals made by the painter Minas who had been trained in the Netherlands and who was assisted by the two Armenian bishops, Joseph and Stephen. While the majority of the paintings betray a clear European inspiration, others are inspired by typical motifs taken from Irânian tapestry and from panels featuring floral decorations and arabesques that were popular during the later Safavid period. The murals represent a unique blending of European 17th century painting technique with typical Irânian art patterns. The top register shows numerous scenes from the Old Testament starting with Adam and Eve, the middle ones many scenes from the New Testament ending with the Crucifixion. On the parts just below the cupola, four-winged angels are depicted. In the lowest register finally the life of Saint Gregory the Illuminator is shown, including his martyrdom and his conversion of King Tiridates III in AD 301. The murals above the entry finally feature the Last Judgement emphasizing the pleasures of paradise as well as the torments in Hell. The paintings, as well as the scene of the Last Judgement above the entrance door, were given to the cathedral by an Armenian merchant named Avadich who is said to have had great difficulty in getting them accepted by the rest of the community. The interior of the dome is painted in Persian style with very elegant blue and gold designs.

A museum of Armenian culture has been set up in a building next to the cathedral. It contains a variety of objects related to the Armenian community in Esfahân, including Safavid costumes, embroidery, tapestries, European paintings brought back by Armenian merchants and a remarkable collection of illuminated manuscripts dating mainly from the 12th to the 17th centuries. Just outside the museum are several carved stones representing scenes from the Bible.

A second Christian church, the **Church of Bethlehem** (kelisâ-ye Bethlehem), is on Nazar-e Sharqi Avenue, near the junction with Haft-e Tir Avenue. This huge church of the same size as the Cathedral was founded in 1628 and contains murals painted in a slightly naïve, yet quite artistic way. This impression derives from the

The pol-e Khâju, built in 1650 by Shâh Abbâs II, and which also serves as a sluice gate, is Esfahân's most famous and picturesque bridge

fact that the artists attempted for the first time to paint the walls in the miniature-style of painting taken from the famous 17th century miniature-illuminations from New Jolfâ. They show many episodes of the life of Christ, various saints such as St. Stephen, St. Christopher carrying Jesus, the Apostles, and the Martyrdom of St. Gregory as well as Armenian patriarchs. The resurrected Saviour is shown enthroned in the main cupola.

Of the more than a dozen further Armenian churches in Esfahân only the small one dedicated to Mary is worthwhile visiting. Its murals date from the late 18th century and are less interesting when compared to those in the Cathedral and the Bethlehem Church.

EXCURSIONS AROUND ESFAHÂN

On Azâdegân Avenue, which forms part of the ring road around the south of the city (just before Basij-e Mostazafin Square, is the **tomb of Bâbâ Rokn od-Din** (ârâmgâh-e Bâbâ Rokn od-Din). This mausoleum, with its rather original ten-sided conical roof and drum, was built in 1629 by Shâh Abbâs to commemorate a theologian who died in the 14th century. Unfortunately a large part of the tilework, both inside and outside, has now disappeared.

In the western suburbs of Esfahân, on the main road out to Najaf Âbâd and Hamadân, are the famous **Shaking Minarets** (menâr-e Jonbân) which belong to a small 14th-century Mongol mosque. As their name suggests, these minarets have the unusual feature of moving from side to side when shaken vigorously: as soon as one of them shifts, the movement is transmitted to its twin. Several theories have been put forward to explain this phenomenon but none are completely satisfactory. Although the minarets themselves date to the 18th century and have little artistic value, the eivân (1317) beneath them is more interesting and contains the tomb of a Sufi shaykh who died in 1338.

A few kilometres further on along the same road one can see the remains of a **Zoroastrian fire temple** (âteshgâh) of the Sasanian dynasty on top of a hill to the right of the road. The climb up to the ruins from the road is quite steep and requires good shoes.

FÂRS PROVINCE

The province of Fârs, in southwestern Irân near the Persian Gulf, has played such a major role in the country's ancient history that it is considered the centre of Irânian identity. It is this province that gave its name to the Persian language spoken today, Fârsi.

In the first millennium BC, when the Indo-European tribes, ancestors of the Persians, arrived in Irân after a long migration from the north, they settled in the Bakhtiâri Mountains, to the northeast of present-day Fârs, in a region then known as Parsumash. King Teispes (675–640 BC) of Parsumash annexed the kingdoms of Parsa and Anshân, which correspond roughly to the modern province of Fârs. The city of Anshân, about 40 kilometres (25 miles) north of Shirâz, had been one of the capitals of the Elamite Empire, along with Susa. Anshân became the seat of one of the two branches of the Achaemenian royal family, founded by Cyrus I, and it was from there that Cyrus II (559–530 BC) set out on his conquest of the Median and Assyrian empires. Later, the Achaemenian rulers were to establish their capitals in newly-conquered cities such as Susa and Ecbatana, but Fârs appears to have held a special significance. The construction of Pasargadae and Persepolis, which served for the main politico-religious ceremonies, and of the royal tombs at Naqsh-e Rostam, reflects the sacred character of the whole region.

During the Parthian and Seleucid dynasties, many foreign cultural influences entered Irân, but one region in particular kept the old traditions alive: Fârs. When the Sasanian Ardeshir I, whose family came from Istakhr near Persepolis, set out against Artabanus V, the last Parthian ruler, he presented himself as the legitimate heir of the Achaemenians, the restorer of Persian values. For the Sasanians too, Fârs appears to have held particular religious and political significance, and some of their most important bas-reliefs were carved near Persepolis. As for Istakhr, where the temple dedicated to the goddess Anâhitâ was located, it was one of the main Zoroastrian centres of the empire.

In the north of the province, the Zagros Mountains rise steeply to over 3,000 metres (9,000 feet) in height, but south of Shirâz they become progressively lower, eventually forming basins which are well adapted to cultivating crops such as cereals, cotton and vines. To the south and east lie the *garmsir*, or warm land, once winter pastures used by the nomadic tribes and which mark the transition between the inland plateau and the coastal region along the Persian Gulf. Until the second half of the 20th century, nomadism was the main way of life for a large proportion of the

(Following pages) *Citadel of Karim Khân, Shirâz*

population of Fârs, particularly in the east and north of the province. The largest nomadic group were the Qashqâi, who travelled seasonally between the garmsir and the mountains to the north of Shirâz. Organized into a tribal confederation, they held considerable power at regional level but were disarmed and forced to settle by Rezâ Shâh in the 1960s. A second confederation, the Khamseh, which was artificially created in the 19th century from groups of diverse ethnic origins, used to live in the region between Shirâz and the Persian Gulf.

SHIRÂZ

To an Irânian, the very mention of the name of Shirâz will evoke a eulogy to a unique sophistication, an art of living present nowhere else in the world, the product of an ancient and learned civilization. Shirâz is an opulent oasis of greenery and culture in an otherwise barren landscape; it is the town of roses, of nightingales, of love and, at one time, of wine. But above all, Shirâz is the town of poetry, of Sa'adi and of Hâfez. The popularity of these poets is such that their verse provokes tears and sighs of admiration, and most Irânians carry collections of their poetry and are able to recite lines pertinent to every aspect of life. Their writings have been immortalized in the form of innumerable proverbs and aphorisms.

The foreign visitor who arrives in Shirâz today, and for whom the town is not as evocative as it is for an Irânian, may wonder at its reputation. Many of its famous gardens have long since disappeared and few of its buildings pre-date the 18th century. The charm of Shirâz is subtle, poetic, insubstantial.

Shirâz was founded in the Achaemenian Dynasty; under the Sasanians it became one of the main cities of the province, without ever rivalling Istakhr in importance. It was only after the Arab invasion that Shirâz emerged as the major town of the region and was used as a base for the Arab armies attacking Istakhr (684). Shirâz benefited from the decline of Istakhr and, in 693, became the provincial capital. Under the Saffârid Dynasty (867–963), and under the Buyids (945–1055), Shirâz played an important political role. It was at this period that its fortifications, which it was to keep until the 20th century, were first built. Unlike so many other towns in Irân which suffered from the invasions of Genghis Khân (1220) and Tamerlane (1387), Shirâz was left unharmed, its rulers having preferred to surrender rather than fight. From the 13th century, the town became the literary centre of all Persia, thanks in large part to the reputation of two of its most famous citizens, the poets Sa'adi (c.1207–1291) and Hâfez (c.1324–1389). Shirâz had a long tradition of painting which flourished in the 14th century with the development of its own style.

Hâfez

The world to me has been a home;
Wherever knowledge could be sought,
Through differing climes I loved to roam,
And every shade of feeling caught
From minds, whose varied fruits supply
The food of my philosophy.
And still the treasures of my store
Have made my wanderings less severe;
From every spot some prize I bore,
From every harvest gleaned an ear,
but find no land can ever vie
With bright Shirâz in purity;
And blest for ever be the spot
Which makes all other climes forgot!

Hâfez, from The Rose Garden of Persia,
freely adapted by Sir William Jones, 1795

Shams al-Din Muhammad Hâfez was a native of
Shirâz who lived c. 1324–1389. The brilliance,
energy and originality of his poems have carried his
fame throughout the world.

The tomb of Hâfez, Shirâz

During the reign of Shâh Abbâs (1587–1629), the governor of Fârs, Emâm Qoli Khân, set out to transform the town. Taking as a model the recent work that had been carried out in Esfahân, he had a wide avenue built flanked by pavilions, palaces and *madraseh*. Few of these buildings can be seen today as Shirâz later fell into decline, a situation aggravated by a series of natural and man-made disasters. For example, in 1729 the town was sacked by the Afghân army, then again in 1744 by Nâder Shâh as a reprisal for the rebellion of the province's governor. But from 1750, Karim Khân, the ruler of the new Zand Dynasty, transferred his capital to Shirâz and set about making extensive changes, including the building of a royal quarter and the Regent's Mosque and Bazaar. Zand rule was short-lived and after the death of the last ruler, Lotf Ali Khân, his successors, the Qâjâr, moved to Tehrân. Shirâz remained an important stop on the caravan routes from the port of Bushehr on the Persian Gulf but this role declined in the 20th century with the modernization of the country, and as rail and motorized road transport replaced donkeys and camels. Today, Shirâz is still not yet linked to the national railway system and the town is mainly an administrative and university centre.

Masjed-e Vakil (the Regent's Mosque), Shirâz

The main monuments in Shirâz are to be found in the centre of town, on the south bank of the Khoshk River. The old royal quarter of the Zand, built in the 18th century, has been cut in two by the Karim Khân Zand Avenue which crosses town from east to west, and only a few of the original buildings can still be seen today. The imposing **citadel of Karim Khân** is at Shohadâ Square; today it houses the municipal offices (*shahrdâri*) and is not open to visitors. Opposite the citadel, Karim Khân laid out a landscaped garden; one of its pavilions has been turned into the **Pars museum**. Once a reception hall, this small octagonal building was also briefly Karim Khân's mausoleum until Âghâ Mohammed Qâjâr ordered the body removed. The *haft rangi* decoration on the outer walls with its floral motifs and hunting scenes in shades of blue, beige, green and pink, is typical of the period. Inside is a small collection of excellent manuscripts, and a variety of objects, some relating to the life of Karim Khân.

Another building from the same period is the **Regent's Mosque** (masjed-e Vakil), further east on Zand Avenue, next to the Regent's Bazaar. Both buildings are named after the title of Regent, or 'Vakil', which Karim Khân took when he came to the throne and which he preferred to the more usual title of Shâh. The mosque was restored in the 19th century and its main interest lies in its *haft rangi* decoration, done in the same style as that of the Pars museum, with the distinctive pink and

green used by the Shirâz school. The *mehrâb* hall is quite remarkable with its 48 barley-sugar columns, and its *membar* carved out of a single block of white marble.

The old Regent's Bazaar was cut in two when Zand Avenue was built. The larger of the two halves, covered with a series of very fine brick vaults, is to the south of the avenue; the northern section has been renamed bâzâr-e No (the New Bazaar).

A second group of monuments, older than the ones mentioned above, can be seen around Âyatollâh Dastgheib Avenue. North of the avenue is the *madraseh-ye Khân*, built in 1615 by Emâm Qoli Khân, the Safavid governor of the province who hoped to reproduce in Shirâz the type of large-scale transformations that Shâh Abbâs had carried out in Esfahân. The *madraseh* has been heavily restored after earthquake damage and only the octagonal hall that can be seen from the entrance is original. The interior is designed in traditional style with a central court with trees surrounded by arcades which lead into the students' rooms. The south *eivân* is decorated with blue and pink tiles in stylized designs of flowers and birds.

The **New Mosque** (masjed-e No or masjed-e Shohadâ, the Martyrs' Mosque), on Dastgheib Avenue, was built by the local ruler Sa'd ibn Zangi, patron of the poet Sa'adi, at the end of the 12th century (it was finished in 1218). Its plan is the usual four-*eivân* one but with a much larger courtyard. The mosque was renovated in the 16th century but was quite extensively damaged by earthquakes in the 18th and 19th centuries.

Not far away on the other side of Ahmadi Square (Hezarat Street) is the **Mausoleum of Shâh Cherâgh** (ârâmgâh-e Shâh Cherâgh), which has a bulbous

(Top) Cenotaph of Ahmed ibn Musâ; (right) The Mausoleum of Shâh Cherâgh, Shirâz

dome set on a tall thin drum and a small golden-roofed minaret. Inside is the cenotaph of Ahmed ibn Musâ, brother of Emâm Rezâ, who died in Shirâz in 835. The first buildings erected here in his honour were built in the 13th century and modified later. In the 19th century an earthquake destroyed the original dome which was rebuilt as it is today, decorated with large beige and turquoise floral designs. This mausoleum is an important pilgrimage site for Shi'a Muslims.

Nearby is a second mausoleum, built in the Qâjâr period, that of Seyyed Mir Muhammed, another brother of Emâm Rezâ. Again, the dome is set on a very narrow drum and is decorated with a lozenge design.

Further east is the **Nâser ol-Molk** Mosque, one of the most successful Qâjâr buildings of the 19th century. Its outer walls, and in particular the south *eivân*, are decorated with the characteristic predominantly pink flower motifs of the period. Inside, under the arches of the winter mosque, the vaults are decorated with geometric patterns and the twisted pillars with stylized palmettes. From the roof of the mosque one has a good view over the above-mentioned tombs.

Further south, the old Friday Mosque or **masjed-e Atiq** was built on the site of a Saffârid mosque (ninth century) of which a few remains can be seen in the *mehrâb* hall (part of the decoration and brickwork). The present buildings are much more recent and were heavily renovated in the 17th century. The tilework on the western walls are 16th century. One interesting feature of this mosque is its House of Korans (beit ol-Moshaf) or House of God (Khodâ-khâneh), a square building with a tower at each corner, set in the centre of the courtyard. Built in the 14th century and restored in the 20th century, it is said to have housed copies of the holy book. The very fine relief inscription around it is attributed to Yahyâ al-Jamali, a famous 14th-century calligrapher.

Shirâz still has a number of parks and gardens which are particularly pleasant to wander through in summer or after a long drive through

Tomb of Sa'adi

Entrance to the prayer hall, Mausoleum of Shâh Cherâgh

the desert. One of the most popular gardens is the **Bâgh-e Erâm** in the northwest part of town, which is known for its cypress trees. In the middle of the garden, reflected in the pool in front of it, stands a Qâjâr palace (19th century) decorated with figurative scenes and animals.

The tombs of the poets Sa'adi and Hâfez are also on the north bank of the river. To most Irânians, these are the most important monuments in Shirâz. The **tomb of Hâfez** is the closest to the centre of town (entrance on Golestan Boulevard, opposite Melli Pârk). Rebuilt in 1953 in a garden, the mausoleum is a small open pavilion; inside it is a marble tombstone on which are carved several of the poet's verses. Shams od-Din Muhammad—or Hâfez, 'he who knows the Qur'ân by heart'—was born in Shirâz between 1317 and 1326. He spent most of his life in his native town and died there in 1389. As a court poet, Hâfez was subjected to the vagaries of political life, going through periods of disgrace, and even exile. His poems have been collected in a *Divân*, or anthology, of some 500 *ghazals*, a poetic

form of complex metre and a single rhyme. Hâfez is considered the undisputed master of the *ghazal*, and his poems reflect a richness and a subtlety unequalled even by that other great talent, Sa'adi. Hâfez' work has led to very diverse interpretations; in his *Divân*, mystical poems associated with a profound symbolism are found with others, which deal with love and wine. But should one to read the literal meaning of the words, or should an attempt be made to uncover the poet's esoteric message? When does the word 'love' refer to carnal love, and when is it the ideal love of God, union with the Divine? The freedom given to the reader to make his own interpretation and the subtlety of the language go a long way to explain the great popularity of Hâfez' poetry. Indeed, his *Divân* has become a book of consolation and divination: when opened at random, it allows one to predict the future—providing that the verses are correctly interpreted, of course!

Do not miss the opportunity to visit the little châikhâneh in the park for a cup of tea and a rose water ice cream. The entrance to the teahouse is in the back wall of the garden.

Sa'adi's tomb, also set in a pleasant garden, is in the northeast of Shirâz, at the end of Bustân Boulevard. The present tomb was built in 1952 and replaces an earlier, much simpler construction. Unlike Hâfez, Mosleh od-Din Sa'adi, born in Shirâz in 1189, travelled extensively in Iraq and Syria, where he claims to have been taken prisoner by the Crusaders. After his travels, he returned to his native Shirâz where he finished his two most famous works, the *Bustân* (The Orchard) and the *Golestân* (The Rose Garden), collections of moral tales with witty maxims, written either in verse or in a mixture of prose and verse. Sa'adi also wrote a number of *qasidas* and exquisite *ghazals*. The main theme of his *ghazal* is love, both physical and mystical, which he treats in an elegant manner, in simple but expressive terms. Sa'adi is said to have died in 1290 at the age of over 100.

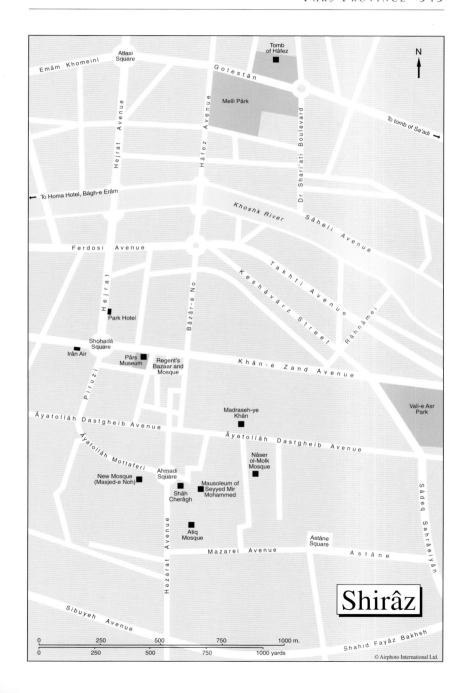

N

Emâm Khomeini

Atlasi Square

Tomb of Hâfez

Golestân

Melli Pârk

Hejrat Avenue

Hâfez Avenue

Dr Shari'ati Boulevard

To tomb of Sa'adi

To Homa Hotel, Bâgh-e Erâm

Khoshk River

Sâheli Avenue

Ferdosi Avenue

Hejrat

Bâzâr-e No

Keshâvârz Street

Takhti Avenue

Rahnâmei

Park Hotel

Shohadâ Square

Irân Air

Pârs Museum

Regent's Bazaar and Mosque

Khân-e Zand Avenue

Piruzi

Madraseh-ye Khân

Vali-e Asr Park

Âyatollâh Dastgheib Avenue

Âyatollâh Dastgheib Avenue

Âyatollâh Mottaferi

Nâser ol-Molk Mosque

New Mosque (Masjed-e Noh)

Ahmadi Square

Shâh Cherâgh

Mausoleum of Seyyed Mir Mohammed

Sâdeq Sahrâei yân

Hezarat Avenue

Atiq Mosque

Astâne Square

Mazarei Avenue

Astâne

Sibuyeh Avenue

Shiraz

0   250   500   750   1000 m.

0   250   500   750   1000 yards

Shahid Fayâz Bakhsh

© Airphoto International Ltd.

THE PHILOSOPHY OF LIFE

OF THE CUSTOMS OF KINGS

*T*hey have related that at a hunting seat they were roasting some game
for Nushirowan, and as there was no salt they were despatching a
servant to the village to fetch some. Nushirowan called to him, saying, 'Take
it at its fair price, and not by force, lest a bad precedent be established and
the village desolated.' They asked, 'What damage can ensue from this trifle?'
He answered, 'Originally, the basis of oppression in this world was small,
and every newcomer added to it, till it reached to its present extent: Let the
monarch eat but one apple from a peasant's orchard, and his guards, or
slaves, will pull up the tree by its root. From the plunder of five eggs, that
the king shall sanction, his troops will stick a thousand fowls on their spits.'

ON THE PRECIOUSNESSS OF CONTENTMENT

*T*wo dervishes of Khorasan were fellow-companions on a journey. One
was so spare and moderate that he would break his fast only every
other night, and the other so robust and intemperate that he ate three meals
a day. It happened that they were taken up at the gate of a city on suspicion
of being spies, and both together put into a place, the entrance of which was
built up with mud. After a fortnight it was discovered that they were
innocent, when, on breaking open the door, they found the strong man
dead, and the weak one alive and well. They were astonished at this
circumstance. A wise man said, 'The contrary of this had been strange, for
this one was a voracious eater, and not having strength to support a want of
food, perished; and that other was abstemious, and being patient, according
to his habitual practice, survived it. When a person is habitually temperate,
and a hardship shall cross him, he will get over it with ease; but if he has
pampered his body and lived in luxury, and shall get into straitened
circumstances, he must perish.'

ON THE BENEFIT OF BEING SILENT

Some of the courtiers of Sultan Mahmud asked Husan Maimandi, saying: 'What did the king whisper to you today on a certain state affair!' He said: 'You are also acquainted with it.' They replied: 'You are the prime minister; what the king tells you, he does not think proper to communicate to such as we are.' He replied: 'He communicates with me in the confidence that I will not divulge to anybody; then why do you ask me!' A man of sense blabs not, whatever he may come to know; he should not make his own head the forfeit of the king's secret.

OF THE DUTIES OF SOCIETY

Riches are intended for the comfort of life, and not life for the purpose of hoarding riches. I asked a wise man, saying: 'Who is the fortunate man, and who is the unfortunate?' He said: 'That man was fortunate who spent and gave away, and that man unfortunate who died and left behind: Pray not for that good-for-nothing man who did nothing, for he passed his life in hoarding riches, and did not spend them.'

Sa'adi, The Gulistan, c. 1280, translated by James Ross, 1900

Sa'adi began life as a student of the Qur'ān in Shirâz, and later graduated to higher Islamic learning, including Sufism, in Baghdâd. He travelled widely before returning to Shirâz in his old age. There he wrote the *Bustân* and the *Golestân* (*Gulistan*), which are filled with anecdotes and maxims in which he presents himself as having travelled to Kashgar in Chinese Turkestan and Somnath in Indian Gujarat, as well as having contracted an unsuitable marriage to escape forced labour for the crusaders in Syria.

Palace of Darius, Persepolis

PERSEPOLIS (TAKHT-E JAMSHID)

Persepolis is undoubtedly the most impressive of all the archaeological sites in Irân, not only because of its sheer size but by the nature of the ruins themselves which display some of the finest examples of Achaemenian carving to be seen anywhere. Unlike Susa and Pasargadae, where a considerable mental effort on the part of the visitor is required to grasp the original layout of the palaces, it is possible here to picture a part of the Achaemenian world.

The site of Persepolis is extensive and a good two to four hours minimum are needed for the visit. Allow at least a half-day's excursion from Shirâz (120 kilometres [75 miles] there and back) and more if you want to visit the other sites nearby. Be careful in summer as the sun is very hot and the ruins offer little shade.

Around 518 BC, as soon as work on Susa was finished, Darius I began the construction of a new capital in the plain of Marv-e Dasht, near Pasargadae, Cyrus the Great's capital. Parsa (better known in the West by its Greek name, Persepolis) never had an administrative or commercial role but is generally thought to have served for the New Year celebrations. These were the most important festivities in the Mazdean calendar when envoys from all the vassal states of the Achaemenian Empire came to present tribute to the King of Kings. (It should be pointed out, however, that this interpretation is not unanimously accepted and that some scholars prefer to see Persepolis simply as a residence and treasury located near the royal tombs at Naqsh-e Rostam.)

Relief carving of a procession of Persian officials

The site of Persepolis was carefully chosen: the palatial complex was built to impress those who came to it and symbolized the power of the Achaemenian rulers. The trip each year from Susa, the administrative capital some 500 kilometres (311 miles) away, would have been a long and difficult one, and this isolated position would have accentuated the prestige and glory of the king. Indeed, beginning with the reign of Darius, the whole region of Fârs appears to have taken on a sacred character linked to the religious beliefs which lay behind the very principle of royalty: the Achaemenian kings held their power directly from the god Ahura Mazda, and the political and religious aspects of the coronation ceremonies, held nearby at Pasargadae, and of the New Year ceremonies are therefore difficult to separate from one another. It is in this context that the decision was taken to site the royal cemetery at Naqsh-e Rostam, a few kilometres away from Persepolis.

Thanks to the numerous inscribed tablets that have been found, it has been possible to establish a detailed chronology of the construction of Persepolis, which lasted from its foundation under Darius until its destruction under Alexander the Great. The terrace, âpâdânâ, monumental staircases and Darius' palace (*tachara*) were all built during Darius' reign (522–486 BC). Xerxes I (486–465 BC) added the great Gate of All Nations and his own palace (*hadish*); he also began work on the Hall of a Hundred Columns which was finished in the reign of Artaxerxes I

(465–423 BC). But the construction of Persepolis was never really completed and several buildings, including Artaxerxes II's palace (359–338 BC) were left unfinished. The term 'palace' given to some of the buildings may be debatable, since the Achaemenian rulers lived at Persepolis mostly during the New Year celebrations. Excavations carried out in the plain at the foot of the terrace have uncovered buildings belonging to a lower city. Even in the king's absence, a minimum staff of priests and soldiers would most probably have remained at Persepolis all year round to protect the buildings and ensure their upkeep.

Alexander the Great entered Persepolis in January 330 BC. The town had surrendered without a fight but it was sacked and the royal treasure taken away, although the buildings appear to have been left intact and were guarded by Macedonian soldiers. Much controversy has arisen over the destruction of Persepolis: were the palaces deliberately burnt on Alexander's orders, or was the fire that destroyed them an accidental consequence of one of the conqueror's orgies? The event is interpreted by some as Greek revenge for the destruction of the temples of Athens by the Persians in 480 BC, but it has rightly been pointed out that Alexander, who was not in the habit of destroying the cities he conquered, had absolutely nothing to gain from the burning of Persepolis. Whatever the real reasons behind the fire, the city was entirely destroyed and abandoned thereafter.

Europe rediscovered Persepolis at the beginning of the 17th century when travellers brought back descriptions of the ruins, but it was not until the early 19th century that the first excavations were carried out. The Oriental Institute of Chicago began systematic digs under the direction of Ernst Herzfeld from 1931 to 1934. These excavations were continued by Eric Schmidt until 1939, and then taken over by the Irânian Archaeological Service.

VISITING PERSEPOLIS

On arrival at Persepolis one is confronted by an impressive wall, completely smooth and plain, about 15 metres (49 feet) tall: this is the artificial terrace on which the palaces were built. From the ground, the ruins can hardly be seen except for the very tallest columns and the Gate of All Nations. It is only as one climbs the monumental staircase that the rest of the site is progressively revealed in all its splendour.

This vast terrace of Persepolis, some 450 metres (1,476 feet) long and 300 metres (984 feet) wide, was originally fortified on three sides by a tall wall. The only access was from the **monumental staircase** which leads to the **Gate of All Nations**.

(Preceding pages) *View of the āpādānā, Persepolis;* (right) *Doorway of the Throne Hall, Persepolis*

This gate, built by Xerxes I, is a square room, open on three sides. The east and west doorjambs are decorated with large sculptures of guardian winged bulls with human heads, strongly influenced by Assyrian sculpture (in Assyria, however, the bulls have five legs whereas here the Achaemenian artist has only given them four). From the south door of the Gate of All Nations one can proceed directly to the âpâdânâ, while the west door leads to a broad avenue and a second monumental gate (left unfinished).

Column capital, Persepolis

The **âpâdânâ**, begun by Darius but finished only in Xerxes' reign, was the great audience hall where the King of Kings received delegations from the vassal nations. In this immense hall, measuring 75 square metres (807 square feet) stood six rows of six columns. Each column, some 20 metres (66 feet) tall, ended in a capital in the shape of griffons, bulls or lions set back to back. The âpâdânâ was flanked on three sides by porticos and on the fourth side by small chambers.

Two **monumental staircases** on the north and east sides lead up to the âpâdânâ. Both are decorated with carvings which, in the case of the east staircase, are in exceptional condition through having been buried for centuries under layers of ash and earth. This staircase is without a doubt one of the most remarkable works of art left to us from the Achaemenian period. It presents a summary of one of the ceremonies held during the New Year festivities: the great procession before the Achaemenian ruler of the delegations from the various vassal nations and the presentation of their tribute. It is well worth taking a little time to look at the details of some of these carvings: carpets and chairs being carried on servants' backs; the expression on the face of a young lion or ram; the sometimes touching way in which the men are shown talking among themselves or holding hands; and everywhere a wealth of detail of clothes and hats which represent better than anything the great diversity of peoples that formed the empire.

Gate of All Nations, Persepolis

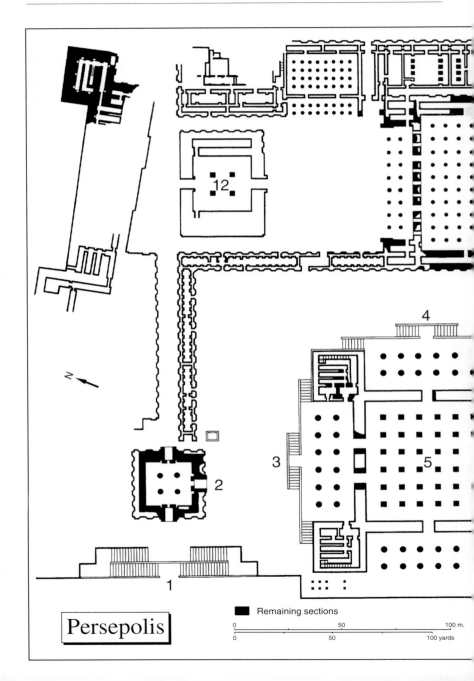

Persepolis

Remaining sections

0   50   100 m.
0   50   100 yards

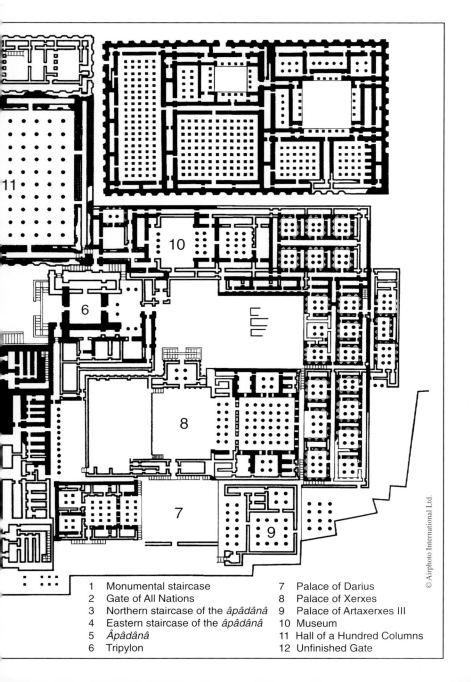

© Airphoto International Ltd.

1 Monumental staircase
2 Gate of All Nations
3 Northern staircase of the *âpâdânâ*
4 Eastern staircase of the *âpâdânâ*
5 *Âpâdânâ*
6 Tripylon
7 Palace of Darius
8 Palace of Xerxes
9 Palace of Artaxerxes III
10 Museum
11 Hall of a Hundred Columns
12 Unfinished Gate

A procession of Bactrian tributaries, from the region of modern-day Afghânistân

In the centre, between the two ramps of the staircase, stand eight guards facing each other. Above them is the symbol of the god Ahura Mazda, the winged sun, and, to each side, a fight between a lion and a bull. The surface of the side walls is divided into three horizontal rows: to the right of the stairs are long lines of Persian and Median guards accompanied by cavalry, infantry and archers; to the left is the procession of the vassal states, each group accompanied by a Persian or Median official. The exact identity of some of the nations represented is still unclear but the generally accepted interpretation is the following (from right to left): in the top row are the Medes, who were given the honour of leading the procession, followed by the Elamites, bringing lions; the Parthians with camels and pelts; the Sogdians from Central Asia (or the Arachosians from Afghânistân) also bringing camels and pelts; the Egyptians with a bull; possible Bactrians with a camel and vessels; and finally probably the Sagartians with clothes and a horse.

In the second row, still from right to left, are the Armenians leading a horse and carrying a large vase; the Babylonians with a bull, lengths of cloth and cups; the

Lion and bull motif, staircase of the âpâdânâ, Persepolis

Cilicians (or a Central Asian people) with rams, pelts and cups; the Scythians, wearing pointed hats, with a horse and armbands; the Assyrians with a bull and spears; and the Chorasmians of Central Asia with a horse, armbands and axes.

In the bottom row are the Lydians with vases and a chariot; the Cappadocians with a horse and clothes; the Ionians with lengths of cloth and plates; the Bactrians (or the Arachosians of Afghānistān) leading a camel; and the Indians carrying baskets with vases and leading a donkey.

The staircase to the left of the central stairs is decorated, from the bottom up, with Ethiopians, or Kushites, carrying an elephant's tusk and leading an okapi or a giraffe; the Somalis with an antelope and a chariot; the Arabs with a dromedary and cloth; and the Thracians with shields, spears and a horse. The figures with a bull, shield and lance are perhaps Drangians from Sistān and Afghānistān.

To the left of the east staircase of the âpâdânâ is another smaller set of stairs, which leads to the **tripylon**. Here, the carvings include a variation on the theme of the lion and bull fight, a sphinx and processions of guards and dignitaries, but there are no representations of the vassal nations. The doorjambs of the north and south doors of the tripylon show King Darius followed by two servants holding a fan and a parasol, while the opening of the east door shows the king seated on his throne

under the winged symbol of Ahura Mazda, and held up by the twenty-eight vassal nations.

From the south corner of the âpâdânâ, one enters **Darius' palace**, or *tachara*. This building, composed of a central hall with columns surrounded by smaller rooms, was also finished by Xerxes. The central hall is sometimes called the Hall of Mirrors because of the highly polished surface of the stones. The doorjambs that lead into it are decorated with large bas-reliefs of the king fighting a lion, a bull and a chimera, as well as servants carrying various objects. The west and south stairs to the palace are decorated with representations of the Immortals (the royal guard) and of vassals bringing tribute.

The south staircase of the *tachara* leads to the unfinished palace of Artaxerxes III, which is in bad condition, and to Xerxes' palace, the *hadish*, built on the highest terrace of the site. This is once again a square room with 36 columns, surrounded by side chambers and with a portico on the north side. A few bas-reliefs still remain on the door jambs showing the king followed by servants carrying parasols, vases and incense burners. From the *hadish* one goes on to the so-called harem, built by Xerxes and left incomplete (the exact function of the building is not clear, it may have been a storage area for the treasury but most probably was not a harem). An excellent small museum here exhibits various objects found at the site as well as Islamic ceramics and glassware from Istakhr nearby. The welcome tree-shade of the café next to the museum, alas, no longer shelters the tired tourist, who must exit the site to take refreshments in the new tourist complex built outside the archaeological area. The lavatories, are, however, still operational.

The largest hall at Persepolis is known as the **Hall of a Hundred Columns**, or Throne Room. It is very likely that an important ceremony was held here as the north portico gives onto a vast courtyard of some 4,000 square metres (43,056 square feet) behind which is an unfinished monumental gate and the avenue which leads to the Gate of All Nations. Several theories have been put forward as to the function of this hall, including that of a storage room for the tribute brought at the New Year celebrations: after a procession in the courtyard, the vassal delegations would have placed their tribute at the feet of the King of Kings, seated in the hall.

A path leads from the ruins to two **tombs** dug in the cliff face behind the terrace. On the left is the tomb said to be of Artaxerxes II (405–361 BC) and on the right that said to be of Artaxerxes III (361–338 BC). Both tombs are shaped like those at Naqsh-e Rostam (see below) and are decorated on the outer façade with bas-reliefs of the king held up by the twenty-eight vassal nations and standing

Detail of a relief carving of Persian officials, Persepolis

Procession of tributary nations:

The Scythians, recognizable by their pointed hats, lived near the Black Sea and were gifted horsemen and blacksmiths. Very few vassal nations retained the privilege of bearing weapons in the prescence of the Achaemenian King of Kings

Lydia (present-day Western Turkey), the land of King Croesus, owed its proverbial wealth to trade and gold mines. The bowls and vases carried here in tribute closely resemble exhibits in the Rezâ Abbâsi Museum in Tehrân

The delegation from the Indus Valley is lead by a Persian official. The Indus marked the eastern limit of the Achaemenian Empire. The gold pannings contained in the baskets would have come from the tributaries of the great river

(Left) *A Lydian tribute-bearer, Persepolis;* (following pages) *Stairway of the âpâdânâ, Persepolis*

before a regnal fire altar; above him are the winged symbol of Ahura Mazda, or more probably the royal glory (*farr-e yazdāni*), the sun and the moon. To the extreme south of the terrace a third tomb, unfinished, of Darius III Codomanus (336–330 BC).

Very near the site of Persepolis are the carvings of **Naqsh-e Rajab**, which date to the Sasanian period. The province of Fārs is particularly rich in Sasanian rock carvings, the most famous of which are those at Naqsh-e Rostam and Bishâpur. Here, at Naqsh-e Rajab, are two investiture scenes, those of Ardeshir I (AD 224–241) and of Shâpur I (AD 241–272), as well as a bas-relief of Shâpur I on horseback, followed by a group of noblemen and foot soldiers. This last scene is accompanied by an inscription in Pahlavi and Greek. The investiture scene is one of the most frequently represented subjects in Sasanian bas-reliefs, and although the details vary from one example to another, the basic composition is always the same: the ruler receiving a diadem, symbol of royalty, from the hands of a god, usually Ahura Mazda. The figures are shown either standing, as in the case of Ardeshir here, or on horseback, as in the case of Shâpur. Secondary figures may also appear: Ardeshir is accompanied here by his son Shâpur and by a page carrying a fan (standing behind him) as well as by two children, set between the king and the god.

Relief carving of Kartir, the Zoroastrian High Priest, late 3rd century AD, Naqsh-e Rajab

Relief carving of the Sasanian King, Shâpur I, at Naqsh-e Rajab

The last carving at Naqsh-e Rajab is of a man with his face turned sideways, raising a finger. Under it is an inscription in Pahlavi, a shorter version of a text which appears at four other sites, including Naqsh-e Rostam, and which is attributed to Kartir, the famous Zoroastrian Magus who served six different shâhs between AD 240/41 and 294 and was responsible for the establishment of a religious state orthodoxy under the Sasanians. These inscriptions relate the main events in Kartir's life, describing his ascension through the clerical hierarchy, and his attacks on non-Zoroastrian religions as follows: 'I removed and destroyed the teachings of Ahriman [the spirit of Evil] and of the demons: the Jews, the Buddhists, the [Hindu] Brahmins, the Nazareans [the Eastern Syriac Christians], the Krystiyân [the Greek speaking prisoners of war], the Baptists and the Manichaeans are annihilated in the Empire. Their idols are broken and their temples destroyed.' The figure shown next to the inscription represents Kartir.

NAQSH-E ROSTAM

Naqsh-e Rostam, about four kilometres (2.5 miles) north of Persepolis, is one of the most important Achaemenian and Sasanian sites in Irân. It is here in the rock face that Darius I and three of his successors had their tombs dug. Like the later tombs of the two Artaxerxes at Persepolis, which were modelled on these, their outer façade, in the shape of a cross, has an opening in the centre which leads to the funerary chamber. The lower part of the façade is plain, while the central section echoes the architecture of columns and capitals, and the upper part has representations of the king beside a fire altar, held up by the vassal nations. The central tomb on the cliff bears a lengthy inscription which identifies it as that of Darius I (521–485 BC). The single tomb on the far right is generally attributed to Darius II (425–405 BC), while the remaining two tombs (from left to right) are thought to be those of Artaxerxes I (465–424 BC) and Xerxes I (485–465 BC).

Opposite the Achaemenian tombs is a square stone structure, known as the **Kab'eh-ye Zardusht**, or Cube of Zoroaster, which might have been an Achaemenian fire temple, or more probably a royal tomb. The walls on three sides have niches set in them which resemble windows while, on the fourth side, steps lead to a door high on the main wall of the building. This tower, probably built during the reign of Darius I, is one of only very few of its type still standing. In 1936, while the base of the tower was being excavated, inscriptions were discovered on the outer wall. The first one, written in Middle Persian, is one of the four versions of the priest Kartir's text (a longer version of this appears at this same site on the carving of Shâpur's victory over the Romans). The second inscription, written in Parthian Pahlavi, in Sasanian Pahlavi and in Greek, tells of Shâpur's campaigns against Rome which ended in one case in the death of the Emperor Gordian, in another in the

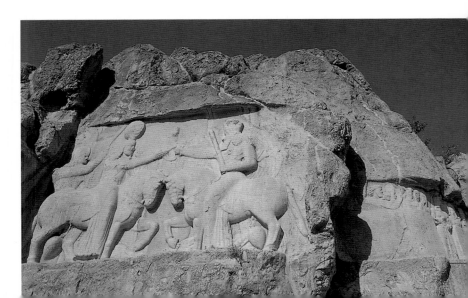

*Triumph of Shâpur I over the Roman Emperors Philip the Arab (kneeling)
and Valerian, Naqsh-e Rostam*

defeat of a Roman army 60,000 strong under Philip the Arab and in the capture of
Antioch, and in the last case in the capture of the Roman emperor Valerian in AD
260. The importance of these inscriptions for the understanding of Sasanian history
is vital: indeed, without Kartir's inscriptions his very name and the role he played
in the development of Zoroastrianism would be completely unknown to us. As for
Shâpur's text on his Roman campaigns, it is as important as Darius' Achaemenian
text at Bisotun.

On the same rock face as the Achaemenian tombs are eight **Sasanian bas-reliefs**.
The choice of this site by the Sasanian rulers was hardly a chance one and they most
probably hoped to benefit from the divine emanations, or *khwarna*, of their predecessors at this spot which had become sacred for the Achaemenians. To the far left of
the site, beside the road, are two small Sasanian altars carved into the rock. They are
pyramidal in shape, with small columns at the corners and a hollow in the top in
which fire may have been lit, or more probably, bones might have been contained.

The investiture of Ardeshir by Ahura Mazda, Naqsh-e Rostam

The cliff at Naqsh-e Rostam with the tombs of the Achaemenian kings

The first bas-reliefs are on the far left of the rock face, before the Achaemenian tombs. The first carving shows the investiture of Ardeshir I (AD 224–241), the founder of the dynasty. The king and the god Ahura Mazda handing him the beribboned diadem are both represented on horseback. Under the hoofs of the horses are the bodies of their enemies, Artabanus V, the last Parthian king, and Ahriman, the God of Evil. Inscriptions in Middle Persian and Greek give the identity of the four figures. The scene is carved in very high relief, with the horses almost free-standing, and is considered to be among the finest examples of Sasanian carving.

The second scene shows Bahrâm II (276–293) with members of his family and dignitaries. Its most interesting feature is that it was carved over a much earlier Elamite bas-relief, dated between the ninth and seventh centuries BC. Only the two figures at each end of the carving remain. This, along with the carving at Kurangun near Bishâpur, is one of the rare examples of Elamite rock carving to have survived in Irân.

The third bas-relief, under the furthest tomb on the left, shows Bahrâm II on horseback and in combat. Next are two carvings set one above the other. The top one, which is badly damaged, represents Shâpur II (309–379) leaning on his sword; the lower one shows Hormizd II (303–309) unseating an enemy with his spear. The sixth relief commemorates Shâpur's (241–272) victories against the Romans: the figure kneeling before Shâpur's horse is believed to be Emperor Philip the Arab, while standing behind him is Emperor Valerian, who was captured at the battle of Edessa in 260. Note the billowing and heavily pleated clothes which are characteristic of Shâpur's reign, a sharp contrast to the more austere style of Ardeshir seen in the first bas-relief. The next carving, dated to the reign of Bahrâm II, shows a fight on horseback set in two registers separated by a horizontal line. The last carving represents the investiture of Narses (293–302) receiving the diadem from the hands of the goddess Anâhitâ, or possibly granting it to his wife Shapurdokht.

PASARGADAE

On the road to Esfahân and Yazd, about 70 kilometres (43 miles) from Persepolis, are the ruins of another Achaemenian city, **Pasargadae** (Pâsârgâd). It was here, in the Murghab Plain, that Cyrus the Great (r. 550–529 BC) decided to build his capital, on the same spot, according to legend, where he defeated the Median army led by Astyages in 550 BC. This decisive battle marked the beginning of the years of conquest which lead to the formation of the Achaemenian Empire. It has been suggested that the city was built on the site of earlier constructions which could date back to the very first Achaemenian rulers of Anshân in the 7th century BC. Although this theory has yet to be verified by further excavations, the ruins of Pasargadae nonetheless represent the earliest known examples of Achaemenian architecture.

Many fundamental questions concerning the role of Pasargadae still remain unanswered because of the lack of detailed documentation and the state of the ruins. Was the city an administrative or religious centre, or was there a sharing of these functions between Pasargadae and Ecbatana, the old Median capital which Cyrus had taken over? In any event, it appears that the construction work at Pasargadae, like at Persepolis, was never completed, perhaps because of Cyrus' untimely death in battle in 529 BC.

With the accession to the throne of Darius I in 522 BC, who belonged to a different branch of the Achaemenian family, Pasargadae was relegated to a secondary role and the new ruler quickly began building other cities, first Susa and then Persepolis. Pasargadae was used mainly for the investiture ceremonies of the Achaemenian kings.

The ruins of Pasargadae are much less well preserved than those of Persepolis and are dispersed over a wide area across the plain. The first building that one comes to, a small gabled structure set on a stepped platform, is identified as the **tomb of Cyrus**, and known locally as the tomb of Solomon's mother. Set apart from the other ruins, the mausoleum, which is built of white limestone, is simple and austere. Around the tomb were the remains of the columns of a temple built at a later date, which have now been removed. Classical historians recorded how distressed Alexander the Great was when he arrived in front of the tomb in the spring of 324 BC, only to find that it had been desecrated: the bones of the body were scattered on the ground and there was no trace of the king's clothes and jewellery, his gold sarcophagus, or the rich draperies which Alexander's soldiers had described when they had visited the tomb some years previously. The Macedonian, who considered himself to be the heir of Cyrus, ordered that the tomb should be repaired and sealed to prevent further profanations.

A road leads from the tomb to the ruins of Pasargadae. Although the buildings appear at first sight to be haphazardly placed in relation to one another, they were in fact originally carefully integrated into extensive landscaped gardens, of which only traces of the water channels now remain. The largest of the buildings, known as Cyrus' royal residence, is composed of a central hall of five rows of six columns, flanked on two sides by long porticos. This hall illustrates well one of the characteristic building techniques seen at Pasargadae, the use of alternating blocks of black and white limestone for the column bases. Fragments of carvings are still visible on the openings of some of the doors and the large corner pillar carries a short inscription in three languages, bearing the name of Cyrus. A second, slightly smaller building, surrounded by porticos on all four sides, can be seen a few hundred metres to the south. Near it, stands a gatehouse which is notable for the decoration of one of the door jambs (now under cover). This unique sculpture, 2.7 metres high (8.9 feet), representing a four-winged genie, is the oldest intact Achaemenian carving to have been found. From these ruins one can see the remains of a square tower in the distance, known as Solomon's Prison, similar to the one at Naqsh-e Rostam.

About 200 kilometres (124 miles) further along the same road that leads to Esfahân, one comes to the small but very picturesque village of **Izad Khâst** (between Âbâdeh and Amin Âbâd). Above the modern village which spreads out at the foot of a cliff, are the ruins of an ancient fortified settlement, perched on a rocky outcrop. There is also a Safavid câravânsarai by the stream.

EXCURSIONS FROM SHIRÂZ

The road which leaves Shirâz towards Bandar-e Bushehr, on the Persian Gulf, and Ahvâz, in Khuzestân, passes by the site of **Bishâpur**, known for its bas-reliefs and the ruins of a Sasanian city. The trip through some superb mountain scenery with grandiose gorges and wooded valleys can easily be done as a day's excursion from Shirâz (130 kilometres [81 miles] one way). The site of Bishâpur itself is very attractive: the bas-reliefs are carved on the rock face overlooking the Shâpur River and are surrounded by trees which provide welcome shade in summer.

The first two carvings are on the left bank of the river (on the right-hand side as one enters the gorge). Both represent Shâpur I's victories over the Romans. The subject matter here is the same as at Naqsh-e Rostam but is treated slightly differently. The first bas-relief is badly damaged and the details no longer visible; the second one, however, shows the king receiving the crown not from Ahura Mazda but from a putto, an element borrowed from Western iconography. Unusually, this scene is not restricted to the main protagonists but is accompanied on either side by several registers of figures in an overall design reminiscent of many Roman scenes of triumph.

To reach the carvings on the other bank, cross the river by the road bridge and follow the path which leads into the woods. The third bas-relief once again shows Shâpur's victory over the Romans: here, the two horses are trampling the bodies of Emperor Gordian III and the god Ahriman underfoot, while Philip the Arab kneels before the king. The absence of Valerian from this scene suggests that it was carved before the year 260 and that it therefore predates the two bas-reliefs on the other bank.

The fourth carving shows Bahrâm II (AD 276–293) accepting the submission of Arab nomads who have come with their horses and camels. This carving has been damaged by a later irrigation channel which was once attached to the rock face. The fifth bas-relief shows the investiture of Bahrâm I (273–276) in the now familiar composition, similar to the investitures at Naqsh-e Rostam and Naqsh-e Rajab.

The last relief is treated in a slightly different manner: the king, in the centre, is shown from the front, leaning on his sword. On the left are two registers of court dignitaries and soldiers, while on the right stand prisoners and servants carrying booty. This scene, dated to the reign of Shâpur II (309–379) is the latest one at the site.

On the heights above the river are the ruins of the ancient **Sasanian royal city** of Bishâpur built from AD 266 by Shâpur I. The excavations here were carried out by French archaeologists under the direction of Georges Salles and Roman Ghirshman in the 1930s and 1940s and then taken over by Irânian archaeologists.

On approaching the city, one notices first of all the old stone walls with their semicircular towers. Behind them is the palatial complex and, below, a fire temple. The temple is composed of a central square room surrounded by tall walls which were originally over 14 metres (46 feet) high. Each wall has a single door in it which leads to a dark covered corridor. At the top of the stairs, on the right, is the door to a long hall where mosaic fragments, strongly influenced by Roman styles, were found during the excavations (they are now in the Archaeological Museum in Tehrân and the Louvre in Paris). At the back of this hall another corridor leads to the palace. The walls of this cross-shaped room were divided into 64 niches decorated with carved and painted stucco, still visible in a few places.

About 500 metres (1,640 feet) to the west of the temple is another series of buildings of unknown purpose as well as a votive monument made up of two columns topped with Corinthian capitals. In front of them a third base originally held a statue of Shâpur I. An inscription in Parthian and Sasanian Pahlavi dates the monument to AD 266.

Another interesting visit to be made in the area, which could be combined with a trip to Bishâpur (about 70 kilometres [43 miles] from Bishâpur), is to the bas-relief at **Kurangun**, one of the rare examples of Elamite carving to be seen in Irân. It is dated between the 15th and the 11th century BC and represents a seated god and goddess surrounded by priests or worshippers. It is thought to be an older version of the Elamite relief at Naqsh-e Rostam, damaged by a Sasanian carving. From Bishâpur, continue on the Nur Âbâd and Yâsuj road. Kurangun is near Sih-Talu, 15 kilometres (9.3 miles) to the northwest of Fahliyân.

Further Sasanian ruins and bas-reliefs can be seen at **Firuz Âbâd**, 120 kilometres (75 miles) south of Shirâz, an excursion which takes just over half a day there and back. About 20 kilometres (12 miles) from Firuz Âbâd, the road enters the impressive Tangâb gorge, overlooked by the fortifications of a Sasanian castle, the **Qâl'eh-ye Dokhtar** (Maiden's Castle), built about 100 metres (328 feet) above the road by Ardeshir I (AD 224–242). A bit further on, after the remains of a Sasanian bridge, one comes to the first of two bas-reliefs carved in the rock face, a representation of the investiture of Ardeshir I, accompanied by his son Shâpur. The second relief is carved two kilometres away. Its subject matter is classic and represents once again Ardeshir's victory over the Parthian king Artabanus V; its composition, however, is highly original and shows the decisive moment in battle when Ardeshir (in the lead) killed Artabanus (depicted falling from his horse). Unlike the other stereotyped and rather static Sasanian bas-reliefs, this one is full of vigour and movement.

The ruins of the ancient Sasanian city of **Gur** are a few kilometres further on, at Firuz Âbâd. The city was circular and surrounded by walls and a moat. In the centre are the remains of a large building, perhaps a fire temple. Ardeshir's palace was located outside the town; today there is very little left of the great vaulted halls and enormous walls of this edifice.

NORUZ

The most popular festival in Irân is Noruz, the New Year celebration. This very ancient festival, which is closely tied to Mazdean beliefs, has its origins already celebrated in the Achaemenian period, when the kings marked the return of Spring each year with great festivities held at Persepolis.

The preparations for Noruz begin long before the actual day: this is mainly a family holiday or one to be spent with close friends and which lasts thirteen days in all. It is an occasion when traditions are re-enacted such as the *chahârshambeh suri*: on the last Wednesday before the New Year, small bonfires are lit in the streets and people, both old and young, jump over them to bring health in the coming year.

In every house, a special New Year's table is set, known as the *haft sin* table, or 'seven S's', seven symbolic objects beginning with the letter 'S'. In the centre, are the *sabzi*, germinating seeds of wheat or lentils, symbols of renewal. Around these are placed garlic (*sir*), apples (*sib*), jujubes (*senjed*), vinegar (*serke*), a type of halva made from walnuts (*samanu*) and a gold coin (*sekeh*). A mirror, a Qur'ân, bread, a goldfish, a bowl of water with leaves floating in it, coloured hard-boiled eggs and various sweets finish off the table around which the family will sit to see in the New Year.

The twelve days that follow New Year's Day are traditionally spent visiting friends and acquaintances, with much eating and exchanging of presents. The thirteenth day after Noruz, known as *sizdah bedar* or 'thirteenth outside', is spent on a large family picnic. Custom has it that on this day the *sabzi*, the germinating seeds that had been kept in the house since New Year's Day, are thrown out to ensure early marriage and fertility for the daughters of the family. On this day, everyone leaves their houses to picnic in the country and parks.

A typical house in Yazd

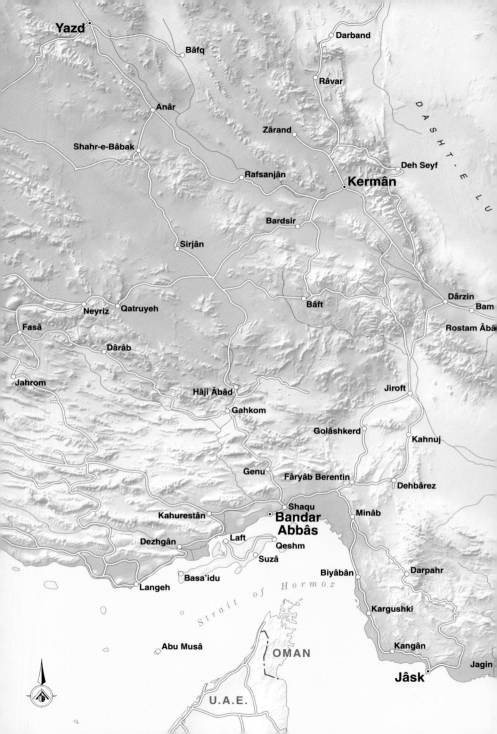

SOUTHEAST
IRÂN

0   50   100 Kilometres

0   50   100 Miles

Nehbandân

Zâbol

AFGHANISTAN

Zâhedân

Mirjâveh

PAKISTAN

Eskel Âbâd

Khâsh

Bazmân

Sarâvân

Irânshahr

Kuhak

Bandan

Nikshahr

Hodâr

Jekegur

Konârak

Châbahâr

Airphoto International Ltd.

THE SOUTHEAST: THE DESERT AND THE STRAITS OF HORMUZ

The southeast of Irân, which includes the provinces of Kermân, Sistân and Baluchestân, and Hormuzgân, is dominated by large areas of desert, and by high mountains chains which occasionally reach over 4,000 metres (12,000 feet) in height. To the south, the desert and the mountains open out onto a narrow coastal plain along the Straits of Hormuz and the Sea of Oman and onto the main port of the region, Bandar Abbâs. The province of Yazd, located between Esfahân and Kermân provinces and geographically similar to the latter, will also be dealt with in this section.

YAZD

The geographical location of **Yazd** (1,230 metres [4,035 feet]), surrounded by salt lakes and built in the middle of an apparent wilderness between two deserts—the Dasht-e Kavir to the north and the Dasht-e Lut to the east—may seem an unlikely

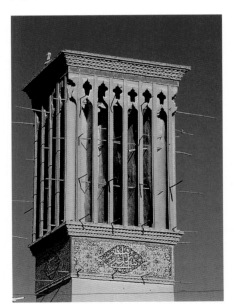

one for the development of a large settlement. But Yazd has made the most of its position halfway between Esfahân and Kermân, on the main route that leads to Pakistan and Afghânistân. The early history of the town is unclear but the site would appear to have been occupied by the Sasanian period. In AD 642 it was conquered by the Arabs. Unlike so many other Irânian towns, Yazd was spared by the invading Mongol armies of Genghis Khân (12th century) and by those of Tamerlane (14th century), although the period of great prosperity it enjoyed after this date, when it was famous for its carpets and its weaving, was brought

A wind tower, Yazd

to an abrupt end by the Afghân invasion in the 18th century. Today, Yazd is the main provincial town and an important centre with some 260,000 inhabitants. The recent construction of a university just outside town should contribute further to its future development.

As in all the towns of the region, buildings in Yazd are traditionally of brick and pisé and have flat or domed roofs, on top of which are low rectangular towers, the walls of which are pierced at intervals to catch the wind. These are the wind towers (*bâdgir*), a very efficient ventilation system which allows air to circulate within the houses. Traditionally, the most important room in the house was the coolest one, a covered patio with a fountain in the centre. The entrance to the house often gave directly onto this room, and from it one had access to the bedrooms, a communal room and the terrace. The wind tower, placed above the water basin, created a draught which kept the room at a comfortable temperature.

The wind towers serve not only as ventilation shafts in the houses but also to cool water. Yazd is built at the foot of the Shir Mountains and for centuries the town's water has been brought down from these hills by a complex system of *qanâts*. In the desert around the town, large brick domes flanked by two wind towers indicate the presence of an underground reservoir, some of which are very deep, in which the water is cooled by the draft created between the towers. Once a commonplace feature of Irânian architecture, the windtower is unfortunately gradually disappearing. Old, eroded towers are no longer systematically replaced or repaired as more highly-priced, electrically operated methods of cooling and ventilation are slowly reaching even the smallest villages.

The most interesting buildings in Yazd are the Islamic ones, built within the town, and the Zoroastrian ones, mainly located outside it. In the centre of town is the gateway to the **Chahâr Suq Bâzâr**, built in the 19th century, and easily recognizable by its three rows of arcades, one above the other, and its two tall minarets. Opposite it, on the other side of the square, is the **Mir Chaqmâq Mosque** (1437), named after a well-known Timurid governor of the town (it contains a very fine marble *mehrâb*). Near the bazaar stood the complex of the **Vaght-o-Sa'at** Mosque (Mosque of Time and the Hour) which included a *madraseh*, a library and an observatory. Today only the tomb-chamber itself, built in 1325, is still standing. Its most interesting feature is the stucco and tile decoration of the dome chamber and *mehrâb*.

In the northern part of town (take Emâm Khomeini Avenue from Dr. Beheshti Square) is the entrance *pishtâq* of the **Friday Mosque** (masjed-e Jomeh) which was built in the 14th century. The gateway, topped by two minarets, has an unusually tall and narrow *eivân* covered on the inner surface with stalactites. The dome of the main hall and the stalactite *mehrâb* (1375), which are entirely decorated in glazed tilework, are very fine. Near the mosque is the **Tomb of the Twelve Emâms** (boq'eh-ye Davâzde Emâm), a small 11th-century Saljuq building with carved stucco decoration around the *mehrâb*.

THE ZOROASTRIAN COMMUNITY

Although Zoroastrians were, with difficultly, recognized as *ahl al-dhimma*— Protected minorities—after the Arab conquest and were therefore free to worship in their own manner (see page 143), a large number nevertheless were forced to convert to the Islamic faith. Conversion brought with it a number of important financial and social advantages, including the avoidance of the poll-tax paid by non-Muslims and the opportunity of holding an administrative post. Periodic toughening of the Islamic position towards Zoroastrianism caused mass conversions and large-scale emigration to India from the eighth century on. Zoroastrian communities in Irân and India have remained in contact since this time, and in the 20th century the Parsis (the Indian Zoroastrians) have given considerable financial support to their fellow Zoroastrians in Irân.

The Friday Mosque, Yazd

The Zoroastrians, despite their relatively large numbers, have experienced a certain amount of discrimination, generally in the form of confiscation of belongings or property, arbitrary taxation or profanation of their sanctuaries. However, in the rural areas well removed from the large Muslim centres, and particularly in the Yazd region which was considered strategically unimportant, Zoroastrian traditions were kept alive. The Zoroastrian community in Yazd is currently estimated at slightly over 10,000, making it the largest in the country.

There is still a **Zoroastrian fire temple** (*âteshgâh*) in Yazd where the sacred fire is kept burning permanently. Worshippers and visitors can watch the fire through a glass window, as entry into the hall is forbidden except for the guardians of the fire. The fire was brought to Yazd around 1940 and is said to have burned without interruption for 1,500 years since c. AD 400. The temple itself is a modern building, built especially to house the holy flame, and includes a small exhibition of Zoroastrian writings; on the wall hang the portraits of two of the donors who provided funds for the construction of the temple. Above the door on the outside is the winged symbol of Ahura Mazda, the *Faravahar*, in blue and yellow glazed tiles, the same emblem that appears in Acheamenian architecture. The temple is located on Âyatollâh Kâshâni Avenue, near the centre of town.

Zoroastrian Fire Temple, Yazd

According to Zoroastrian beliefs, Earth is one of the elements associated with the divinities known as Amesha Spenta, and it cannot be soiled by contact with a dead human body, as death is an evil brought about by Ahriman, the spirit of Evil. For the same reason, Fire, the most holy of the elements, must not come into contact with dead bodies either. As burial in the ground and cremation were prohibited, Zoroastrians adopted the practice of exposing the bodies of their dead in large open-air circular constructions, known as **towers of silence**, or *dakhmeh*. A few hours after a death, the body would be brought to the foot of the tower where a ritual ceremony would be held in the presence of relatives and friends of the deceased. The body was then carried by the priests into the tower where it was laid out on flat stones on the ground—thus avoiding any contact with the earth. In a short time the body would be torn apart by vultures and crows; the bones were then thrown into a circular pit in the centre of the tower.

At Yazd, the towers of silence are built on the hilltops outside the town. At the foot of the towers stand the remains of the buildings which once served for the funerary ceremonies. When the towers were still used for Zoroastrian burials, only the priests were allowed into them. Nowadays, however, some of them have been opened to the public. In the 1970s, the custom of exposing bodies in the towers was gradually replaced by burial in the ground (to avoid all contamination of the earth,

Disused Zoroastrian buildings outside Yazd

THE ZURKHÂNEH

O utside Irân, the *zurkhâneh*, or 'Houses of Strength', are little known and yet they perpetuate one of the country's most distinctive cultural expressions. The *zurkhâneh* itself is a small, spartan gymnasium, basically a shallow octagonal hollow about a metre deep, with a beaten-earth floor in which the young men of the neighbourhood meet to exercise and train. Unlike Western gymnastics, the exercises in the *zurkhâneh* are a collective sport with specific rituals, formal competitions, and strict moral and ethical rules. The athletes, or *pahlavân*, work together to the sound of a drum played by the *morshed* (the 'guide') from a raised seat in a corner of the room, who also chants from the *Shâhnâmeh* epic. The precise movements of each exercise are carried out by all the participants in the same order and at the same rhythm. The equipment used is very simple, based on ancient weapons and adapted to the restricted space of the *zurkhâneh*. Small planks of wood and heavy clubs, weighing between four and 40 kilos (88 pounds), are used for the loosening-up exercises while the more advanced athletes use large wooden shields which can weigh 60 kilos (132 pounds) each. Another exercise consists of turning around on the spot, arms stretched out, a bit like the whirling dervishes.

But the *zurkhâneh* is much more than a demonstration of strength and skill; its origins go back to the pre-Islamic period. Certain moral qualities (courage, abnegation) were required of the *pahlevân* as well as absolute fidelity to the Prophet and the Emâms. The *zurkhâneh* reached its zenith during the Safavid dynasty when Shi'ism became the state religion, but it declined afterwards and was artificially revived by the government in the 20th century, not so much for its religious aspects as for its ancient Irânian origins and the nationalism that accompanies it. For a while the *zurkhâneh* was seen as manipulated by the government, but this ended after the 1968 assassination by the secret police of a well-known *pahlevân* who had become a national hero. Today, the *zurkhâneh* is still frequented in the popular quarters of Tehrân and Esfahân, even if it does have fewer supporters than the other national sport of football.

Zoroastrian Tower of Silence, Yazd

the graves were lined with an 'inert' substance such as cement). The towers were used until about 1978, after which all Zoroastrian dead were buried in the cemetery at the foot of the towers.

The road from Yazd to Taft and Shirâz passes through the small oasis of **Abarkuh**, located in a desert depression of the same name. Once a prosperous centre along the trade routes that linked the Persian Gulf, Central Asia and Turkey, Abarkuh has a half-abandoned air about it today. Its Friday Mosque, in the centre of the town, dates back to the 13th or 14th century. Although relatively badly preserved, it does contain a carved stucco *mehrâb* (14th century) with a fine interlaced decor. On a hill just outside town stands the **Gonbad-e Ali**, an octagonal funerary tower built in 1056 for Hezârasp ibn Nasr, the ruler of a local dynasty. Unlike most funerary towers which are built of brick, this one is of stone and is in very good condition. Its *muqarnas* cornice is the oldest example of this type of exterior cornice and probably originally held up a pyramidal roof. Except for the inscription under the cornice, the walls are plain.

KERMÂN PROVINCE

Kermân is the third largest province in the country but has only just over a million and a half inhabitants, and has always been considered one of the poorest regions of Irân. Its climate and topography certainly do not encourage dense human settlement: the Dasht-e Lut encroaches onto the north of the province, while the centre is taken up by a huge mountainous massif, of which several summits reach over 4,000 metres (12,000 feet) high. Here in particular, the survival of the villages and towns depends heavily on the qanât system dug into the mountains, which provides water even in the hottest of summers. Thanks to this, each year the oases of Kermân produce large crops of cereals, dates, oranges and pistachios (the pistachios of Rafsanjân are said to be the best in the country).

Despite being located away from the main political centres, which has enabled it to maintain a certain political autonomy, Kermân Province has not escaped the successive invasions that have swept into Irân. It was first pillaged in the 12th century by the Ghuzz Turks, then by the Mongols and more recently by the Afghâns and Baluch. Because overland travel into Kermân from the interior of the country is difficult, the province has had close links with the south and Bandar Abbâs, the main port on the Sea of Oman in the Straits of Hormuz. Two important caravan routes linked this port to the towns of Sirjan and Sabzvârân, and trade between India and the Persian Gulf, which was encouraged by the Safavids, ensured a

Regent's Bazaar, Kermân

constant movement of travellers and merchants through Kermân. In the last hundred years, the province has benefited considerably from being joined up to the national railway network and from improvements in the road system, especially those sections between Yazd and Zâhedân which pass through Kermân and Bam, and continue on to Pakistan.

At the beginning of the Islamic period, and until the tenth century, the provincial capital was Sirjân, a town located at a strategic point on the roads east to Shirâz and south to Bandar Abbâs. Besieged from 1393 to 1396 by Tamerlane's army, the castle of Sirjân—of which a few remains are still visible—finally fell, and its inhabitants were deported. Partially occupied again in the 14th century, the site was then abandoned; the modern town of Sirjân is built very near the old one.

The present capital of the province is the city of **Kermân** (250,000 inhabitants), located in a valley to the north of the mountains, at an altitude of 1,800 metres (5,905 feet) which gives it a relatively cool climate even in summer. Kermân is

(Following pages) *The ancient city of Bam, destroyed by an earthquake on December 26th, 2003*

thought to be a very ancient city and to have been founded by the Sasanian king Ardeshir I in the third century. The town was governed successively by Arabs, Turks, and Mongols, and became quite prosperous under the Safavids thanks to trade with India. However, it suffered in the 18th century during Nâder Shah's military campaigns and from the devastation caused by the Qâjâr ruler Âghâ Mohammed (1794).

Kermân's most interesting monument is its **Friday Mosque** (masjed-e Jomeh), built in 1348 by the local Mozaffarid dynasty and considerably rebuilt during the Safavids, in the 16th century. The entrance *pishtâq* and the tall and narrow *eivân* are decorated with blue and white floral motifs. Unlike Esfahân where the twisted columns around the arch are a monochrome turquoise, here they are decorated in polychrome geometric designs.

Near the mosque is the **Bâzâr-e Vakil** (Regent's Bazaar) which dates in large part to the Safavid period. South of it, is the **Emâm Mosque** (ex-masjed-e Malek), a Saljuq mosque of the late 11th century which has been restored several times since. To the north of Dr Shari'ati Avenue, stands a third mosque, the **masjed-e Pâ Menâr**, which is of interest for the decoration of its entrance gate (14th century). Also to the north of the main avenue, near Falastin Street, are the ruins of the **Gonbad-e Sabz**, or Green Dome, a mausoleum of the Qara-khitay princes (13th century) badly damaged by an earthquake in 1896.

About 40 kilometres (25 miles) southeast of Kermân in the small town of **Mâhân**, is the mausoleum of Shâh Nematollâh Vali (died in 1431), who founded a dervish order patronised by a Muslim Indian king of the Deccan. Built in the 15th century, the tomb was restored under the Safavids (dome and main gate) and enlarged by the Qâjârs, who added the minarets (see picture p. 7).

BAM—FROM GHOST TOWN TO NECROPOLIS

On December 26th 2003, a violent earthquake destroyed the modern city of **Bam** as well as the ancient city named Arg-e Bam, one of the world's best preserved cities built out of clay bricks located 190 km (120 miles) south-east of Kermân at the edge of the desert Dasht-e Lut. Within 20 seconds the ancient city was destroyed which had been built over a time span of almost 2000 years. Since the earthquake occurred at 5.30 am, the inhabitants were caught by surprise in their sleep; out of 120,000 inhabitants, at least 35,000 were killed, 16,000 injured, 7,500 children became orphans and virtually all survivors lost their homes, properties and employment. This was not only a human and cultural tragedy but also an economic one, for the

The citadel of Bam

oasis of Bam relied to a great extent on the income generated from tourism. For this reason, the former president of Irân, Ali Akbar Hashemi Rafsanjâni, who had already initiated the yet unfinished restoration of the Arg, declared that it should be rebuilt within the next decade. But the reconstruction of the modern city is more urgent, otherwise the survivors, especially the younger ones, will feel tempted to emigrate to other Irânian cities. Since most urban buildings throughout Irân are not really earthquake-proof, one doesn't dare to imagine what would happen in the case of a strong earthquake in Tehrân or Tabriz, Irân's two largest cities, numbering more than 12 million people althogether, which are both located in active seismic regions. (The following text describes Bam's status before this catastrophic earthquake. While it is not recommended to enter the Arg, an impressive overview can be gained from the top of the southern main gate.)

The foundation of Arg-e Bam goes back to the Sasanian Dynasty (224–650). The fortuitous discovery of Parthian coins suggest that there was on top of the citadel's hill already a settlement under the Parthians (250 BC–AD 224). Bam was located at a strategically important place on a branch of the Silk and Spice Roads linking the plain of the Indus with Central Irân and Mesopotamia. Near Bam another trading road branched southwards to Hormuz, Irân's most important harbour till 1622 when the new harbour of Bandar Abbâs was founded opposite the island of

Hormuz. The fortress of Bam was the centre of a network of smaller forts and watchtowers built at intervals of around 30 km (20 miles) which guarded the trade routes; the communication between them was assured by smoke signals during the day and fire signals at night.

Bam was conquered in the 7th century by the Arabs who expanded it and built mosques, whilst allowing a large Zoroastrian population to flourish for many centuries. In 1002, Bam resisted a three month long siege by Mahmud the Great, leader of the Ghaznavid Empire (based in modern-day Afghânistân). This long resistance was only possible because the city housed twenty wells and a windmill to grind grain. Although Mahmud attempted to break down the walls of the city by diverting the river Tamrud against them, he only succeeded in breaching the outer wall; the inner wall dividing the citadel proper from the city remained impregnable. The Saljuqs, who followed in the 11th century, and the Mongols in the 13th century both spared the city. In the 16th century the Safavids (1501–1732) further enlarged it; virtually all the remaining constructions date from that time. In 1719 and 1721 Bam was twice looted by Afghân warlords. In 1794 the last Zand ruler, Lotf Ali Khân sought refuge in Bam from the first Qâjâr ruler, the Turkoman Âghâ Mohammed Khân (1779–1797) The cruel Qâjâr caught the fugitive, had him blinded and killed and then slaughtered the inhabitants of Bam and Kermân who had sheltered the fugitive. In 1840 Mohammed Shâh (1834–1848) occupied Bam in

order to catch a rebellious governor. When peace returned, the inhabitants of the Arg left their dwellings and settled outside along the river Tamrud. Only the garrison remained inside until the beginning of the 20th century.

Since the ancient city has never been archaeologically excavated—even the great explorer Sir Aurel Stein was forbidden to conduct research in Bam when he visited it in 1932—its early history remains quite in the dark. Another unsolved riddle is the question what happened with the dead, for no ancient cemetery has been found so far. While tradition maintains that dead children were buried under private houses or in courtyards, no such burial has been found yet. It is to be hoped that archaeological investigations will be conducted within the framework of the expected reconstruction of the Arg.

Ancient Bam was fortified by a complex system of six walls. The innermost one protected the citadel itself and the governor's palace; the second one separated the military from the civilian quarters and the third, almost two km long, the present ruins. The first two walls were strengthened with nine round bastions up to 7 m high, the third one with 29 which brings the total to 38 towers. A few remains of the forth and fifth ring are still visible in the north near the ice house (see below) while the sixth ring has virtually disappeared. It is said that it sheltered during Bam's heyday in the 17th century up to 13,000 people living in a 6 sq. km urban area. This relatively large population consisted only of the administration, the garrison, merchants and craftsmen, while the farmers lived outside the city walls.

(Top) *The ice-house of the citadel of Bam;* (left) *a section from the third wall of the citadel*

The construction of a city only out of clay bricks was only possible due to the extremely arid climate and the scarcity of rain. To enhance the stability of the buildings, they were armoured with the strong trunks of palm trees. Without this wooden armour, nothing would have survived the earthquake.

Since Bam lay on the Silk Road, it is not surprising that it developed a thriving sericulture and cotton industry. The 10th century traveller and geographer Ibn Hawqal praised the high quality of the garments manufactured in Bam which were exported to Khorâsân, Iraq and Egypt. The silk exports lasted till the end of the 18th century when the mulberry trees were struck down by disease, while the cotton trade sharply declined in the middle 20th century due to fierce price competition. The industrious people of Bam then switched to the cultivation of dates, but these were also hit in the late 1980s by another attack of pestilence. For this reason, many farmers have now switched to the cultivation of oranges.

Entering Bam through the southern gate, one comes immediately to the **bazaar**. At its end stands to the right a **takiyeh**, a kind of large theatre where religious plays were performed in honour of Emâm Hosein's martyrdom during the month of Moharram. In the south-eastern corner of the city stands the Saffârid **Friday**

Zoroastrian tombstone at the cemetery of Poschtrod near Bam, 20th century

Mosque, founded in the 9th century, the Mirzâ Nâ'im complex with its Koranic school, a large *zurkhâneh* (sports gymnasium) and the ruins of a câravânsarai. Continuing from the bazaar northwards, the visitor passes to his right several large residencies and to his left another mosque before arriving to the second wall. Passing the only gate and climbing towards the citadel, one comes to the large stables, the armoury and the barracks, the palaces of the governor and the military commander and finally reaches the signal tower and the large residence called Chahâr Fasl (four seasons).

At the east of the Arg, just outside the third wall, stands the **ice house**. In the past, every desert city had one or several ice houses; today those of Bam and Kermân are the best preserved examples. Ice houses had extremely thick mud walls built in a 7 to 8 m high conical shape to protect the ice from the heat. The water was stored inside in a 10 m deep cistern built in grades. The water froze in winter and did not melt even in the summer.

About 5 km to the north of the Arg lies the new **Zoroastrian cemetery of Poschtrod**. Its oldest tomb dates from 1931, the latest from 1976. Although the teachings of Zoroastrianism prohibit both burial in the earth and cremation, the Zoroastrians came, in the 20th century, under increasing pressure to forego their tradition of exposing dead bodies to vultures and to bury them instead; this eventually became law in 1970. In order not to pollute the earth, the dead are placed in a tomb made of cement. The tombstones, like those in the much larger Zoroastrian cemetery of Yazd, follow the same pattern: On top is featured the faravahar, the symbol of Ahura Mazda in the shape of a winged king and two inscriptions saying "he is eternal" and "pure thought, pure speech and pure action", the Zoroastrian imperative. Under the wings of the faravahar, vessels with the eternal fire are carved and cypresses, a symbol of eternity. Further below there is a brief description of the deceased.

For those interested in the early development of mosques in Irân, a visit to the Friday Mosque at **Fahraj**, 50 kilometres (31 miles) east of Bam, is recommended. Although relatively little known, this mosque is nevertheless important as it was probably built in the second half of the ninth century, making it one of the oldest in the country. Similar to the Tarik Khâneh in Dâmghân, this is a hypostyle mosque with no *eivân*, but with a deep portico along the *qebleh* wall. The columns are rectangular with half-columns at each corner, and, like most mosques of this period, the building is almost completely unadorned.

Shores of Hormuzgân Province, Bandar Abbâs

HORMUZGÂN PROVINCE

Hormuzgân Province is the coastal province that faces the Sultanate of Oman and the United Arab Emirates across the Straits of Hormuz, only 53 kilometres (33 miles) away. Because of a very hot climate and an average annual precipitation level below 100 millimetres, the province is almost entirely a desert. Easy communication between the coast and the hinterland is hampered by the presence of a mountain chain, which for centuries has been difficult to cross. Even today, the provinces of Kermân and Fârs are linked to Hormuzgân only by three main roads, of which two lead to Bandar Abbâs, the main port of the region.

At the beginning of the 14th century, the prince of Hormuz, in flight from advancing Mongol troops, founded a town on a small island 18 kilometres (11 miles) offshore, opposite the modern port of Bandar Abbâs. The town and the island, both named **Hormuz**, quickly became a prosperous trading post. In 1514, Hormuz was conquered by the Portuguese navigator Alfonse of Albuquerque and became one of the main Portuguese bases along their sea route to India and the Far East. Thanks to its strategic position in the straits, Hormuz controlled all shipping entering and leaving the Persian Gulf. This Portuguese monopoly on trade in the region inevitably aroused the jealousy of the other great powers and, in 1622, Shâh Abbâs succeeded, with help from British ships, in landing on the island and capturing the fort. In return for this help, the Safavid ruler granted the British East India Company trading rights in Persia. The French merchant Jean-Baptiste Tavernier, who visited the island in 1665, described it in the following terms: 'There grows here neither tree nor grass, and the land is everywhere covered in salt which is good and as white as snow, so that it is absolutely sterile. There is no fresh water either except that which falls from the sky and is collected in tanks.'

Hormuz lost its economic importance and a new settlement, **Bandar Abbâs**, built opposite the island on the mainland, rapidly emerged as the main port of the Safavid Empire. At the end of the dynasty, however, the port declined and was abandoned by the European trading companies who preferred to move further west along the coast, to Bushehr. From 1793 to 1868, Bandar Abbâs belonged to the territory of the Sultan of Muscat (Oman). Today it is once again the main port of Irân (accounting for 52 per cent of maritime commercial traffic in 1988), largely as a result of the war with Iraq which temporarily closed down its main rival, Bushehr, in Khuzestân.

The islands in the Persian Gulf and the Straits of Hormuz may be visited by boat from Bandar Abbâs. The first of these islands is **Hormuz** itself (42 kilometres [16 miles]) where the castle built by the Portuguese in 1515 still stands. The castle, and its well preserved ramparts, can be reached on foot from the town of Hormuz. Qeshm, on the west coast of the Straits, is the largest of the Irânian islands; although still very underdeveloped at the moment, it will soon undergo quite drastic changes if the plans to transform it into a tourist centre and an economic investment area are ever implemented. The main town, Qeshm, is on the northeast point of the island.

Further west in the Persian Gulf is the island of **Kish**, the only free port in Irân. In the 12th and 13th centuries, Kish was an important Arab port, known for the quality of its pearls. Supplanted by Hormuz, it fell into oblivion until the 1960s when the last Shâh turned it into a luxury holiday resort complete with a casino and an international airport. Since the Revolution, Kish has become a popular destination with Irânians who come here for duty-free shopping, in particular for electronic goods which are much cheaper than on the mainland. The hotels and restaurants, however, are very expensive on Kish and most visitors stay only a short while. In addition to the boat links with Bandar Abbâs and Bushehr, there are flights from Kish to Tehrân and Shirâz. Tickets, however, are difficult to buy at short notice because of high demand.

SISTÂN AND BALUCHESTÂN PROVINCE

Because of the harshness of its climate and its geographical isolation, this province of the far southeast of Irân is one of the poorest in the country and the most underdeveloped. The road which runs south along the Afghân border from Mashhad (1,000 kilometres [621 miles] away from Zâhedân) was only built after World War II; until then the only link with the rest of the country had been the road that goes to Kermân.

The province of Sistân and Baluchestân owes its name to its two main regions. **Sistân** is a deep basin in the north which extends into Afghânistân as far as Qandahâr. It has an average altitude of 500 metres (1,640 feet) above sea level and is surrounded in the east by the Palangan chain of mountains. In the centre, several lakes collect the waters of the Hirmand-rud, the main river of the basin which springs up in the Kuh-e Bâbâ Mountains of Afghânistân. This region is the ancient Drangiana, the country of Rostam, hero of the epic *Shâhnâmeh*. Once extremely fertile due to an efficient irrigation system, it turned into a desert after Tamerlane's invasion in 1383 when the dams and *qanât* were deliberately destroyed, and also as a result of long-term salination of the soil. Entire towns had to be abandoned and even today only the area around Zâbol is inhabited. The problem of obtaining water is still an important one in Sistân: the construction of a dam on the Hirmand in Afghânistân has considerably reduced the volume of water in the river to the extent that the largest of the lakes, the Hâmun-e Sâberi (or Lake Sistân) was almost dry during the winter of 1976 and has still not yet fully recovered.

The proximity of the Afghân border makes travel in Sistân difficult for foreigners. Drug trafficking across the border is a major problem and consequently the police and the locals are wary of outsiders. The atmosphere in the main town, **Zâbol**, is frankly unpleasant and it is not advisable to stay there any longer than is strictly needed. It may be necessary, however, to pass through to reach **Kuh-e Khwâjeh** (pronounced Khâjeh), a Parthian site a few kilometres southwest near the village of Divâneh. This ancient citadel dates back to the first century AD and was built on a basalt outcrop in the centre of a lake. In winter, when the water level is low, it is usually possible to walk out to the island, but in spring one has to take a *tuten*, the local form of punt made of reeds. The frescoes on the walls of the citadel for which this site is famous were taken away long ago, but the ruins of the palace and a fire temple can still be visited.

Baluchestân, in the south of the province, is an arid and mountainous region with occasional large basins. A first chain of mountains stretches from Khorâsân along the Pakistani border. Its highest points are Mount Taftân (4,042 metres, 13,258 feet), an active volcano just south of Zâhedân, and Mount Bazmân (3,503 metres, 11,490 feet). A second, lower chain, the Makran Mountains (rising 1,000–2,100 metres, 3,000–6,800 feet) stretches from east to west, separating the coastal basin from the Bampur River and the large salt lake of Jâzmuriân. It is in this basin, linked by road to Kermân and Zâhedân, that the old provincial capital, Irân Shahr, is located. From Irân Shahr, one can drive to the small port of Châbahâr on the Sea of Oman, on the other side of the Makrân Range. This whole coastal region is very underdeveloped and until the recent construction of an airport at Châbahâr, the port was almost completely isolated. Its only real link with the rest of the country was the main road to Irân Shahr. Even today there is no proper road along the coast either towards Pakistan or towards Hormuzgân and Bandar Abbâs.

Thanks to the presence of underground rivers and extensive irrigation, crops such as sugar cane, cereals, tobacco, banana trees and citrus fruit can be grown in oases in the valleys of central Baluchestân, despite very low rainfall (85 millimetres [3.5 inches] a year on average in Zâhedân). The coast, on the other hand, is extremely arid, and the local economy is heavily dependant on sea fishing. The inhabitants of this area, known as Gedrosia, were called the Ichthyophagai by classical authors because of their habit of eating fish raw. No story illustrates better the harshness of the coastal climate than that of the return of Alexander the Great from the Indus in the autumn of AD 325. Two months after setting out, suffering desperately from thirst and heat, his army managed to reach Kermân; almost two-thirds of the men perished on the way. The troops who had taken a northern route along the Hirmand Valley and through Sistân, hardly lost a single man.

The main ethnic minority in the province are the Baluch who live principally in Sistân and in the southwest, around Irân Shahr and Sarâvân, although isolated pockets of Baluch are still found further west, even as far as Hormuzgân and Kermân provinces. Chased out of northern Khorâsân by the Turko-Mongol invasions in the 12th century, the Baluch settled in southeastern Irân and in western Pakistan where they lived a nomadic life. They mixed with the local population, including the Brahui, a Dravidian people who are thought to have formed part of the waves that swept down into India in the third millennium BC. The absorption of the Brahui by the Baluch has been so complete that it is difficult today to tell them apart. However, a few pockets of Brahui are thought to exist still between

Sarâvân and the coast. As for the Baluch, they were forced into a more settled life style in the second half of the twentieth century, and now work in the main urban centres such as Zâhedân and Irân Shahr.

Zâhedân, the provincial capital, is of little interest other than being located about 100 kilometres (62 miles) away from the Pakistani border. It is here that the train from Quetta (Pakistan) arrives. The frontier post is located at Taftan (Pakistani side) and Mirjâve (Irânian side). There are also bus services between Zâhedân and Mirjâve, and between Taftan and Quetta. At Zâhedân it is possible to get visas both for India and Pakistan at the consulates of those countries (the Pakistani Consulate is on Shahid Moqadam Avenue, tel 23389; and the Indian Consulate is on Emâm Khomeini Avenue, tel 2337).

Although Zâhedân is not yet linked to the Irânian railway system—which begins only at Kermân, 541 kilometres (336 miles) away—it does have an airport with regular flights to other cities in Irân, including Tehrân, Esfahân and Mashhad. These might prove useful to those travellers who want to avoid crossing the desert by road.

HOTELS

Most hotels in Irân now have room prices in US$ for foreign tourists (and expect to be paid in dollars). These prices are much higher than those paid in riâl by Irânian nationals. With the development of tourism, it is likely that there will be price increases in the near future. For this reason, the hotels below are placed in three categories: superior (US$80-US$200 for a double room); moderate (US$80–US$30); and budget (less than US$30). As a general rule, hotels in Tehrân and Esfahân are more expensive than those in other cities. See the section on accommodation on page 110.

TEHRÂN (CODE 021)

SUPERIOR

Azâdi Grand Hotel (ex-Hyatt), Chamrân Expressway, at Evin. Tel 207 3021/9; fax 207 3038. Restaurants, coffee shop, shops, bank. Rather a long way from the centre of town but convenient for the International Fair Centre.

Esteqlâl Hotel (ex-Hilton), Chamrân Expressway, at the corner of Vali-e Asr Avenue. Tel 204 0021/5; fax 204 7041. In the same area as the Azâdi Grand. Offers similar services.

Homâ Hotel (ex-Sheraton), Vali-e Asr Avenue, Vanak Square, Shahid Khodâmi Street. Tel 877 3021/9; fax 879 7179. Also a long way from the city centre. Recently renovated.

Lâleh Hotel, Dr Fatemi Avenue. Tel 8966021/9; fax 8965517. Located in a corner of Lâleh Park near the Carpet Museum and the University.

Kiyân Hotel, Vali-e Asr Avenue, Zartosht Street. Tel 650 237; fax 653 236.

MODERATE

Tehrân Grand Hotel (Bozorg-e Tehrân), Ostâd Motahari Avenue, at the corner of Vali-e Asr Avenue. Tel 872 1656/9; fax 871 3857. Still quite far from the centre but a very decent hotel.

Kosar Hotel, Vali-e Asr Avenue, Khusro Khâvar Street.
Tel 890 8371/5; fax 889 1615. A comfortable hotel located near the city centre with restaurant.

Evin Hotel, Chamran Highway, Evin intersection. Tel 207 8606/9; fax 209 0425. Next door to the Azâdi Grand. Comfortable and the staff are friendly. Restaurant.

Hotel Bozorg-e Ferdosi (Ferdosi Grand), at the corner of Ferdosi Avenue and Mesri Street. Tel 6719991/3; fax 6711449. A new hotel very well situated in the centre of town, near the Archaeological Museum.

BUDGET
Rãmãtiã Hotel, Vali-e Asr Avenue, Hejdahom Street.
Tel 871 7856; fax 871 8593. A bit far from the centre but perfectly good.

Irân Hotel, Vali-e Asr Avenue, Kâryâbi Street.
Tel 893 161/5. A comfortable hotel near the city centre.

Irânshahr Hotel, 75 South Irânshahr Avenue, by Mahzâd Street.
Tel 8846650; fax 8821924.

Bolvâr Hotel, Keshâvarz Boulevard. Tel 650 533, 654 716. Located between Lâleh Park and the University.

AHWAZ (CODE 0611)
Hotel Fajr
Tel 2220091/5; fax 2218677, Shahid Abedi Alley, 24 Metri Street.

BAM (CODE 0344)
Azadi Hotel
Tel 2222097/9; fax 2222099.

BANDAR ABBÂS (CODE 0761)
Homâ Hotel
Tel 5564038/9; fax 5551732, Mearaj Ave, Pasdaran Blvd.

CHALUS (CODE 0191)
SUPERIOR
Caspian Enqelâb Hotel (Enqelâb Khazar Hotel), 12 kilometres (7 miles) on the road to Ramsar, Châlus. Tel 2222001/9; fax 2222012. Although it was built about 20 years ago, this is still one of the best hotels in the country. Very comfortable but quite expensive.

HAMADÂN (CODE 0811)

SUPERIOR

Bu Ali Hotel, Bu Ali Avenue, just north of Azâdi Square.
Tel 8250788, 8250856; fax 8252824. Good rooms but a bit expensive; make sure to choose rooms overlooking the garden.

MODERATE

Azadi Hotel, Eram Boulevard. Tel 825001/4; fax 8260035.

ESFAHÂN (CODE 0311)

SUPERIOR

Abbâsi Hotel (ex-Shâh Abbâs Hotel), Shahid Âyatolollâh Madani Avenue. Tel 2226011/9; fax 2226008. The most famous hotel in town, located in an old câravânsarai to which a modern wing has been added. Unfortunately not quite up to standard now and very expensive. The garden and teahouse are well worth visiting.

Kowsar Hotel, Bustan-e Mellaat, near the Si-o-Se Bridge. Tel 6240230/7; fax 6249975. On the south bank of the river. Restaurants, shops. Comfortable but quite expensive.

Âli Qâpu Hotel, Chahâr Bâgh Avenue, five minutes away from the Si-o-Se Bridge. Tel 2211377; fax 2216049. Very central, friendly and very comfortable. Restaurants, shops.

Suite Hotel, Bustan-e Aemieh, near Si-o-Se Bridge. Tel 616071; fax 613872. Next door to the Kowsar. Less well kept up and more expensive than the Kowsar.

MODERATE

Aryâ Hotel, Shahid Âyatollâh Madani Avenue.
Tel 27242. Very central location near the Abbâsi Hotel.

Azâdi Hotel, Chahâr Bâgh Avenue, near Jamal Abdolrazzâq Avenue.
Tel 204 011, 204 056. A comfortable hotel.

Hajihasani Hotel, Chahâr Bâgh Avenue. Tel 231 282; fax 239 519.

Hotel Sa'adi, Abbas Âbâd. Tel 2203881 2211593.

KÂSHÂN (CODE 0361)

Hotel Amir Kabir, Fin Garden Ave. Tel 25322, 30091/5; fax 30338. Whilst here, visit Delpazir Restaurant, run by Reza Modarresian and his English wife Jane, Malak Âbâd, Âyatollâh Kâshâni Stl, Kâshân.

KERMÂN (CODE 0341)

MODERATE

Akhavan Hotel, Shahid Sadughi Avenue. Tel 2441411/2; fax 2449113. Unpretentious but friendly; serves good local home cooking.

Big Guest House, Jamhuriye Eslâmi Boulevard. Tel 45203/5.

Pars Hotel, Tel. 2119310; fax 2119350. Farhangian Crossroad, Jumhuri Blvd.

KERMÂNSHÂH (CODE 0831)

Hotel Azadegan Tel 4225591/7, fax 4293503; Shahark Taavon.

KISH (CODE 0764)

Hotel Dariush, Tel 442174/9 .

MASHHAD (CODE 0511)

SUPERIOR

Homâ Hotel, Tâleqâni Square, Feyziyeh Avenue. Tel 8432001/9; fax 8437019. The best hotel in town, with shops and restaurants, but a bit far from the centre and quite expensive.

Atrak Hotel, Beit ol-Moqadas Square. Tel 22044/5. A comfortable hotel, well situated.

MODERATE

Asia Hotel, Pâsdârân Street. Tel 20074; fax 58030. A comfortable, central hotel, with a teahouse.

Jam Hotel, Pâsdârân Street. Tel 90045. Opposite the Asia Hotel.

Lâleh Hotel, on the corner of Kushangi, 24. Tel 823010/2; fax 823822.

BUDGET

Irân Hotel, Andarzgu Avenue. Tel 28010/1. Near the bazaar.

Azâdi Hotel, Azâdi Avenue. Tel 51927.

Atlas Hotel, Beit ol-Moqadas Square. Tel 45061/3. Good and well priced.

NÂ'IN (CODE 0323)

Tourist Inn, Jehad-i-sazandegi. Tel 2253081/8; fax 2253665.

RAMZA (CODE 019252)

Hotel Kosar, Sadat Mahalleh, Tel 42102; fax 35202.

RASHT (CODE 0131)

Hotel Kadoos, Manzarieh. Tel 3223075/9; fax 3220050.

SÂRI (CODE 01524)

Hotel Badleh, Tel 222548/50.

SHIRÂZ (CODE 0711)

SUPERIOR

Homâ Hotel, Azâdi Park, Meshkinfâm Street. Tel 2288001/4; fax 2247123. Currently the best hotel in town, with restaurants, a coffee shop, and shops. Opposite Azâdi Park, on the north bank of the river. Renovated in 1998. Avoid rooms overlooking the street.

Parsian Hotel, Roudaki Street, Zand Avenue. Tel 2331000; fax 2337512.

MODERATE

Arg Hotel, Takhti Avenue. Tel 2222889; fax 2221931. Good rooms but the food in the restaurant is uninteresting.

Ariabazan, Roudaki Ave. Tel 2247182/4; fax 2228959.

Dena Motel, Tel 4452212, 25 km along the Shirâz-Persepolis highway, at Zarghân (Near Marvdasht). N.B. Designed by a local engineer and managed by his wife. Good commanding site, separate chalets, very convenient for visiting Persepolis.

BUDGET

Atlas Hotel, Atlas Avenue. Tel 29225, 43877. On the north bank of the river, near the Hâfez mausoleum.

Kosar Hotel, on Zand Boulevard, west of Shohadâ Square. Tel 335724/5.

QAZVIN (CODE 0281)

Hotel Irân (Moderate family-run, currently being upgraded) Khiaban Peighambarieh, on the corner of Sabzeh Maidân (The Central Square). Tel. 2228877.

Hotel Marmar, Âyatollâh Khameneï Blvd, Valiasr Square. Tel 2555771/4; fax 2555771.

TABRIZ (CODE 0411)

SUPERIOR

Tabriz Hotel, (ex-International), Abressan Crossroads.
Tel 3341081/9; fax 3341080. The best hotel in town. Comfortable but a bit far from the centre.

MODERATE

Daryâ Hotel, 22 Bahman Avenue. Tel 4459501/9. Comfortable. Near the train station, to the west of the town centre.

Irân Hotel, 22 Bahman Avenue. Tel 49516. Comfortable. Close to Hotel Daryâ.

BUDGET

Morvârid Hotel, Bâgh Golestân Square. Tel 56398, 60520. A fairly decent hotel, near the centre and Golestân Park.

TAKAB (CODE 0482)

Rangi Hotel, Angelab St. Tel 23179; fax 24650 (Convenient location from which to visit Takht-e Soleimân).

YAZD (CODE 0351)

Enqelâb Hotel, Islamic Republic Boulevard, Nahzat Avenue. Tel 53111; fax 56444.
Safaieh Hotel, Tel 842811. Pretty bungalows. Serves good food.

GLOSSARY

Arg	Citadel
âpâdânâ	audience hall or throne room
ârâmgâh	tomb
âteshgâh	Zoroastrian fire altar
bâdgir	wind tower, traditional ventilation system in houses
borj	tower
boq'eh	mausoleum
châdor	'tent'; long cloth worn by women in public and which covers them from head to foot
dakhmeh	tower of silence
eivân	vaulted room open on one side
emâm	Shi'a: descendants of the Prophet and of Ali, are authorized to interpret the Koran; Sunni: leader of prayer in the mosque
emâmzâdeh	'son of the Emâm'; used for the tombs of the descendants of the Shi'a emâms
gach	carved stucco, often used as decoration in mosques
gonbad	dome
haft rangi	'seven colours'; polychrome painted tiles not formed of mosaic
hejâb	'veil'; term used for the correct dress worn by women in Irân, either a *châdor*, or a scarf covering the head
Hejira	day of the flight of Mahommed from Mecca to Medina in 622; date with which the Islamic calendar begins
hypostyle	area with a roof supported by pillars
Ka'beh	sacred edifice at Mecca which contains the venerated Black Stone
khân	câravânsarai; honorific title
khâtam	marquetry
madraseh	theological college
maqsureh	reserved enclosure in the *qebleh* wall
masjed	mosque
mashhad	place of martyrdom
mehrâb	niche in the *qebleh* wall
menâr	minaret

membar	pulpit of a mosque
minâï	overglaze enamelled ware
Moharram	first month of the Islamic lunar calendar; month of mourning in the Shi'a faith for the commemoration of the death of Emâm Hosein
muqarnas	corner squinches or stalactite decoration
nezâmiyeh	madraseh founded by the vazir Nezâm ol-Molk
pishtâq	tall, formal gateway at the entrance of mosques or bazaars
pol	bridge
qaliân	water pipe
qanât	underground water canals
qebleh	direction of Mecca
sahn	courtyard in a mosque
seyyed	descendant of the Prophet
tâlâr	covered terrace
tappeh	artificial hill
ta'ziyeh	religious plays performed during the month of Moharram
tall	artificial hill, also tappeh

RECOMMENDED READING

An excellent reference book on all aspects of Irânian history, geography and culture is the English-language *Encyclopaedia Iranica* (Routledge & Kegan Paul, ten volumes published to date, continuing).

PHOTOGRAPHIC BOOKS

Good photographic books on present-day Irân are rare. One photographer in particular, Nasrollâh Kasrâiân, stands out for the very high quality of his work. His books on the Tukomans and the Kurds are particularly interesting for the insight they provide into the daily lives of these people.

Kasrâiân, Nasrollâh and Arshi, *Zibâ Torkman-e Irân or Turkomans of Iran*. Persian and English text, (Sekeh Press, Tehrân, 1991).

Kasrâiân, Nasrollâh and Arshi, *Zibâ Sarzamin-e ma Irân or Our Homeland Iran*. Persian and English text, (Sekeh Press, Tehrân, 1992).

Arshi, Ziba and Kasrâiân, Nasrollâh, *Kurdistan*, (Kegan Paul, 1992).

HISTORY

Roy Mottahedeh, *The Mantle of the Prophet*, religion and politics in Iran, (Peregrine, Penguin, 1985). A fascinating glimpse of the world of the Shi'a clergy and of the training of a young *mollah*.

Ferrier, R W, *A Journey to Persia*, (Tauris, 1994). A description of the Persian court and empire in the seventeenth century as seen through the eyes of the French traveller Jean Chardin.

Frye, Richard, *The Heritage of Persia*, (Cardinal 1976, reprinted Mazda 1993). A scholarly study of pre-Islamic Persia.

Frye, Richard, *The Golden Age of Persia, Arabs in the East*, (Weidenfeld & Nicholson, 1993). A very detailed cultural history of Persia from the Arab con quest in the ninth century to the Turkish invasions in the eleventh century.

Lewis, Bernard, *The Assassins*, (Al Saqi Books, 1985). A very readable history of the Assassin movement in Iran and other regions of the Middle East.

Daftary, Farhad, *The Assassin Legends*, (Tauris, 1994). A more recent and detailed work concentrating on the stories that have developed around the Assassins.

Savory, Roger, *Iran under the Savafids*, (Cambridge UP, 1983).

Moin, Baqer. Khomeini : life of the Ayatollah London : I.B. Tauris, 1999.

Farman-Farmaian, Sattareh: *Daughter of Persia London* : Bantam, 1992.

TRAVEL WRITING

Bird, Isabella, *Journeys in Persia and Kurdistan*, 2 vols, (Virago, 1989).

Byron, Robert, *The Road to Oxiana*, (Pan, 1981).

Morier, James, *The Adventures of Hajji Baba of Ispahan*, 2 vols, (Tynron, 1990, fac simile of the 1897 edition).

Smith, Anthony, *Blind White Fish in Persia*, (Penguin, 1990).

Stark, Freya, *Valley of the Assassins*, (Century Travellers, Arrow, 1991).

Stark, Freya, *Beyond Euphrates*, (Century Hutchinson, London 1989).

de Bellaigue, Christopher, In the Rose Garden of the Martyrs, London I B Tauris 2004 poet extract

Browne, Edward Granville, *A Year among the Persians*, London 1893

RELIGION AND PHILOSOPHY

Gibb, H A R, *Islam*, (Oxford paperbacks, 1987). A short, general introduction to Islam.

Goodman L E, *Avicenna*, (Arabic Thought and Culture Series, Routledge, 1992). A fascinating insight into the life and philosophy of one of the world's great meta physicians.

Zoroaster: Life and Work of the Forerunner in Persia, (Grail Foundation, 1996). A good introduction to the teachings of Zoroaster and his times.

LITERATURE

Attar, Farid ud-din, *The Conference of the Birds*, (Penguin Classics, 1984). A won derful allegorical tale, one of the greatest works of Sufi mysticism.

Khayyam, Omar, *The Ruba'iyat of Omar Khayyam*, (Penguin Classics, 1998). A good translation, closer to the original than that of Fitzgerald. Illustrated edition, with useful appendices.

Kordi, Gohar, *An Iranian Odyssey*, (Serpent's Tail, London, 1991). A compelling autobiography told by a blind Kurdish woman who beats all the odds and becomes a student at Tehrân University.

Melville, Charles, ed, *History and Literature in Iran*, (Tauris, 1993).

ART, ARCHITECTURE AND CRAFTS

Ettinghausen, Richard & Grabar, Oleg, *The Art and Architecture of Islam 650–1250*, (Pelican History of Art, Penguin Books, 1992). A detailed account of the early development of art and architecture throughout the Islamic world. Useful for placing Iranian Islamic culture in a wider context. Well illustrated.

Ferrier, R W, *The Arts of Persia*, (Yale, 1989). Comprehensive introduction to all aspects of Persian art and architecture, both pre-Islamic and Islamic. Well illustrated.

Housego, Jenny, *Tribal Rugs, an Introduction to the Weaving of the Tribes of Iran*, (London, 1978).

Khansari M, Moghtader R, Yavari M, *The Persian Garden: Echoes of Paradise*, (Mage, 1998). Wonderful photography illustrating the history of the garden in Persia.

SOCIOLOGY

Beck, Lois, *Nomad—a Year in the Life of a Qashqa'i Tribesman in Iran*, (Tauris, 1991). A fascinating description of the daily life of a nomadic tribe and the breakdown of traditional ways in the modern period.

Haeri, Shahla, *Law of Desire—Temporary Marriage in Iran*, (Tauris, 1991). A very revealing account of a little-known Shi'a institution: that of the temporary marriage, a contractual agreement which may last from a few hours to several years.

LANGUAGE

Elwell-Sutton, L, *Elementary Persian Grammar*, (Cambridge UP, 1974).

Mace, John, *Teach Yourself Modern Persian*, (Hodder & Stoughton, 1989).

Moshiri, Leila, *Colloquial Persian*, with cassette, (Routledge, 1991).

Lambton, Ann, *Persian Grammar*, Cambridge University Press 1984

Pocket dictionaries, as well as larger ones can easily be bought in Tehrân bookshops, including the following:

Farzenegi, Kh, *Djadid English-Persian Dictionary*, (Golshaie, Tehrân, 1989).

Haim, S, *One-volume Persian-English Dictionary*, (Farhang Moaser, Tehrân, 1952).

COOKERY

For those interested in discovering for themselves the unusual but delicate flavours of Iranian cuisine, the following cookbooks in English are recommended:

Hekmat, Forough, *The Art of Persian Cooking*, (Ebn-e-Sina Publishers, Tehrân, (1970).

Mazda, Maideh, *In a Persian Kitchen*, (Tuttle, 1987).

Simmons, Shirin, *Entertaining the Persian Way*, (Lennard Publishing, 1991).

Batmanglij, Najmieh *A taste of Persia : an introduction to Persian cooking*, I.B. Tauris, 1999

USEFUL INTERNET ADDRESSES

Best of Iran: A mine of information related to culture, geography, travel and further links. www.bestirantravel.com

Iran Air: National airline of Iran. www.iranair.nl

Iran Daily: Daily Iranian newspaper in English. www.iran-daily.com

Iranian Dailies: An index of links to Daily Newspapers based in or reporting on Iran. www.iranian.com/Webguide/MediaDailies.html

Irannet: Message board related to culture and business. Hundreds of direct links worldwide, sorted by host country. www.irannet.com

Iran Tourism and Touring Organisation: Helpful overview over travel agencies sorted by provinces. www.itto.org

Map zones: Source of general information linked to Google. www.mapzones.com/world/middle_east/iran

National Library: Homepage of the National Library of Iran. www.nli.bi.ir

Ministry of Foreign Affairs: Official homepage of the Ministry of Foreign Affairs. www.mfa.gov.ir

Netiran: Comprehensive site featuring information on Iran's political, cultural and business environment. www.netiran.com

Oznet: Large photo album of architectural sites, useful for the preparation of a journey. www.oznet.net/iran

Stanford's information on Iran: A valuable cultural information centre. tehran.stanford.edu

Tehrân Times: Daily Iranian newspaper in English from Tehrân. www.tehrantimes.com

Yellow pages: Alphabetical list of Iranian companies. Access is payable. www.iranyellowpages.net

Iran Society: Learned society in London offering lectures and seminars on Iran. www.iransoc.dircon.co.uk

INDEX